ST. DRAGON GIRL

VOLUME FIVE

STARTING WITH VOLUME 5, I'M THE MAIN CHARACTER!

NO, YOU'RE NOT!

REALLY?

Story & Art by **Natsumi Matsumoto**

St. ♥ Dragon Girl

Characters

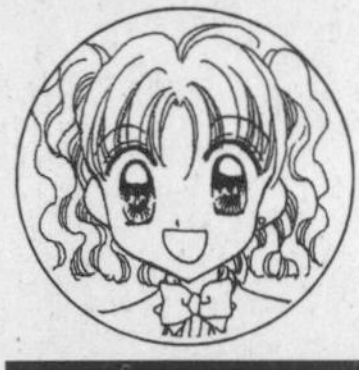

Shunran Kou

Ryuga's cousin and Momoka's best friend. Has psychic abilities.

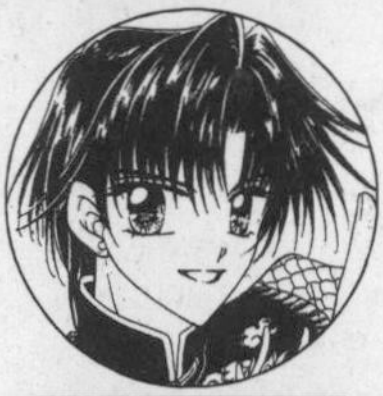

Ryuga Kou

Momoka's childhood friend and magic master.

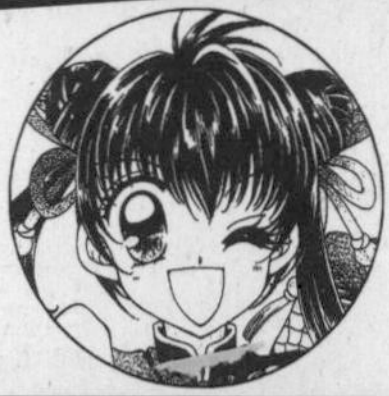

Momoka Sendou

She's possessed by a dragon spirit Ryuga called forth. When the seal on the dragon is broken, she becomes an invincible dragon girl.

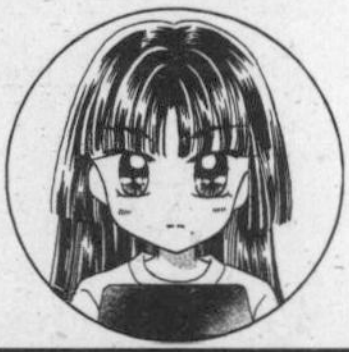

Akira Mikado

A girl onmyouji. She loves Ryuga. ♥

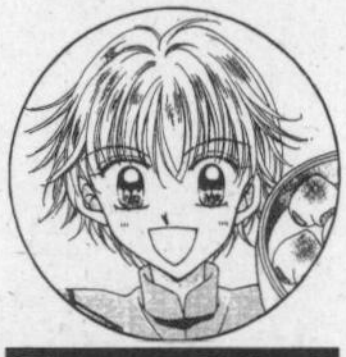

Touya Shirai

He's actually Yutengenyo, but he's reformed now. He loves Momoka. ♥

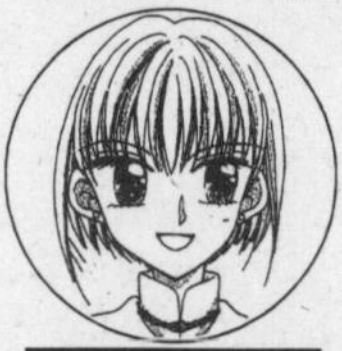

Raika Kou

Ryuga's distant relative. A physical condition causes her to emit electricity.

Story Thus Far

Momoka is a member of the kenpo club at Yokohama's Tourin Academy. She's a very strong girl.

Momoka is childhood friends with Ryuga and Shunran Kou. The Kou family controls dragons and uses magic for banishing evil spirits and purification ceremonies. Ever since the dragon Ryuga summoned possessed Momoka, she's been in danger many times. But every time, they manage to control the dragon and fight together.

One day, however, the clan that opposes the Kou family's Holy Dragon, the Black Dragon Clan, appears. And the enemy is closer than expected... First-year student Touya is the descendant of the Black Dragon Clan, Yutengenyo!

Ryuga can't prevent the reawakening of the Black Dragon, and, while trying to calm it, he gives up his spirit. Touya gives Momoka a pearl that contains the power of resurrection, as well as the capability to test the power of love. And because of Momoka's love, Ryuga is safely revived! But the two can't be straightforward with each other, so things between them are still strange! Just what will happen next?

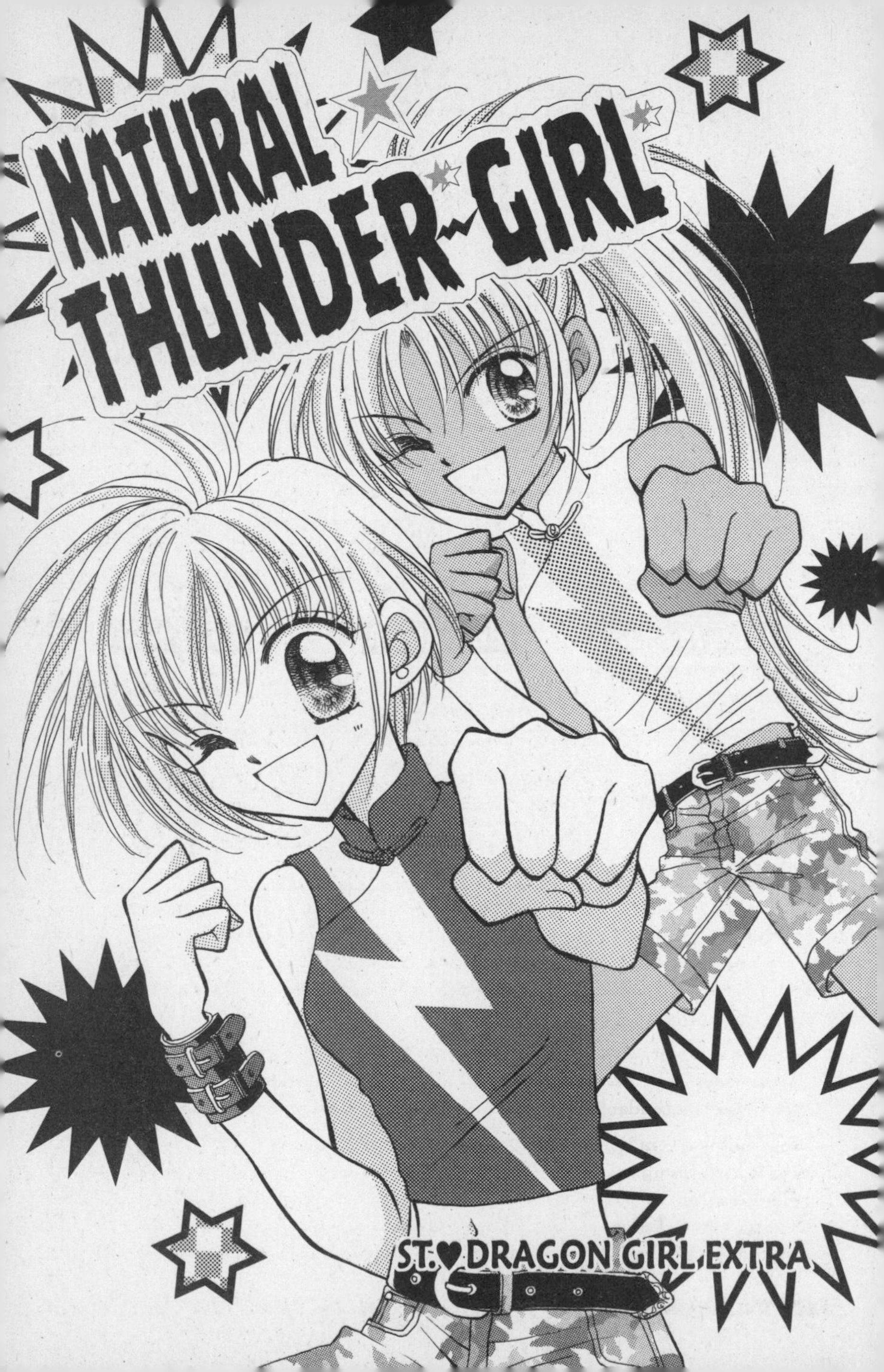

NATURAL THUNDER GIRL
ST.♥DRAGON GIRL EXTRA

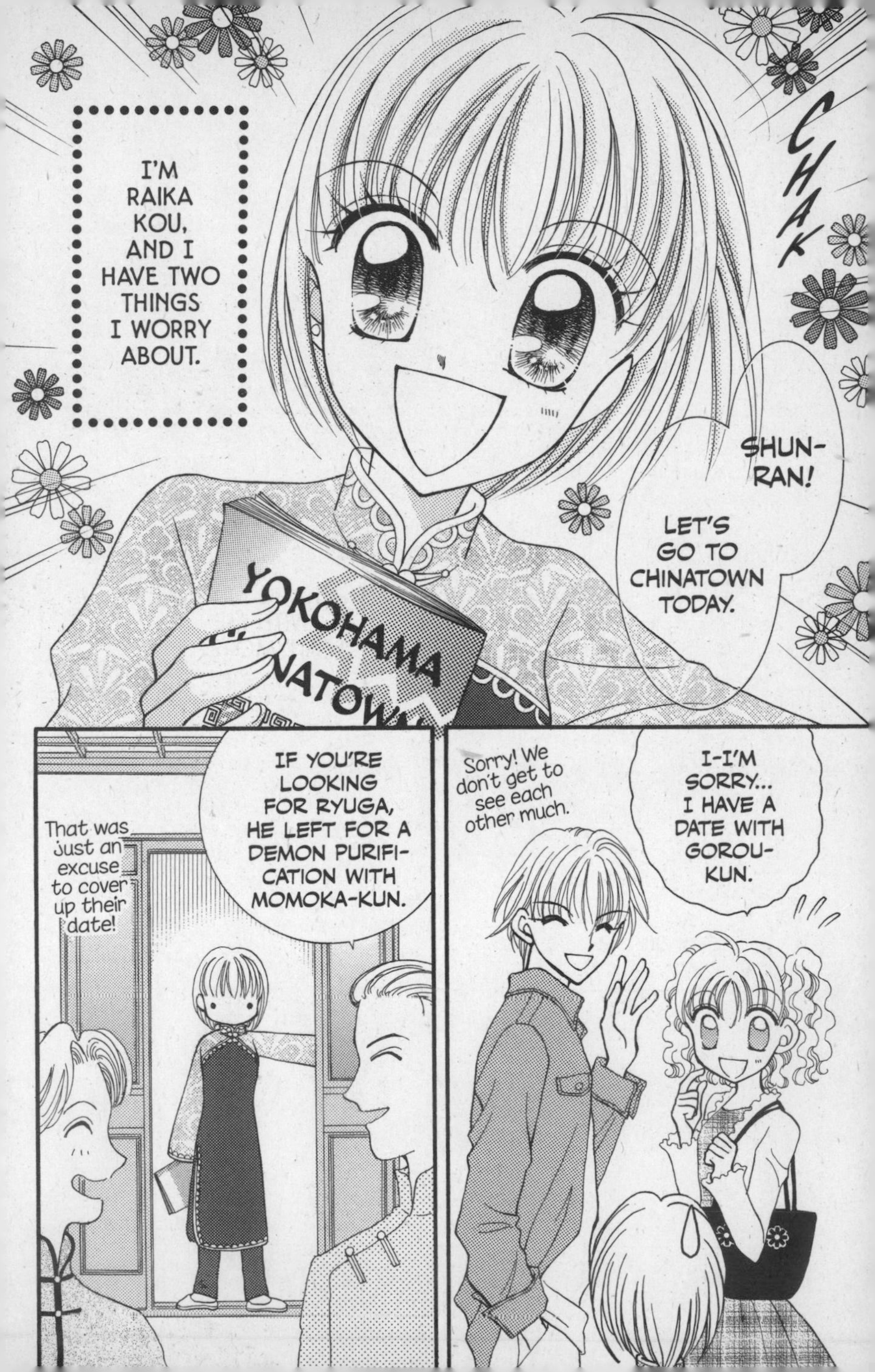
CHAK
I'M RAIKA KOU, AND I HAVE TWO THINGS I WORRY ABOUT.
SHUN-RAN!
LET'S GO TO CHINATOWN TODAY.
YOKOHAMA
I-I'M SORRY... I HAVE A DATE WITH GOROU-KUN.
Sorry! We don't get to see each other much.
IF YOU'RE LOOKING FOR RYUGA, HE LEFT FOR A DEMON PURIFICATION WITH MOMOKA-KUN.
That was just an excuse to cover up their date!

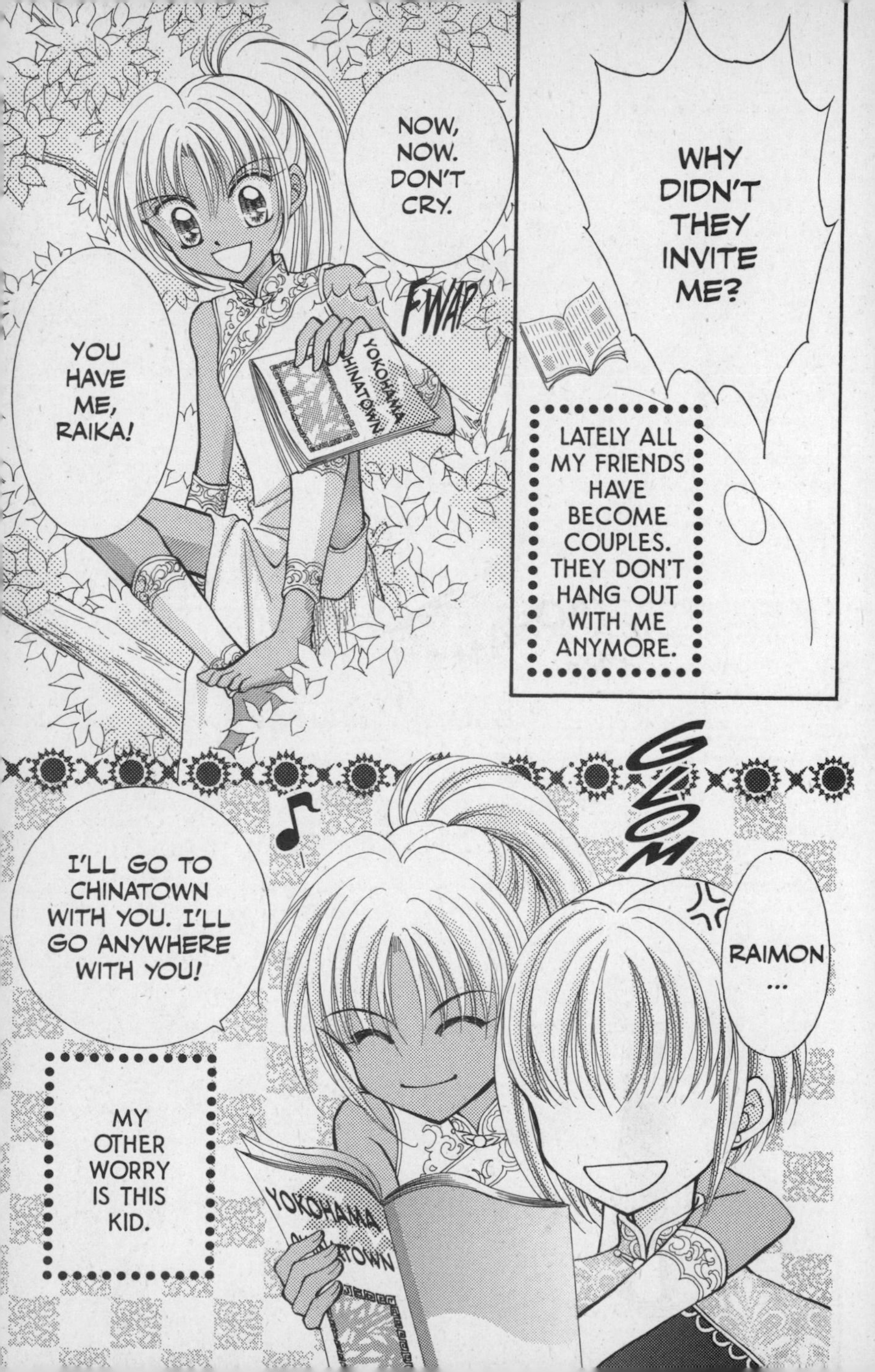
WHY DIDN'T THEY INVITE ME?
LATELY ALL MY FRIENDS HAVE BECOME COUPLES. THEY DON'T HANG OUT WITH ME ANYMORE.
NOW, NOW. DON'T CRY.
FWAP
YOKOHAMA CHINATOWN
YOU HAVE ME, RAIKA!
GLOM
RAIMON ...
I'LL GO TO CHINATOWN WITH YOU. I'LL GO ANYWHERE WITH YOU!
MY OTHER WORRY IS THIS KID.

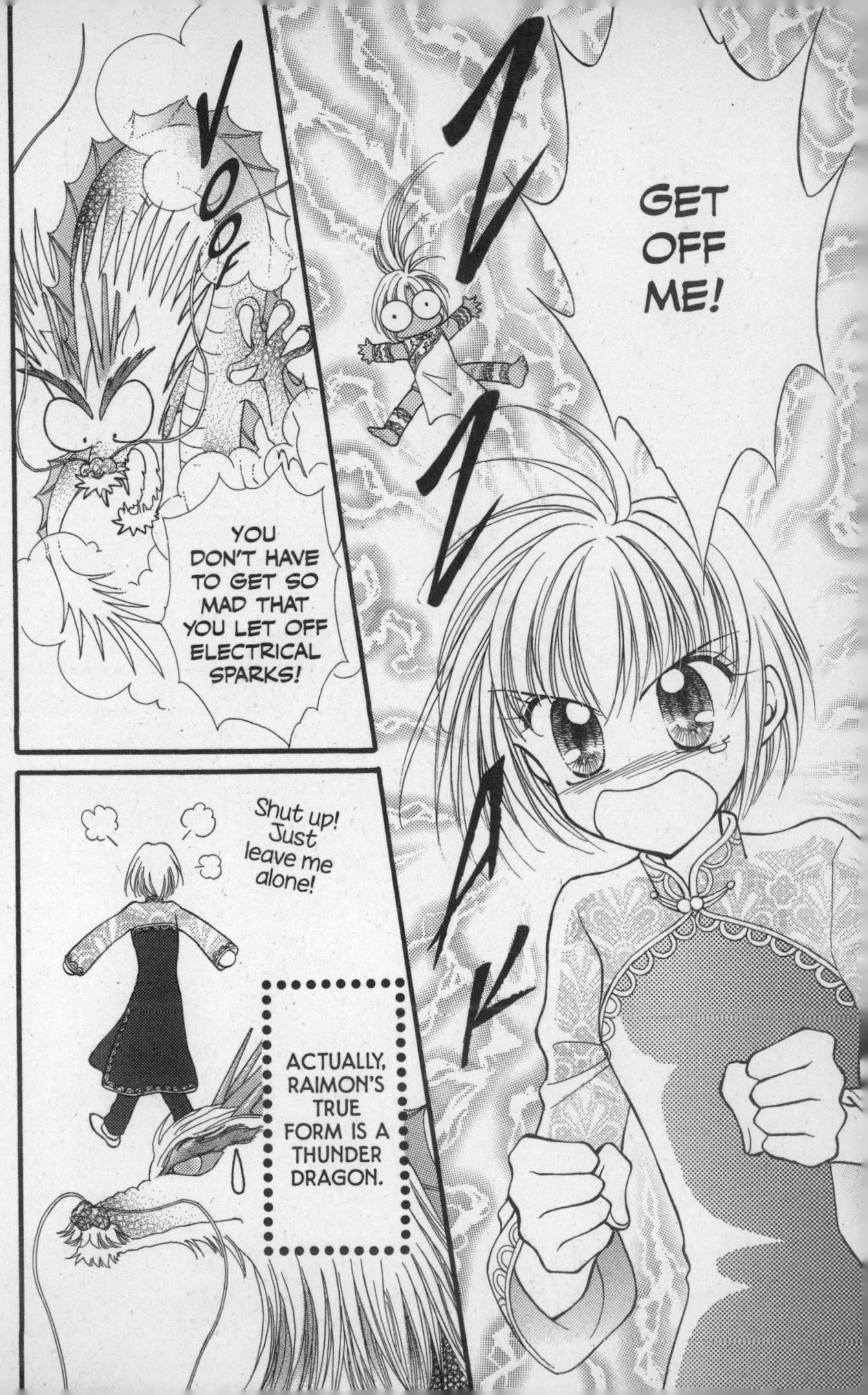
GET OFF ME!
YOU DON'T HAVE TO GET SO MAD THAT YOU LET OFF ELECTRICAL SPARKS!
Shut up! Just leave me alone!
ACTUALLY, RAIMON'S TRUE FORM IS A THUNDER DRAGON.

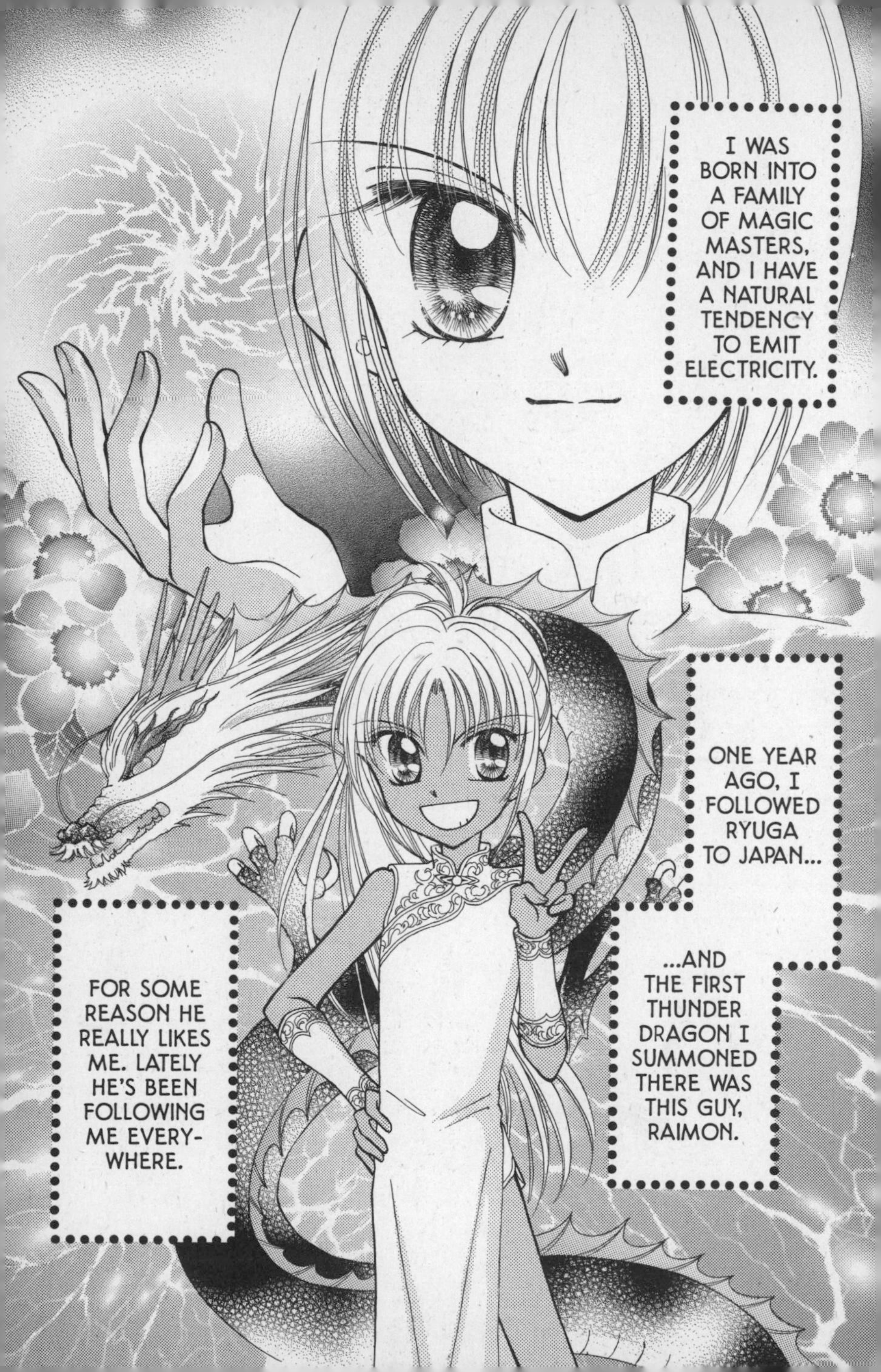
I WAS BORN INTO A FAMILY OF MAGIC MASTERS, AND I HAVE A NATURAL TENDENCY TO EMIT ELECTRICITY.
ONE YEAR AGO, I FOLLOWED RYUGA TO JAPAN...
...AND THE FIRST THUNDER DRAGON I SUMMONED THERE WAS THIS GUY, RAIMON.
FOR SOME REASON HE REALLY LIKES ME. LATELY HE'S BEEN FOLLOWING ME EVERY-WHERE.

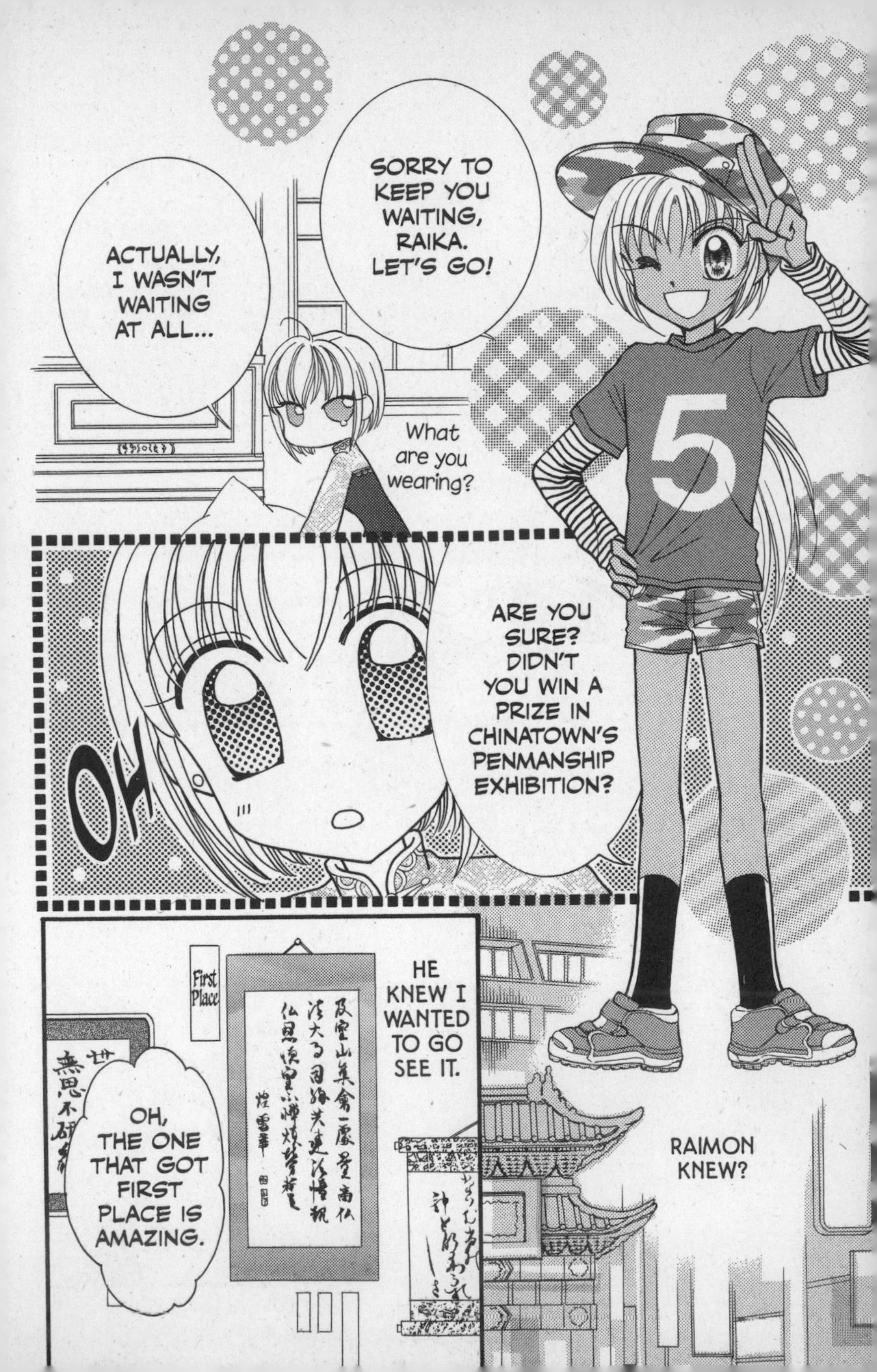
SORRY TO KEEP YOU WAITING, RAIKA. LET'S GO!
ACTUALLY, I WASN'T WAITING AT ALL...
What are you wearing?
ARE YOU SURE? DIDN'T YOU WIN A PRIZE IN CHINATOWN'S PENMANSHIP EXHIBITION?
OH
RAIMON KNEW?
HE KNEW I WANTED TO GO SEE IT.
First Place
OH, THE ONE THAT GOT FIRST PLACE IS AMAZING.

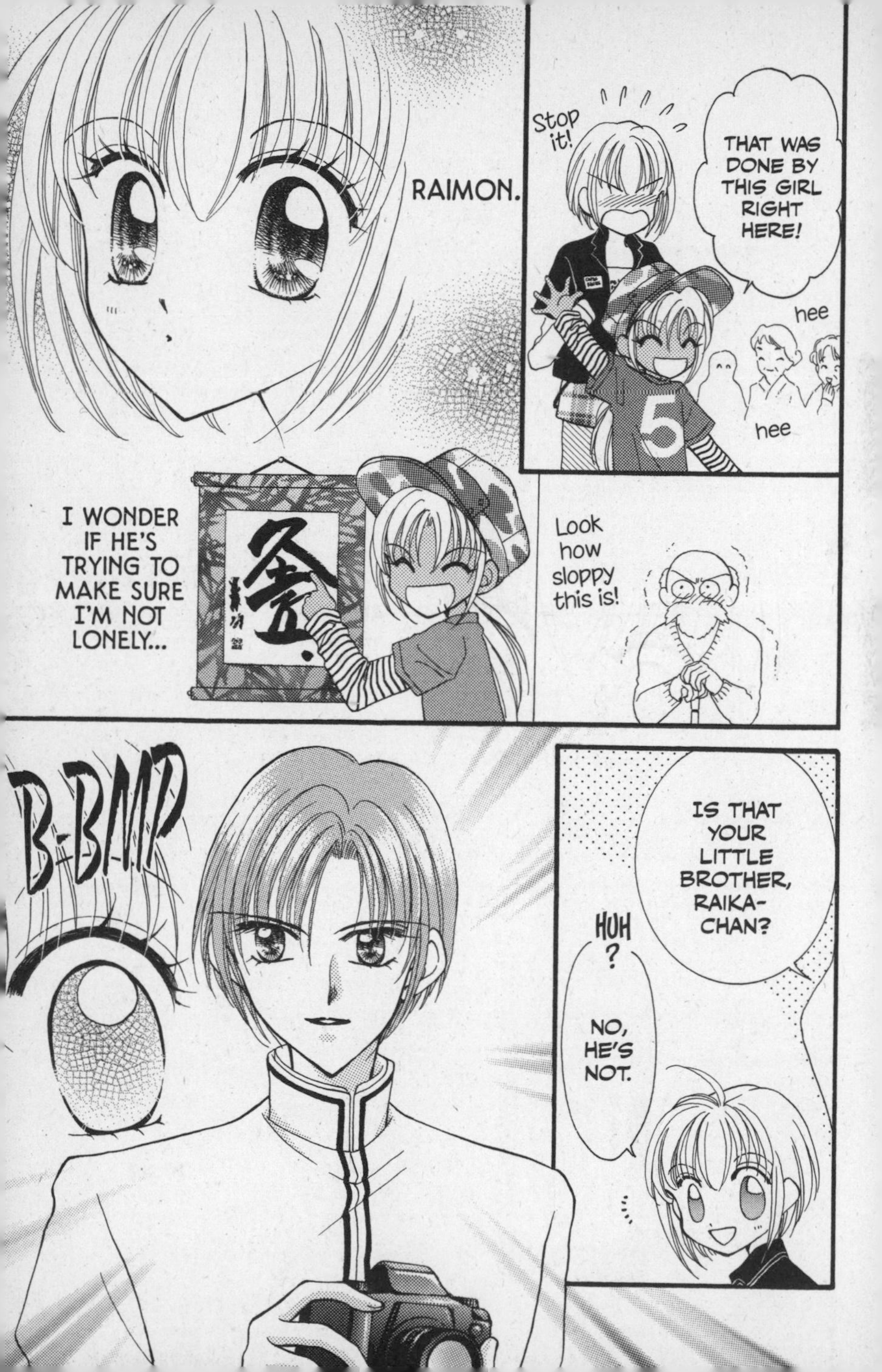
THAT WAS DONE BY THIS GIRL RIGHT HERE!
Stop it!
hee
hee
Look how sloppy this is!
RAIMON.
I WONDER IF HE'S TRYING TO MAKE SURE I'M NOT LONELY...
IS THAT YOUR LITTLE BROTHER, RAIKA-CHAN?
HUH?
NO, HE'S NOT.
B-BMP

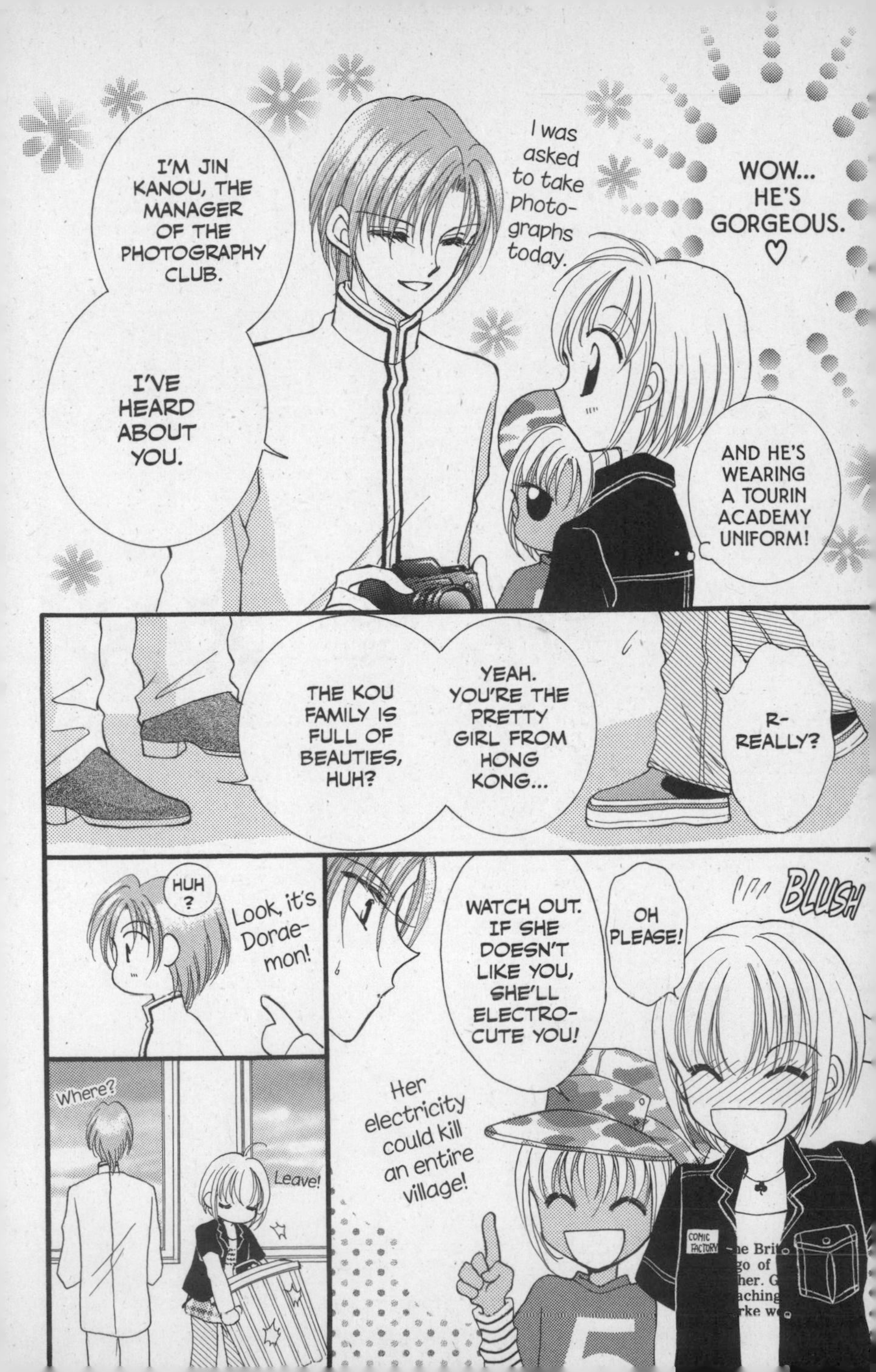
WOW... HE'S GORGEOUS. ♡
AND HE'S WEARING A TOURIN ACADEMY UNIFORM!
I was asked to take photo-graphs today.
I'M JIN KANOU, THE MANAGER OF THE PHOTOGRAPHY CLUB.
I'VE HEARD ABOUT YOU.
YEAH. YOU'RE THE PRETTY GIRL FROM HONG KONG...
THE KOU FAMILY IS FULL OF BEAUTIES, HUH?
R-REALLY?
BLUSH
OH PLEASE!
WATCH OUT. IF SHE DOESN'T LIKE YOU, SHE'LL ELECTRO-CUTE YOU!
Her electricity could kill an entire village!
COMIC FACTORY
HUH?
Look, it's Dorae-mon!
Where?
Leave!

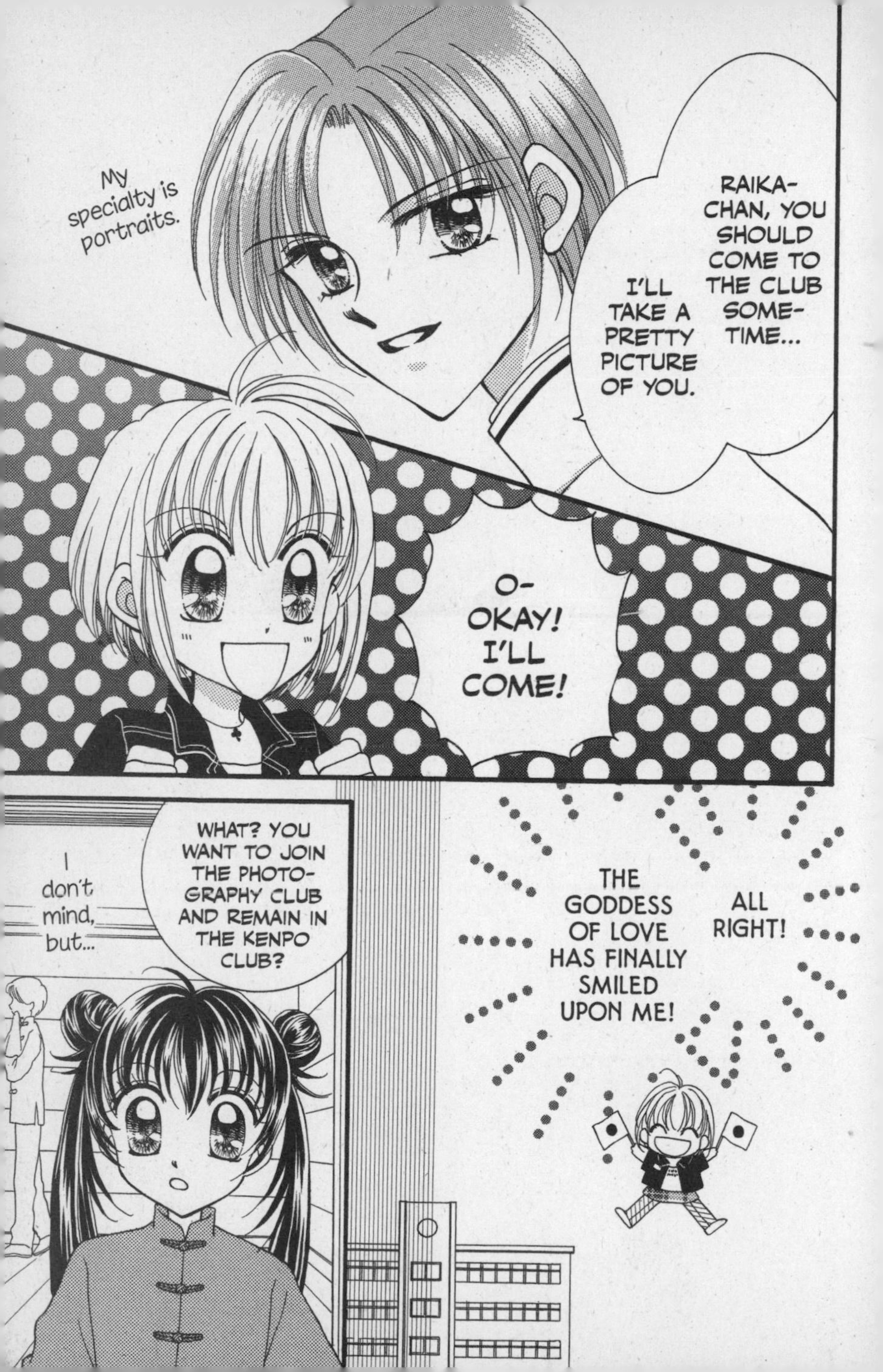
RAIKA-CHAN, YOU SHOULD COME TO THE CLUB SOMETIME...
I'LL TAKE A PRETTY PICTURE OF YOU.
My specialty is portraits.
O-OKAY! I'LL COME!
ALL RIGHT!
THE GODDESS OF LOVE HAS FINALLY SMILED UPON ME!
WHAT? YOU WANT TO JOIN THE PHOTOGRAPHY CLUB AND REMAIN IN THE KENPO CLUB?
I don't mind, but...

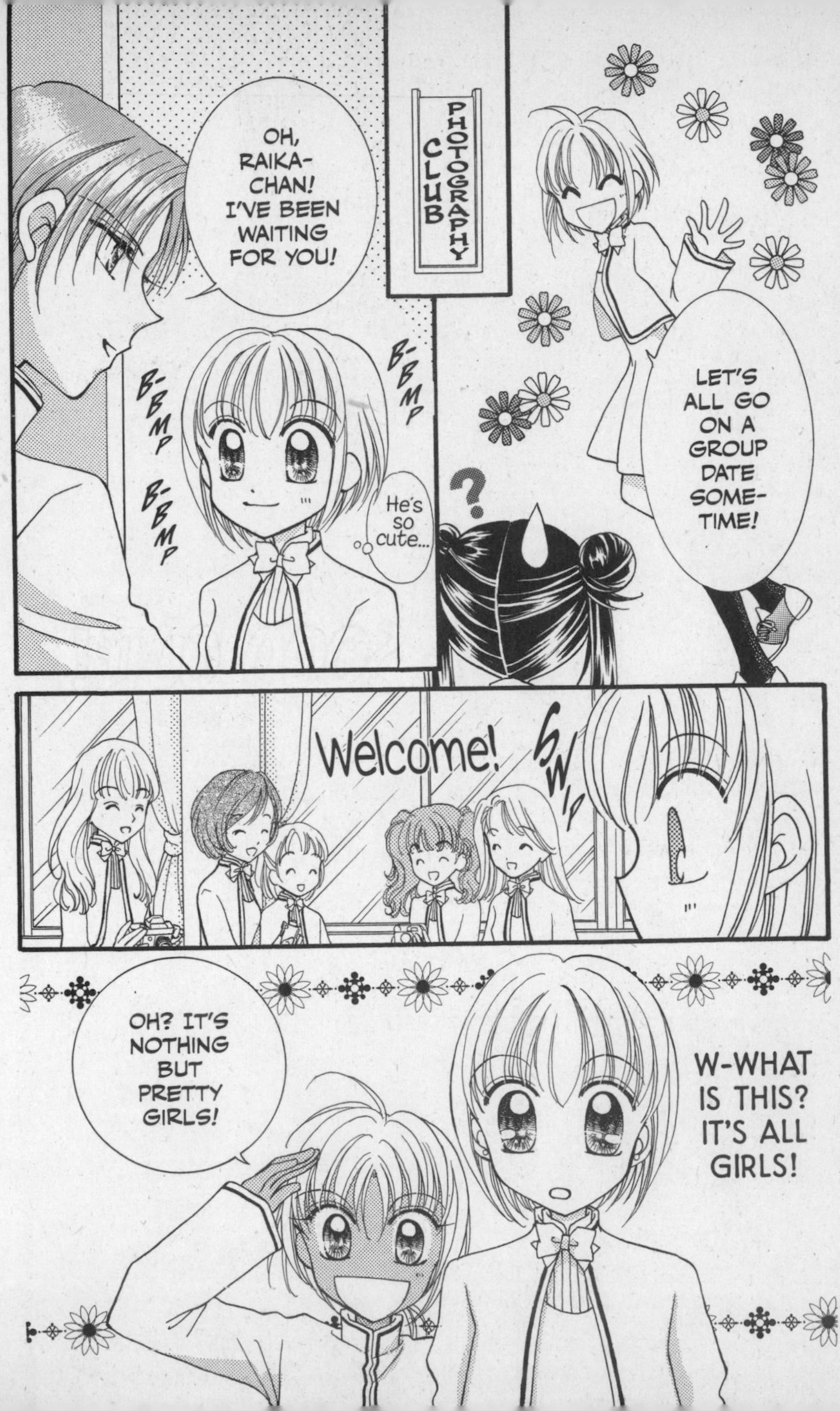
?
LET'S ALL GO ON A GROUP DATE SOMETIME!
PHOTOGRAPHY CLUB
OH, RAIKA-CHAN! I'VE BEEN WAITING FOR YOU!
B-BMP
He's so cute...
B-BMP
B-BMP
SWIP
Welcome!
W-WHAT IS THIS? IT'S ALL GIRLS!
OH? IT'S NOTHING BUT PRETTY GIRLS!

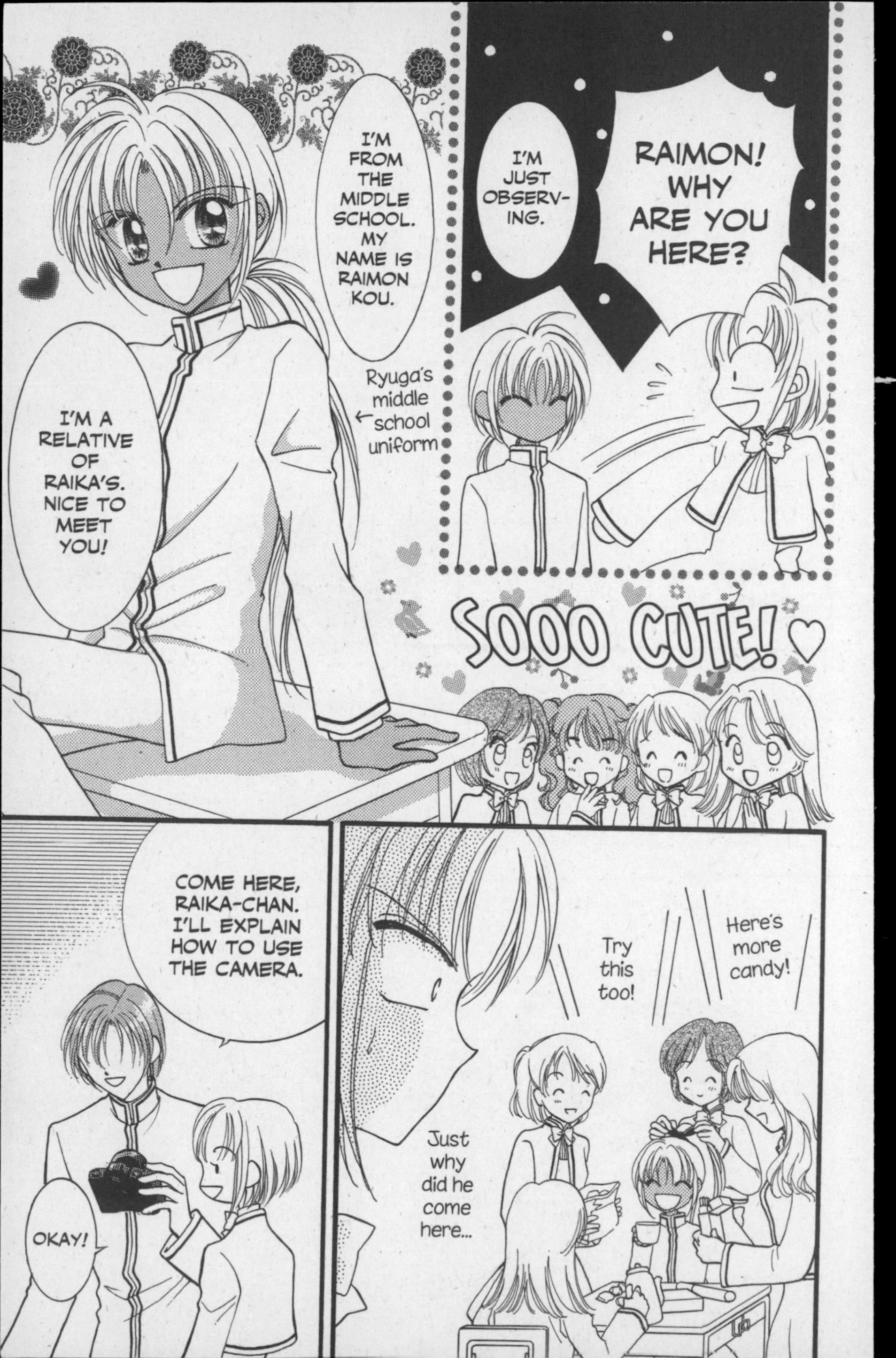
RAIMON! WHY ARE YOU HERE?
I'M JUST OBSERVING.
SOOO CUTE!
I'M FROM THE MIDDLE SCHOOL. MY NAME IS RAIMON KOU.
I'M A RELATIVE OF RAIKA'S. NICE TO MEET YOU!
Ryuga's middle school uniform
Here's more candy!
Try this too!
Just why did he come here...
COME HERE, RAIKA-CHAN. I'LL EXPLAIN HOW TO USE THE CAMERA.
OKAY!

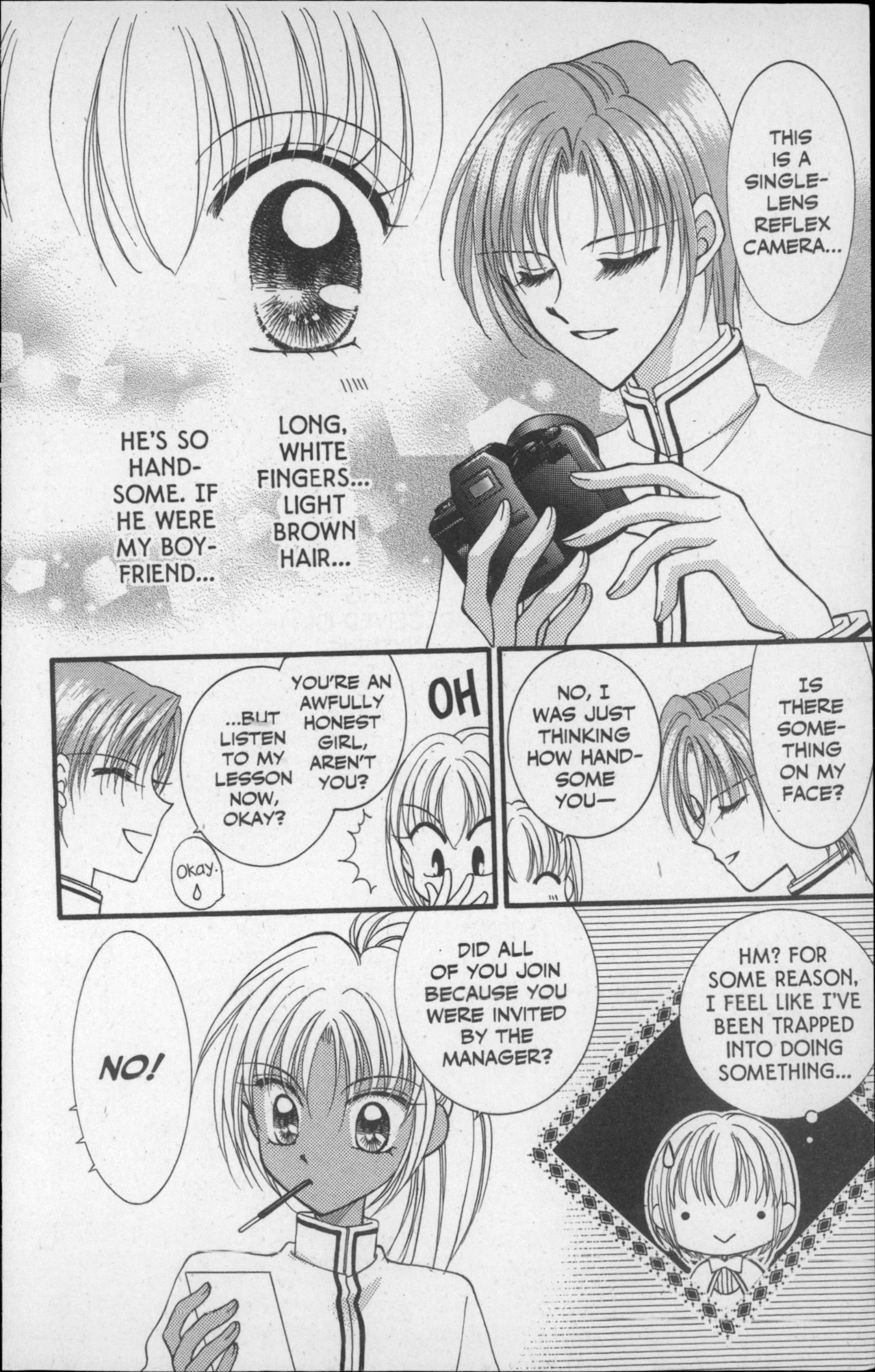
THIS IS A SINGLE-LENS REFLEX CAMERA...
LONG, WHITE FINGERS... LIGHT BROWN HAIR...
HE'S SO HAND-SOME. IF HE WERE MY BOY-FRIEND...
IS THERE SOMETHING ON MY FACE?
NO, I WAS JUST THINKING HOW HAND-SOME YOU—
OH
YOU'RE AN AWFULLY HONEST GIRL, AREN'T YOU?
...BUT LISTEN TO MY LESSON NOW, OKAY?
Okay.
HM? FOR SOME REASON, I FEEL LIKE I'VE BEEN TRAPPED INTO DOING SOMETHING...
DID ALL OF YOU JOIN BECAUSE YOU WERE INVITED BY THE MANAGER?
NO!

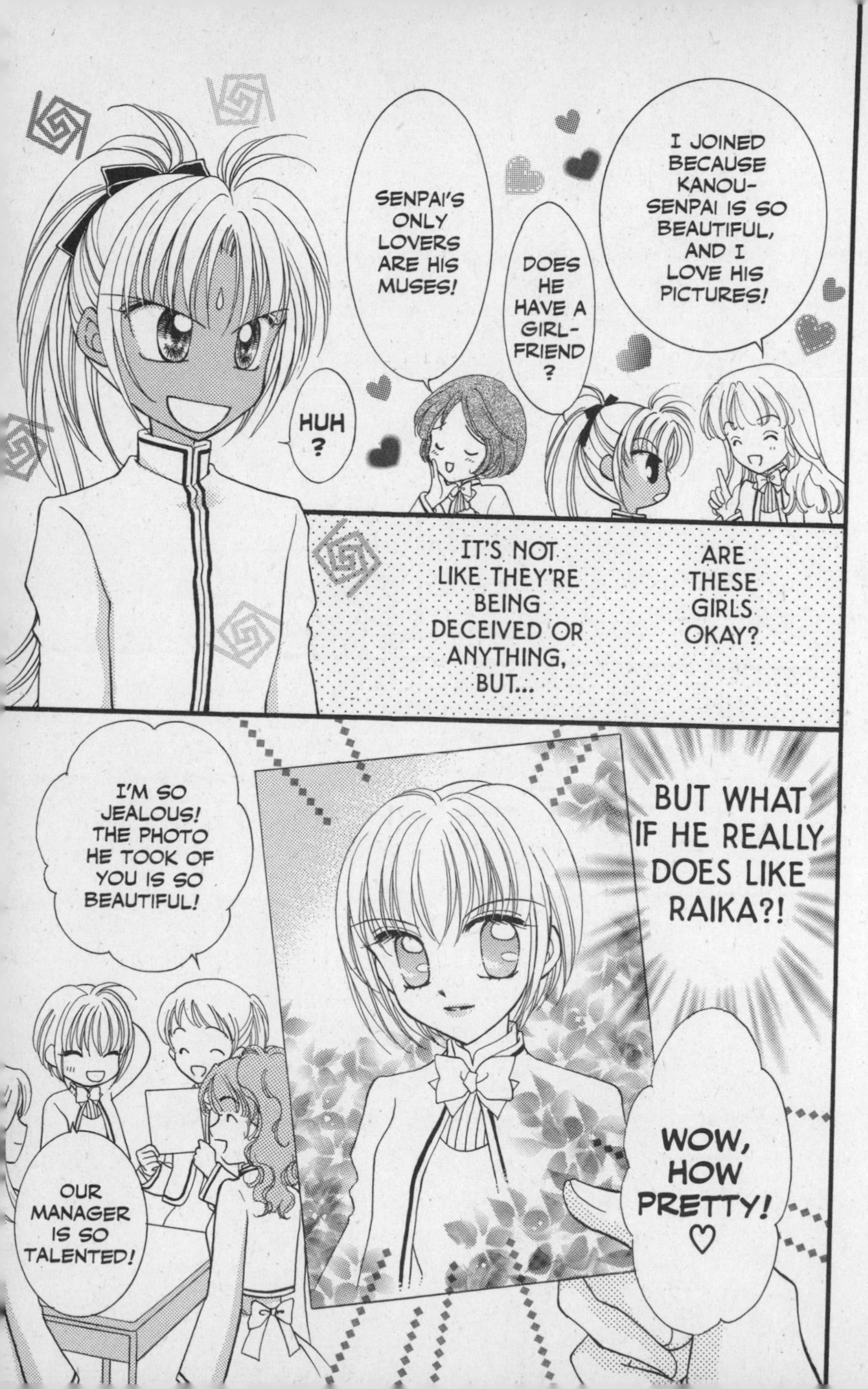

I JOINED BECAUSE KANOU-SENPAI IS SO BEAUTIFUL, AND I LOVE HIS PICTURES!
DOES HE HAVE A GIRL-FRIEND?
SENPAI'S ONLY LOVERS ARE HIS MUSES!
HUH?
ARE THESE GIRLS OKAY?
IT'S NOT LIKE THEY'RE BEING DECEIVED OR ANYTHING, BUT...
BUT WHAT IF HE REALLY DOES LIKE RAIKA?!
WOW, HOW PRETTY! ♡
I'M SO JEALOUS! THE PHOTO HE TOOK OF YOU IS SO BEAUTIFUL!
OUR MANAGER IS SO TALENTED!

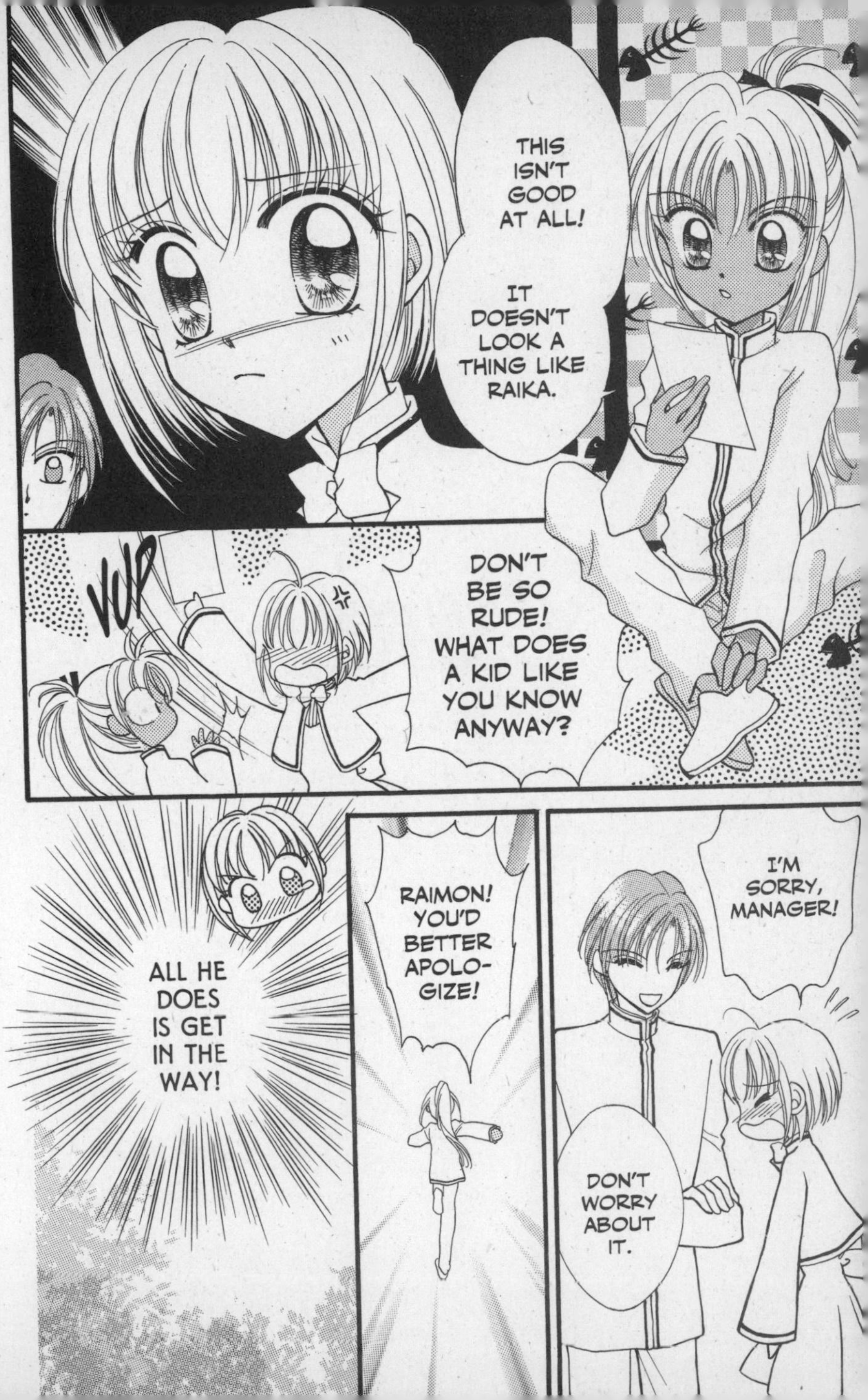
THIS ISN'T GOOD AT ALL!
IT DOESN'T LOOK A THING LIKE RAIKA.
DON'T BE SO RUDE! WHAT DOES A KID LIKE YOU KNOW ANYWAY?
VUP
I'M SORRY, MANAGER!
DON'T WORRY ABOUT IT.
RAIMON! YOU'D BETTER APOLOGIZE!
ALL HE DOES IS GET IN THE WAY!

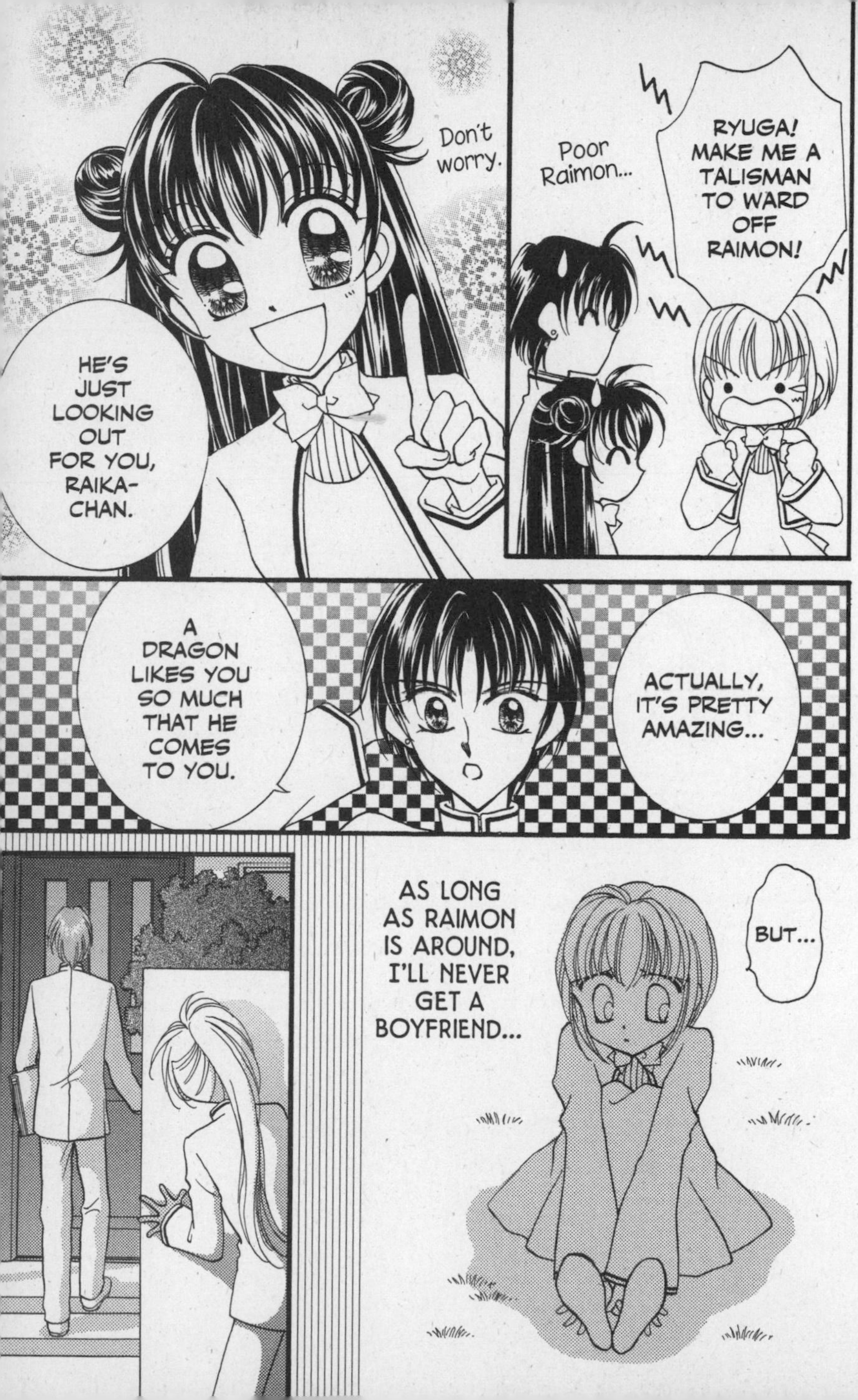
RYUGA! MAKE ME A TALISMAN TO WARD OFF RAIMON!
Poor Raimon...
Don't worry.
HE'S JUST LOOKING OUT FOR YOU, RAIKA-CHAN.
ACTUALLY, IT'S PRETTY AMAZING...
A DRAGON LIKES YOU SO MUCH THAT HE COMES TO YOU.
BUT...
AS LONG AS RAIMON IS AROUND, I'LL NEVER GET A BOYFRIEND...

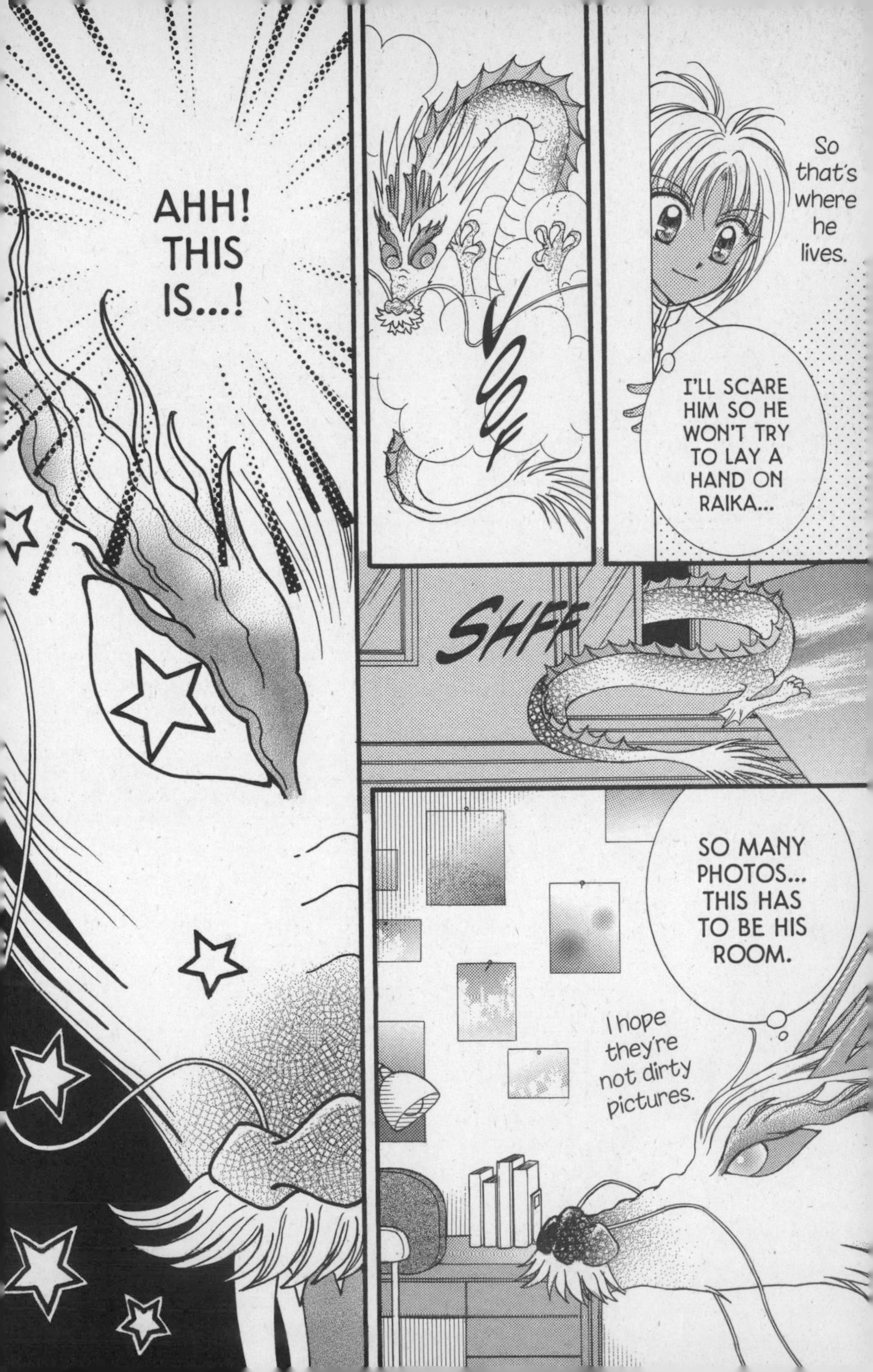
So that's where he lives.
I'LL SCARE HIM SO HE WON'T TRY TO LAY A HAND ON RAIKA...
VOOM
SHFF
SO MANY PHOTOS... THIS HAS TO BE HIS ROOM.
I hope they're not dirty pictures.
AHH! THIS IS...!

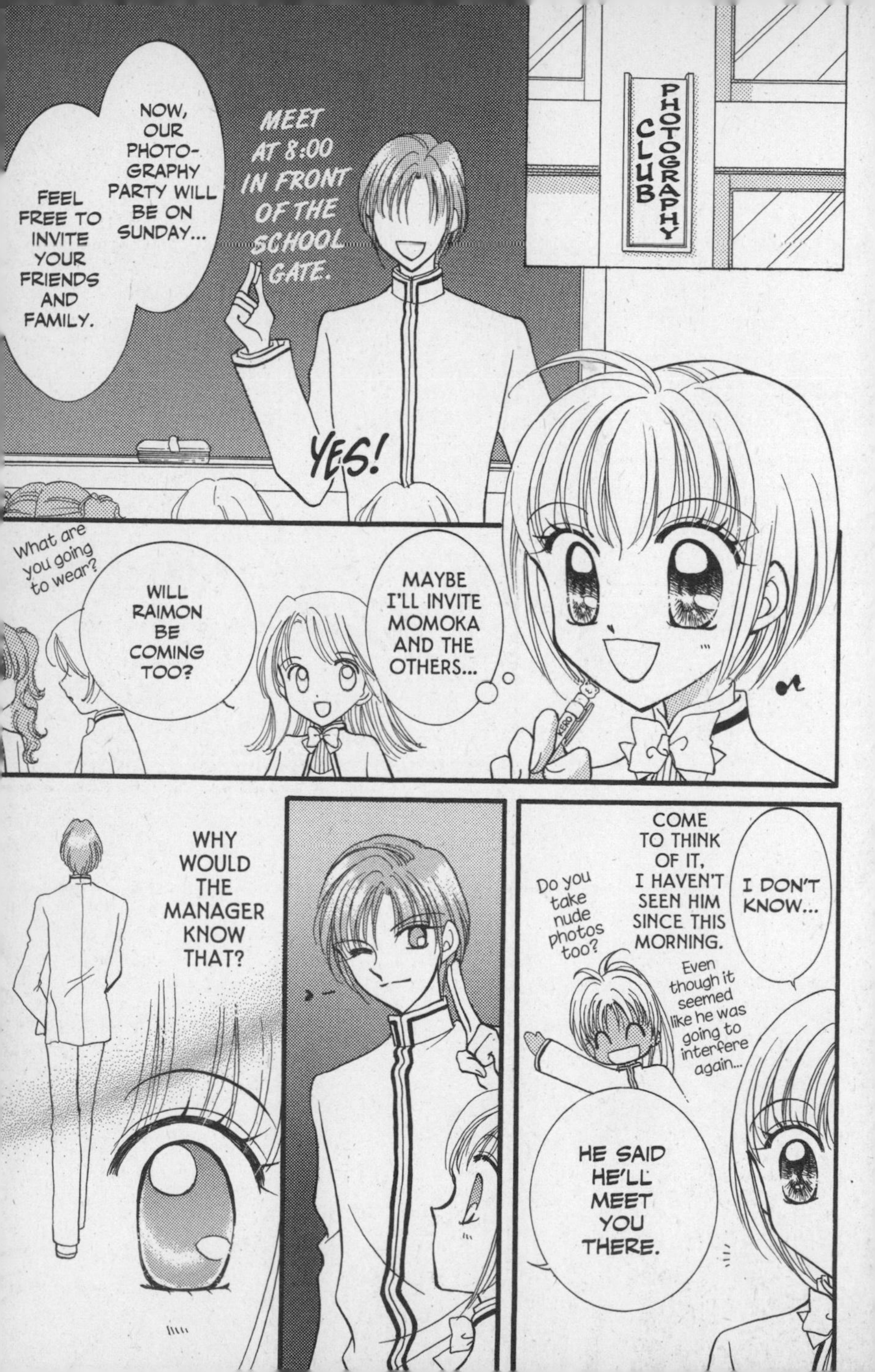
PHOTOGRAPHY CLUB
MEET AT 8:00 IN FRONT OF THE SCHOOL GATE.
NOW, OUR PHOTOGRAPHY PARTY WILL BE ON SUNDAY...
FEEL FREE TO INVITE YOUR FRIENDS AND FAMILY.
YES!
MAYBE I'LL INVITE MOMOKA AND THE OTHERS...
WILL RAIMON BE COMING TOO?
What are you going to wear?
I DON'T KNOW...
COME TO THINK OF IT, I HAVEN'T SEEN HIM SINCE THIS MORNING.
Do you take nude photos too?
Even though it seemed like he was going to interfere again...
HE SAID HE'LL MEET YOU THERE.
WHY WOULD THE MANAGER KNOW THAT?

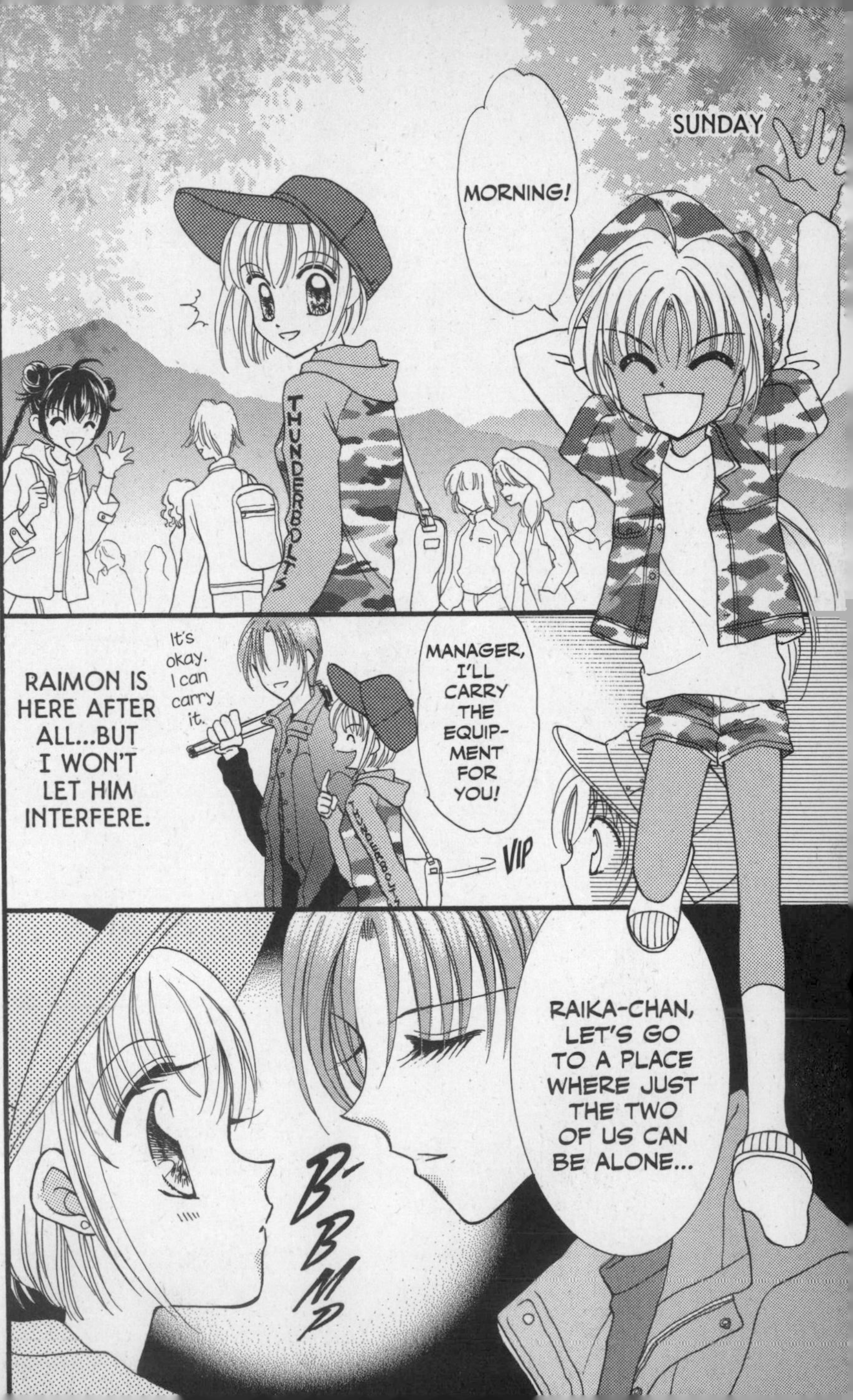
SUNDAY
MORNING!
MANAGER, I'LL CARRY THE EQUIPMENT FOR YOU!
It's okay. I can carry it.
VIP
RAIMON IS HERE AFTER ALL...BUT I WON'T LET HIM INTERFERE.
RAIKA-CHAN, LET'S GO TO A PLACE WHERE JUST THE TWO OF US CAN BE ALONE...
B-BMP

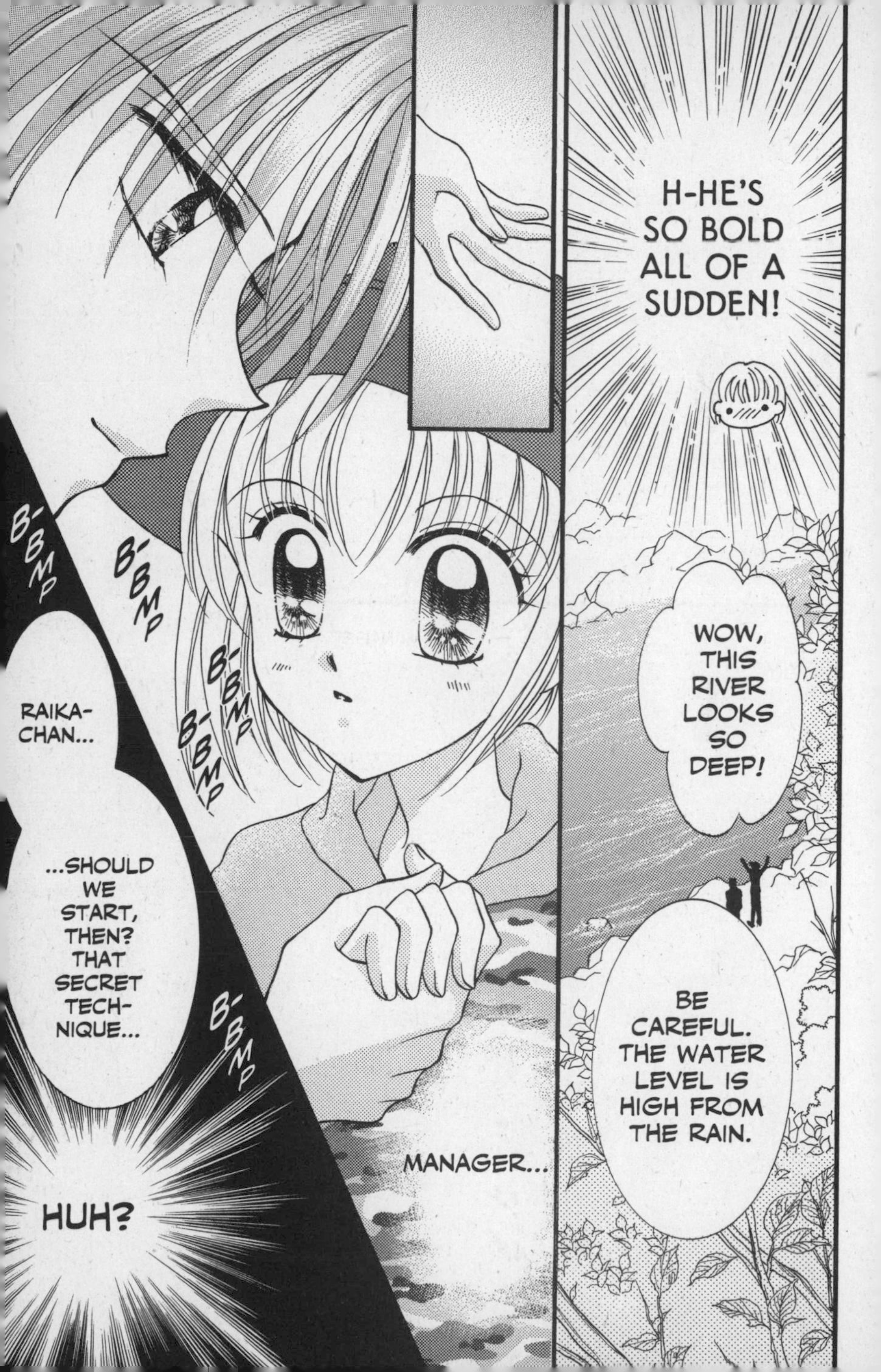
H-HE'S SO BOLD ALL OF A SUDDEN!
WOW, THIS RIVER LOOKS SO DEEP!
BE CAREFUL. THE WATER LEVEL IS HIGH FROM THE RAIN.
B-BMP
B-BMP
B-BMP
B-BMP
RAIKA-CHAN...
...SHOULD WE START, THEN? THAT SECRET TECH-NIQUE...
B-BMP
MANAGER...
HUH?

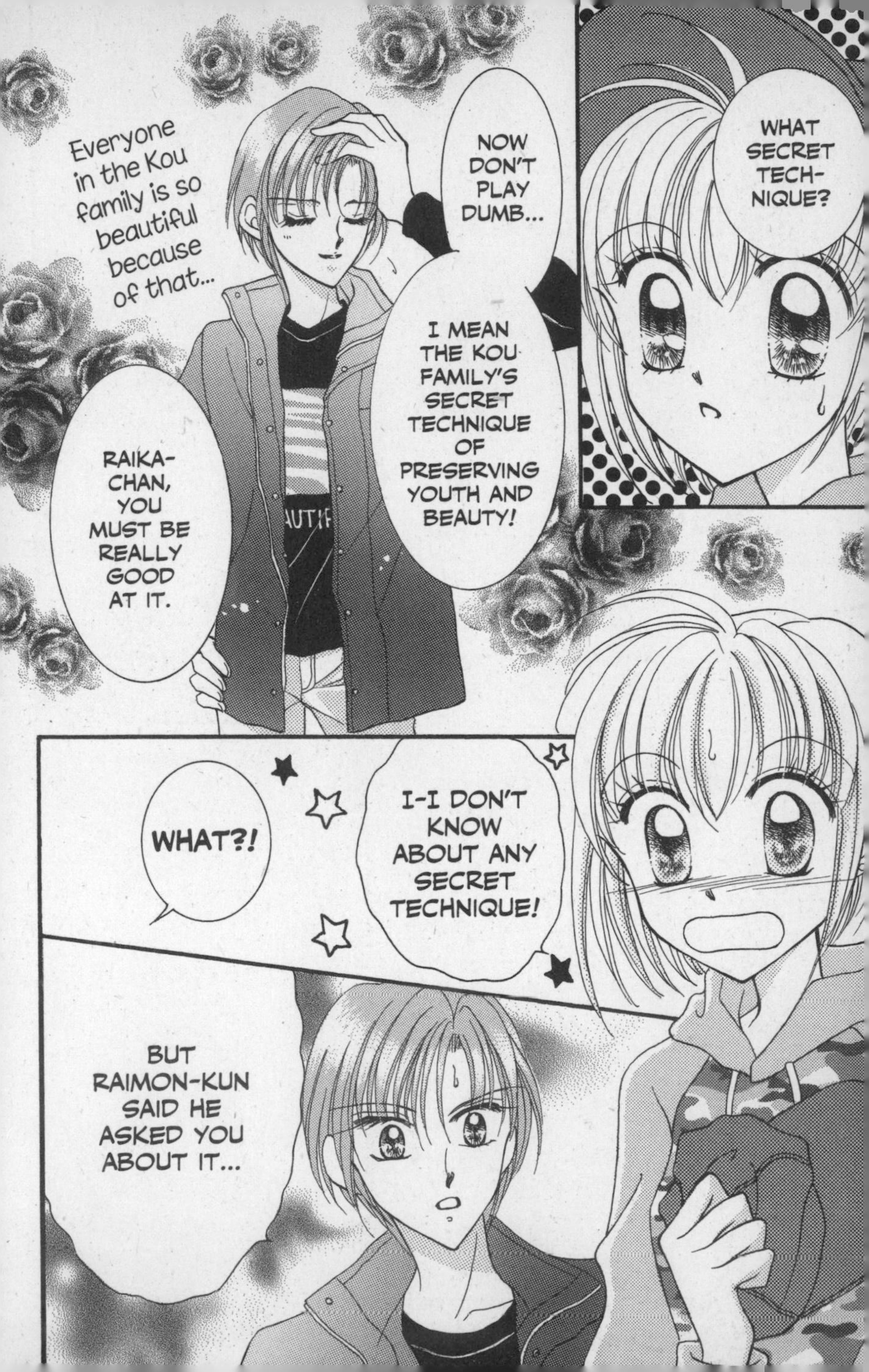
WHAT SECRET TECH-NIQUE?
NOW DON'T PLAY DUMB...
I MEAN THE KOU FAMILY'S SECRET TECHNIQUE OF PRESERVING YOUTH AND BEAUTY!
Everyone in the Kou family is so beautiful because of that...
RAIKA-CHAN, YOU MUST BE REALLY GOOD AT IT.
I-I DON'T KNOW ABOUT ANY SECRET TECHNIQUE!
WHAT?!
BUT RAIMON-KUN SAID HE ASKED YOU ABOUT IT...

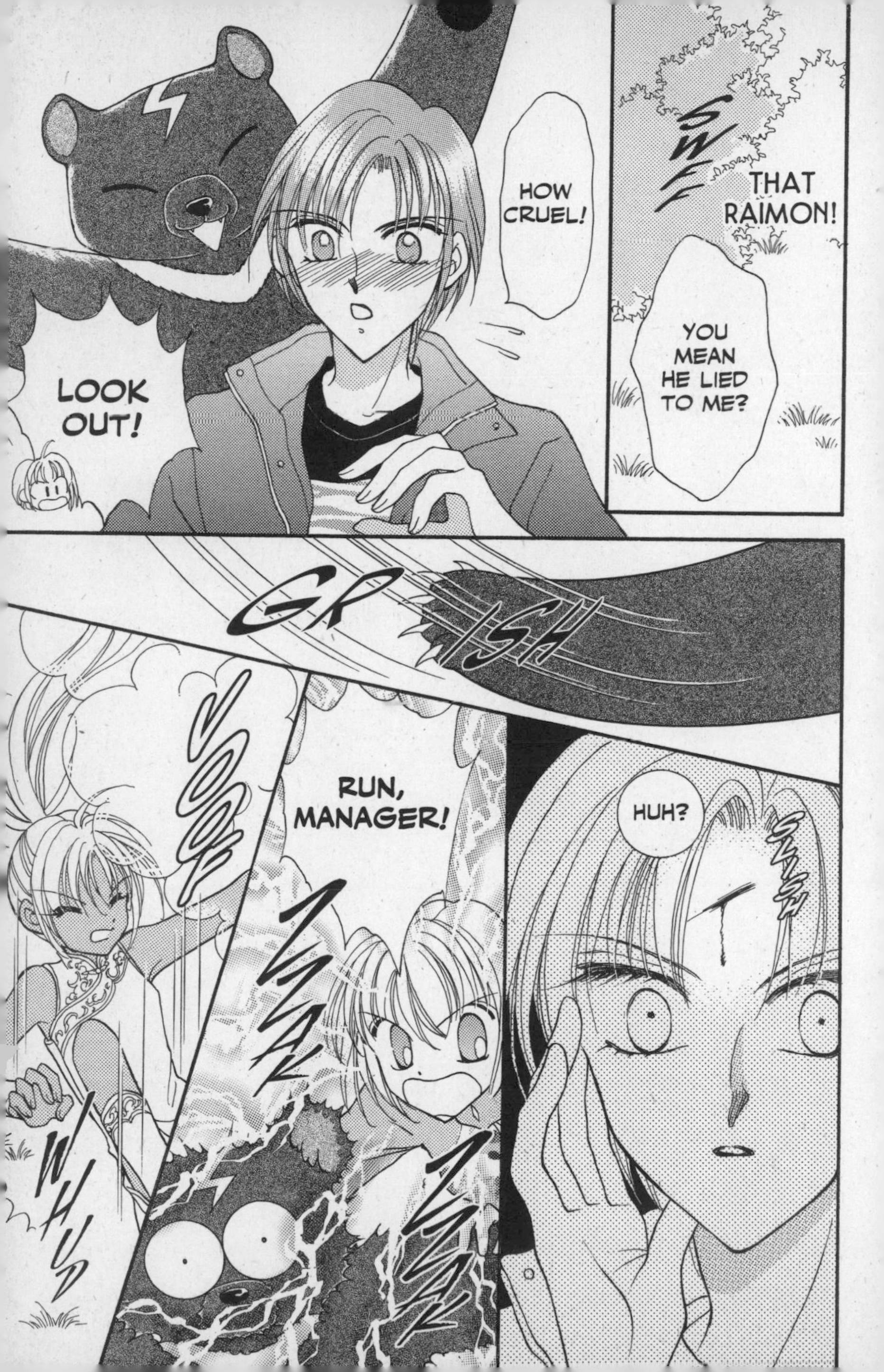
SWF
THAT RAIMON!
YOU MEAN HE LIED TO ME?
HOW CRUEL!
LOOK OUT!
GRISH
HUH?
RUN, MANAGER!

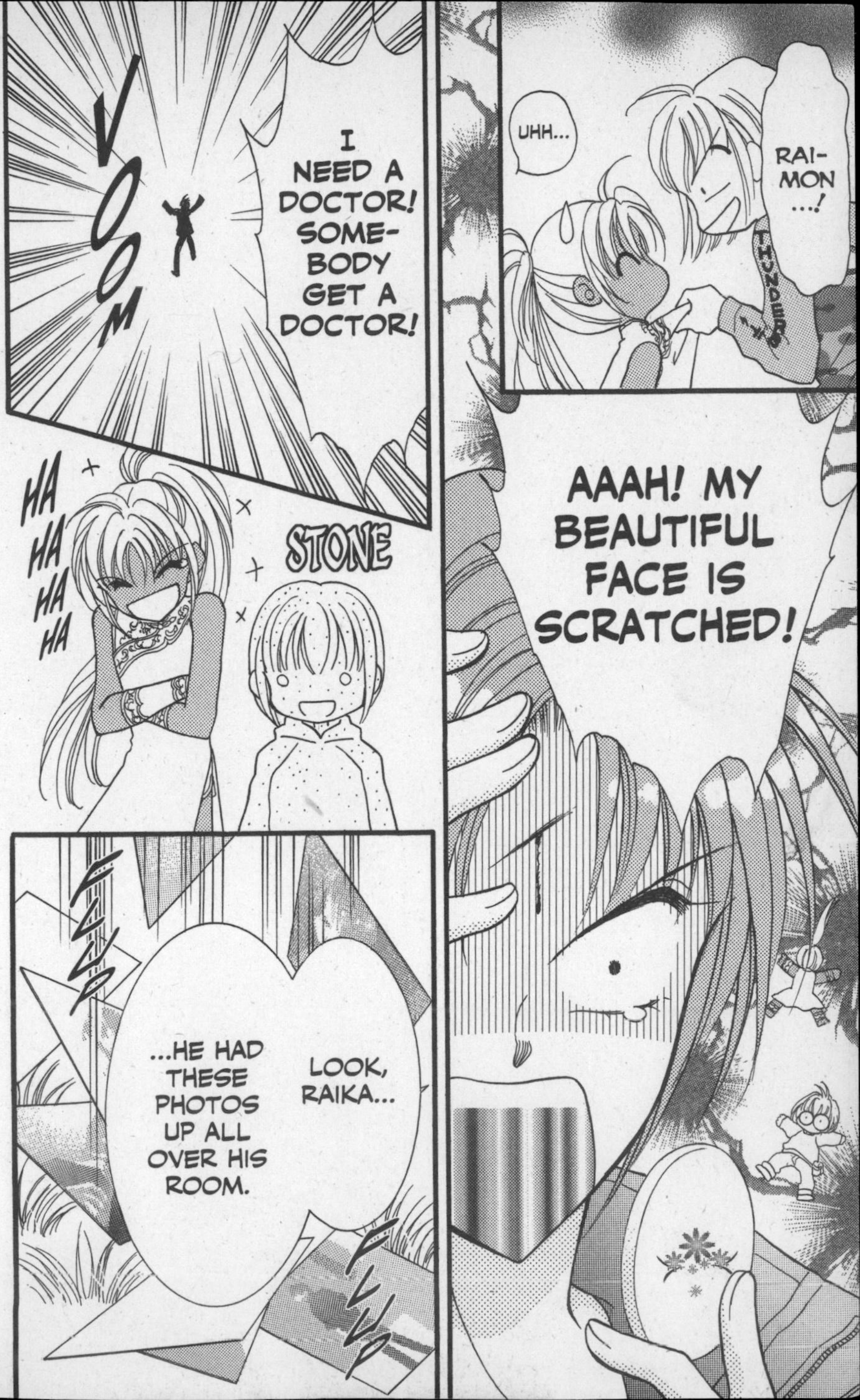
RAI-MON ...!
UHH...
THUNDER
AAAH! MY BEAUTIFUL FACE IS SCRATCHED!
VOOM
I NEED A DOCTOR! SOMEBODY GET A DOCTOR!
STONE
HA HA HA HA HA
FLUP
LOOK, RAIKA...
...HE HAD THESE PHOTOS UP ALL OVER HIS ROOM.
FLUP

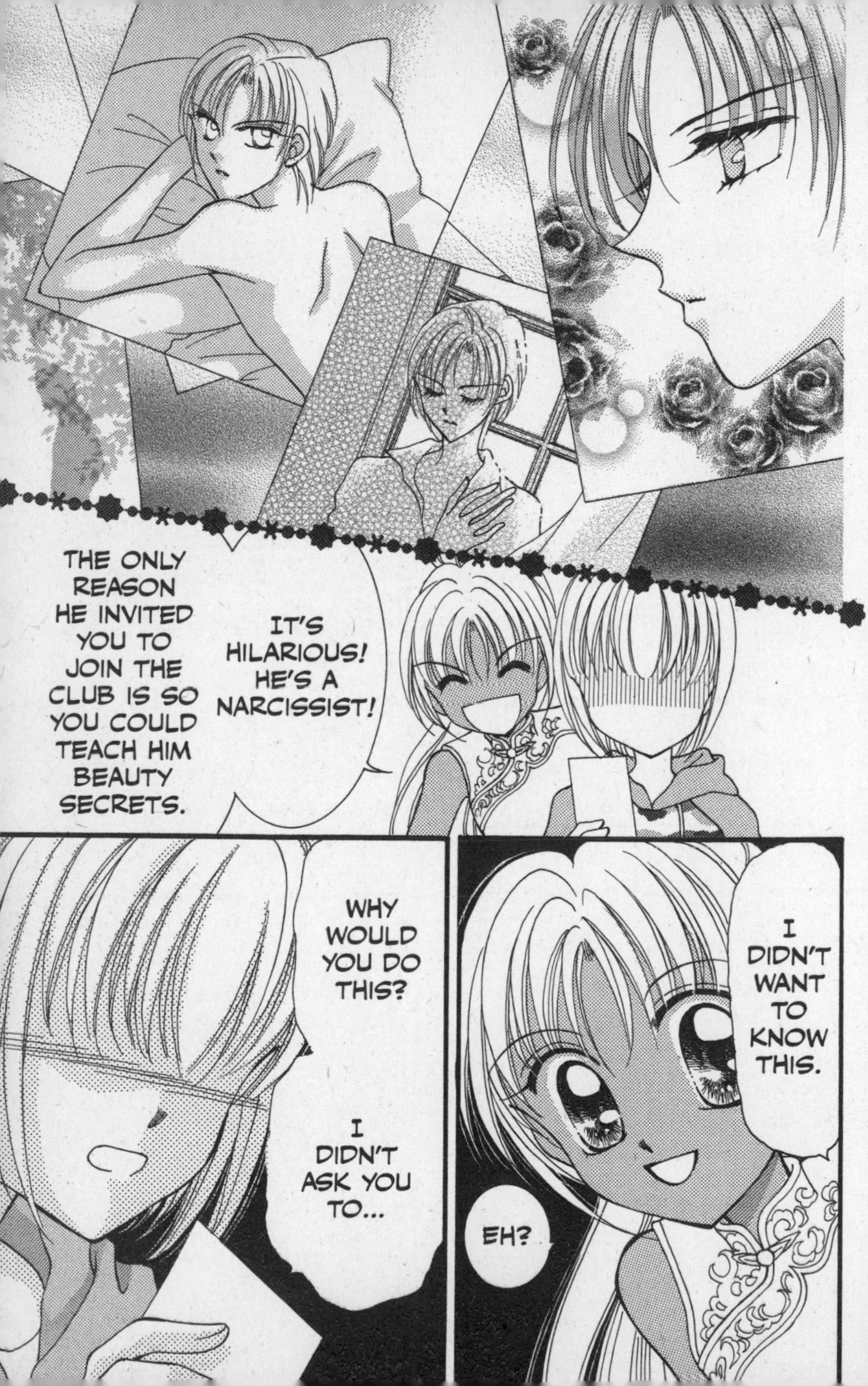
THE ONLY REASON HE INVITED YOU TO JOIN THE CLUB IS SO YOU COULD TEACH HIM BEAUTY SECRETS.
IT'S HILARIOUS! HE'S A NARCISSIST!
I DIDN'T WANT TO KNOW THIS.
EH?
WHY WOULD YOU DO THIS?
I DIDN'T ASK YOU TO...

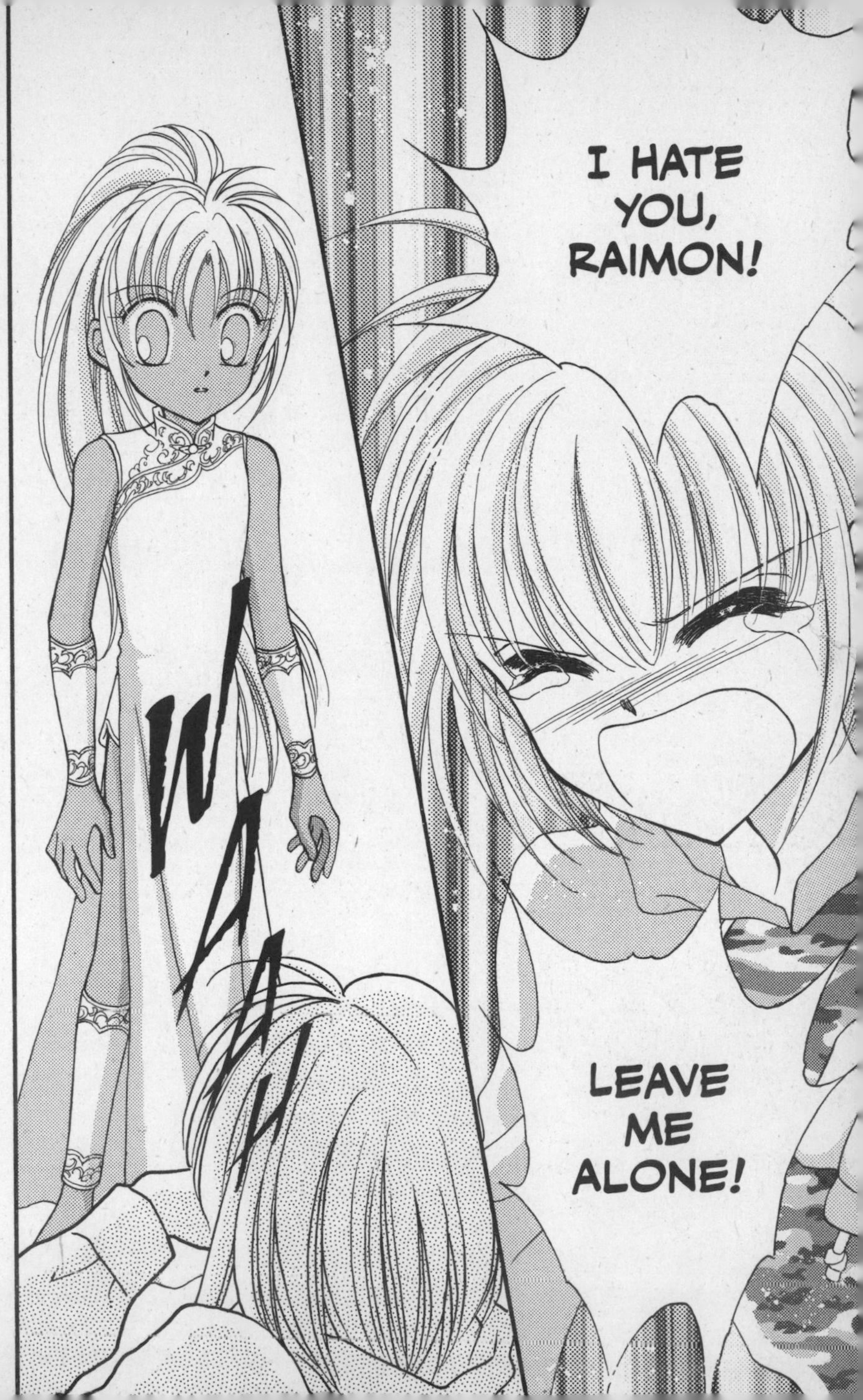
I HATE YOU, RAIMON!
LEAVE ME ALONE!
WAAH

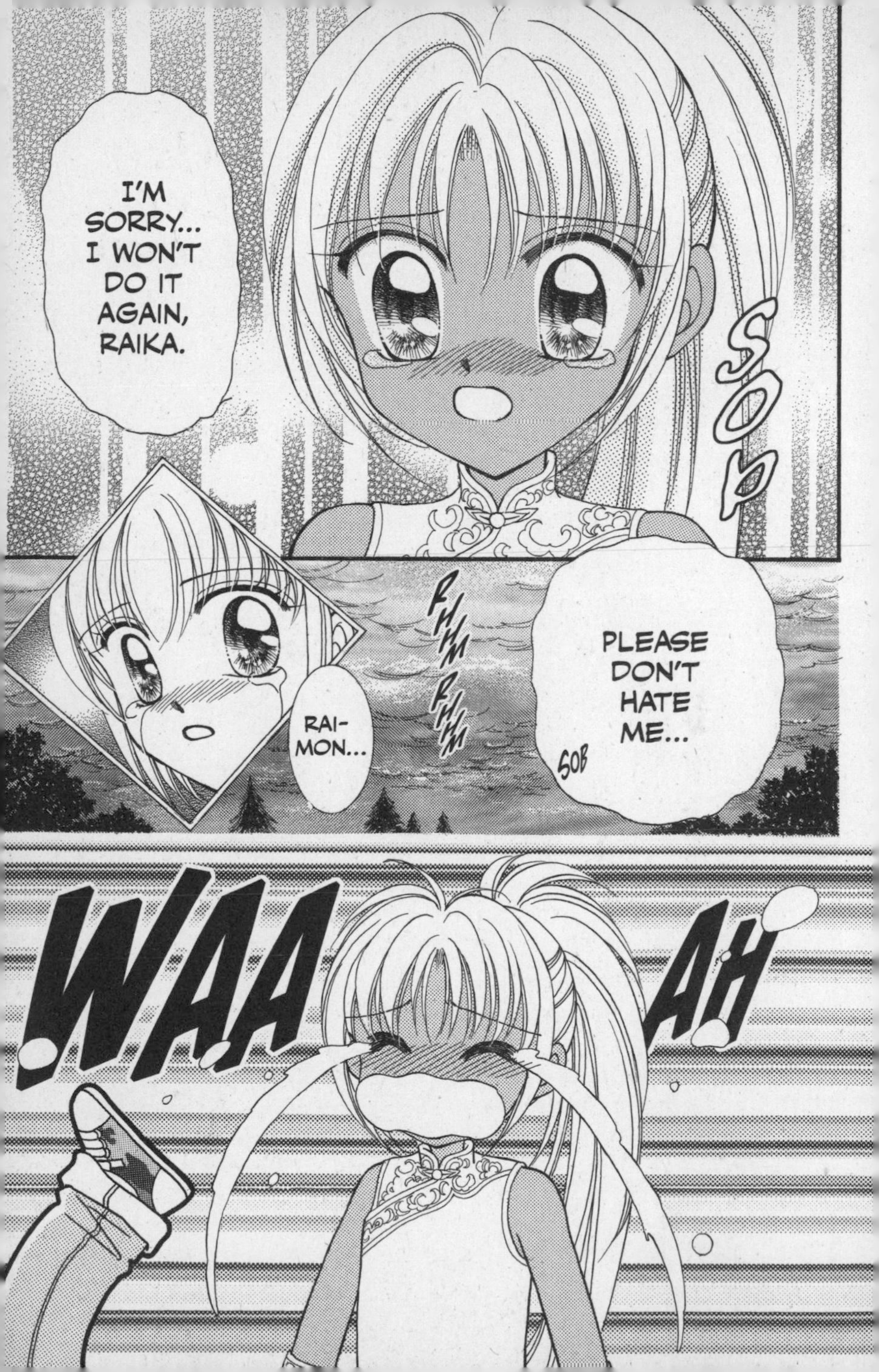
I'M SORRY... I WON'T DO IT AGAIN, RAIKA.
SOB
PLEASE DON'T HATE ME...
SOB
RHHMRHHM
RAI-MON...
WAAAH

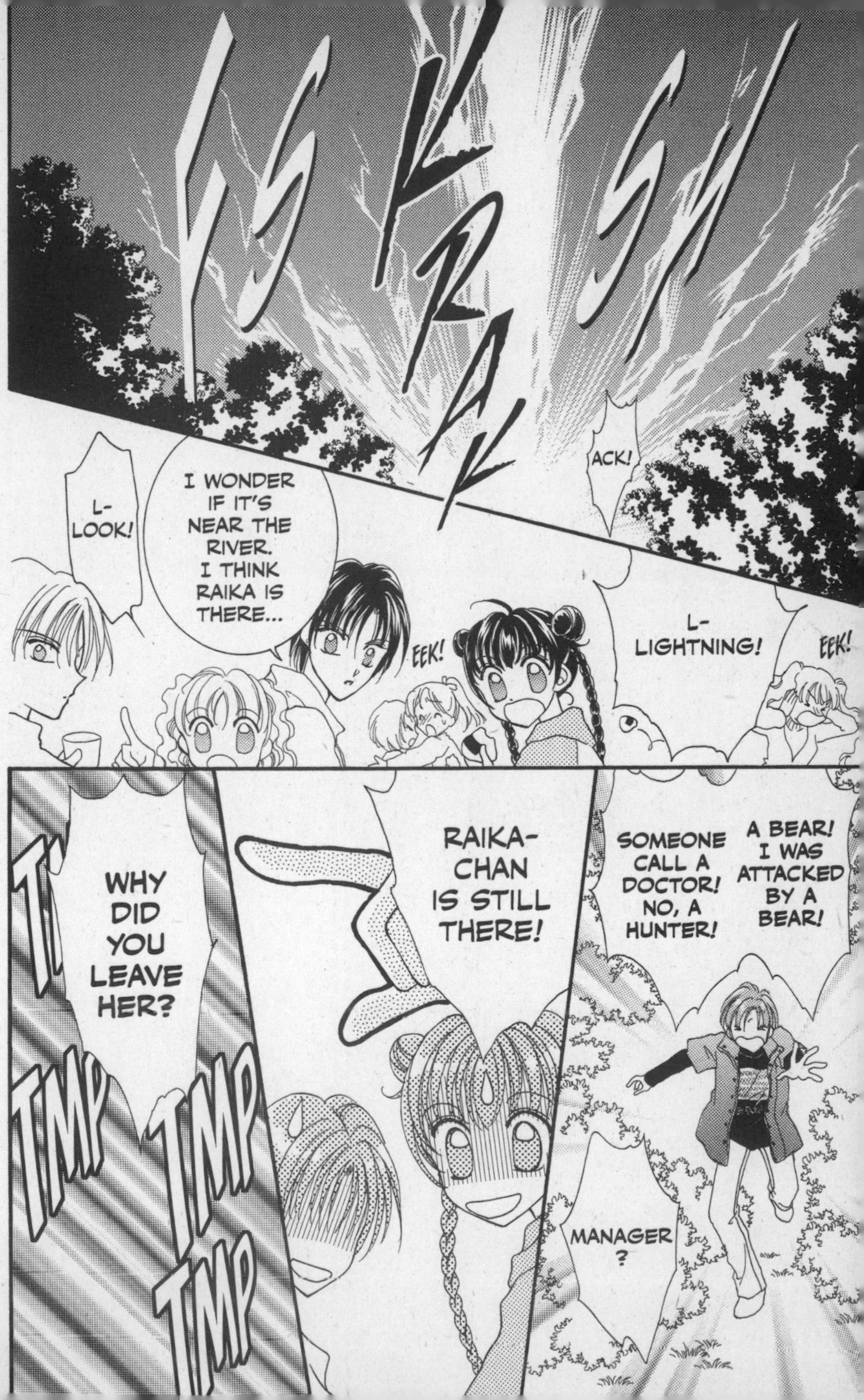
ACK!
EEK!
L- LIGHTNING!
EEK!
I WONDER IF IT'S NEAR THE RIVER. I THINK RAIKA IS THERE...
L- LOOK!
A BEAR! I WAS ATTACKED BY A BEAR!
SOMEONE CALL A DOCTOR! NO, A HUNTER!
MANAGER?
RAIKA-CHAN IS STILL THERE!
WHY DID YOU LEAVE HER?
TMP
TMP
TMP

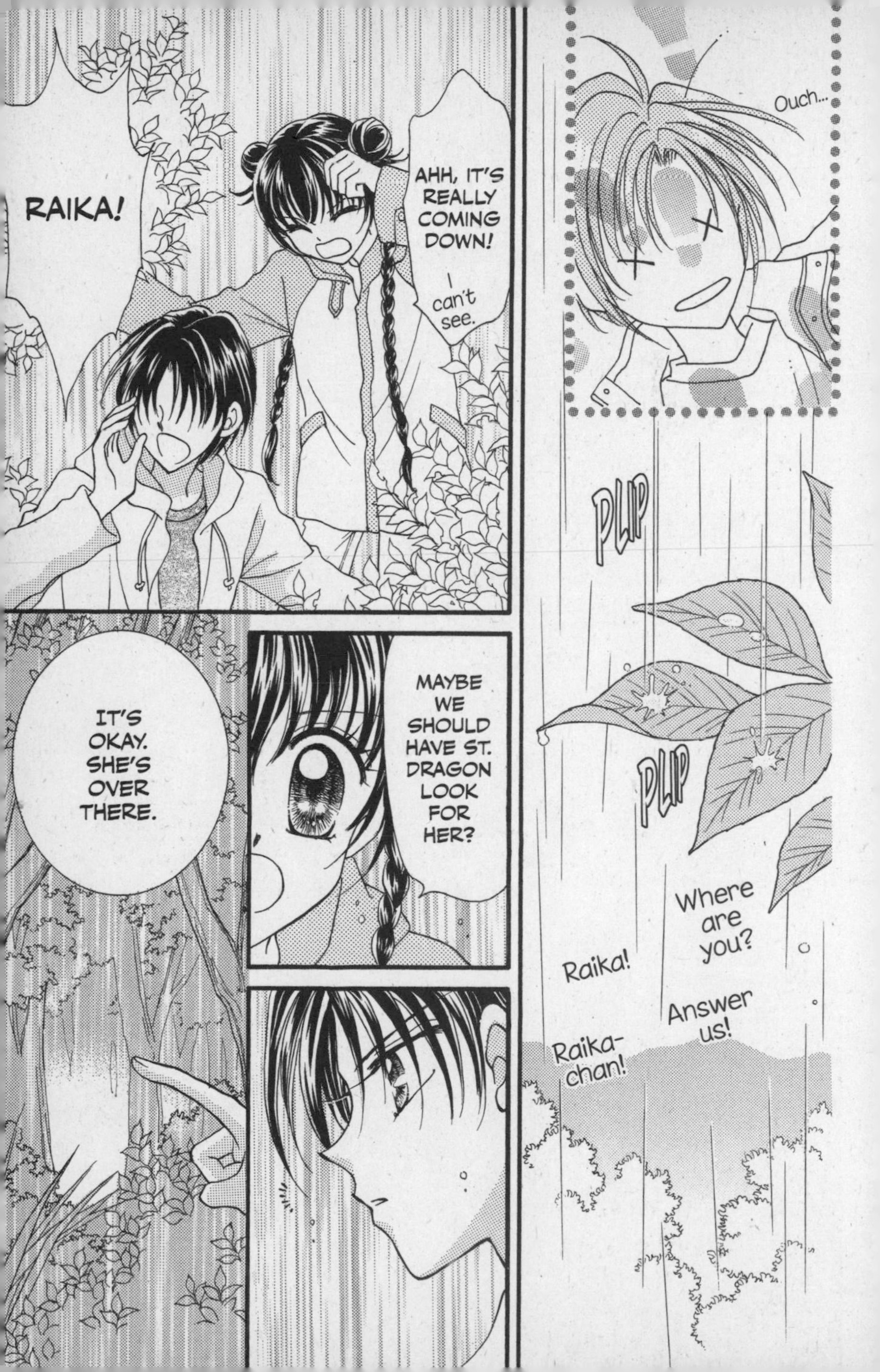
Ouch...
PLIP
PLIP
Where are you?
Raika!
Answer us!
Raika-chan!
AHH, IT'S REALLY COMING DOWN!
I can't see.
RAIKA!
MAYBE WE SHOULD HAVE ST. DRAGON LOOK FOR HER?
IT'S OKAY. SHE'S OVER THERE.

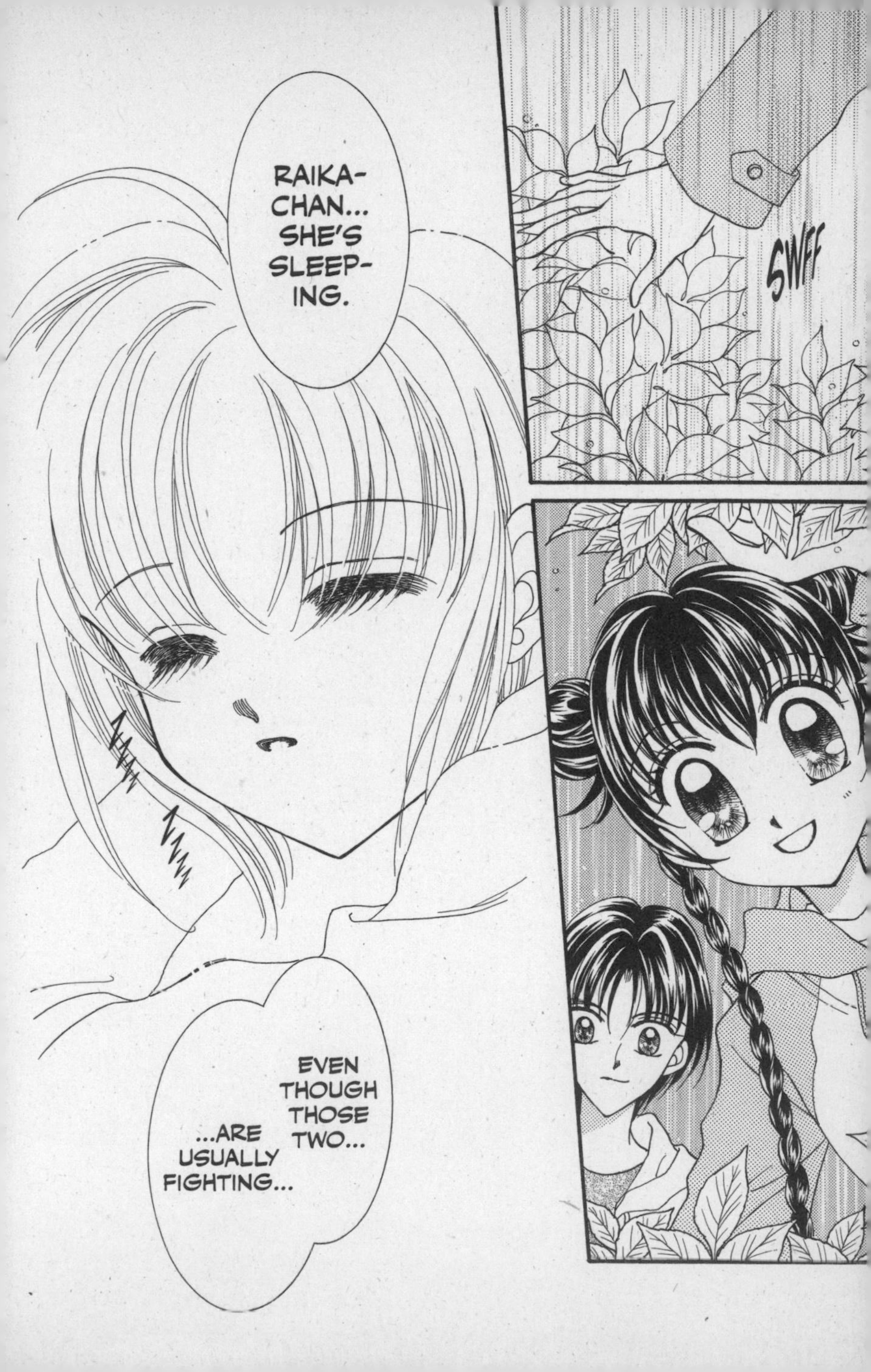
SWFF
RAIKA-CHAN... SHE'S SLEEPING.
EVEN THOUGH THOSE TWO...
...ARE USUALLY FIGHTING...

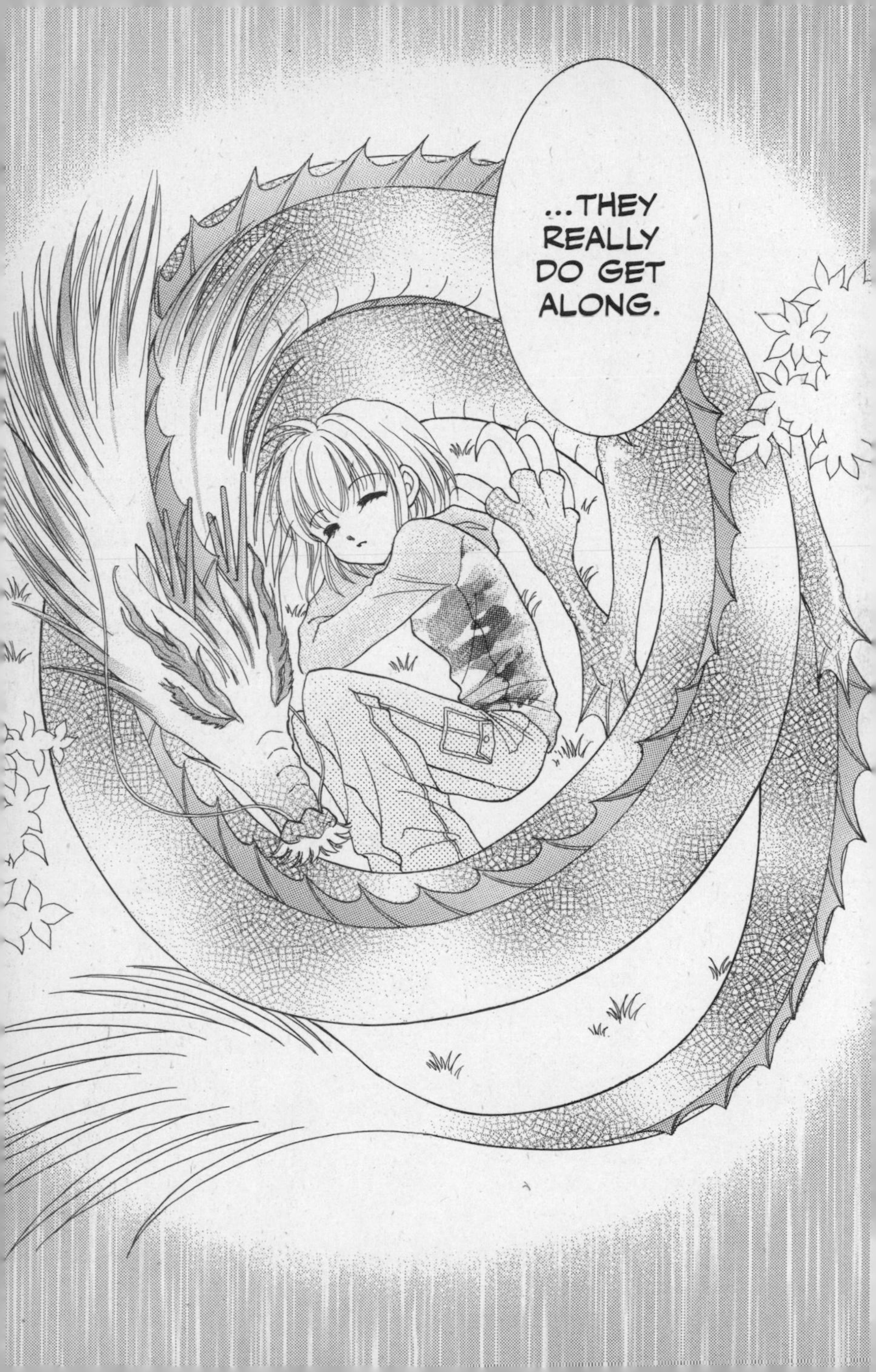
...THEY REALLY DO GET ALONG.

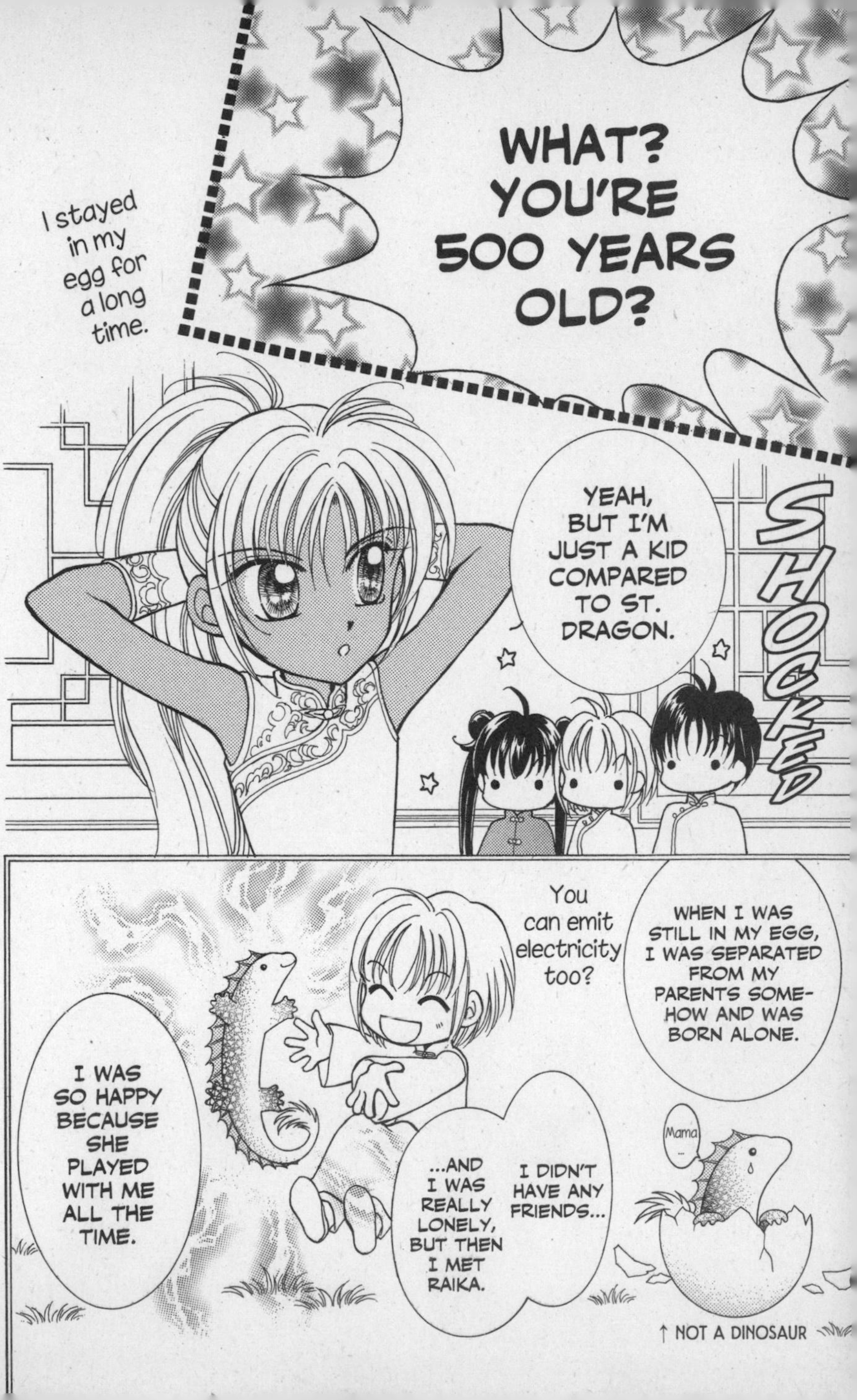
WHAT? YOU'RE 500 YEARS OLD?
I stayed in my egg for a long time.
YEAH, BUT I'M JUST A KID COMPARED TO ST. DRAGON.
SHOCKED
WHEN I WAS STILL IN MY EGG, I WAS SEPARATED FROM MY PARENTS SOMEHOW AND WAS BORN ALONE.
You can emit electricity too?
Mama...
I DIDN'T HAVE ANY FRIENDS...
...AND I WAS REALLY LONELY, BUT THEN I MET RAIKA.
I WAS SO HAPPY BECAUSE SHE PLAYED WITH ME ALL THE TIME.
↑ NOT A DINOSAUR

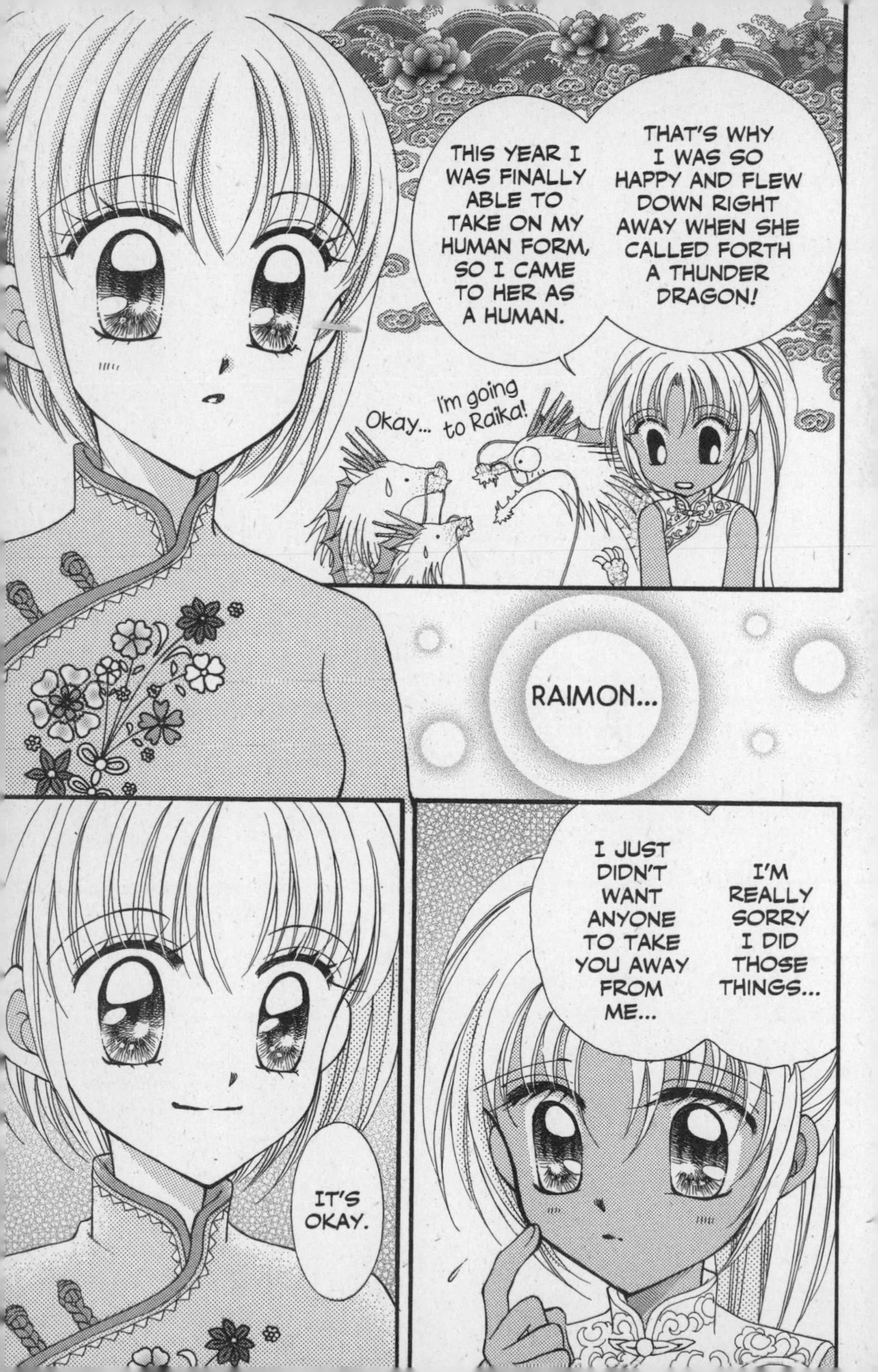
THIS YEAR I WAS FINALLY ABLE TO TAKE ON MY HUMAN FORM, SO I CAME TO HER AS A HUMAN.
THAT'S WHY I WAS SO HAPPY AND FLEW DOWN RIGHT AWAY WHEN SHE CALLED FORTH A THUNDER DRAGON!
I'm going to Raika!
Okay...
RAIMON...
I JUST DIDN'T WANT ANYONE TO TAKE YOU AWAY FROM ME...
I'M REALLY SORRY I DID THOSE THINGS...
IT'S OKAY.

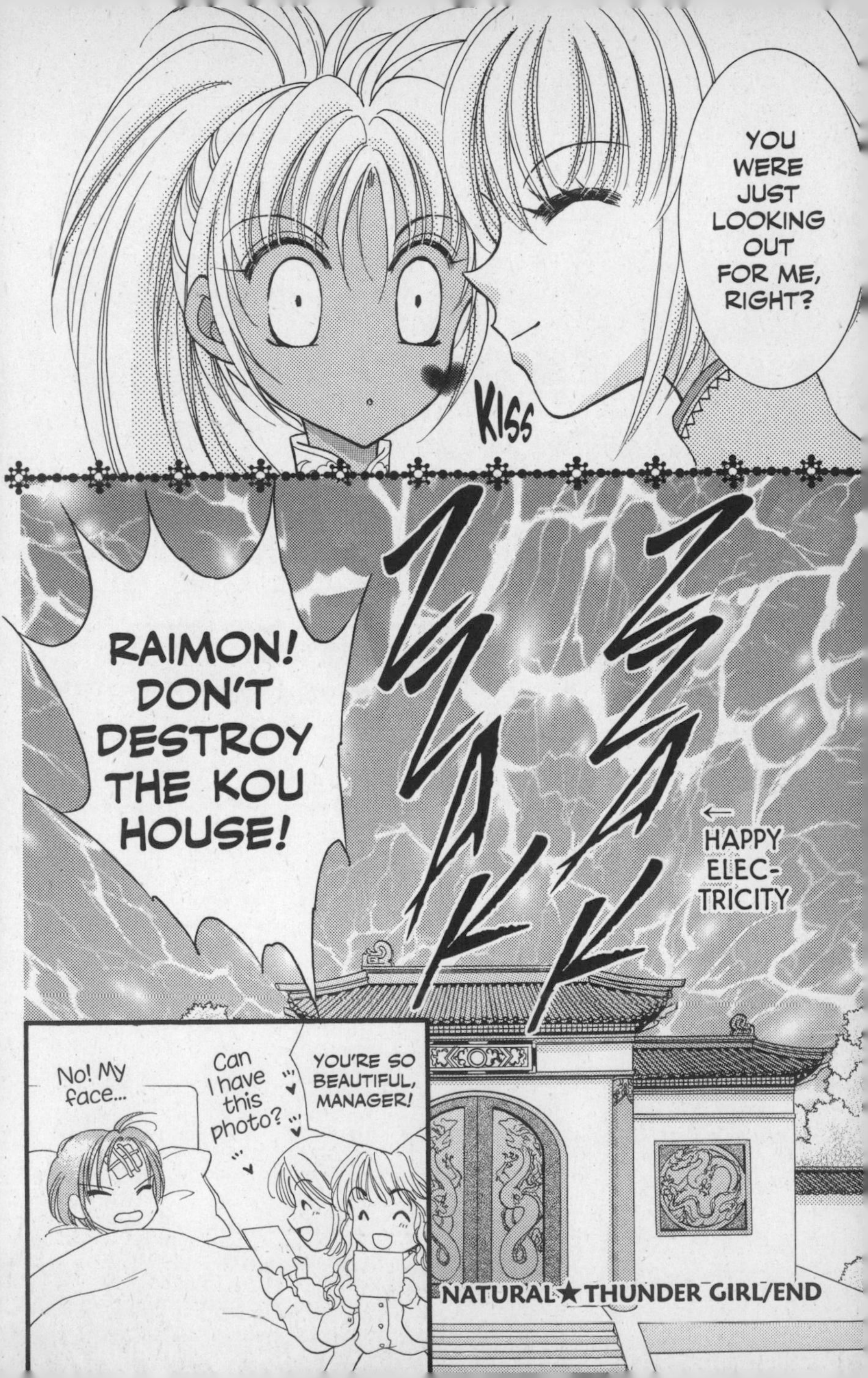
YOU WERE JUST LOOKING OUT FOR ME, RIGHT?
KISS
ZZAAKK
RAIMON! DON'T DESTROY THE KOU HOUSE!
← HAPPY ELEC-TRICITY
NATURAL★THUNDER GIRL/END
YOU'RE SO BEAUTIFUL, MANAGER!
Can I have this photo?
No! My face...

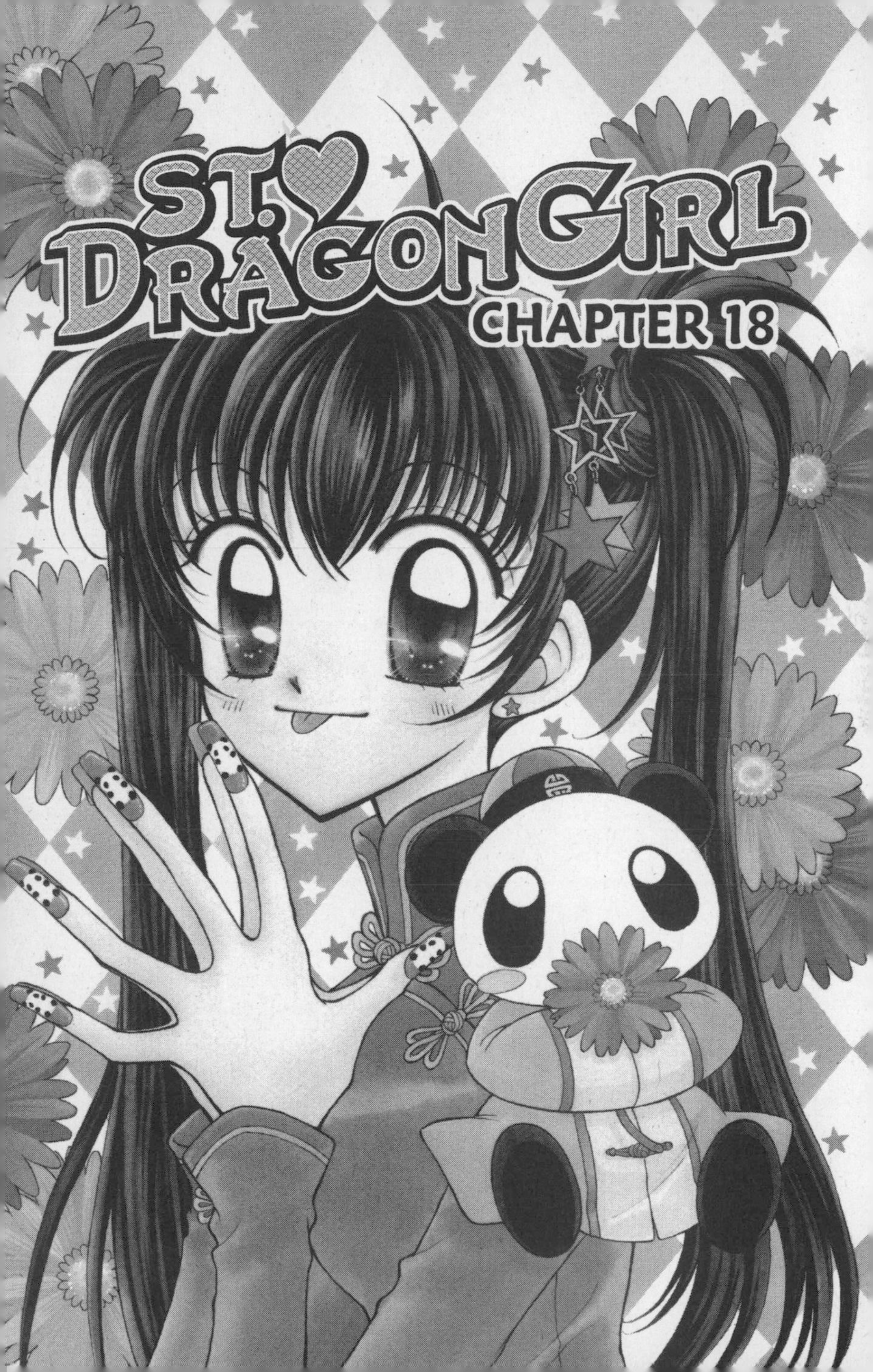
ST. DRAGON GIRL
CHAPTER 18

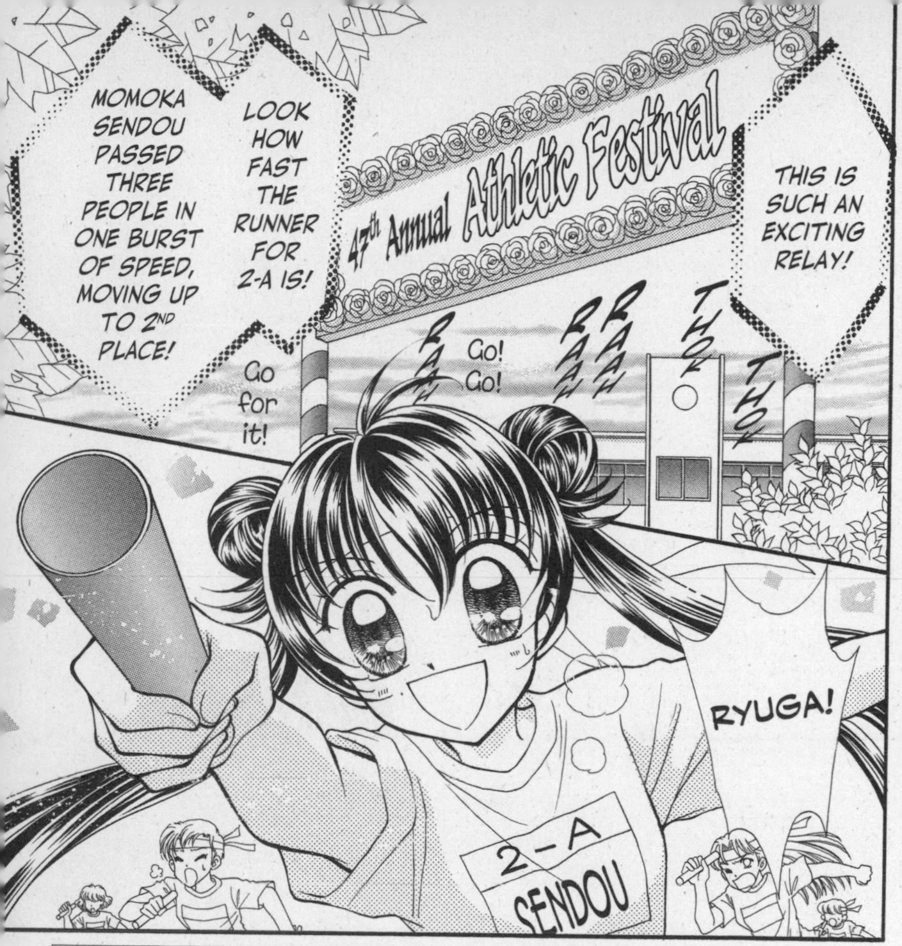
THIS IS SUCH AN EXCITING RELAY!
LOOK HOW FAST THE RUNNER FOR 2-A IS!
MOMOKA SENDOU PASSED THREE PEOPLE IN ONE BURST OF SPEED, MOVING UP TO 2ND PLACE!
47th Annual Athletic Festival
THOM THOM
RAAAH RAAAH
Go! Go!
RAAAH
Go for it!
RYUGA!
2-A SENDOU

Until this volume, I had used this space for character introductions. But there were only ghosts and spirits as the new characters in this volume! So this time I'll use this space to answer questions I get all the time.

- **Please tell me your profile info and what you like to do when you're not working.**

I get this question a lot. I've written profiles for lots of others, but I finally have time for myself in this volume! So this year, if you have any compassion, don't ask me these questions again...(laugh)

Natsumi Matsumoto
Birthday: May 2
Zodiac Sign: Taurus. Blood Type: O
Hometown: Beppushi in Oita Prefecture.
Debuted in 1993 in *Ribon* with "Guuzen Janai Yo."
Favorite Foods: chocolate and curry
Favorite Colors: pink and mint blue
Favorite Celebrities: Kinki Kids and Yousuke Kubozuka
Favorite Flowers: rose, Thunberg spirea, sunflower

Recently I started tai chi. When I don't have to work, I like to watch movies and hang out with friends.

My ambition is to learn how to use computers and cell phones!

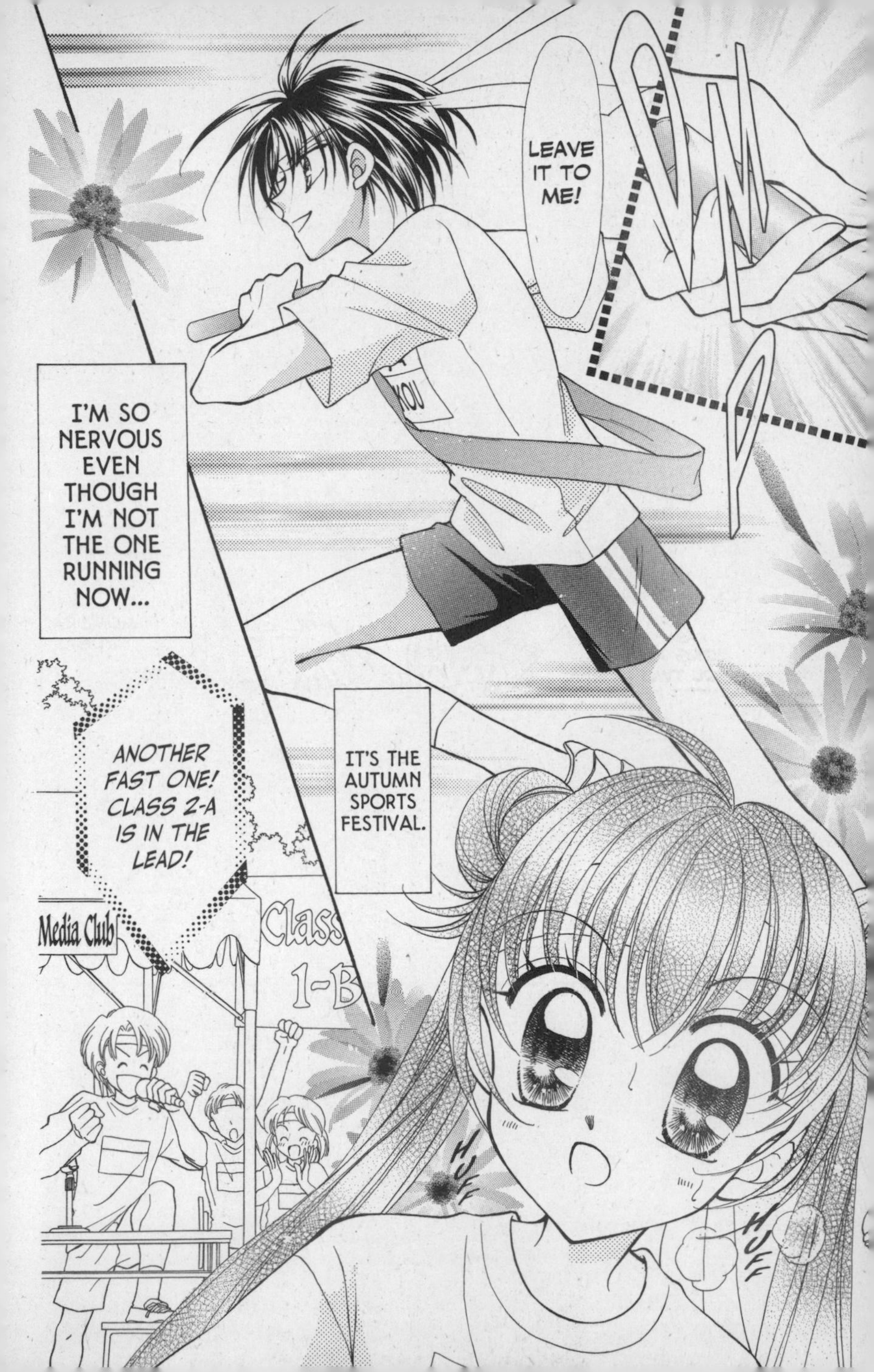
LEAVE IT TO ME!
KOU
I'M SO NERVOUS EVEN THOUGH I'M NOT THE ONE RUNNING NOW...
IT'S THE AUTUMN SPORTS FESTIVAL.
ANOTHER FAST ONE! CLASS 2-A IS IN THE LEAD!
Media Club
Class 1-B
HUFF
HUFF

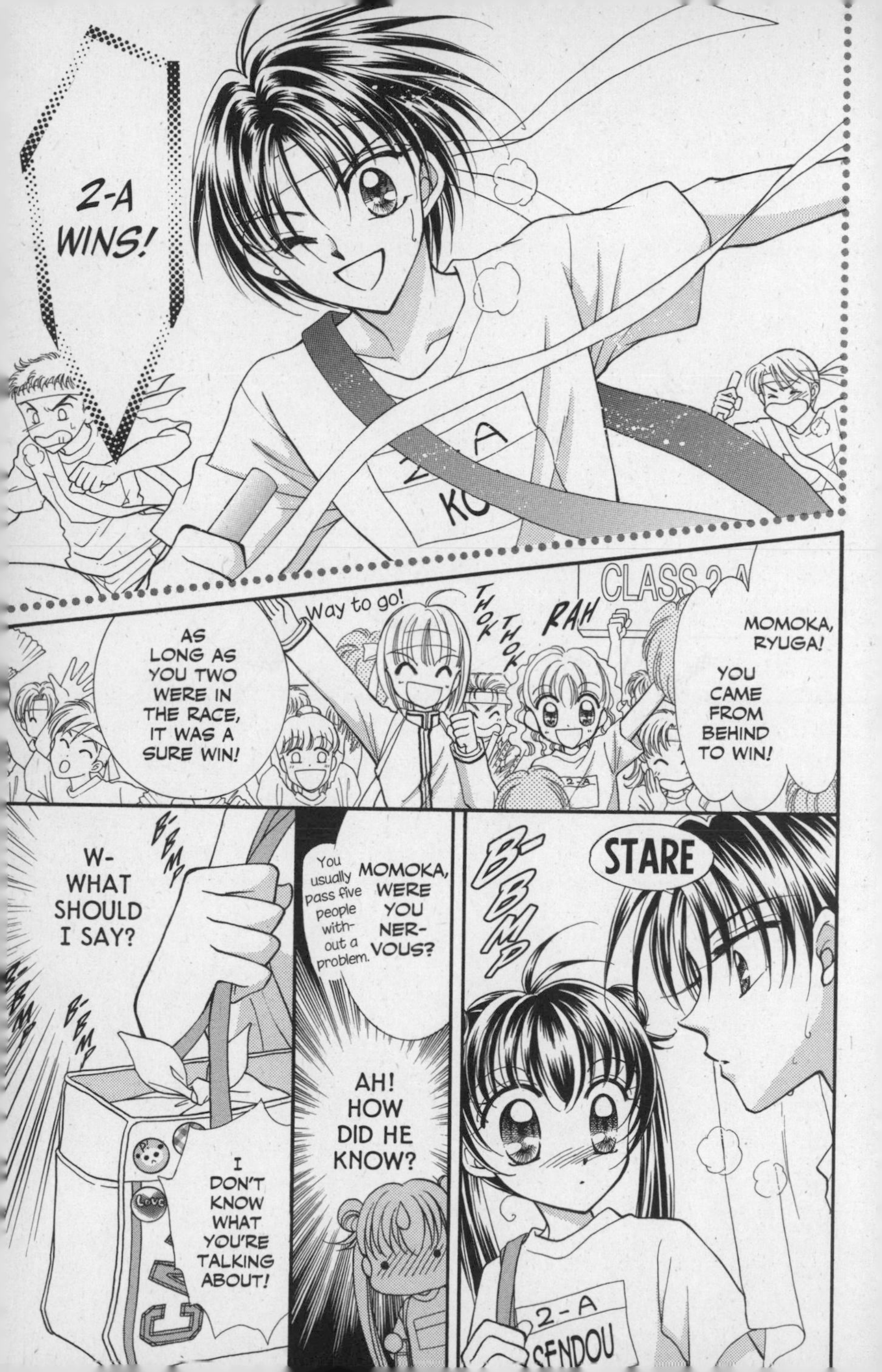
2-A WINS!
MOMOKA, RYUGA!
YOU CAME FROM BEHIND TO WIN!
RAH
THOK THOK
Way to go!
AS LONG AS YOU TWO WERE IN THE RACE, IT WAS A SURE WIN!
STARE
B-BMP
2-A SENDOU
MOMOKA, WERE YOU NERVOUS?
You usually pass five people without a problem.
AH! HOW DID HE KNOW?
W- WHAT SHOULD I SAY?
I DON'T KNOW WHAT YOU'RE TALKING ABOUT!

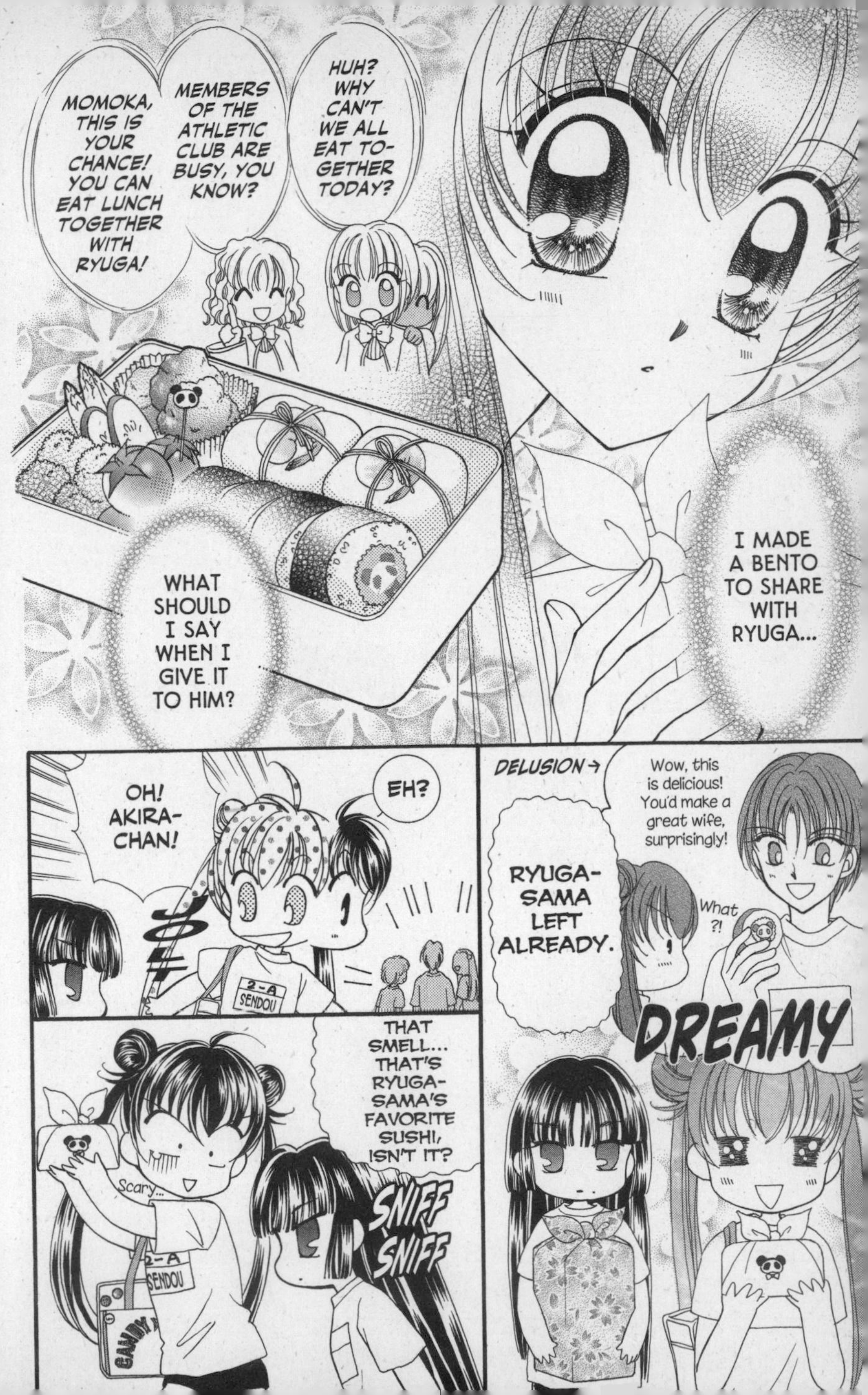
HUH? WHY CAN'T WE ALL EAT TO- GETHER TODAY?
MEMBERS OF THE ATHLETIC CLUB ARE BUSY, YOU KNOW?
MOMOKA, THIS IS YOUR CHANCE! YOU CAN EAT LUNCH TOGETHER WITH RYUGA!
I MADE A BENTO TO SHARE WITH RYUGA...
WHAT SHOULD I SAY WHEN I GIVE IT TO HIM?
DELUSION →
Wow, this is delicious! You'd make a great wife, surprisingly!
What ?!
RYUGA-SAMA LEFT ALREADY.
DREAMY
EH?
OH! AKIRA-CHAN!
2-A SENDOU
THAT SMELL... THAT'S RYUGA-SAMA'S FAVORITE SUSHI, ISN'T IT?
Scary...
SNIFF SNIFF
2-A SENDOU

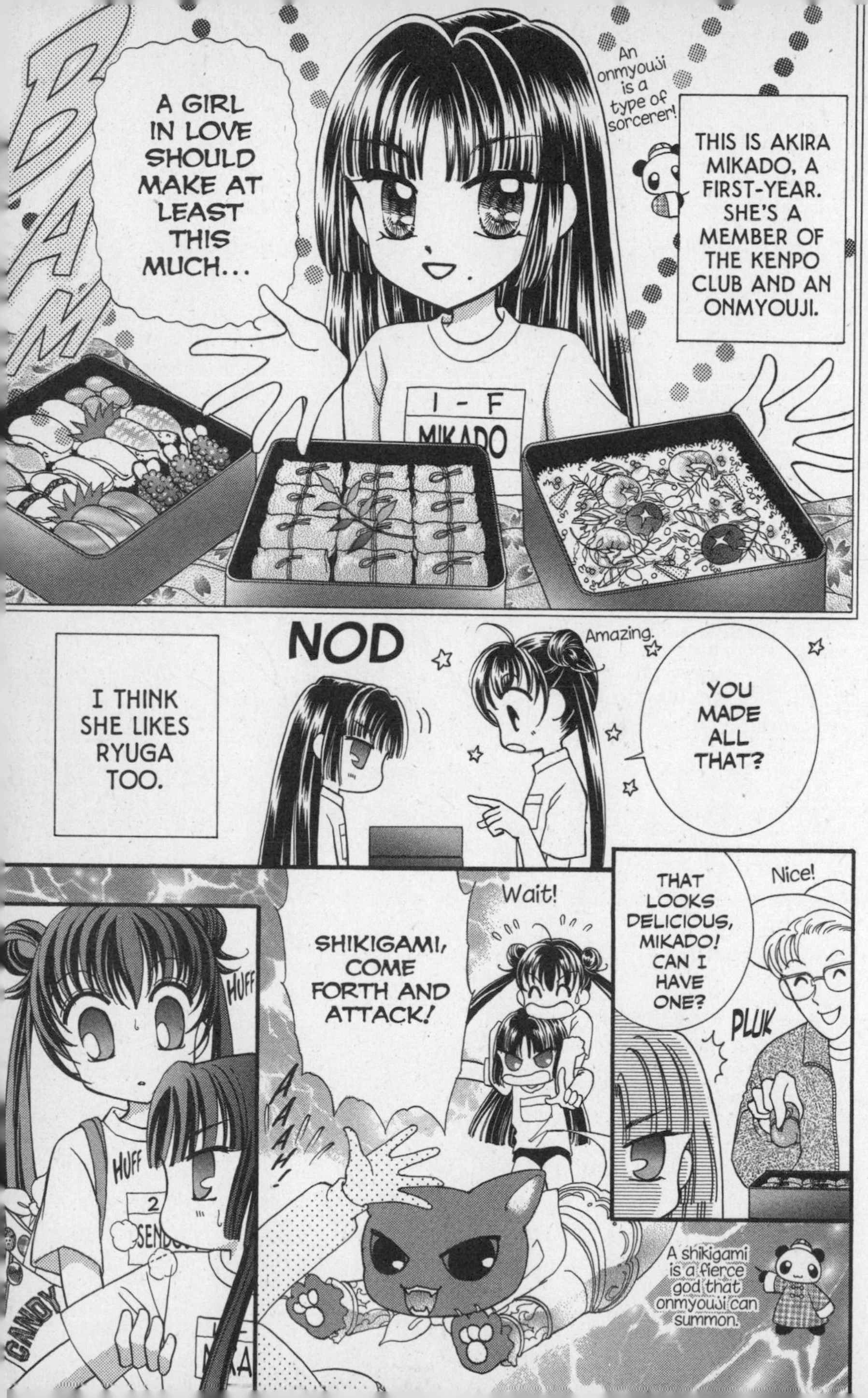
An onmyouji is a type of sorcerer!
THIS IS AKIRA MIKADO, A FIRST-YEAR. SHE'S A MEMBER OF THE KENPO CLUB AND AN ONMYOUJI.
A GIRL IN LOVE SHOULD MAKE AT LEAST THIS MUCH...
BAM
I - F
MIKADO
Amazing.
YOU MADE ALL THAT?
NOD
I THINK SHE LIKES RYUGA TOO.
Nice!
THAT LOOKS DELICIOUS, MIKADO! CAN I HAVE ONE?
PLUK
Wait!
SHIKIGAMI, COME FORTH AND ATTACK!
AAAAH!
A shikigami is a fierce god that onmyouji can summon.
HUFF
HUFF
2
CANDY

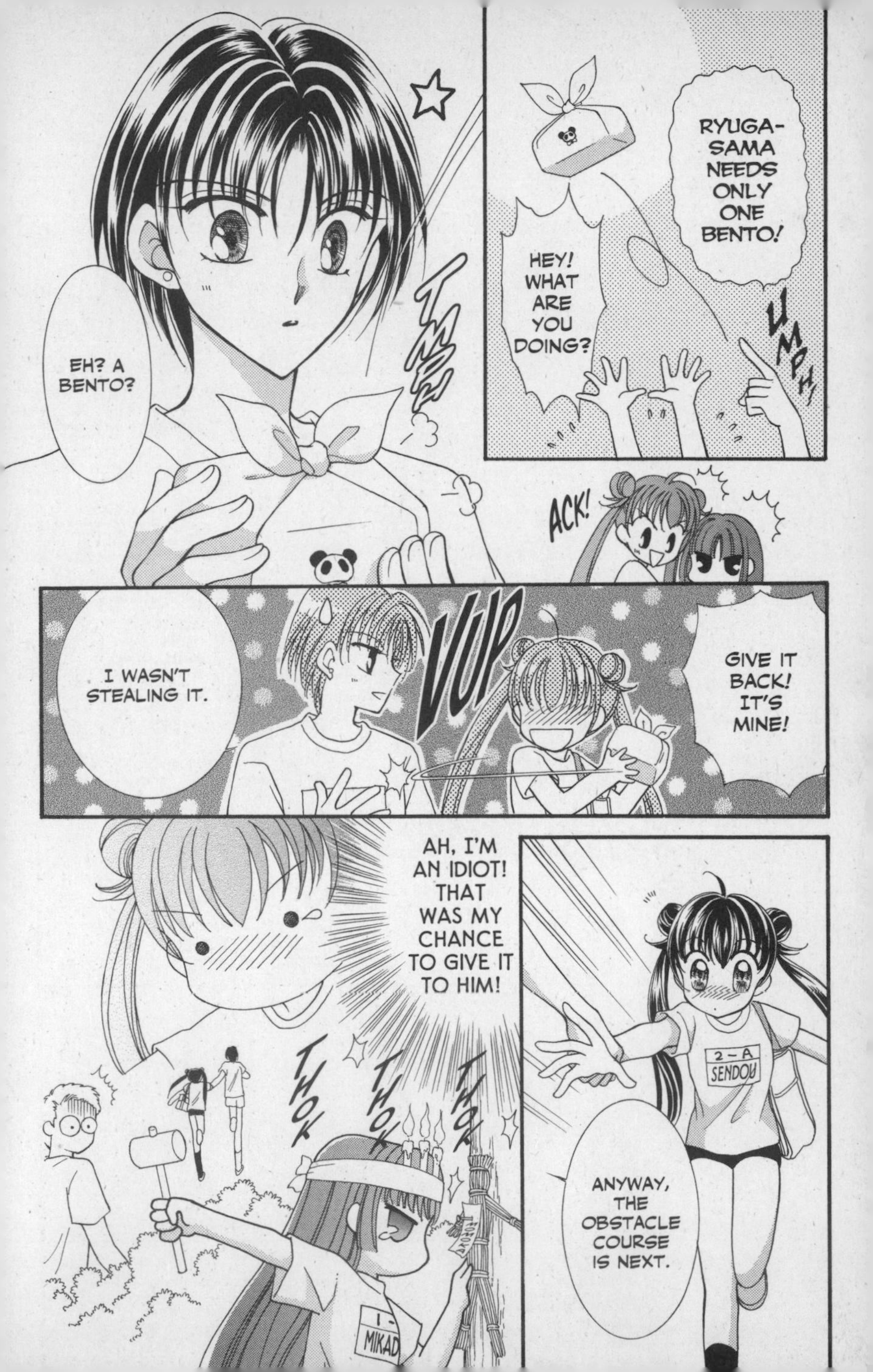
RYUGA-SAMA NEEDS ONLY ONE BENTO!
UMPH!
HEY! WHAT ARE YOU DOING?
EH? A BENTO?
ACK!
GIVE IT BACK! IT'S MINE!
VUP
I WASN'T STEALING IT.
2-A SENDOU
ANYWAY, THE OBSTACLE COURSE IS NEXT.
AH, I'M AN IDIOT! THAT WAS MY CHANCE TO GIVE IT TO HIM!
THOK
THOK
THOK

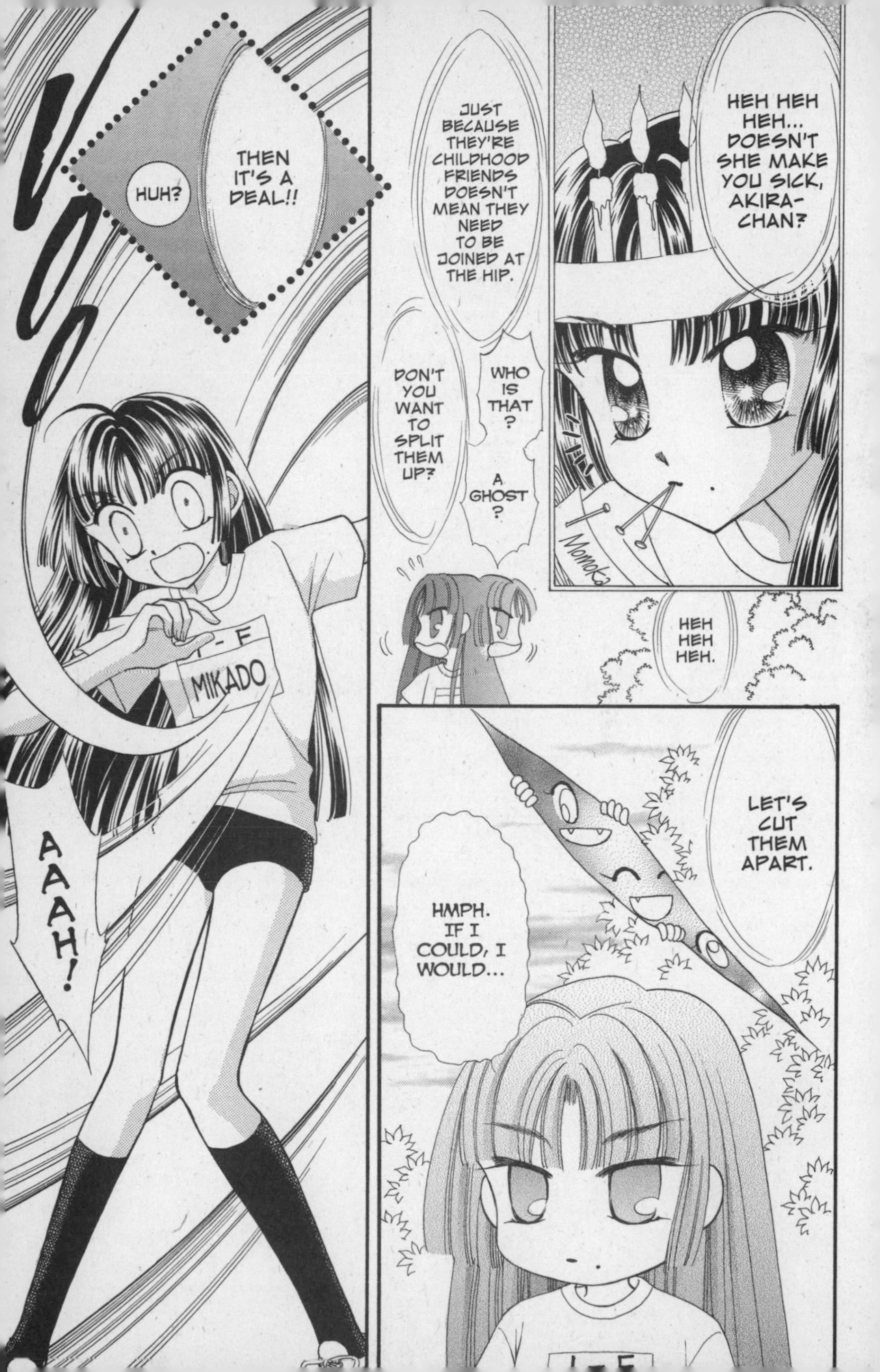
HEH HEH HEH... DOESN'T SHE MAKE YOU SICK, AKIRA-CHAN?
Momoka
JUST BECAUSE THEY'RE CHILDHOOD FRIENDS DOESN'T MEAN THEY NEED TO BE JOINED AT THE HIP.
WHO IS THAT?
A GHOST?
DON'T YOU WANT TO SPLIT THEM UP?
HEH HEH HEH.
LET'S CUT THEM APART.
HMPH. IF I COULD, I WOULD...
THEN IT'S A DEAL!!
HUH?
MIKADO
AAAH!

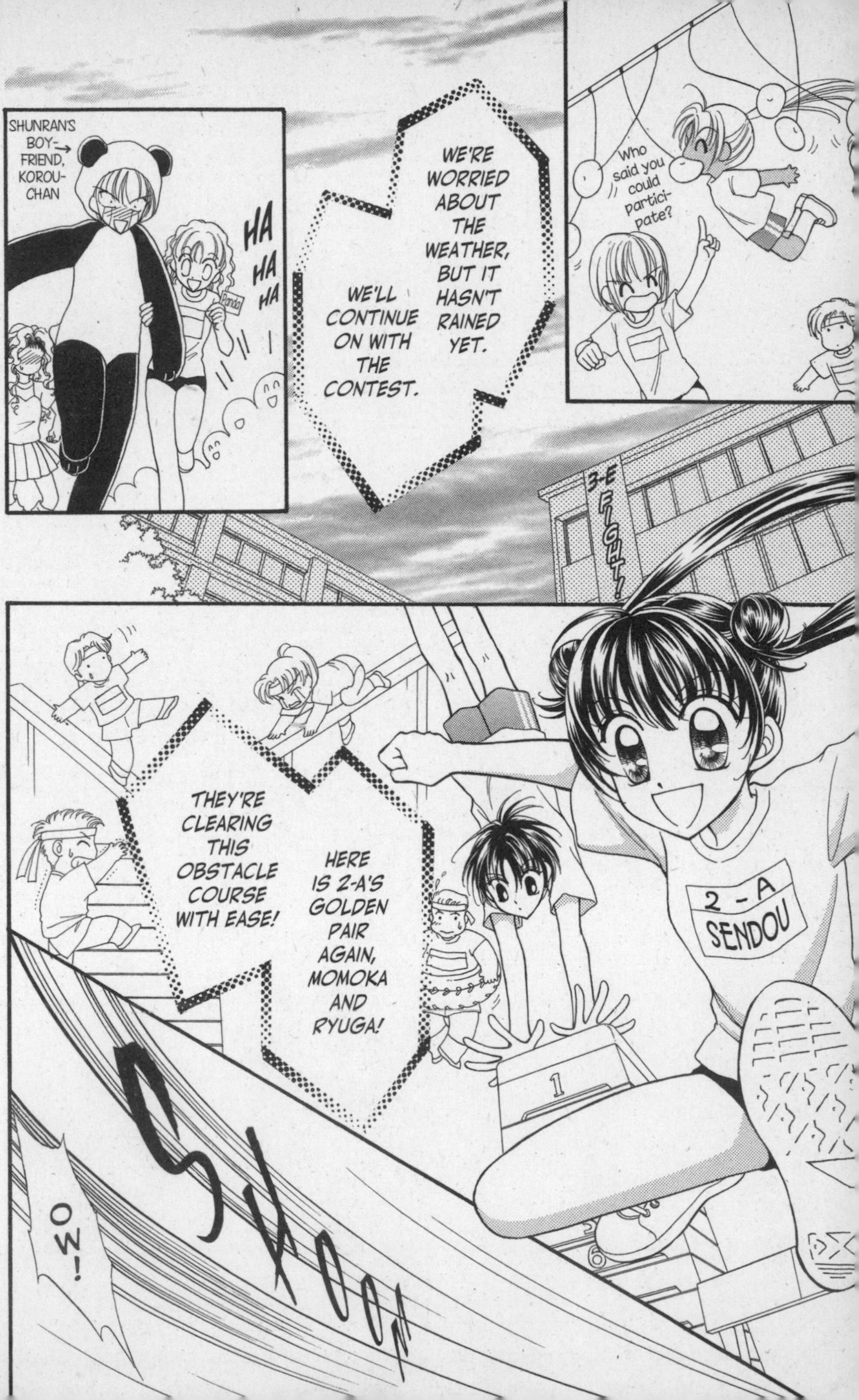
Who said you could partici-pate?
WE'RE WORRIED ABOUT THE WEATHER, BUT IT HASN'T RAINED YET.
WE'LL CONTINUE ON WITH THE CONTEST.
SHUNRAN'S BOY-FRIEND, KOROU-CHAN
HA HA HA
Panda
3-E FIGHT!
HERE IS 2-A'S GOLDEN PAIR AGAIN, MOMOKA AND RYUGA!
THEY'RE CLEARING THIS OBSTACLE COURSE WITH EASE!
2-A SENDOU
1
SHOOP
OW!

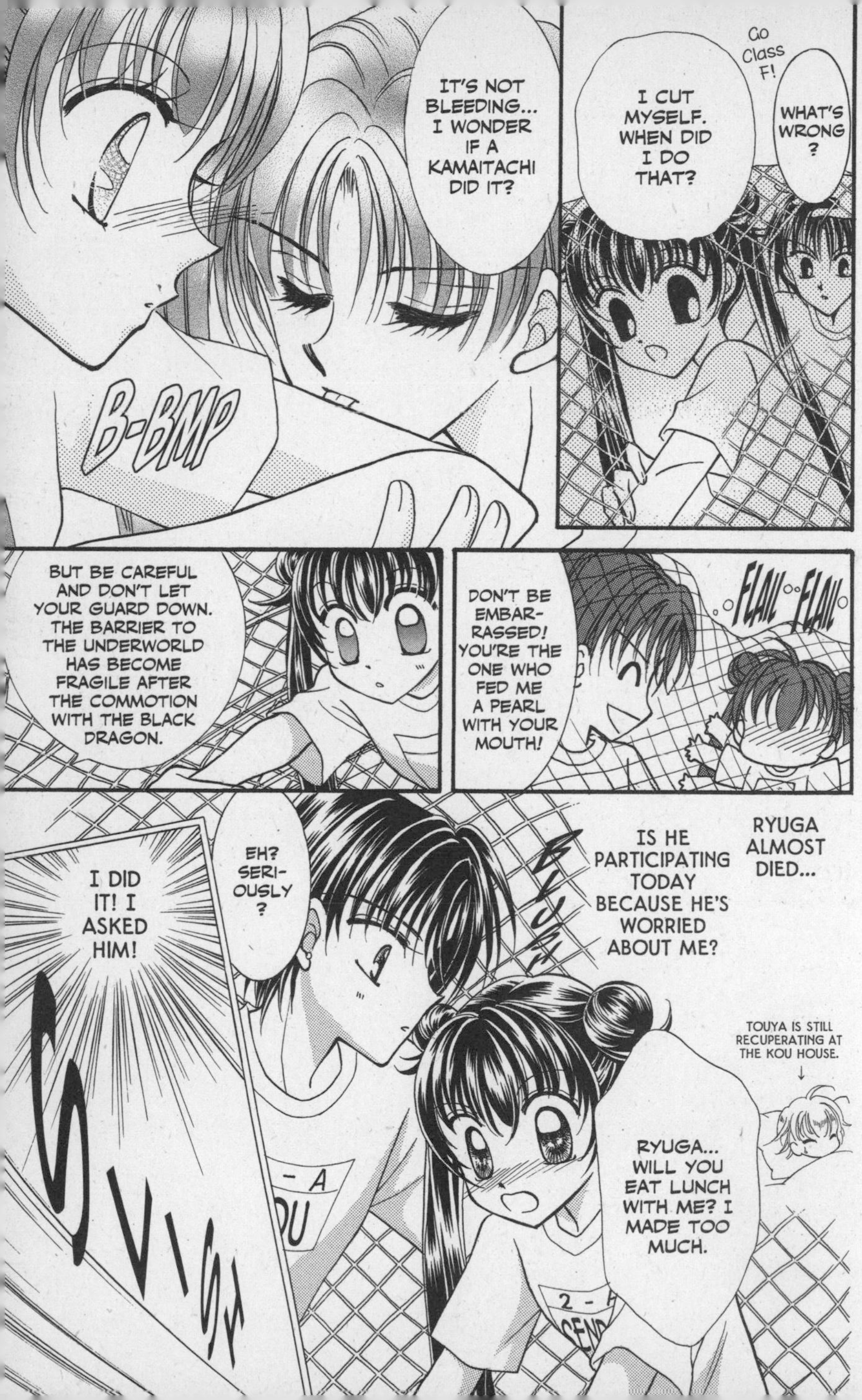
Go Class F!
WHAT'S WRONG?
I CUT MYSELF. WHEN DID I DO THAT?
IT'S NOT BLEEDING... I WONDER IF A KAMAITACHI DID IT?
B-BMP
FLAIL FLAIL
DON'T BE EMBARRASSED! YOU'RE THE ONE WHO FED ME A PEARL WITH YOUR MOUTH!
BUT BE CAREFUL AND DON'T LET YOUR GUARD DOWN. THE BARRIER TO THE UNDERWORLD HAS BECOME FRAGILE AFTER THE COMMOTION WITH THE BLACK DRAGON.
RYUGA ALMOST DIED...
IS HE PARTICIPATING TODAY BECAUSE HE'S WORRIED ABOUT ME?
TOUYA IS STILL RECUPERATING AT THE KOU HOUSE.
RYUGA... WILL YOU EAT LUNCH WITH ME? I MADE TOO MUCH.
EH? SERIOUSLY?
I DID IT! I ASKED HIM!
SWISH

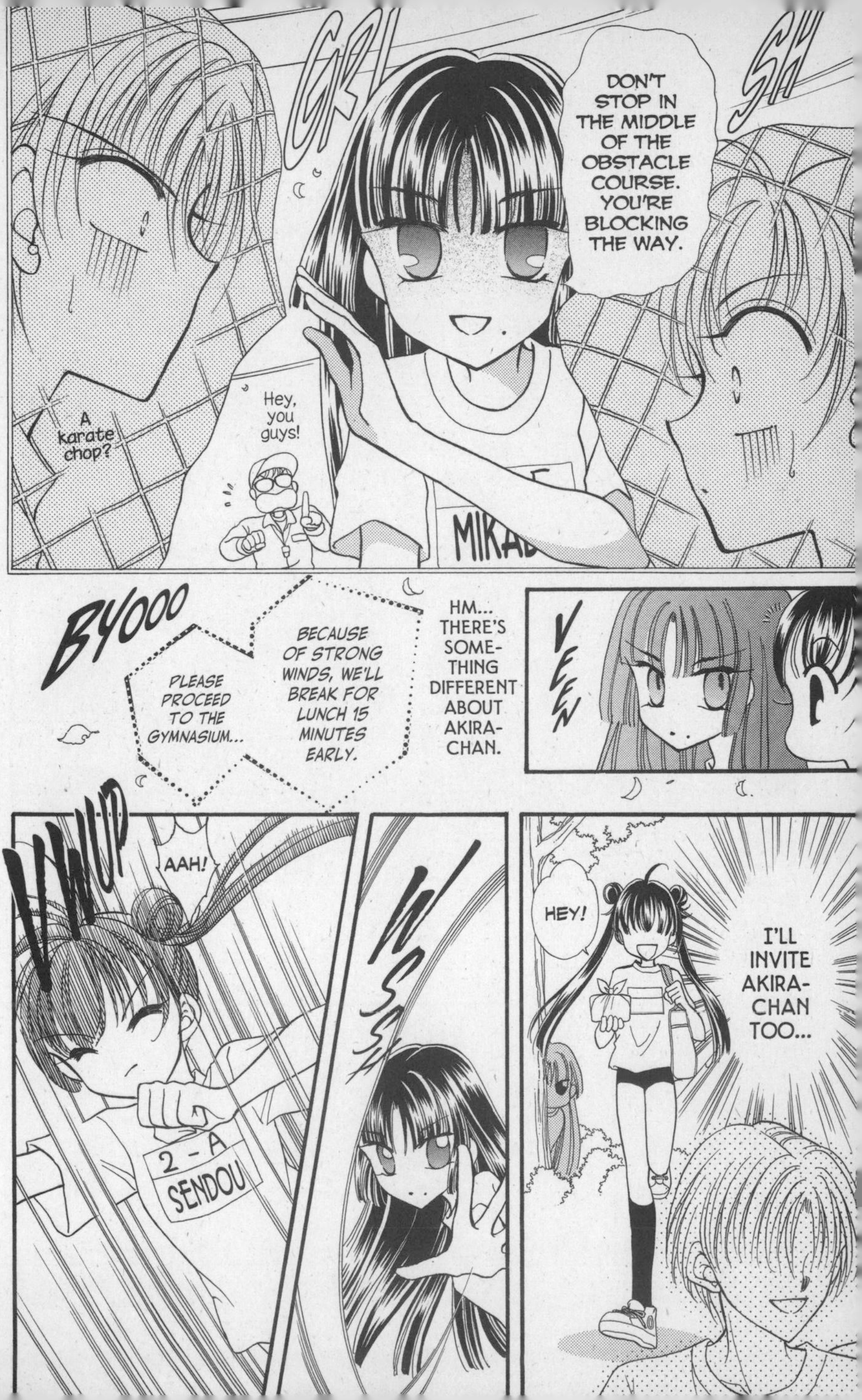
SH
DON'T STOP IN THE MIDDLE OF THE OBSTACLE COURSE. YOU'RE BLOCKING THE WAY.
GRI
Hey, you guys!
A karate chop?
VEEN
HM... THERE'S SOME-THING DIFFERENT ABOUT AKIRA-CHAN.
BECAUSE OF STRONG WINDS, WE'LL BREAK FOR LUNCH 15 MINUTES EARLY.
PLEASE PROCEED TO THE GYMNASIUM...
BYOOO
I'LL INVITE AKIRA-CHAN TOO...
HEY!
VWUP
AAH!
2 - A
SENDOU

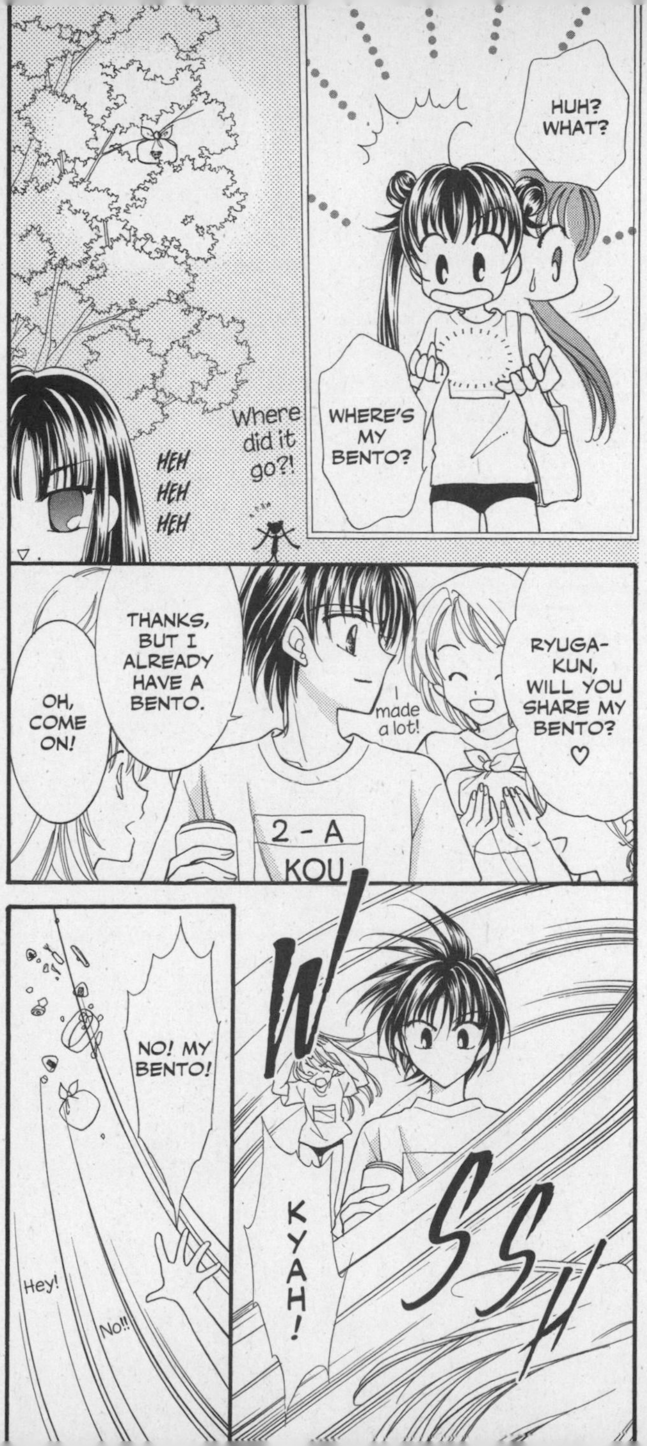
HUH? WHAT?
WHERE'S MY BENTO?
Where did it go?!
HEH HEH HEH
RYUGA-KUN, WILL YOU SHARE MY BENTO? ♡
I made a lot!
THANKS, BUT I ALREADY HAVE A BENTO.
OH, COME ON!
2 - A KOU
W
KYAH!
SSH
NO! MY BENTO!
Hey!
No!!

1

Hello, this is Matsumoto! I hope you're enjoying *St.♥Dragon Girl* volume 5.

I started this volume with a story based around Raika, and I bet a lot of people will be surprised!

Don't worry though. Momoka is still the main character. (laugh)

"Natural☆Thunder Girl" was a bonus story in the November 2001 issue of *Ribon*.

However, *St.♥Dragon Girl* was also in it, so there were two stories of mine in one month... I really worked hard!

Around that time, I was so busy that I barely have any memories of it... I had always wanted to write something about Raimon, so I was glad when I heard I could write a bonus story. It was a lot of work, but it was really fun too!

I really love the combination of Raika and Raimon. I want to write more about them sometime.

I also love that perverted club manager! (laugh)

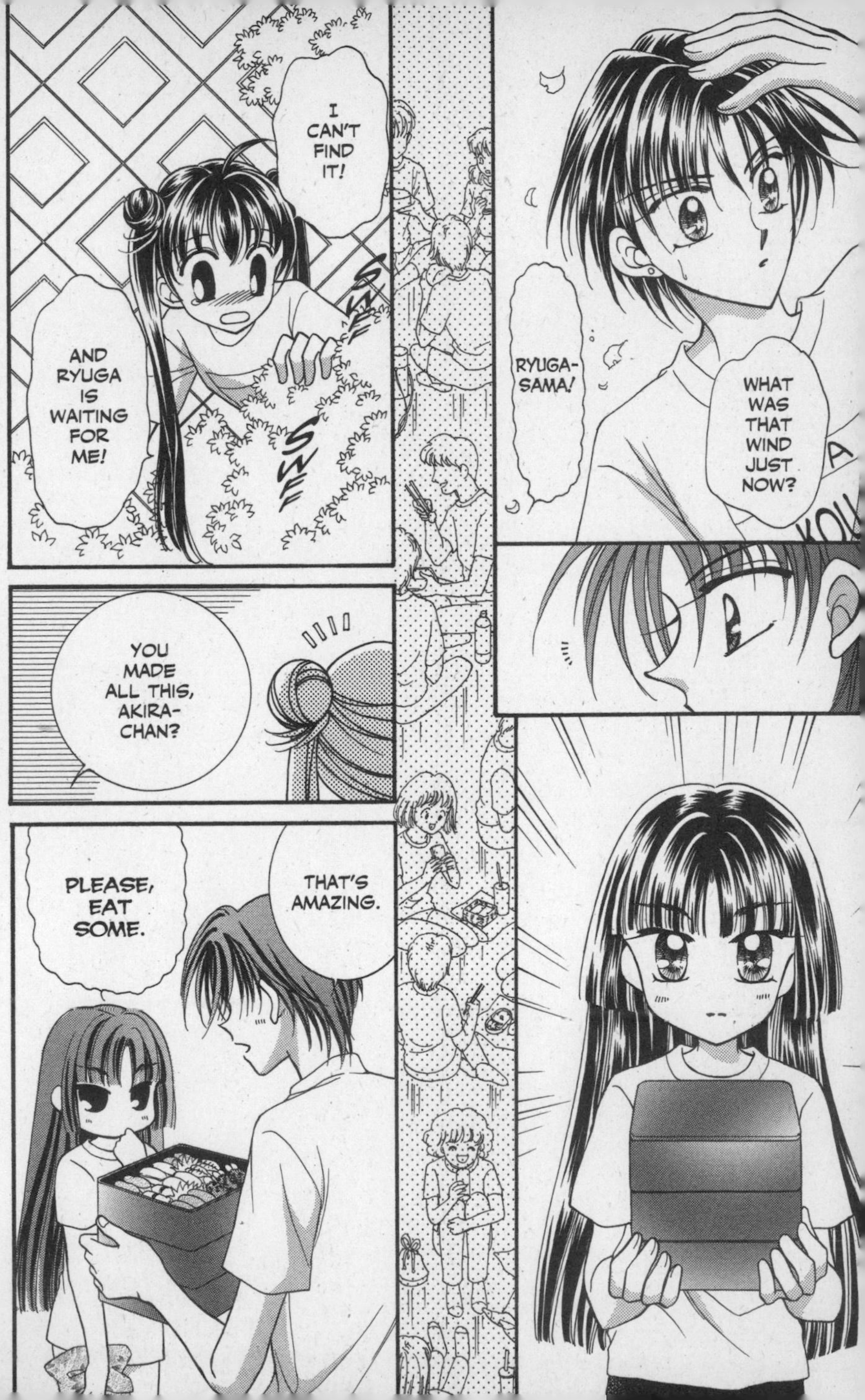
WHAT WAS THAT WIND JUST NOW?
RYUGA-SAMA!
I CAN'T FIND IT!
SWFF
AND RYUGA IS WAITING FOR ME!
SWFF
YOU MADE ALL THIS, AKIRA-CHAN?
THAT'S AMAZING.
PLEASE, EAT SOME.

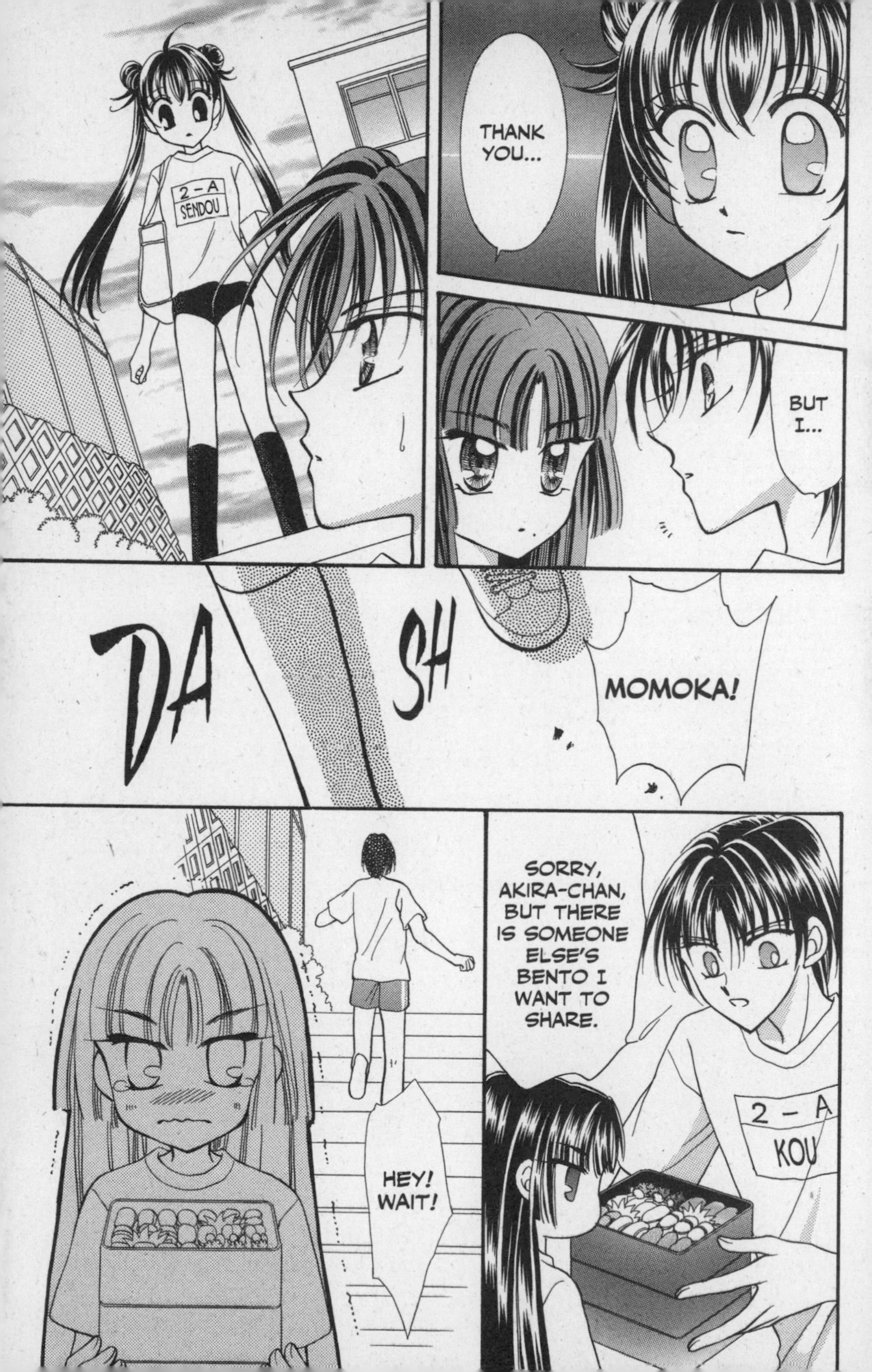
THANK YOU...
BUT I...
2 – A
SENDOU
MOMOKA!
DASH
SORRY, AKIRA-CHAN, BUT THERE IS SOMEONE ELSE'S BENTO I WANT TO SHARE.
2 – A
KOU
HEY! WAIT!

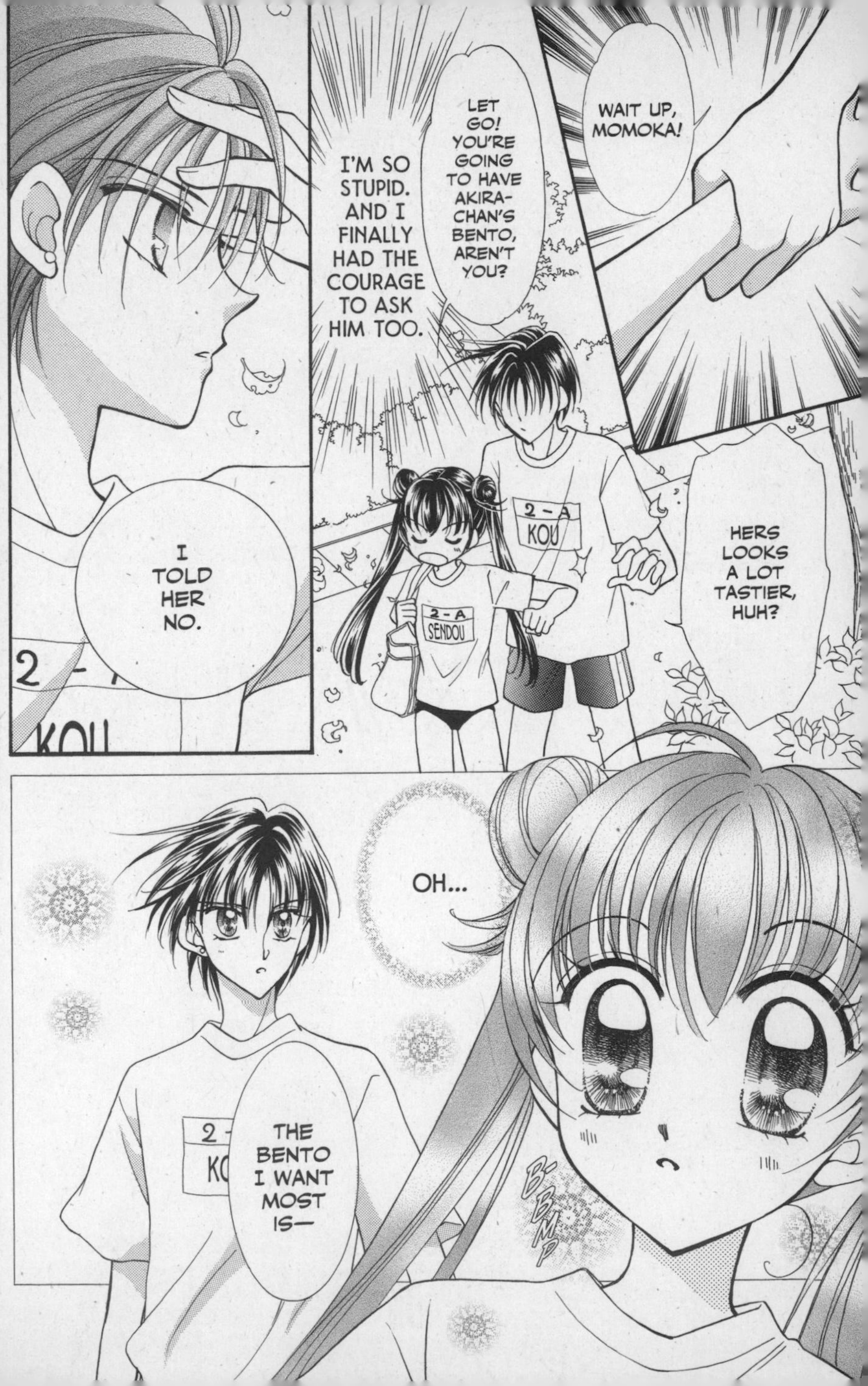
WAIT UP, MOMOKA!
LET GO! YOU'RE GOING TO HAVE AKIRA-CHAN'S BENTO, AREN'T YOU?
HERS LOOKS A LOT TASTIER, HUH?
I'M SO STUPID. AND I FINALLY HAD THE COURAGE TO ASK HIM TOO.
2-A KOU
2-A SENDOU
I TOLD HER NO.
OH...
THE BENTO I WANT MOST IS—
B-BMP

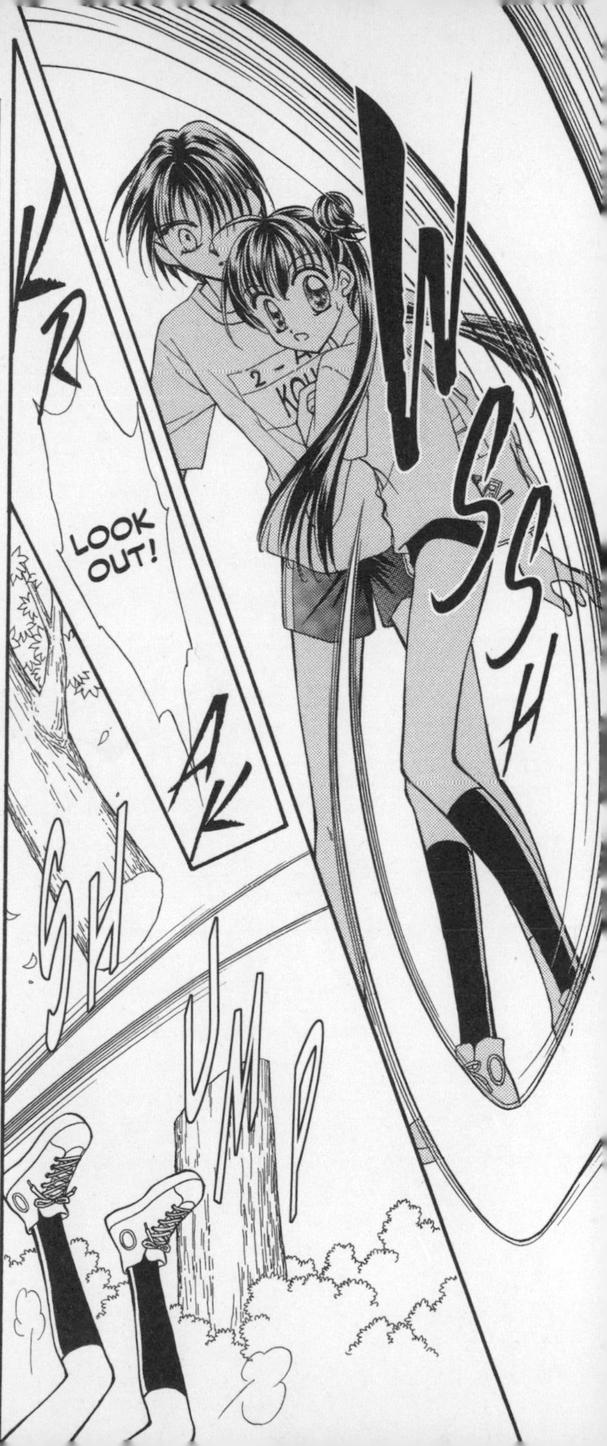
WSSH
LOOK OUT!
KRAK

2

In the October issue, the Yutengenyo storyline ended, and then I started with the regular chapter stories when I wrote about the kamaitachi.

In *Ribon Original*, I got 40-45 pages, but in this magazine I get 32 pages for a story. It was pretty tough, but now that I'm used to it, I think I like this format better.

But I really liked the sequence of stories I did. That's probably because until then, *St.♥Dragon Girl* was one story per chapter.

It's a shame I can't have more action scenes, but I guess it's good to divide it up more. Please give me your opinions too.

Well, this is from the November issue and is about three kamaitachi siblings, the cat god general, and the wind god! Drawing nonhuman characters is so fun! (laugh)

While I was drawing the cat god, I remembered I had originally intended the character of Akira-chan to show up in my other manga "Just Ask Alice!" as the main character's rival.

Her personality was the same. But in that one she was supposed to have come home from England and been a witch with a black cat as her familiar.

(continued in sidebar 3)

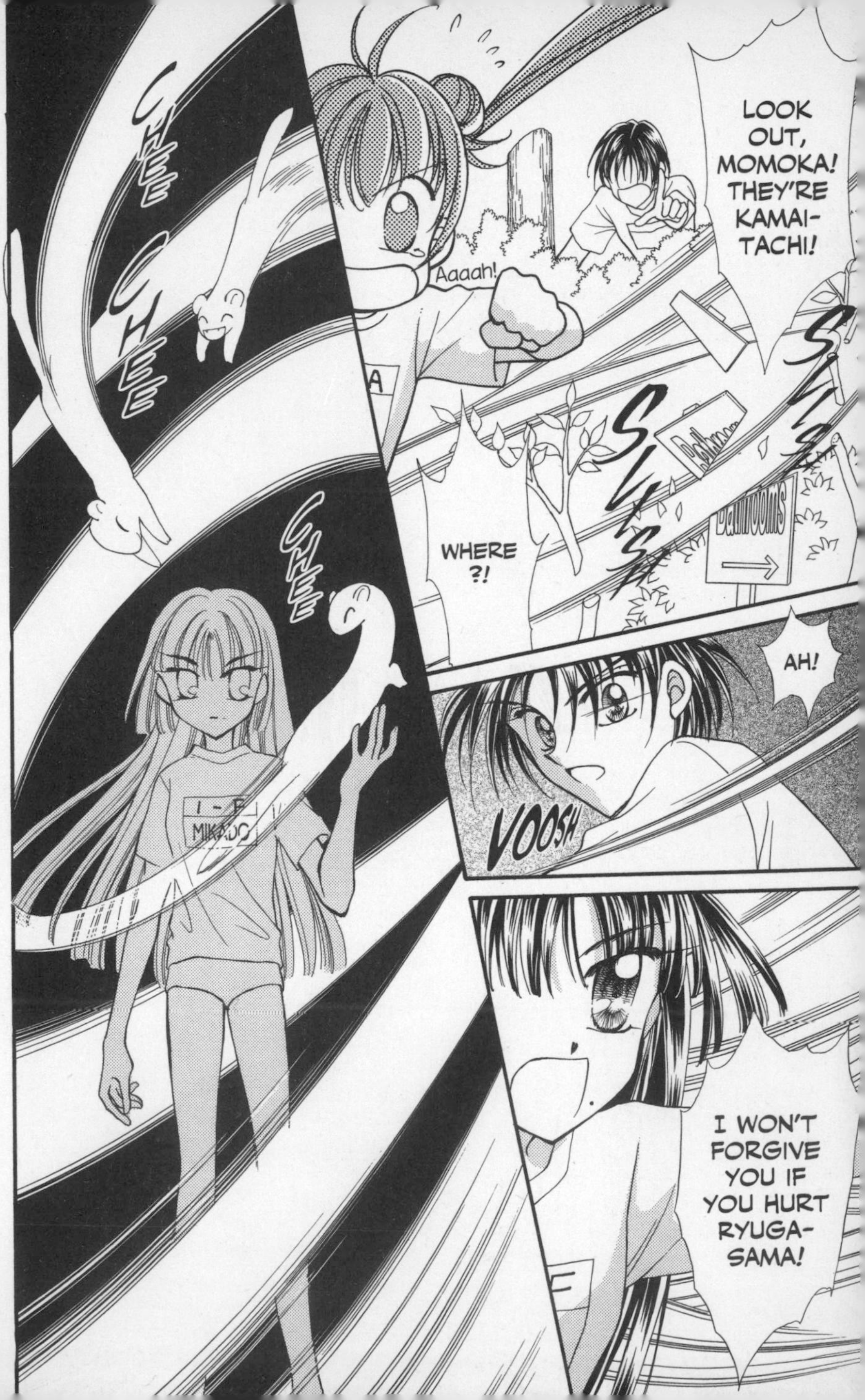
LOOK OUT, MOMOKA! THEY'RE KAMAI-TACHI!
Aaaah!
SLISH
SLISH
WHERE?!
AH!
VOOSH
I WON'T FORGIVE YOU IF YOU HURT RYUGA-SAMA!
CHEE CHEE CHEE
CHEE
MIKADO

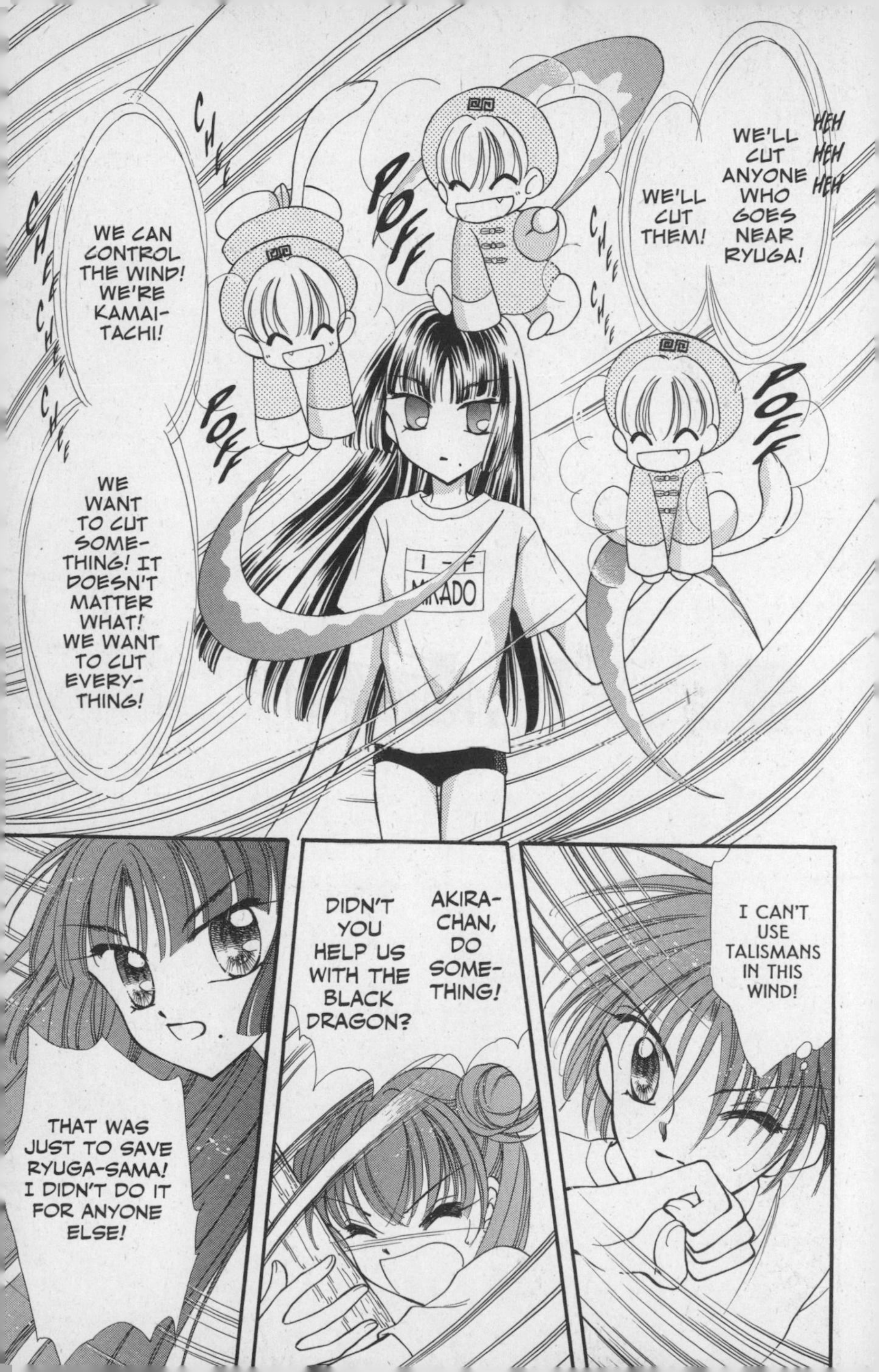
HEH HEH HEH
WE'LL CUT ANYONE WHO GOES NEAR RYUGA!
WE'LL CUT THEM!
CHEE CHEE CHEE
POFF
CHEE
WE CAN CONTROL THE WIND! WE'RE KAMAI-TACHI!
CHEE CHEE CHEE
POFF
POFF
WE WANT TO CUT SOME-THING! IT DOESN'T MATTER WHAT! WE WANT TO CUT EVERY-THING!
I CAN'T USE TALISMANS IN THIS WIND!
AKIRA-CHAN, DO SOME-THING!
DIDN'T YOU HELP US WITH THE BLACK DRAGON?
THAT WAS JUST TO SAVE RYUGA-SAMA! I DIDN'T DO IT FOR ANYONE ELSE!

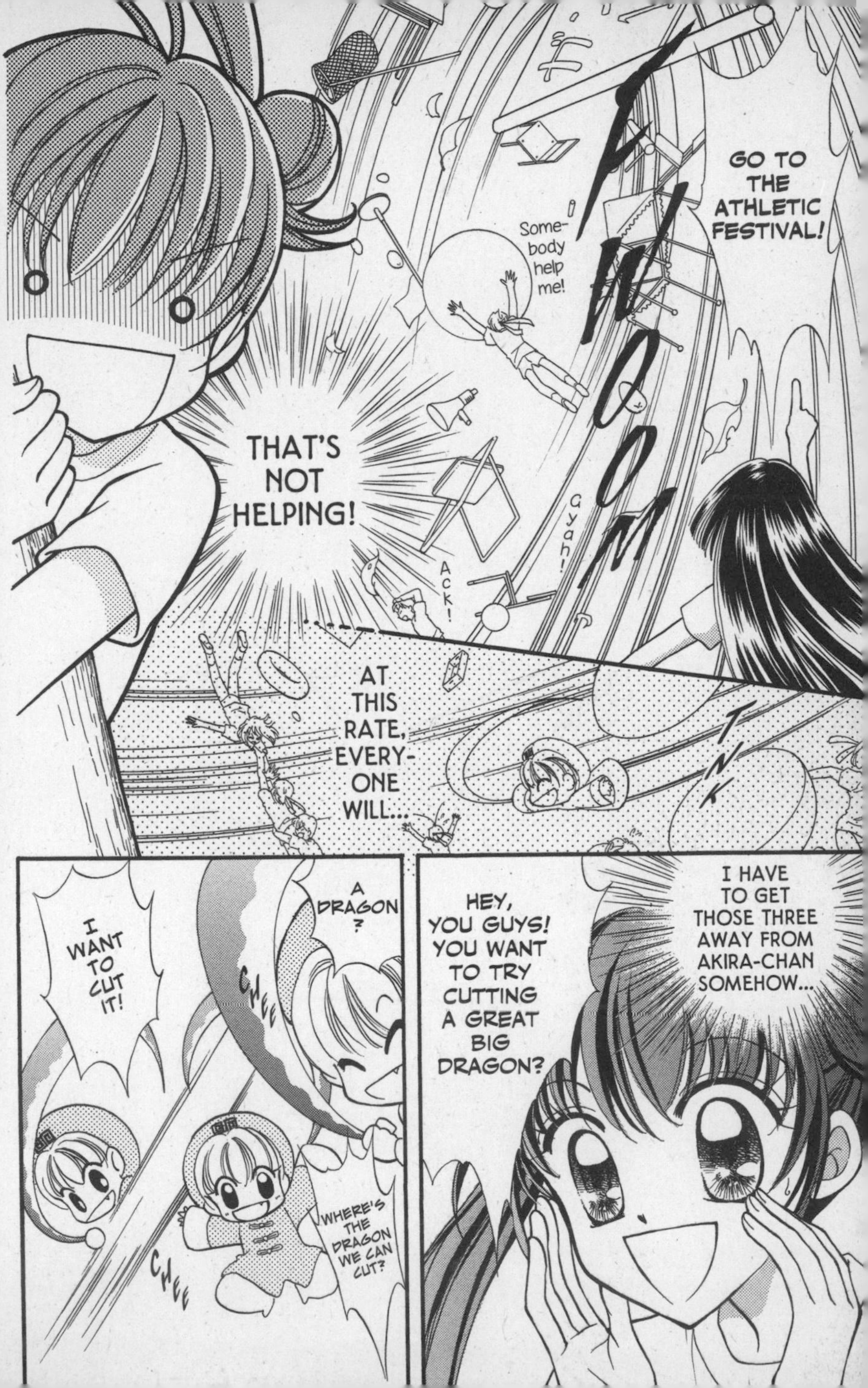
GO TO THE ATHLETIC FESTIVAL!
FWOOOM
Some-body help me!
Gyah!
Ack!
THAT'S NOT HELPING!
AT THIS RATE, EVERY-ONE WILL...
TINK
I HAVE TO GET THOSE THREE AWAY FROM AKIRA-CHAN SOMEHOW...
HEY, YOU GUYS! YOU WANT TO TRY CUTTING A GREAT BIG DRAGON?
A DRAGON?
I WANT TO CUT IT!
CHEE
WHERE'S THE DRAGON WE CAN CUT?
CHEE

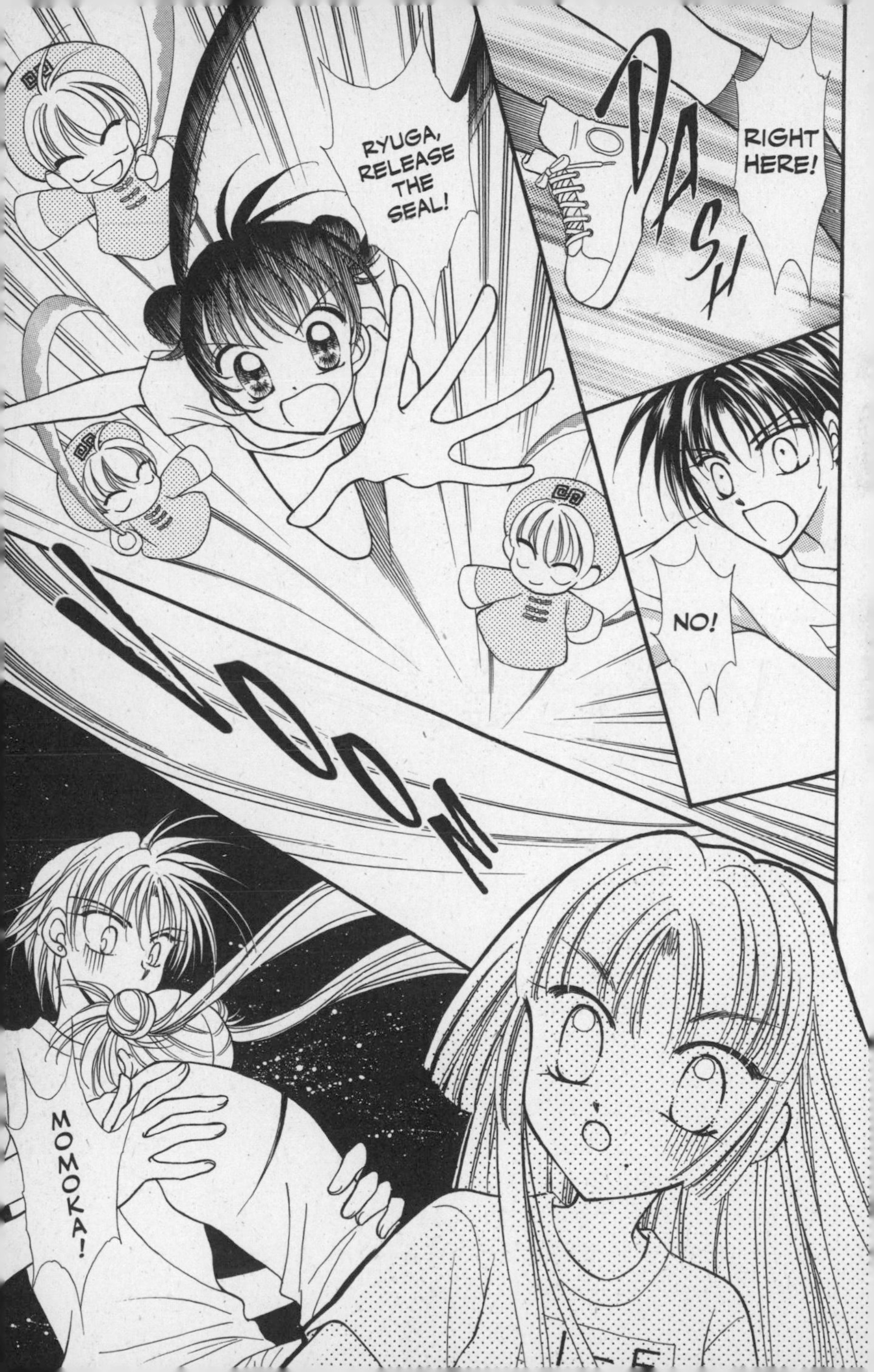
DASH
RIGHT HERE!
NO!
RYUGA, RELEASE THE SEAL!
VOOOM
MOMOKA!

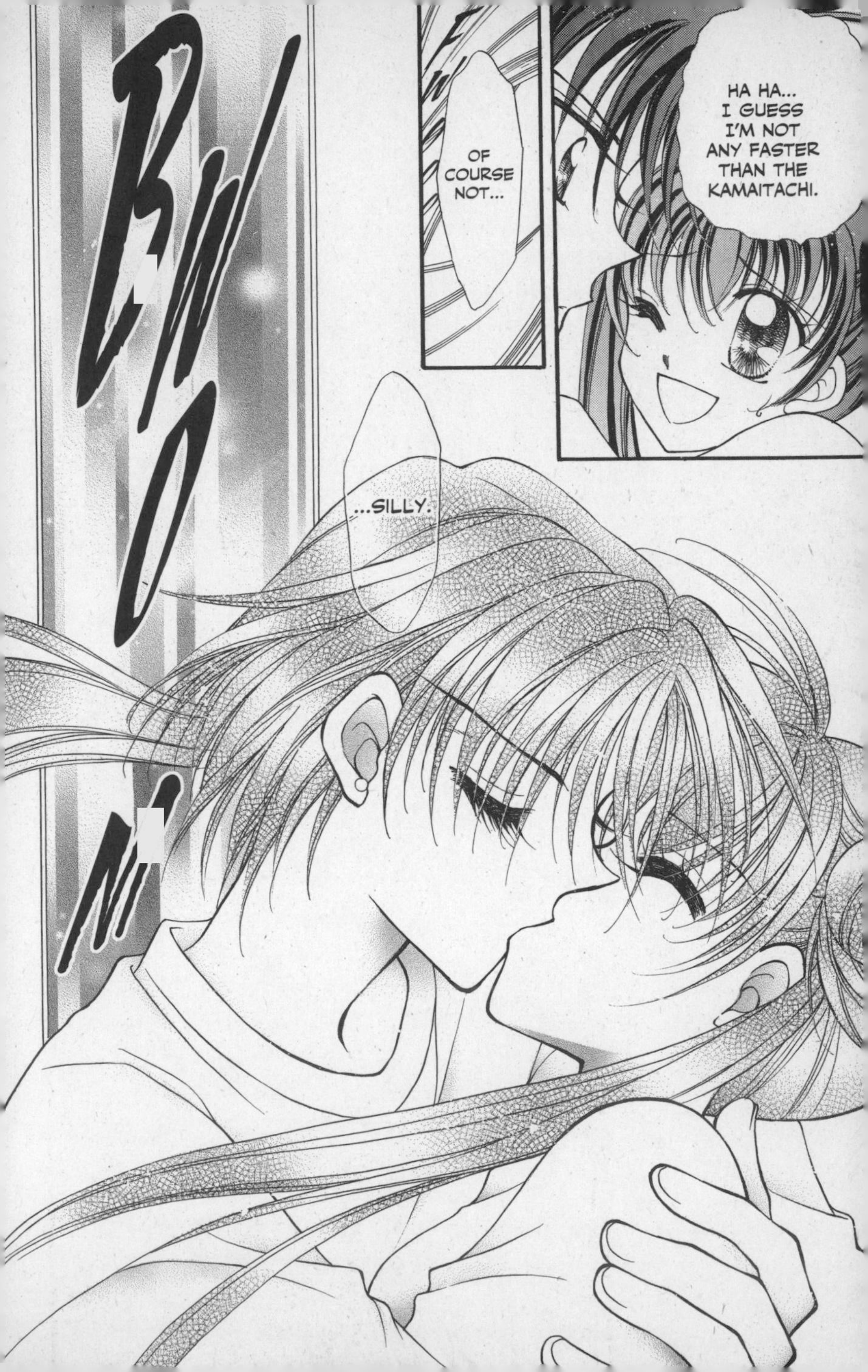
HA HA... I GUESS I'M NOT ANY FASTER THAN THE KAMAITACHI.
OF COURSE NOT...
...SILLY.

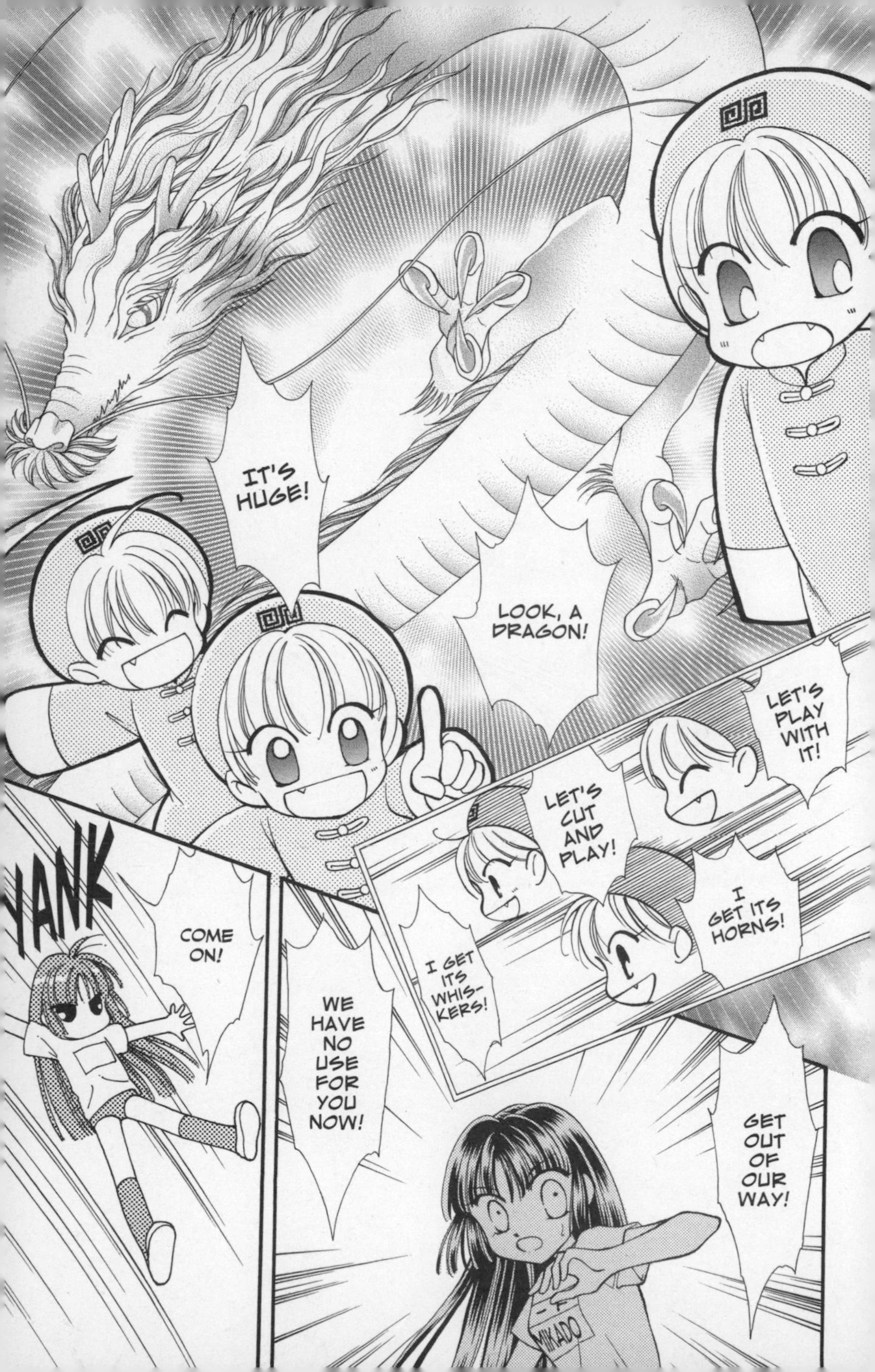
LOOK, A DRAGON!
IT'S HUGE!
LET'S PLAY WITH IT!
LET'S CUT AND PLAY!
I GET ITS HORNS!
I GET ITS WHIS-KERS!
GET OUT OF OUR WAY!
WE HAVE NO USE FOR YOU NOW!
MIKADO
YANK
COME ON!

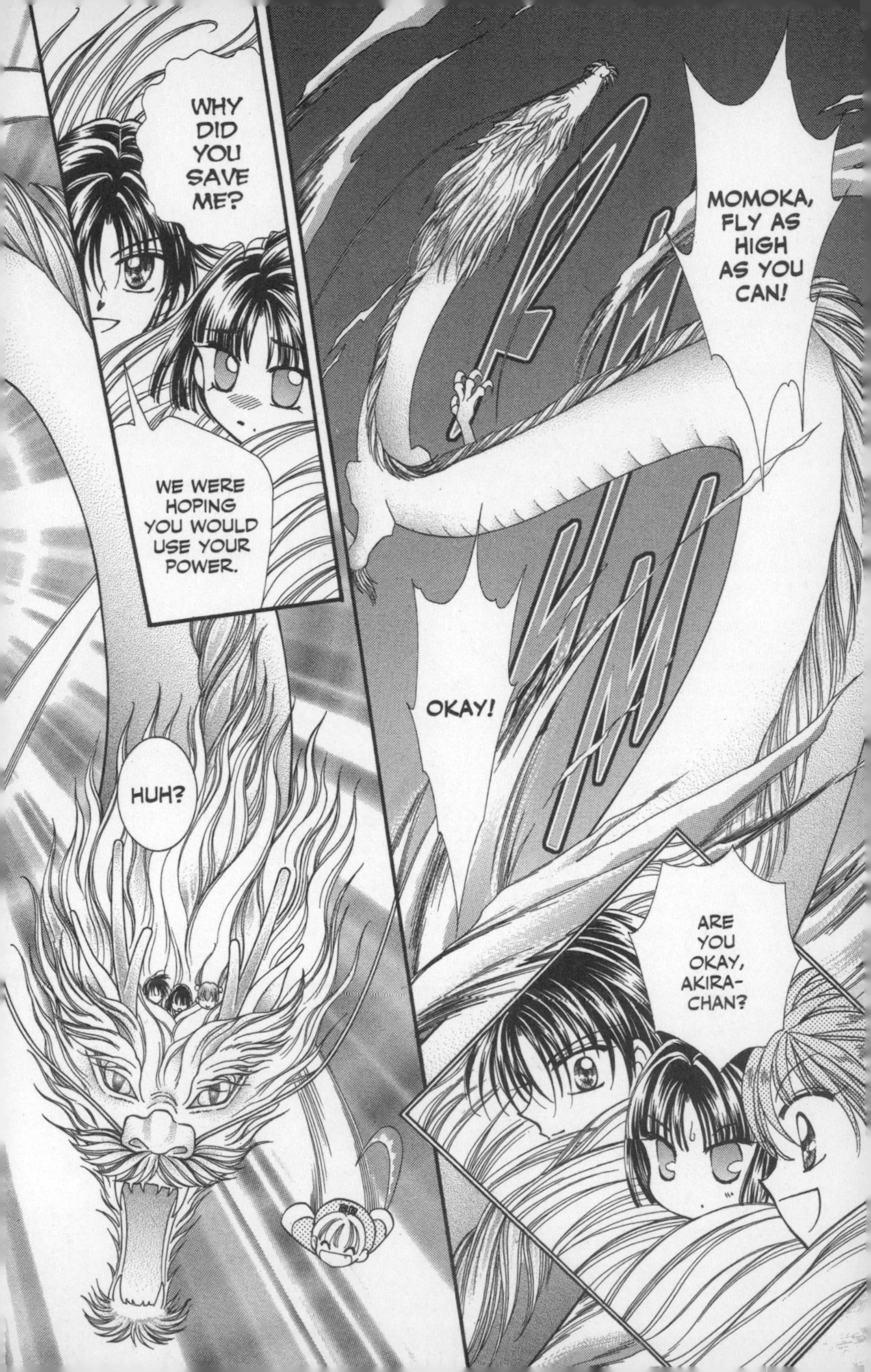
MOMOKA, FLY AS HIGH AS YOU CAN!
OKAY!
ARE YOU OKAY, AKIRA-CHAN?
WHY DID YOU SAVE ME?
WE WERE HOPING YOU WOULD USE YOUR POWER.
HUH?

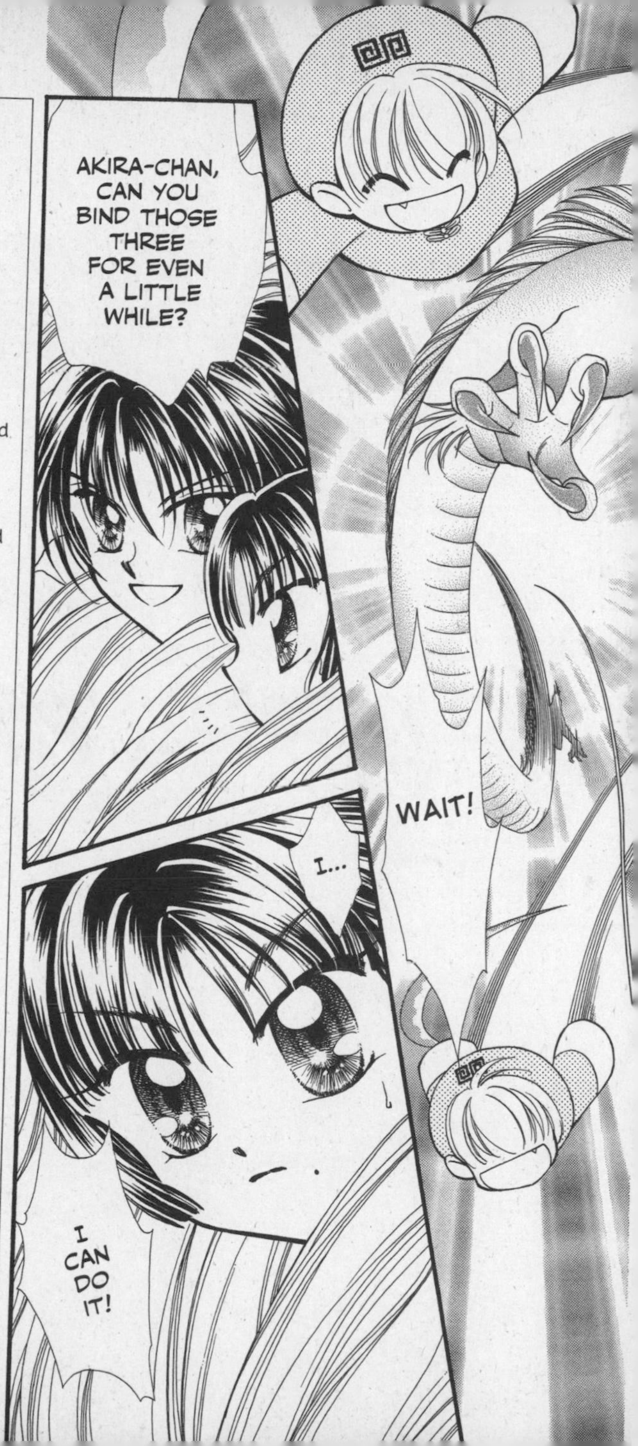
AKIRA-CHAN, CAN YOU BIND THOSE THREE FOR EVEN A LITTLE WHILE?
WAIT!
I...
I CAN DO IT!

3

In *St.♥Dragon Girl*, the witch became an onmyouji, and the familiar became a shikigami.

I never got a chance to use her in "Just Ask Alice!" but I wonder what you would have thought if you would have seen Akira-chan in it? (laugh)

Anyway, she hasn't changed much. I want to write a mini-story soon about Akira-chan and her cat god. What do you think?

After I drew this, I saw the movie *Onmyouji* with my assistants. I really loved the acting in it.

I liked the strength in the villain role that Hiroyuki Sanada played. I generally think it was a good movie, but the budget was so small. The crow shikigami was a little... yeah. It looked totally fake. (It was a little cute though.) Nonetheless, I really liked *Onmyouji*, and I want to see the sequel. The novel it's based on is really interesting too! (It's by Baku Yumemakura-san.) I highly recommend it!

By the way, don't you think using shikigami would be fun? If I could use them, it would be a lot easier drawing my manga! I'd make my shikigami help me with work! (laugh) I'd say, "Finish this chapter," and then I'd go to sleep! (laugh)

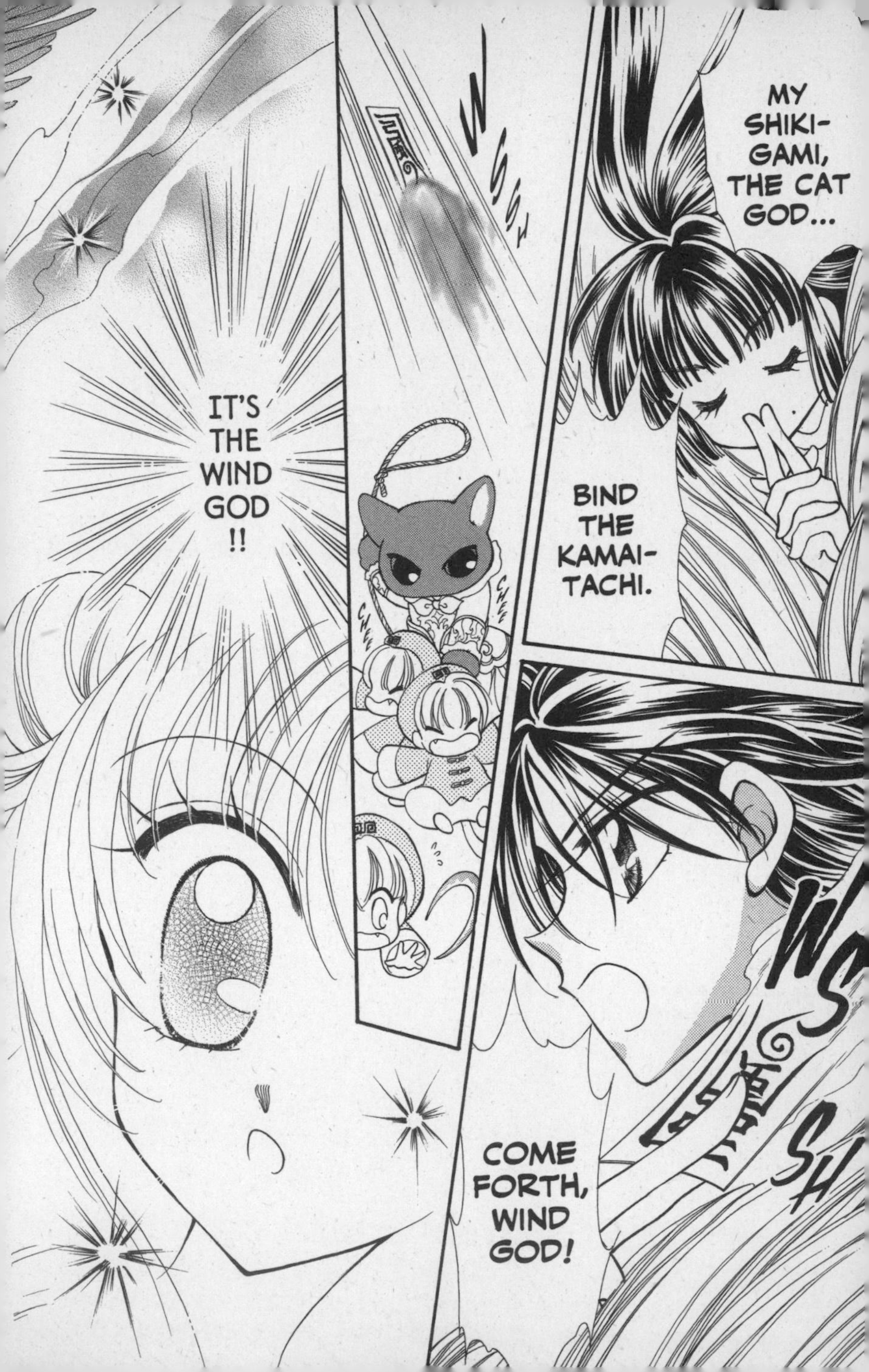
MY SHIKI-GAMI, THE CAT GOD...
BIND THE KAMAI-TACHI.
COME FORTH, WIND GOD!
CHEE
CHEE
IT'S THE WIND GOD !!

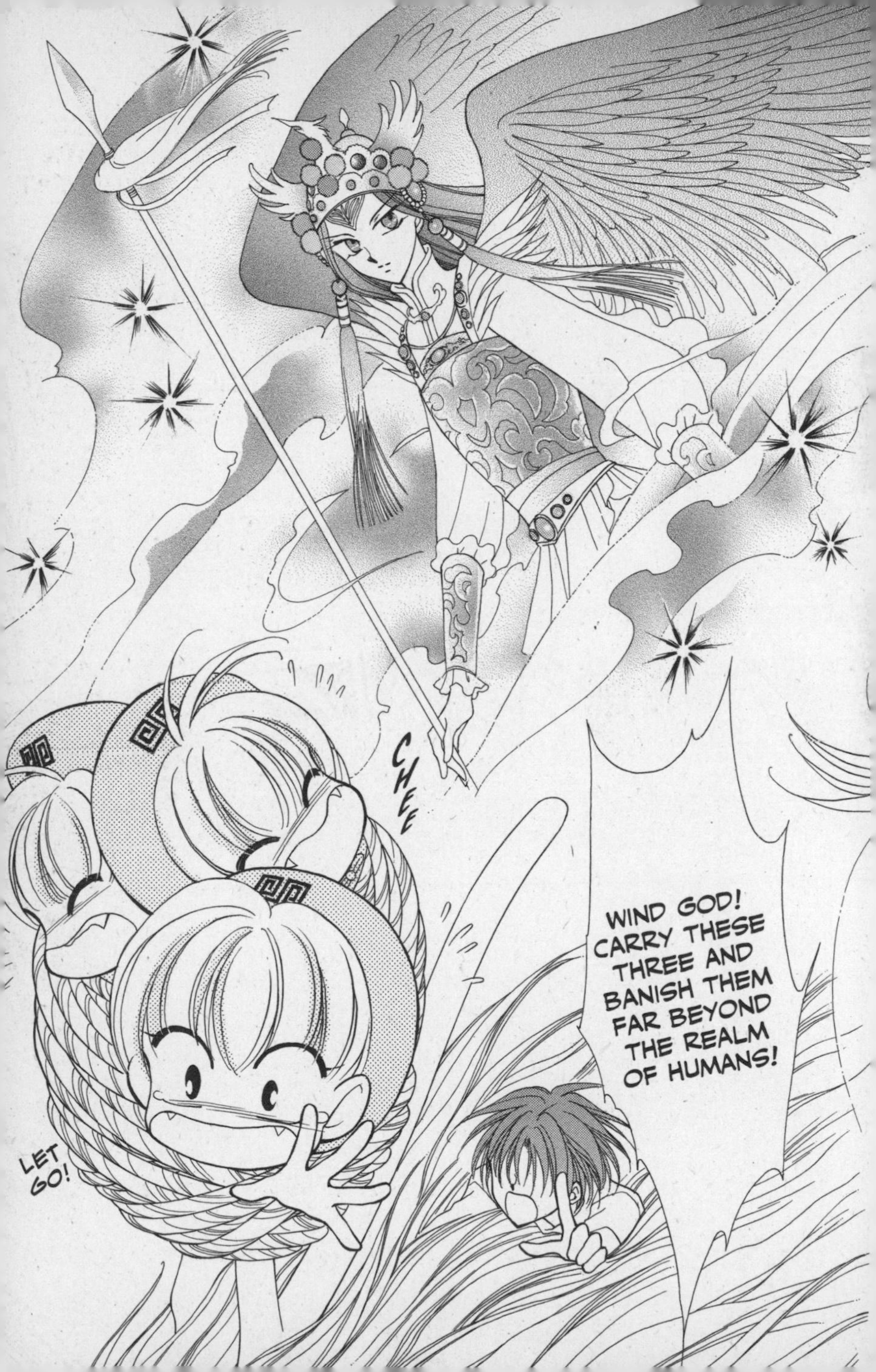
CHEE
WIND GOD! CARRY THESE THREE AND BANISH THEM FAR BEYOND THE REALM OF HUMANS!
LET GO!

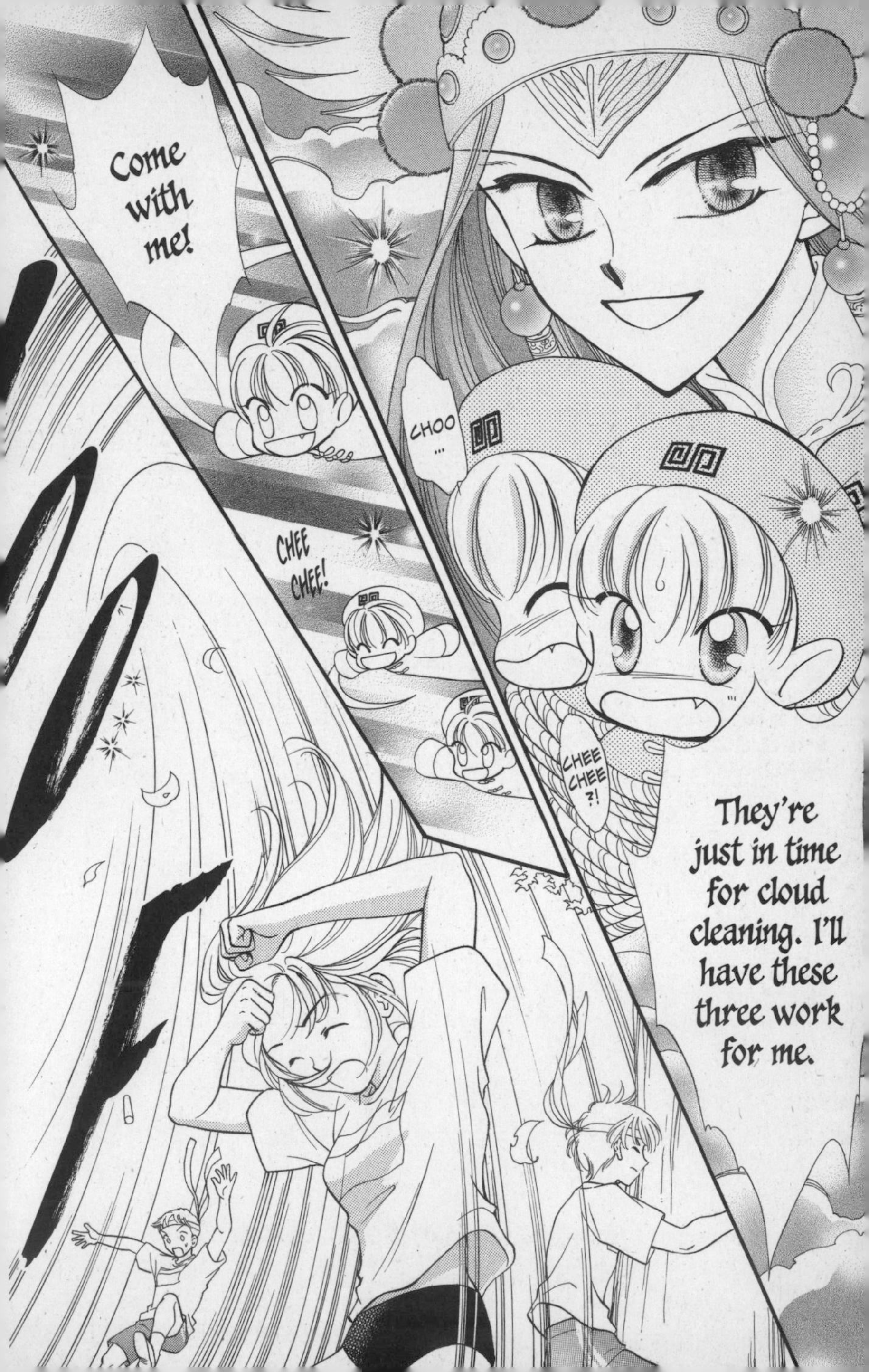

They're just in time for cloud cleaning. I'll have these three work for me.
CHOO ...
CHEE CHEE ?!
CHEE CHEE!
Come with me!

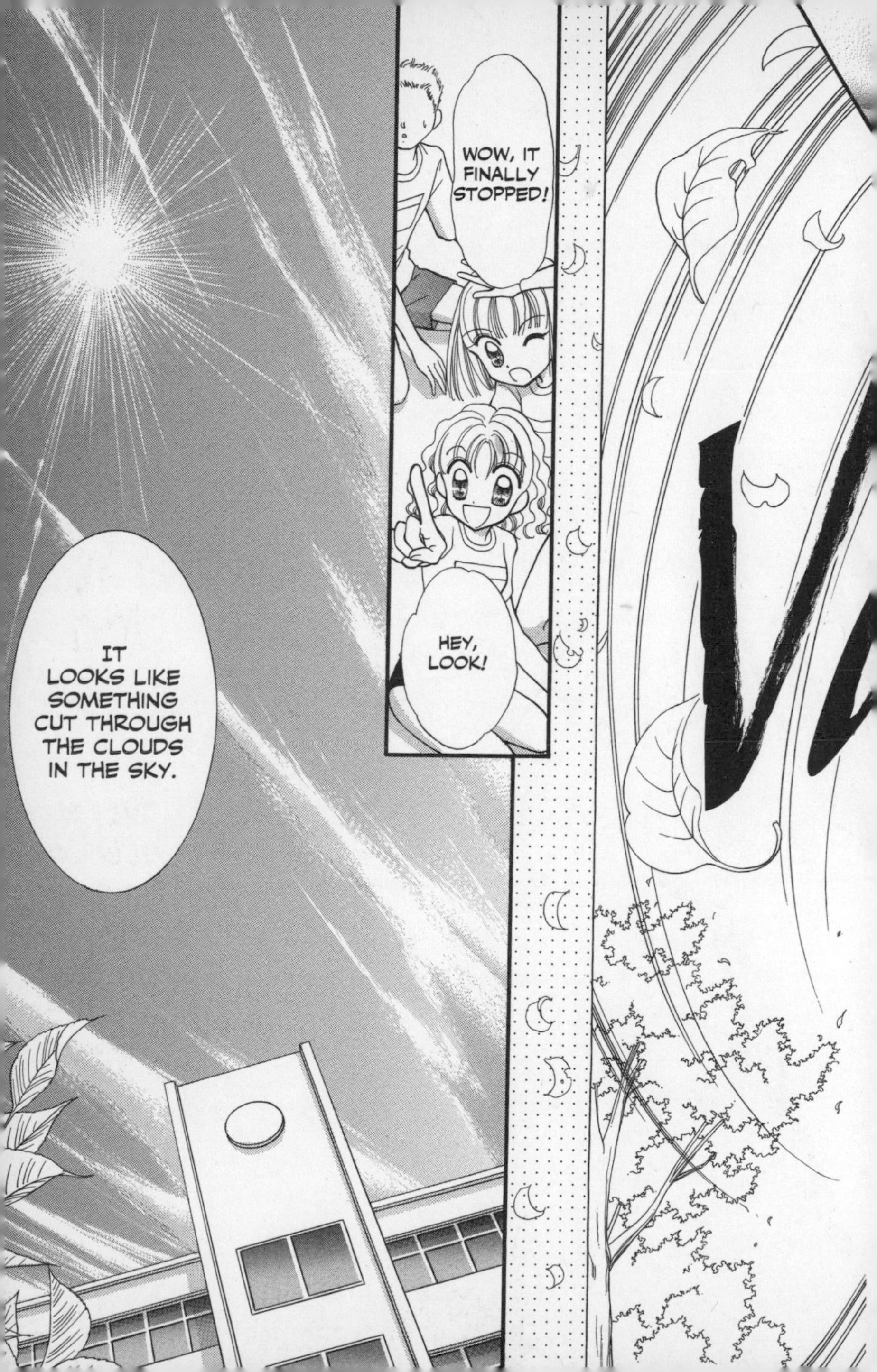
WOW, IT FINALLY STOPPED!
HEY, LOOK!
IT LOOKS LIKE SOMETHING CUT THROUGH THE CLOUDS IN THE SKY.

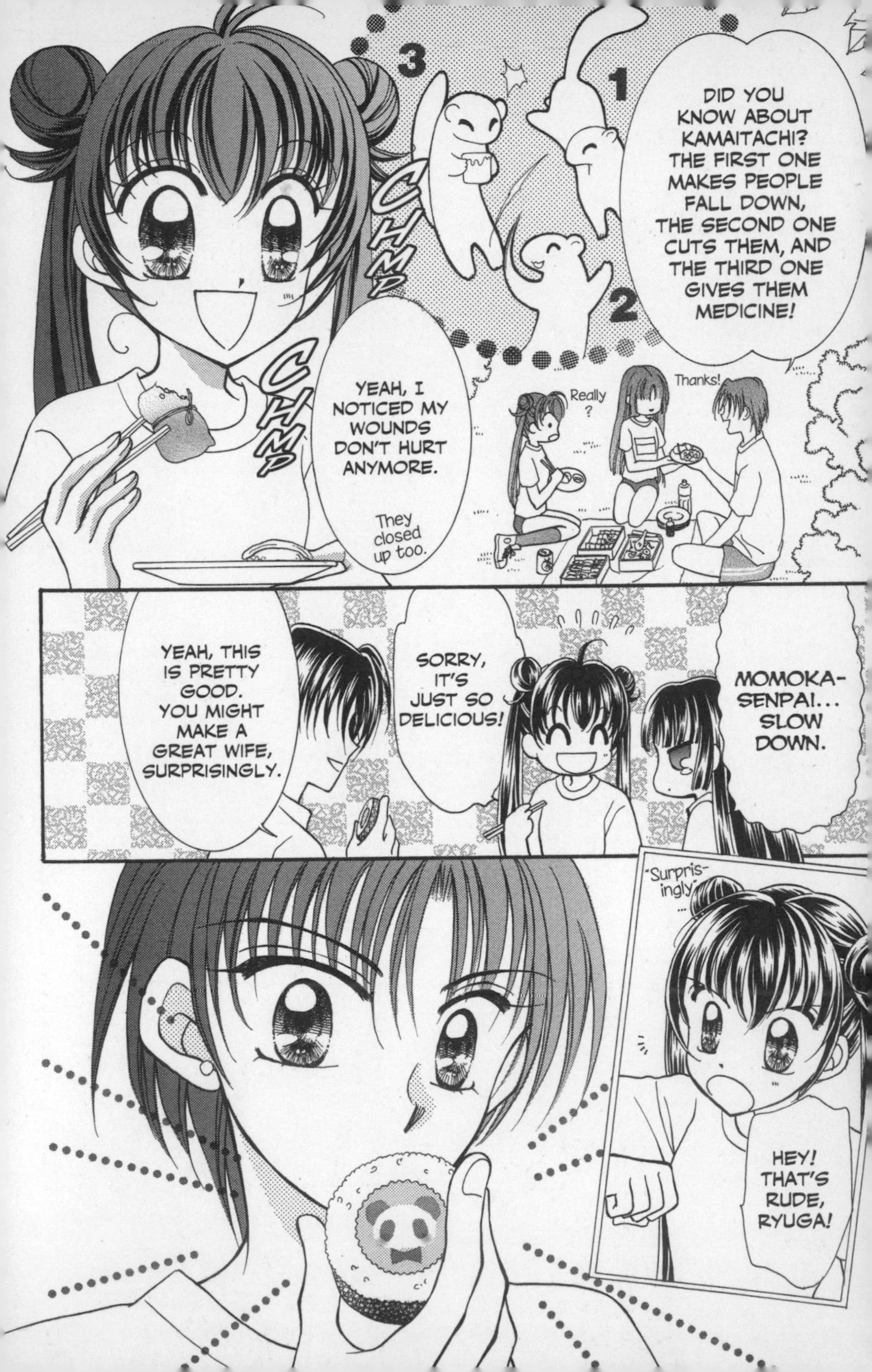
3
1
2
DID YOU KNOW ABOUT KAMAITACHI? THE FIRST ONE MAKES PEOPLE FALL DOWN, THE SECOND ONE CUTS THEM, AND THE THIRD ONE GIVES THEM MEDICINE!
Thanks!
Really?
CHMP
YEAH, I NOTICED MY WOUNDS DON'T HURT ANYMORE.
They closed up too.
CHMP
MOMOKA-SENPAI... SLOW DOWN.
SORRY, IT'S JUST SO DELICIOUS!
YEAH, THIS IS PRETTY GOOD. YOU MIGHT MAKE A GREAT WIFE, SURPRISINGLY.
"Surprisingly"...
HEY! THAT'S RUDE, RYUGA!

FIGHT, DRAGON RANGERS!

BY KODAKA

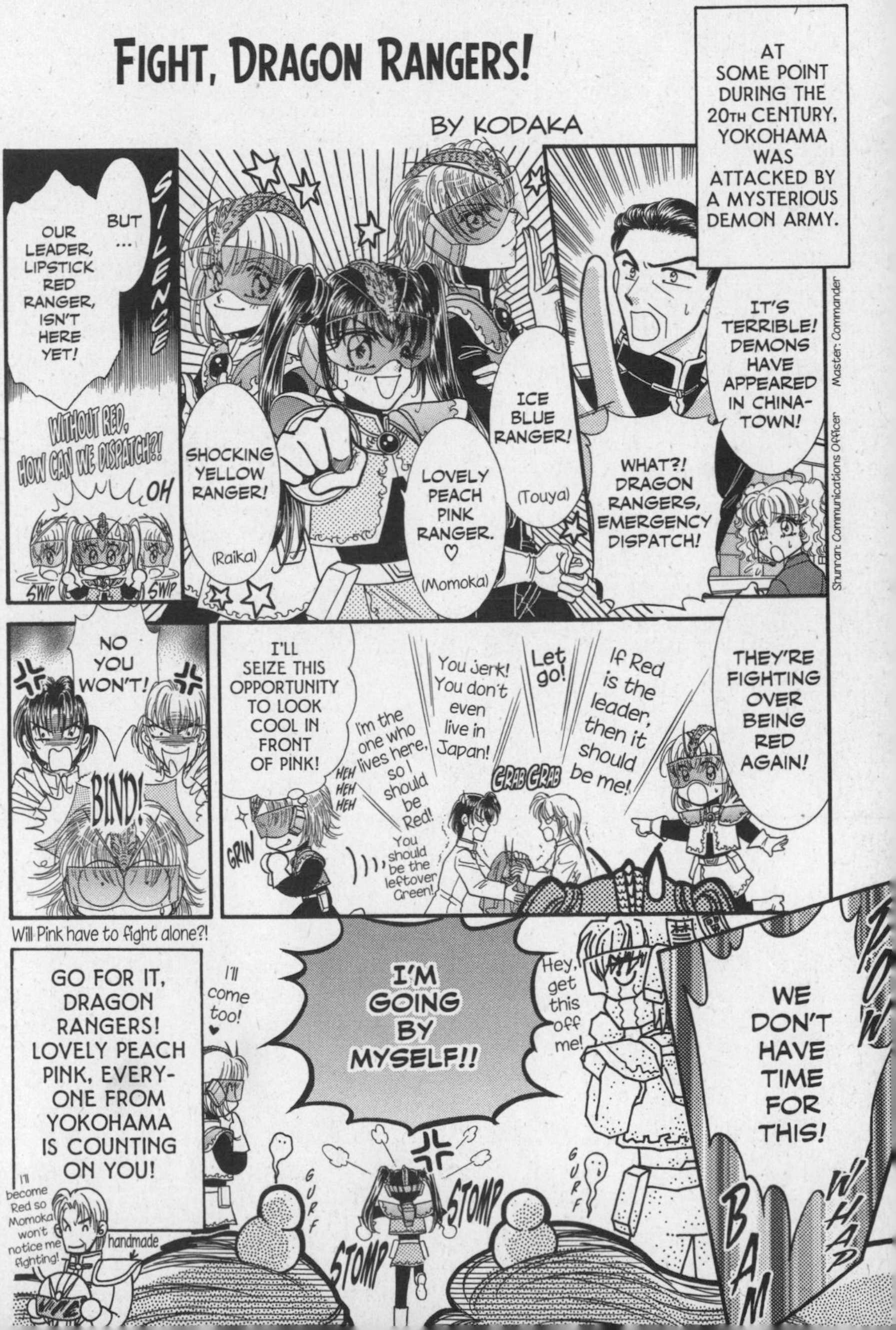

AT SOME POINT DURING THE 20TH CENTURY, YOKOHAMA WAS ATTACKED BY A MYSTERIOUS DEMON ARMY.
Master: Commander
IT'S TERRIBLE! DEMONS HAVE APPEARED IN CHINA-TOWN!
Shunran: Communications Officer
WHAT?! DRAGON RANGERS, EMERGENCY DISPATCH!
ICE BLUE RANGER!
(Touya)
LOVELY PEACH PINK RANGER. ♡
(Momoka)
SHOCKING YELLOW RANGER!
(Raika)
SILENCE
BUT ... OUR LEADER, LIPSTICK RED RANGER, ISN'T HERE YET!
WITHOUT RED, HOW CAN WE DISPATCH?!
OH
SWIP
SWIP
THEY'RE FIGHTING OVER BEING RED AGAIN!
If Red is the leader, then it should be me!
Let go!
You jerk! You don't even live in Japan!
I'm the one who lives here, so I should be Red!
You should be the leftover Green!
GRAB GRAB
I'LL SEIZE THIS OPPORTUNITY TO LOOK COOL IN FRONT OF PINK!
HEH HEH HEH
GRIN
NO YOU WON'T!
BIND!
Will Pink have to fight alone?!
WE DON'T HAVE TIME FOR THIS!
BAM
WHAP
Hey, get this off me!
I'M GOING BY MYSELF!!
GURF
GURF
STOMP
STOMP
GO FOR IT, DRAGON RANGERS! LOVELY PEACH PINK, EVERY-ONE FROM YOKOHAMA IS COUNTING ON YOU!
I'll come too! ♥
I'll become Red so Momoka won't notice me fighting!
handmade

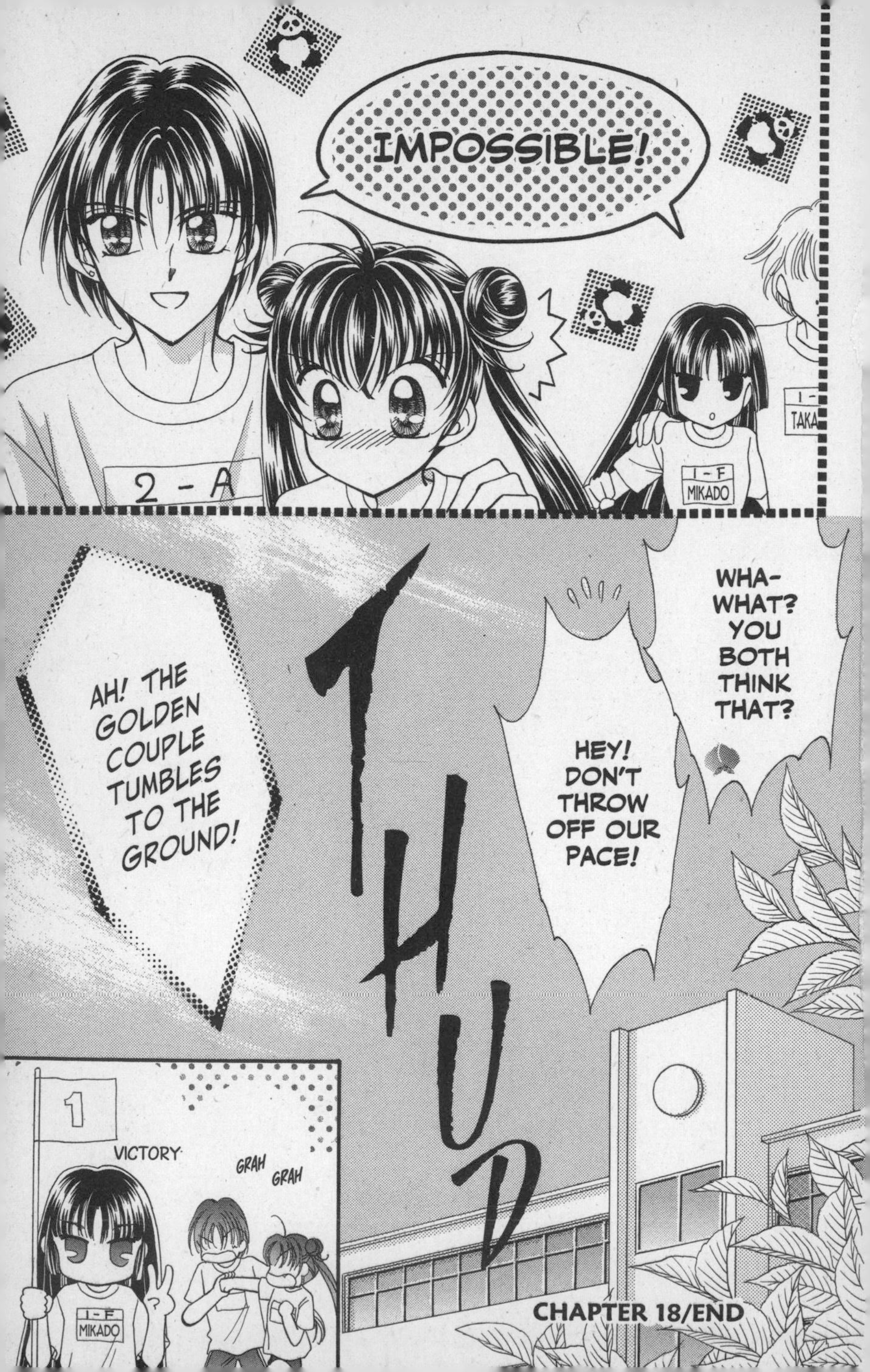
IMPOSSIBLE!
2-A
I-F MIKADO
I-
TAKA
WHA-WHAT? YOU BOTH THINK THAT?
HEY! DON'T THROW OFF OUR PACE!
THUD
AH! THE GOLDEN COUPLE TUMBLES TO THE GROUND!
GRAH
GRAH
VICTORY
1
I-F MIKADO
CHAPTER 18/END

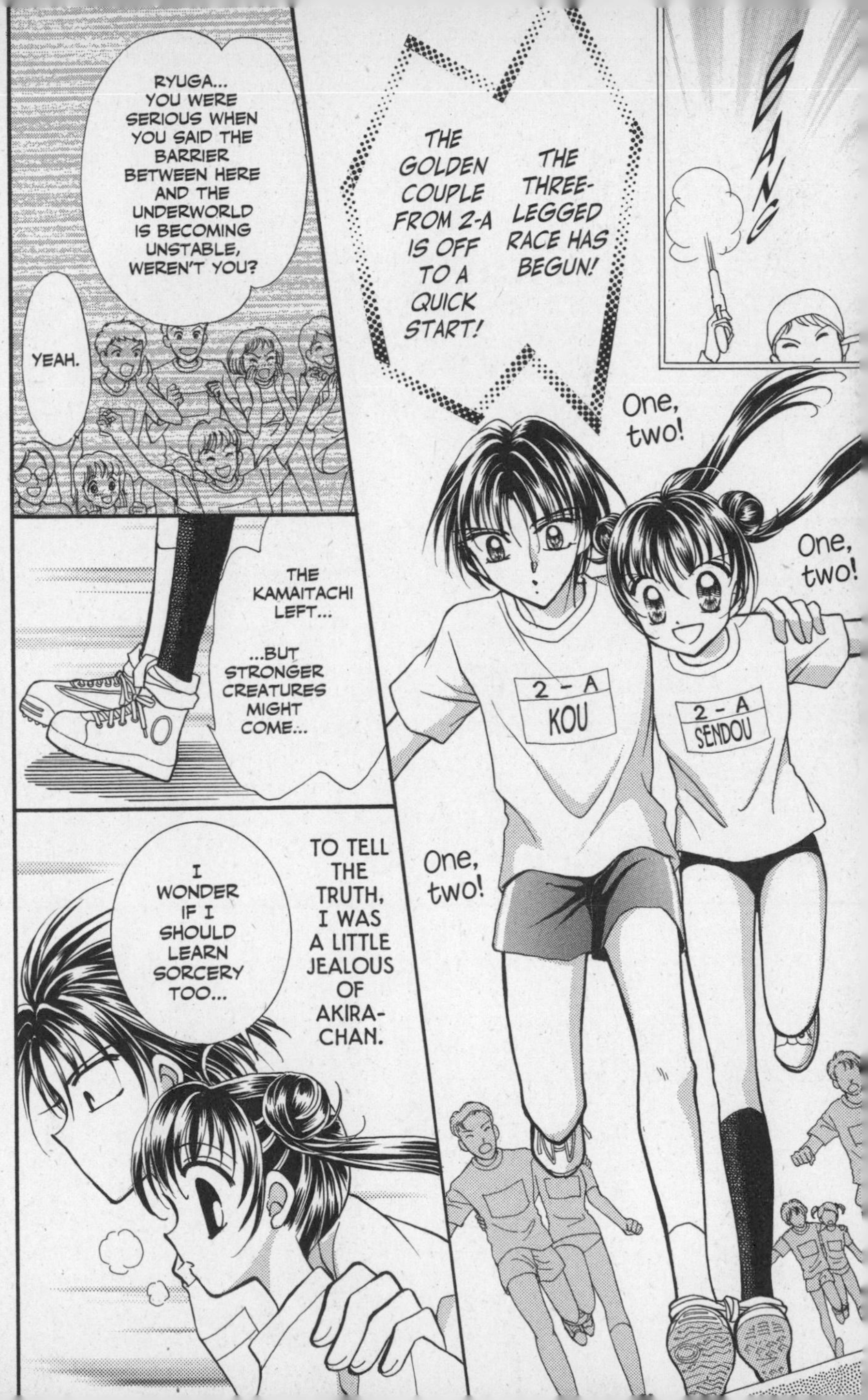
BANG
THE THREE-LEGGED RACE HAS BEGUN!
THE GOLDEN COUPLE FROM 2-A IS OFF TO A QUICK START!
One, two!
One, two!
One, two!
2-A KOU
2-A SENDOU
RYUGA... YOU WERE SERIOUS WHEN YOU SAID THE BARRIER BETWEEN HERE AND THE UNDERWORLD IS BECOMING UNSTABLE, WEREN'T YOU?
YEAH.
THE KAMAITACHI LEFT...
...BUT STRONGER CREATURES MIGHT COME...
TO TELL THE TRUTH, I WAS A LITTLE JEALOUS OF AKIRA-CHAN.
I WONDER IF I SHOULD LEARN SORCERY TOO...

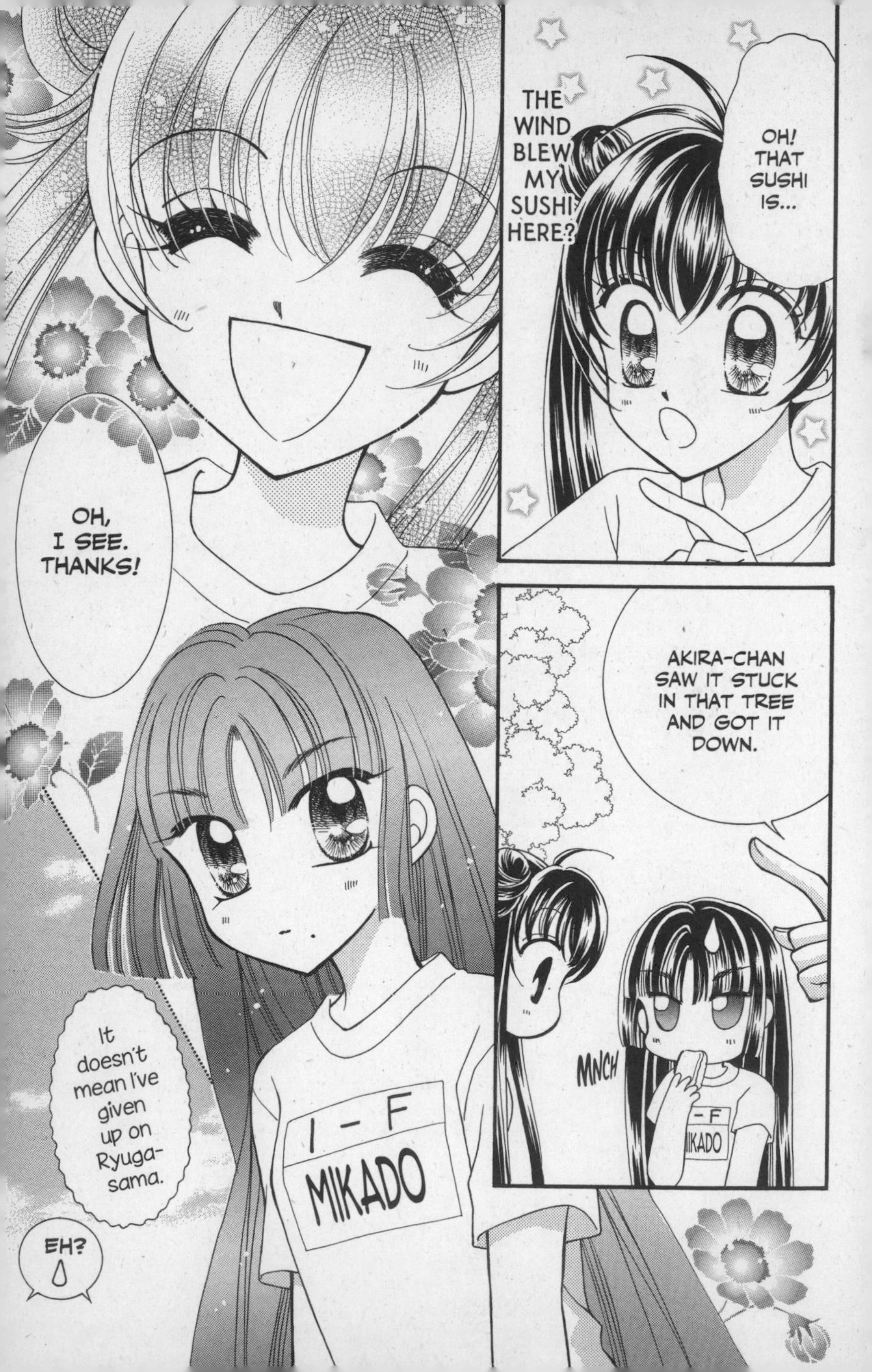
OH! THAT SUSHI IS...
THE WIND BLEW MY SUSHI HERE?
AKIRA-CHAN SAW IT STUCK IN THAT TREE AND GOT IT DOWN.
MNCH
I - F MIKADO
OH, I SEE. THANKS!
It doesn't mean I've given up on Ryuga-sama.
I - F MIKADO
EH?

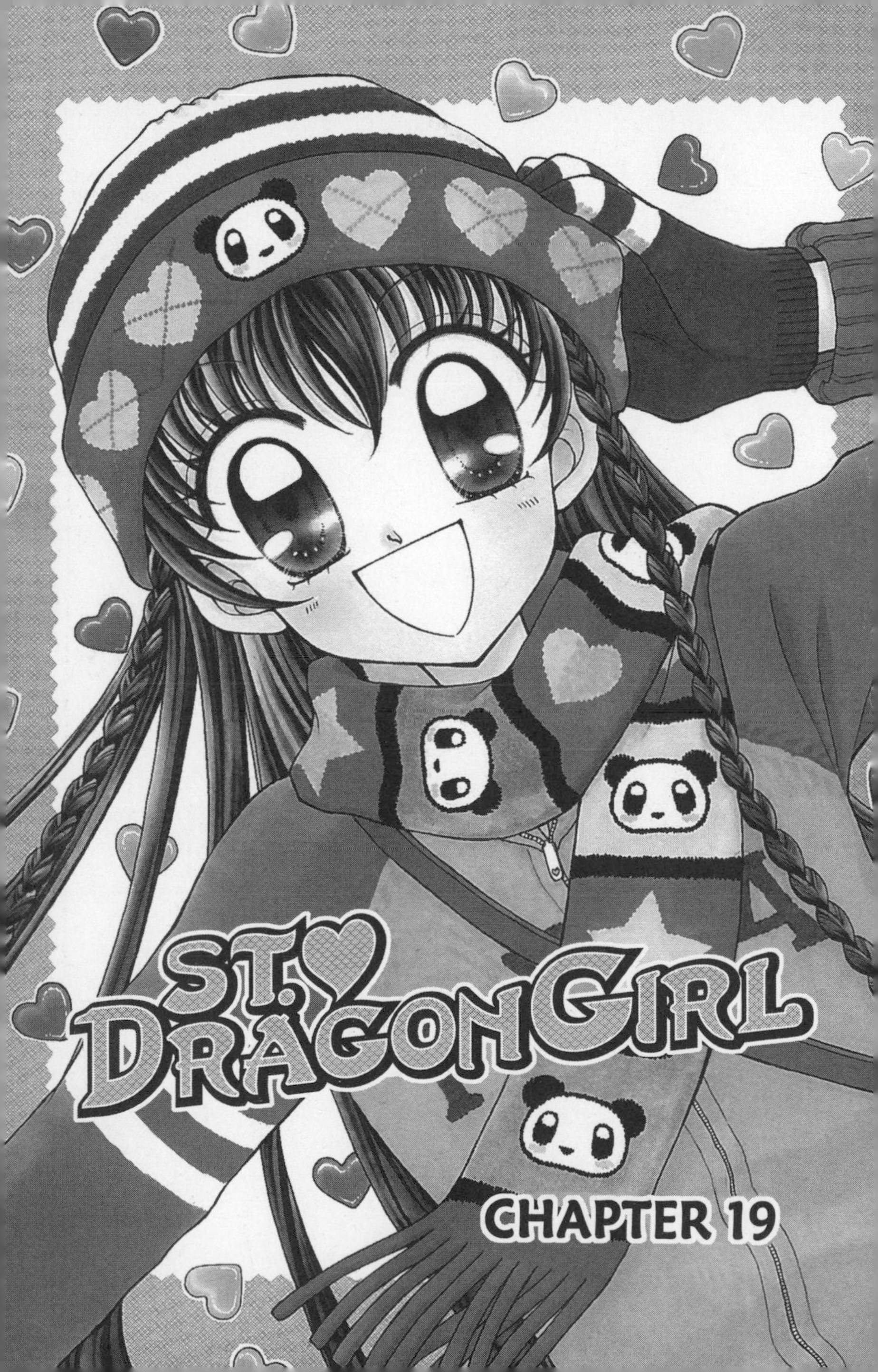
ST.♥DRAGON GIRL
CHAPTER 19

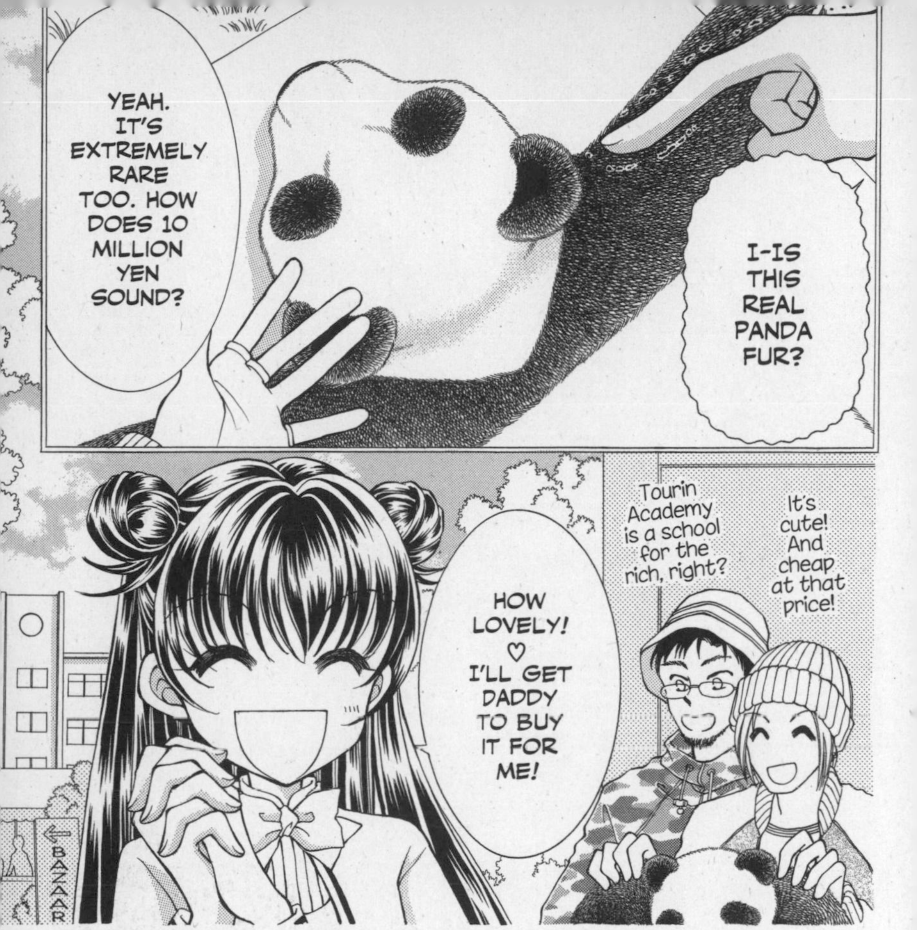
I-IS THIS REAL PANDA FUR?
YEAH. IT'S EXTREMELY RARE TOO. HOW DOES 10 MILLION YEN SOUND?
It's cute! And cheap at that price!
Tourin Academy is a school for the rich, right?
HOW LOVELY! ♡ I'LL GET DADDY TO BUY IT FOR ME!
BAZAAR

- **When you do colored pages, what tools do you use? Also, what paper do you use?**

For colored pages, I usually use "Doctor Matching." For the intricate work, I use a magnifying glass. I also use acrylic painting tools. (And gouache.)

I also use a lot of colortone. For example, for this chapter title page, I used a blue colortone technique for the jagged areas around Momoka.

For the paper, I use Canson. In the past, I tried a lot of different ones like Mermaid, BB Kent, and Watson paper, but I finally settled on Canson. I asked my other mangaka friends, and they all use different ones. The best paper to use is the one that holds the color best.

For coloring, you can pretty much find what you need at the local art supply store. Try many things and see what works best for you. If you find anything really good, let me know! (laugh)

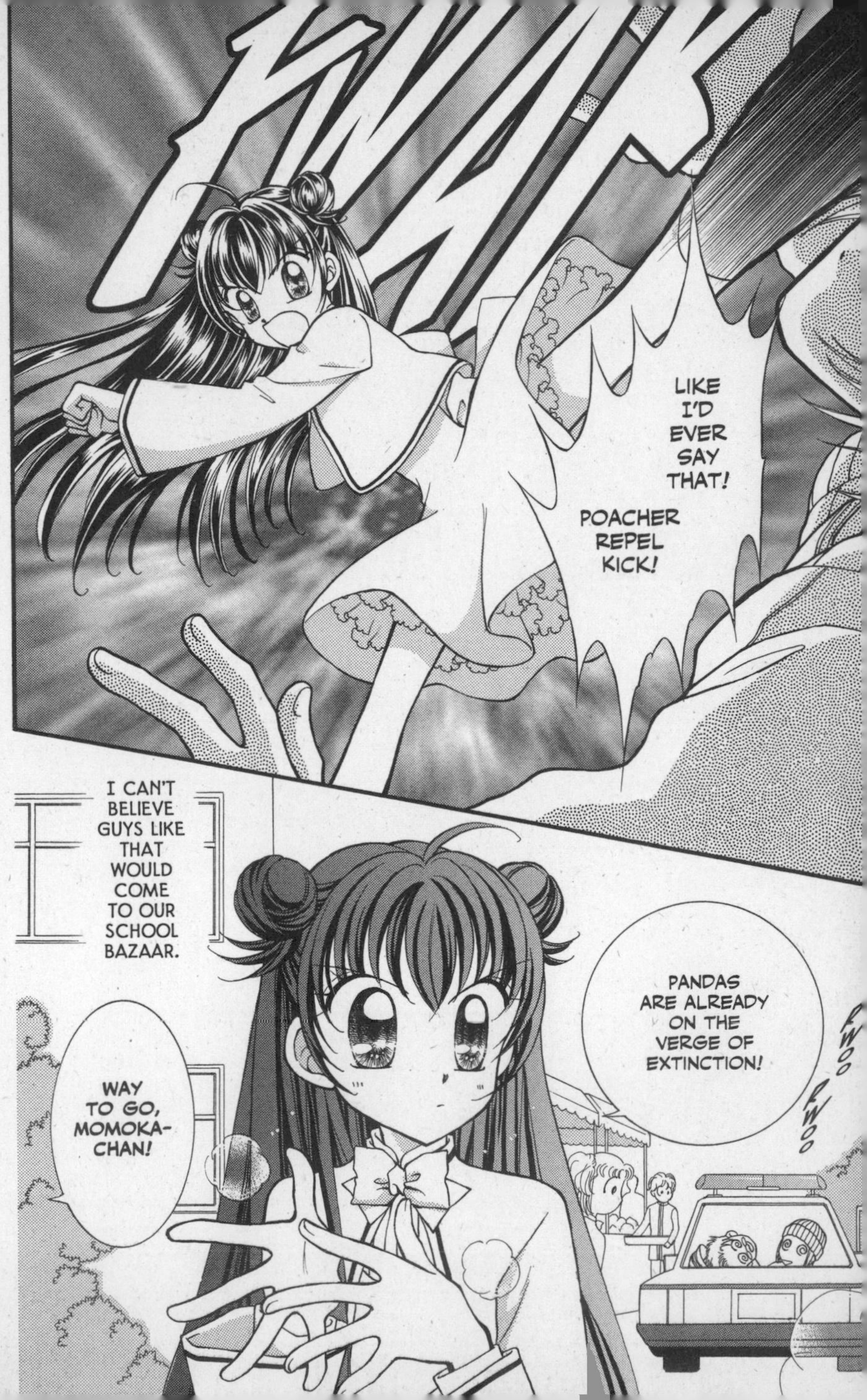
LIKE I'D EVER SAY THAT!
POACHER REPEL KICK!
PANDAS ARE ALREADY ON THE VERGE OF EXTINCTION!
RWOO RWOO
I CAN'T BELIEVE GUYS LIKE THAT WOULD COME TO OUR SCHOOL BAZAAR.
WAY TO GO, MOMOKA-CHAN!

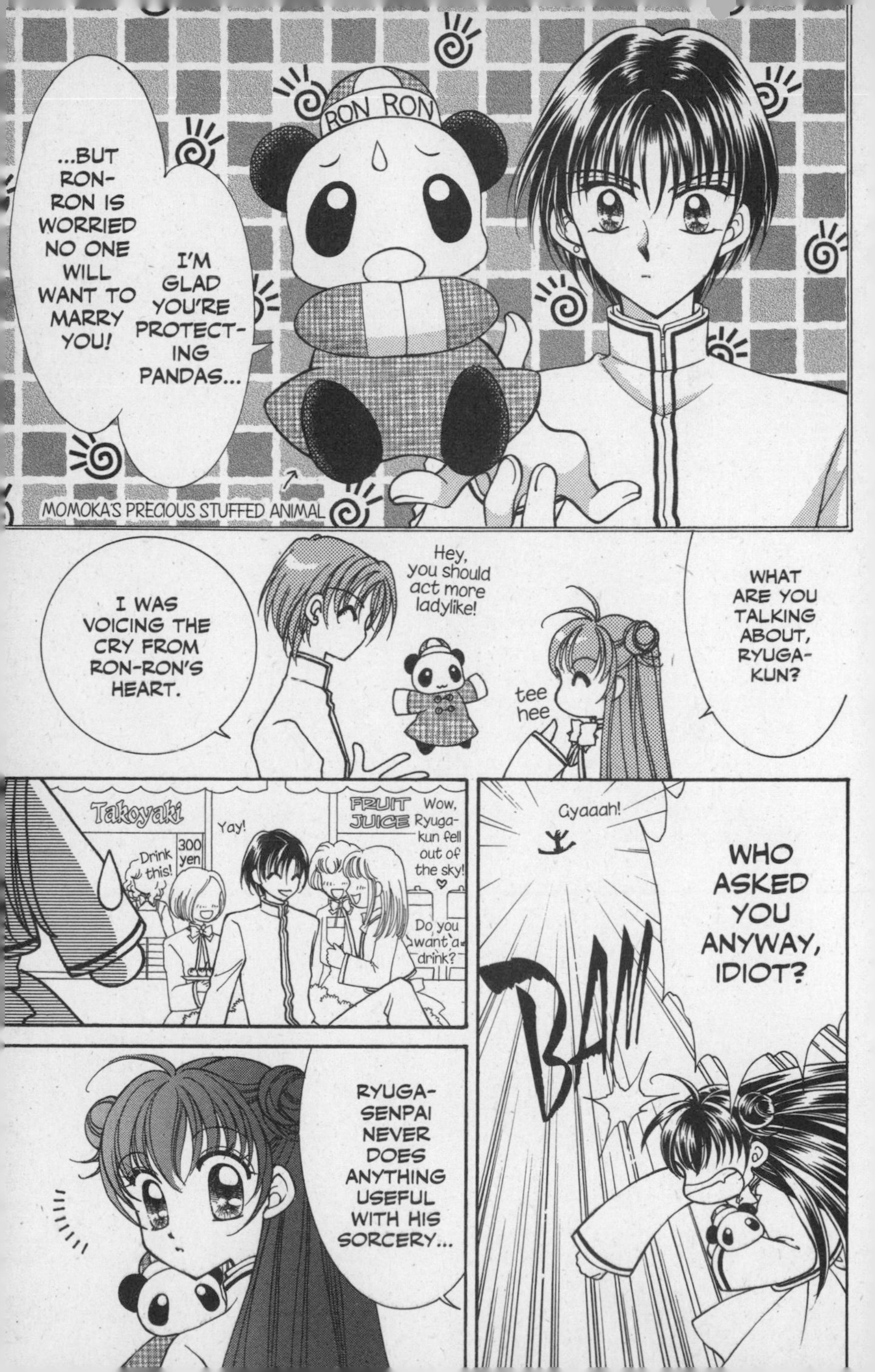
RON RON
I'M GLAD YOU'RE PROTECTING PANDAS...
...BUT RON-RON IS WORRIED NO ONE WILL WANT TO MARRY YOU!
MOMOKA'S PRECIOUS STUFFED ANIMAL
WHAT ARE YOU TALKING ABOUT, RYUGA-KUN?
tee hee
Hey, you should act more ladylike!
I WAS VOICING THE CRY FROM RON-RON'S HEART.
Gyaaah!
WHO ASKED YOU ANYWAY, IDIOT?
BAM
FRUIT JUICE
Wow, Ryuga-kun fell out of the sky!
Do you want a drink?
Takoyaki
Yay!
300 yen
Drink this!
RYUGA-SENPAI NEVER DOES ANYTHING USEFUL WITH HIS SORCERY...

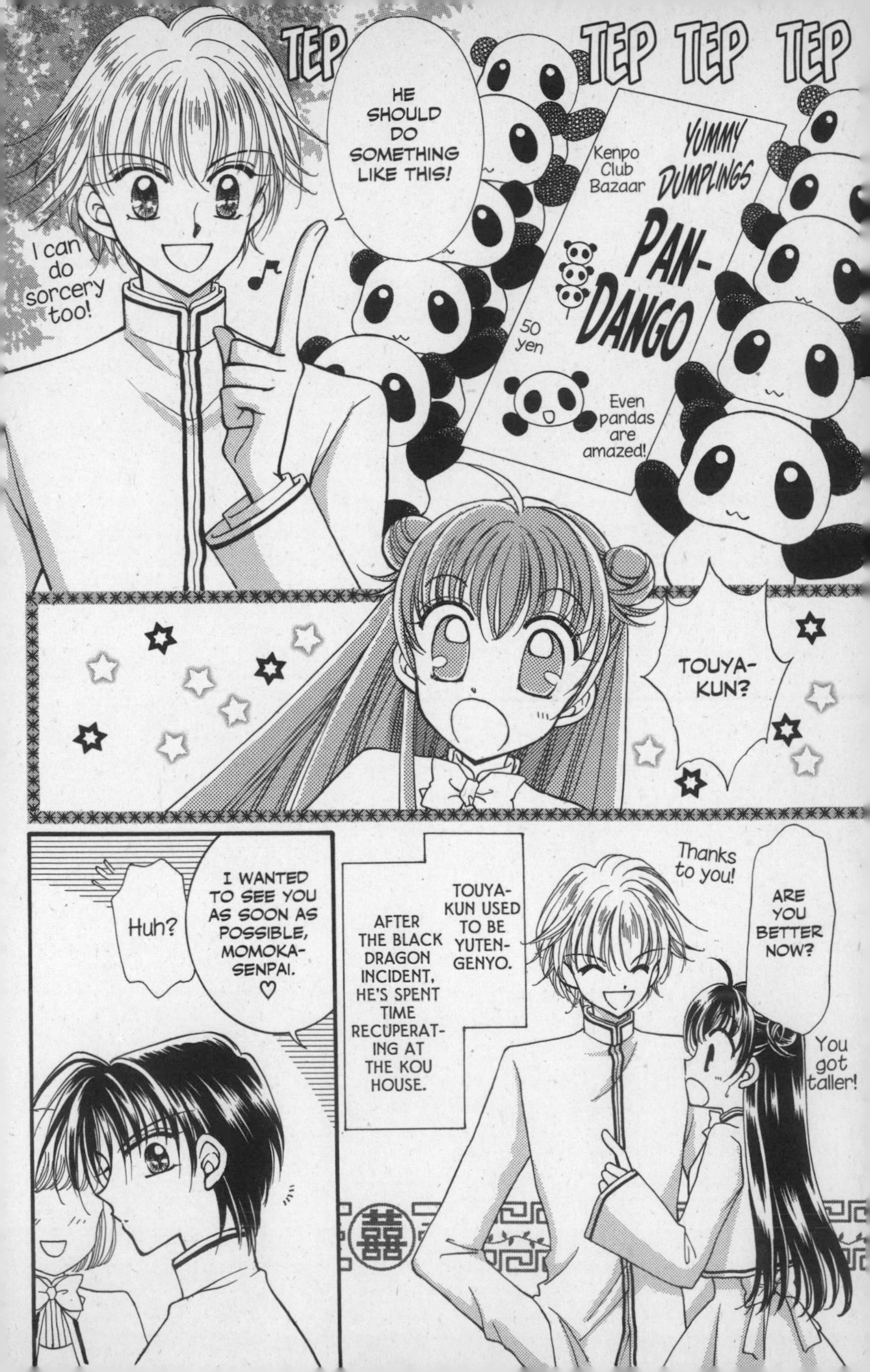
TEP TEP TEP
YUMMY DUMPLINGS
PAN-DANGO
Kenpo Club Bazaar
50 yen
Even pandas are amazed!
HE SHOULD DO SOMETHING LIKE THIS!
TEP
I can do sorcery too!
TOUYA-KUN?
Thanks to you!
ARE YOU BETTER NOW?
You got taller!
TOUYA-KUN USED TO BE YUTEN-GENYO.
AFTER THE BLACK DRAGON INCIDENT, HE'S SPENT TIME RECUPERATING AT THE KOU HOUSE.
I WANTED TO SEE YOU AS SOON AS POSSIBLE, MOMOKA-SENPAI. ♡
Huh?

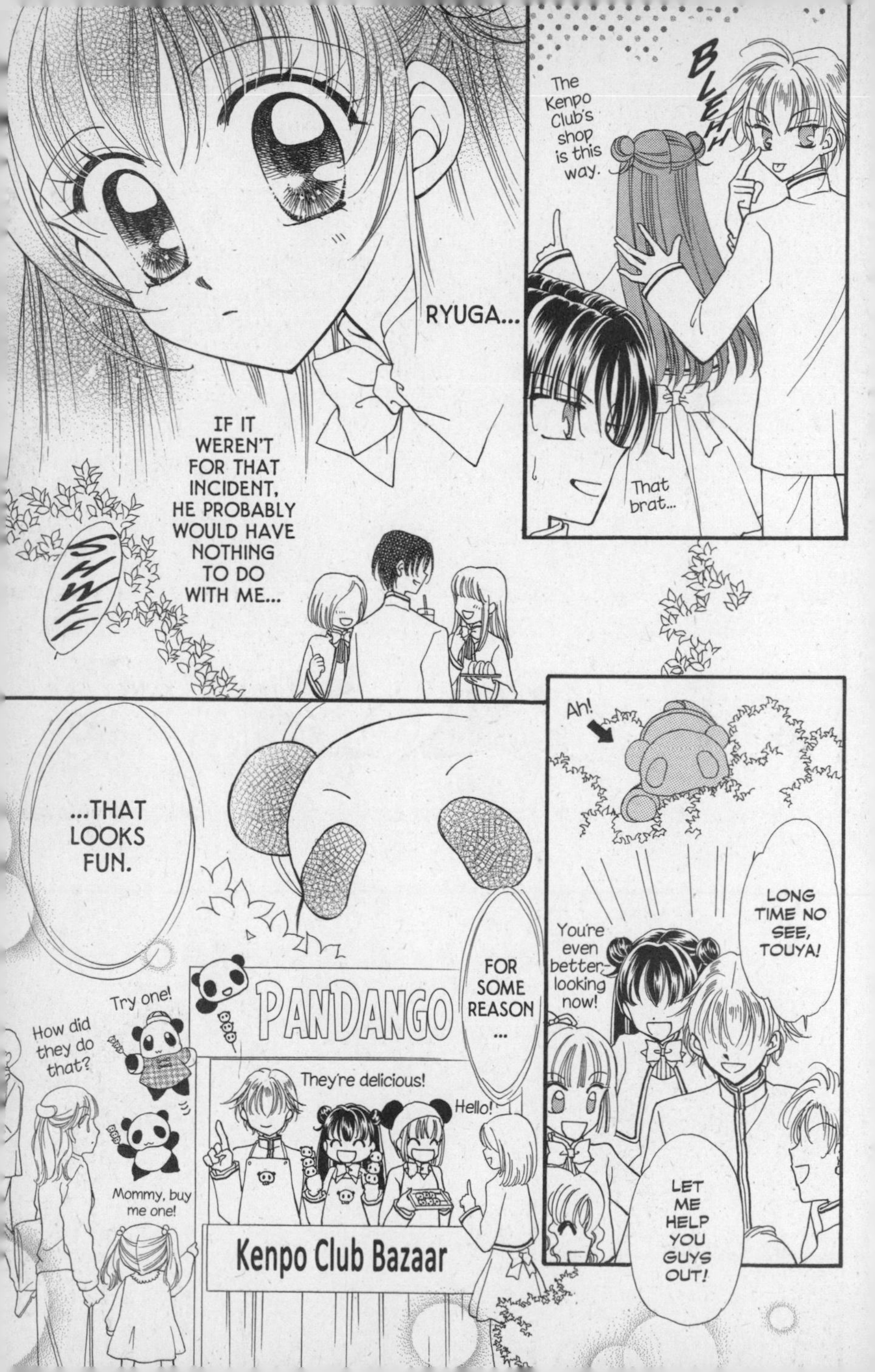
The Kenpo Club's shop is this way.
BLEHH
That brat...
RYUGA...
IF IT WEREN'T FOR THAT INCIDENT, HE PROBABLY WOULD HAVE NOTHING TO DO WITH ME...
SHWFF
Ah!
LONG TIME NO SEE, TOUYA!
You're even better-looking now!
LET ME HELP YOU GUYS OUT!
...THAT LOOKS FUN.
FOR SOME REASON ...
PANDANGO
They're delicious!
Hello!
Try one!
How did they do that?
Mommy, buy me one!
Kenpo Club Bazaar

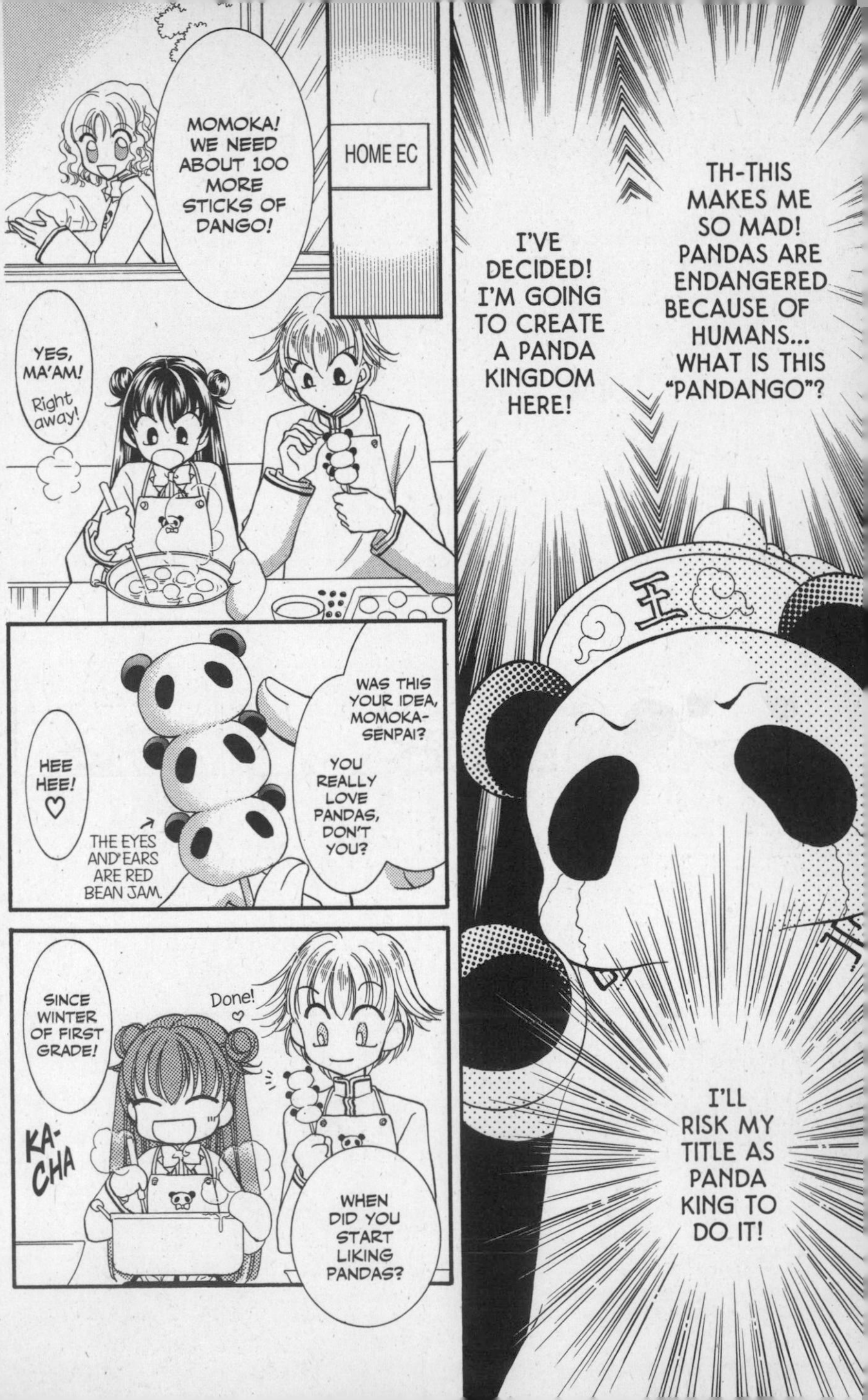
TH-THIS MAKES ME SO MAD! PANDAS ARE ENDANGERED BECAUSE OF HUMANS... WHAT IS THIS "PANDANGO"?
I'VE DECIDED! I'M GOING TO CREATE A PANDA KINGDOM HERE!
I'LL RISK MY TITLE AS PANDA KING TO DO IT!
HOME EC
MOMOKA! WE NEED ABOUT 100 MORE STICKS OF DANGO!
YES, MA'AM!
Right away!
WAS THIS YOUR IDEA, MOMOKA-SENPAI?
YOU REALLY LOVE PANDAS, DON'T YOU?
HEE HEE! ♡
THE EYES AND EARS ARE RED BEAN JAM.
WHEN DID YOU START LIKING PANDAS?
Done! ♡
SINCE WINTER OF FIRST GRADE!
KA-CHA

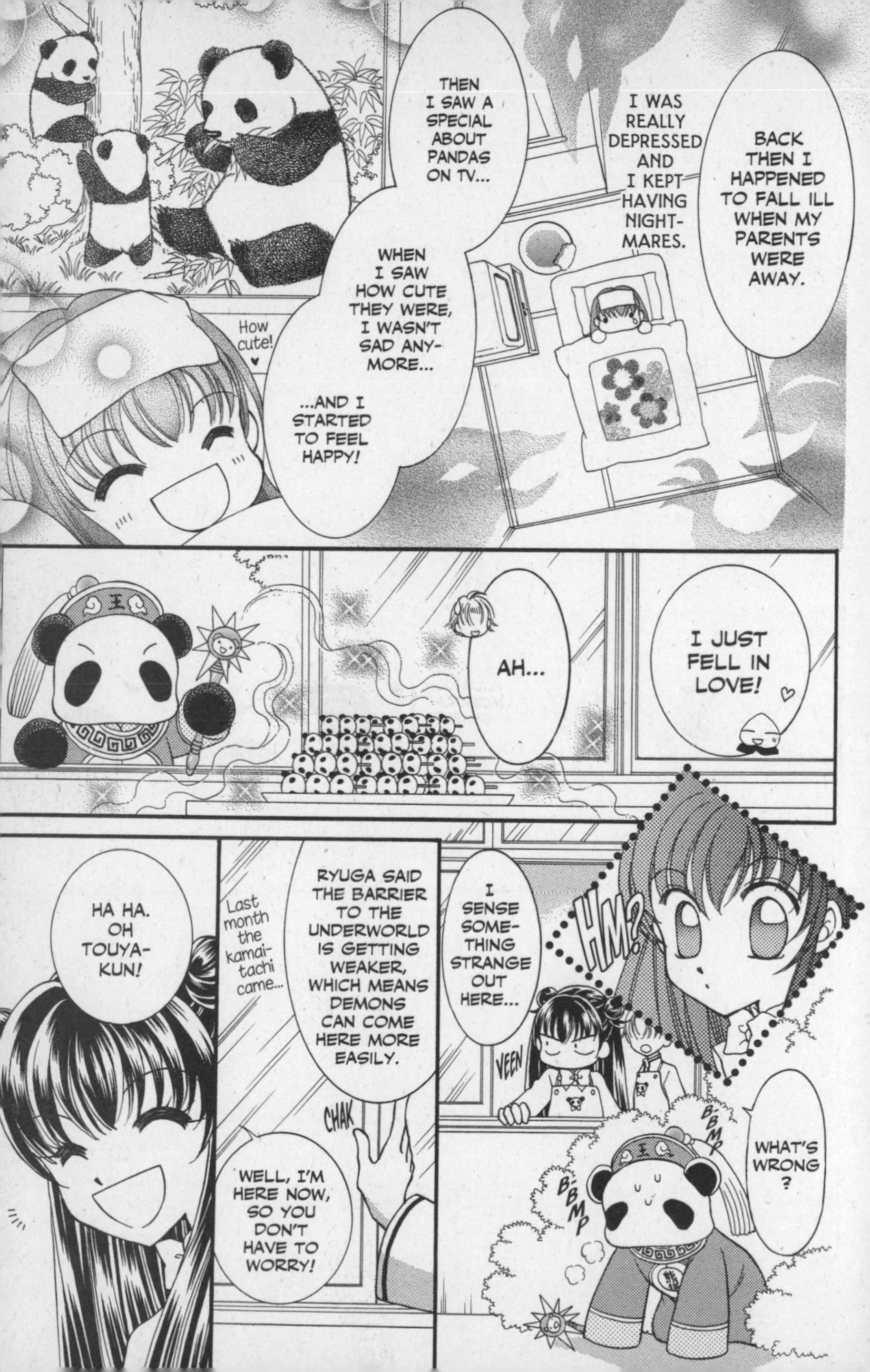
BACK THEN I HAPPENED TO FALL ILL WHEN MY PARENTS WERE AWAY.
I WAS REALLY DEPRESSED AND I KEPT HAVING NIGHT-MARES.
THEN I SAW A SPECIAL ABOUT PANDAS ON TV...
WHEN I SAW HOW CUTE THEY WERE, I WASN'T SAD ANY-MORE...
...AND I STARTED TO FEEL HAPPY!
How cute! ♥
I JUST FELL IN LOVE!
AH...
HM?
WHAT'S WRONG?
B-BMP
B-BMP
I SENSE SOME-THING STRANGE OUT HERE...
VEEN
RYUGA SAID THE BARRIER TO THE UNDERWORLD IS GETTING WEAKER, WHICH MEANS DEMONS CAN COME HERE MORE EASILY.
Last month the kamai-tachi came...
CHAK
WELL, I'M HERE NOW, SO YOU DON'T HAVE TO WORRY!
HA HA. OH TOUYA-KUN!

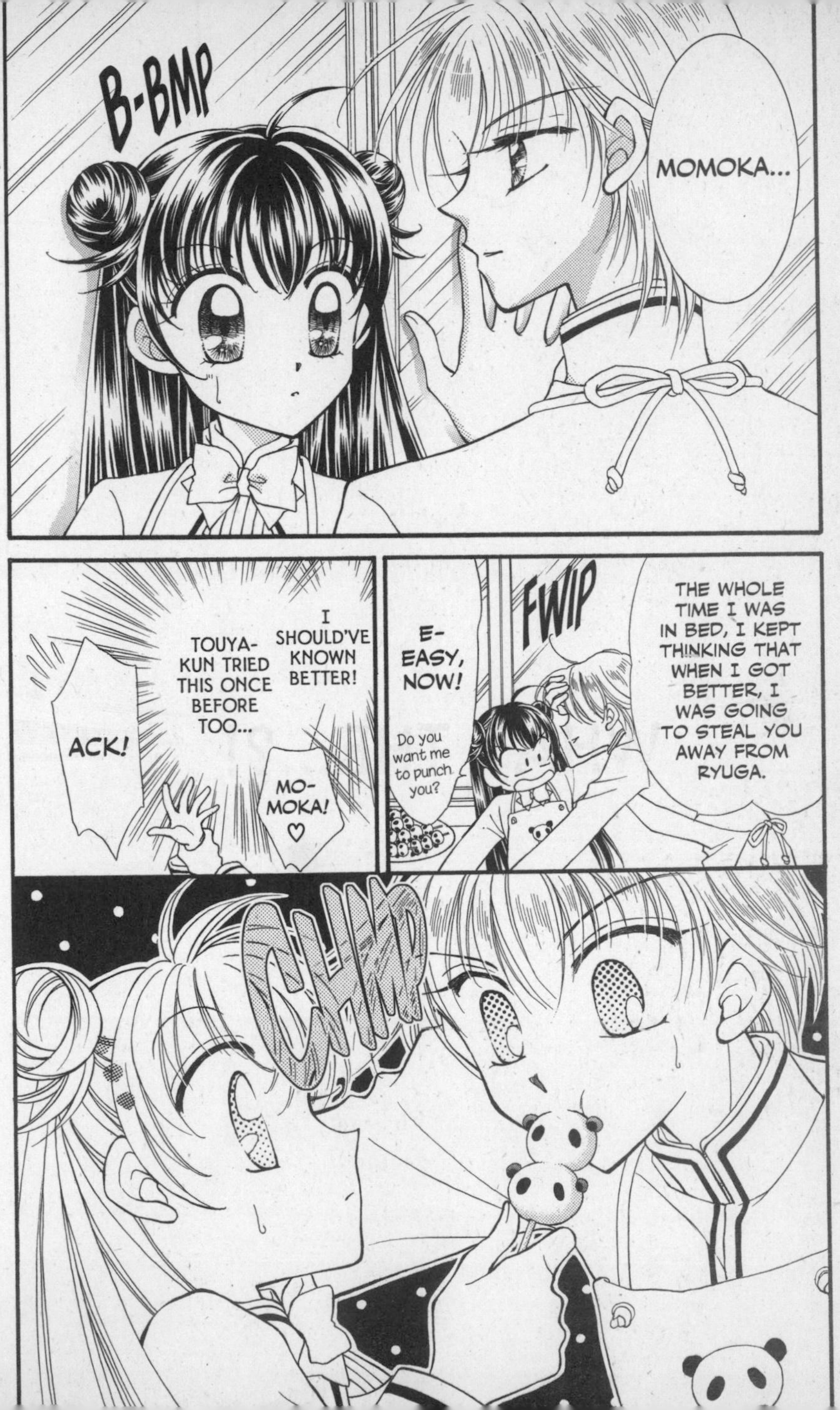
MOMOKA...
B-BMP
THE WHOLE TIME I WAS IN BED, I KEPT THINKING THAT WHEN I GOT BETTER, I WAS GOING TO STEAL YOU AWAY FROM RYUGA.
FWIP
E-EASY, NOW!
Do you want me to punch you?
I SHOULD'VE KNOWN BETTER!
TOUYA-KUN TRIED THIS ONCE BEFORE TOO...
MO-MOKA! ♡
ACK!
CHOMP

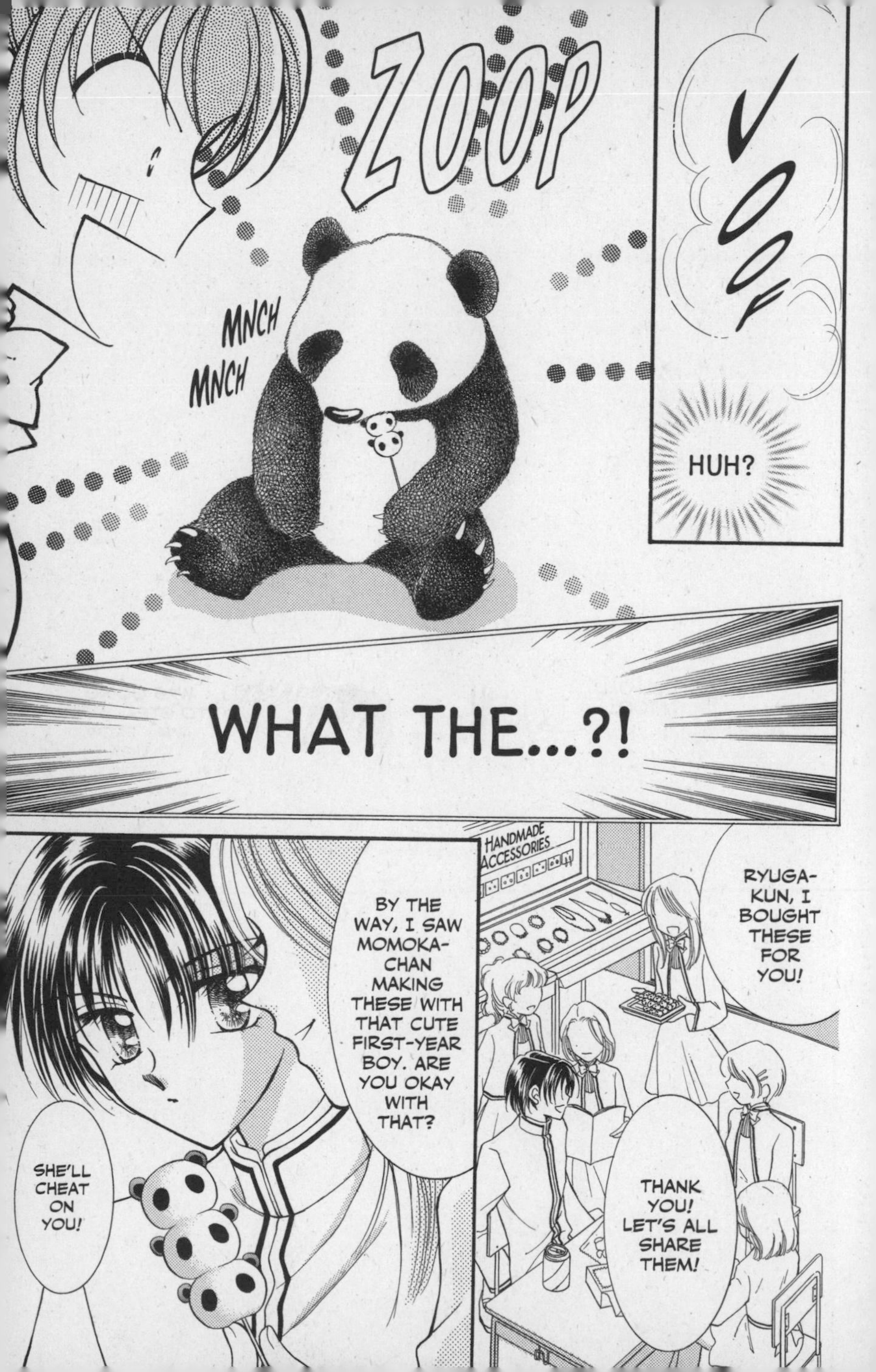
VOOF
HUH?
ZOOP
MNCH MNCH
WHAT THE...?!
HANDMADE ACCESSORIES
RYUGA-KUN, I BOUGHT THESE FOR YOU!
THANK YOU! LET'S ALL SHARE THEM!
BY THE WAY, I SAW MOMOKA-CHAN MAKING THESE WITH THAT CUTE FIRST-YEAR BOY. ARE YOU OKAY WITH THAT?
SHE'LL CHEAT ON YOU!

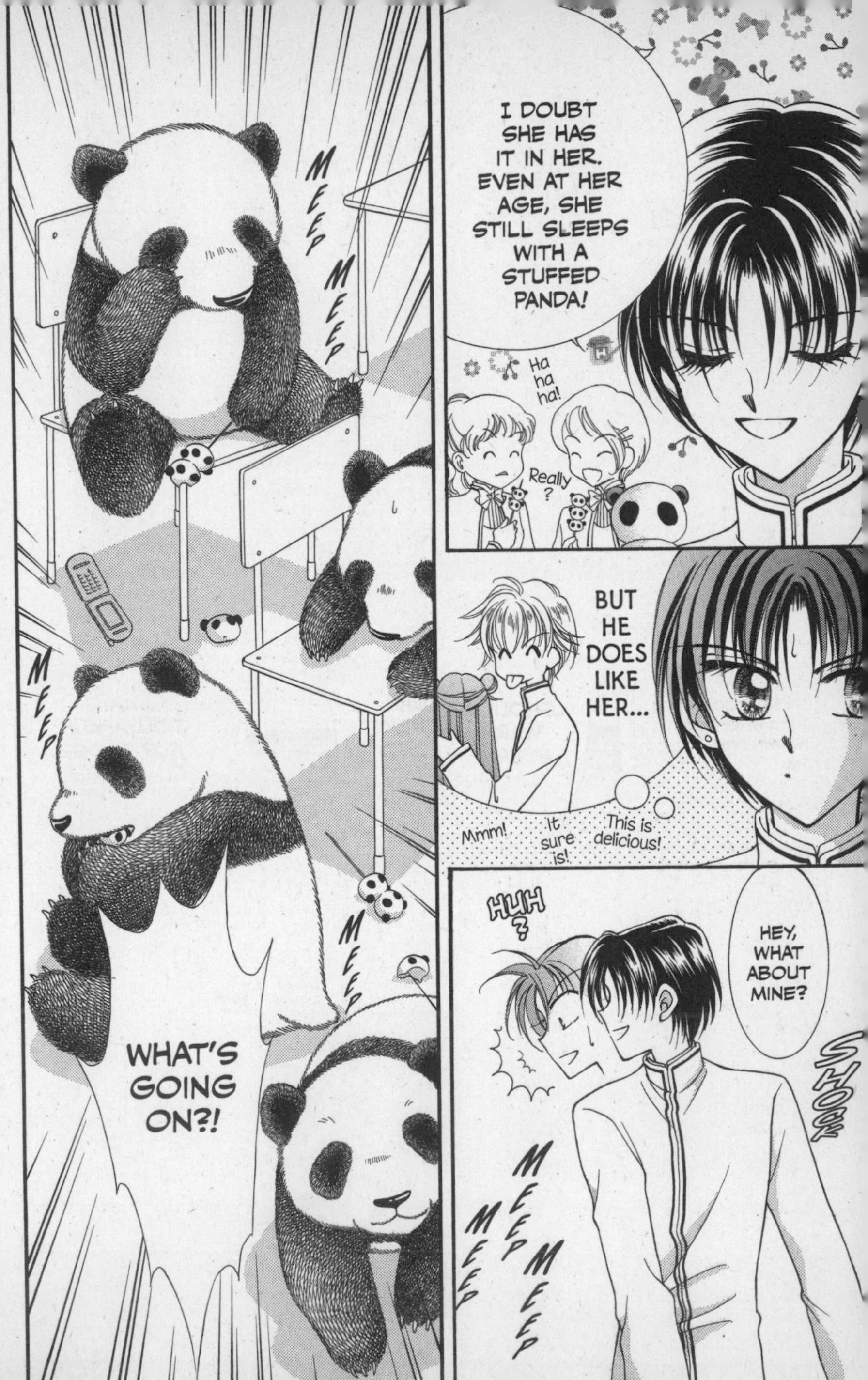
I DOUBT SHE HAS IT IN HER. EVEN AT HER AGE, SHE STILL SLEEPS WITH A STUFFED PANDA!
Ha ha ha!
Really?
BUT HE DOES LIKE HER...
This is delicious!
It sure is!
Mmm!
HEY, WHAT ABOUT MINE?
HUH?
MEEP MEEP
MEEP MEEP
MEEP
MEEP
MEEP
WHAT'S GOING ON?!

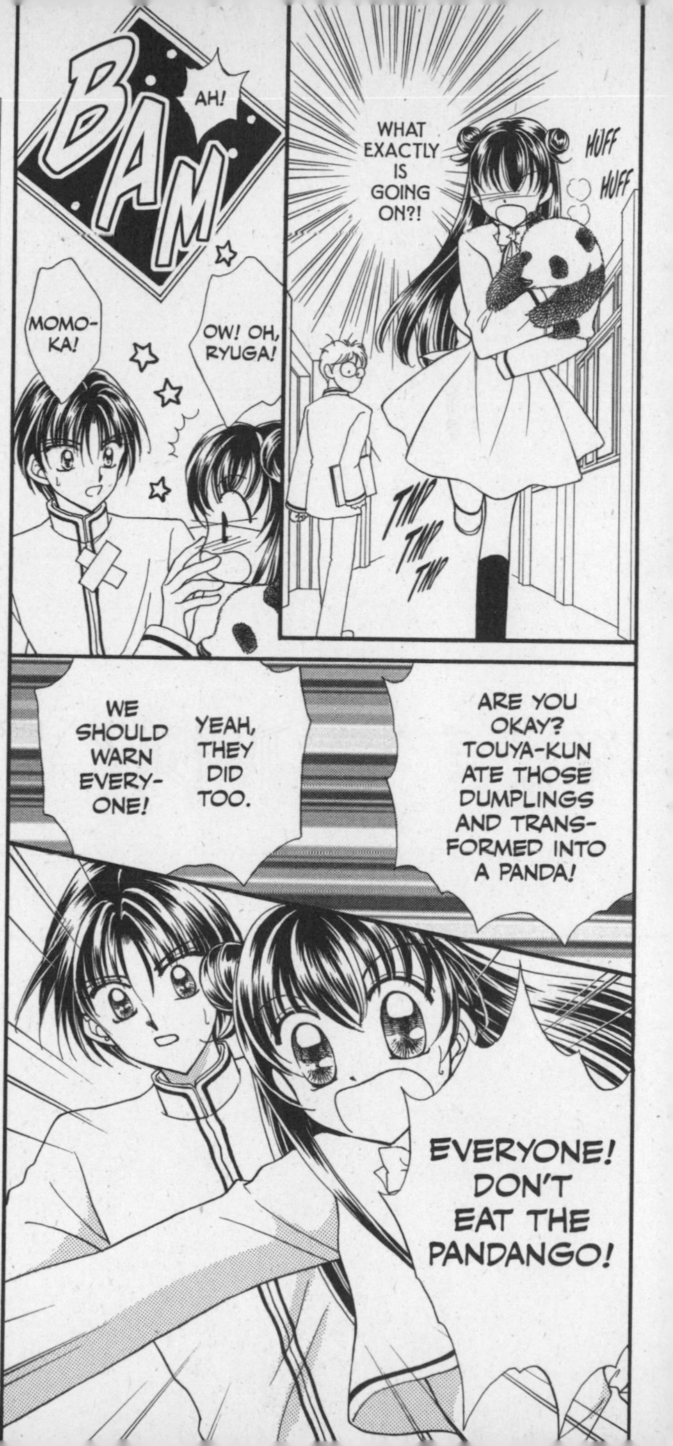
WHAT EXACTLY IS GOING ON?!
HUFF
HUFF
TMP TMP TMP
BAM
AH!
OW! OH, RYUGA!
MOMO-KA!
ARE YOU OKAY? TOUYA-KUN ATE THOSE DUMPLINGS AND TRANS-FORMED INTO A PANDA!
YEAH, THEY DID TOO.
WE SHOULD WARN EVERY-ONE!
EVERYONE! DON'T EAT THE PANDANGO!

4

For the December issue, I wrote the Panda King story, and I got to draw a lot of pandas. It was so fun!

Before I drew this, my assistant recommended a manga called *Panda Adventure* to me.

I was blown away by the baby pandas in it! I decided the next *St.♥ Dragon Girl* would be a panda story!!

Actually, the Panda King was a funny character I'd been thinking about doing for a while. (I just hadn't drawn him yet.)

I never thought he'd actually show up in *St.♥ Dragon Girl*, or that he'd possess Ron-Ron! (laugh) I don't know what will happen with him in the future.

Actually, I wanted to make Ron-Ron come to life earlier!

Also, in the first volume of *St.♥ Dragon Girl*, I had planned to have the Holy Dragon possess Ron-Ron, not Momoka!

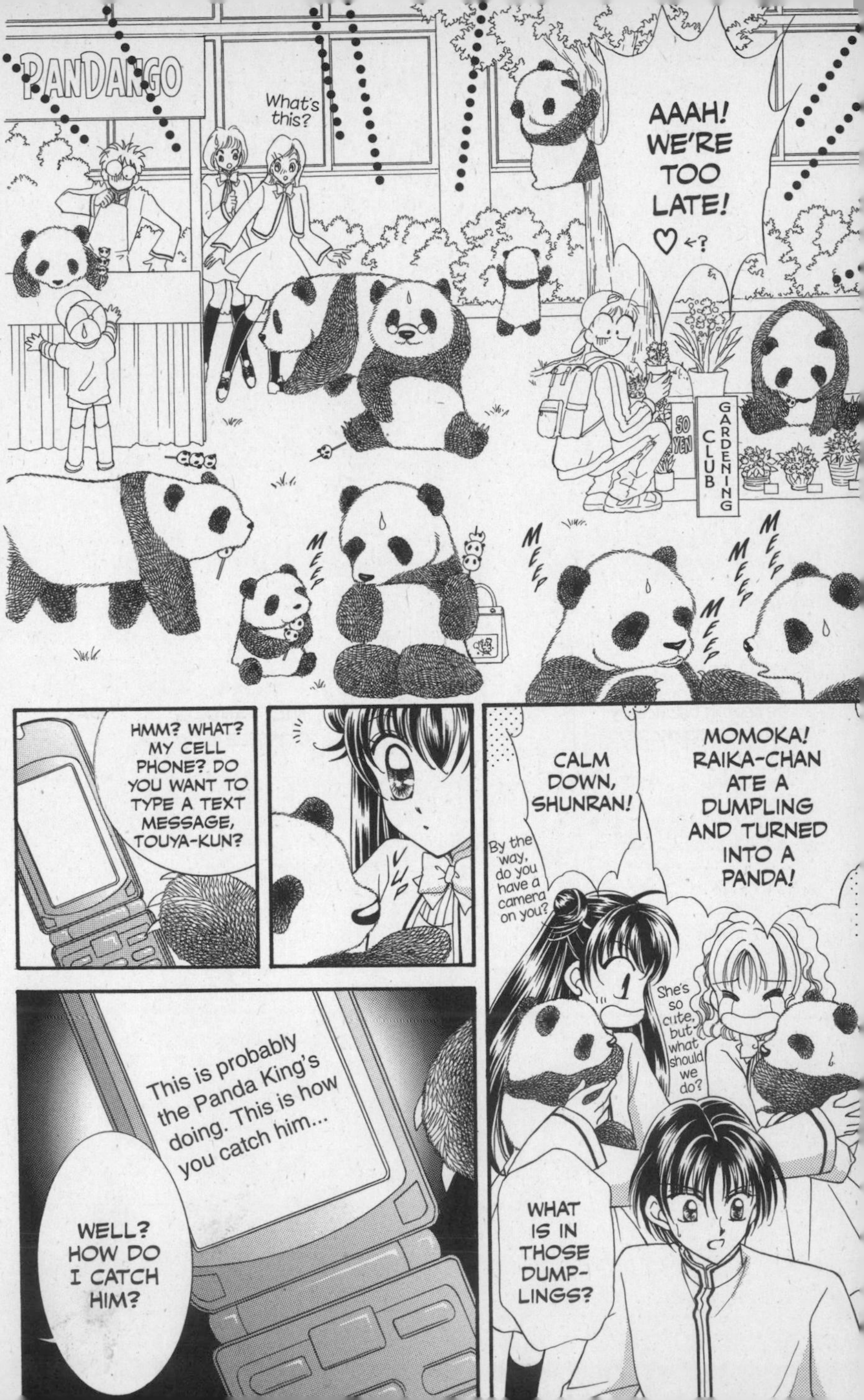
AAAH! WE'RE TOO LATE! ♡ ←?
What's this?
PANDANGO
GARDENING CLUB
50 YEN
MEEP
MEEP
MEEP
MEEP
MEEP
MOMOKA! RAIKA-CHAN ATE A DUMPLING AND TURNED INTO A PANDA!
CALM DOWN, SHUNRAN!
By the way, do you have a camera on you?
She's so cute, but what should we do?
WHAT IS IN THOSE DUMP-LINGS?
HMM? WHAT? MY CELL PHONE? DO YOU WANT TO TYPE A TEXT MESSAGE, TOUYA-KUN?
This is probably the Panda King's doing. This is how you catch him...
WELL? HOW DO I CATCH HIM?

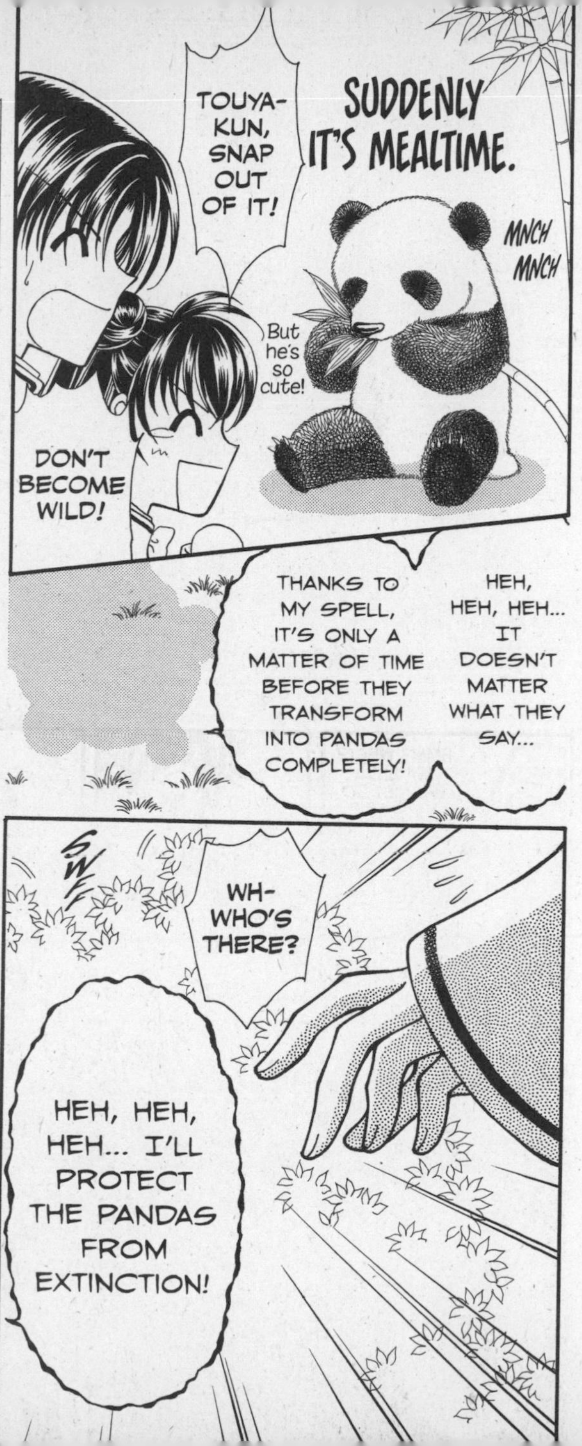
SUDDENLY IT'S MEALTIME.
MNCH MNCH
TOUYA-KUN, SNAP OUT OF IT!
But he's so cute!
DON'T BECOME WILD!
HEH, HEH, HEH... IT DOESN'T MATTER WHAT THEY SAY...
THANKS TO MY SPELL, IT'S ONLY A MATTER OF TIME BEFORE THEY TRANSFORM INTO PANDAS COMPLETELY!
WH-WHO'S THERE?
SWF
HEH, HEH, HEH... I'LL PROTECT THE PANDAS FROM EXTINCTION!

5

But due to the lack of pages, as well as the flow of the story, I thought it would be better to have the dragon possess Momoka. That's why I made Ron-Ron move with Ryuga's and Kouryu's spells at first! (laugh)

The ghost cats Lin-Lin and Len-Len live in Momoka's mirror, and the spirit of the Panda King hangs out in her room! It's like a haunted house now!

Well, Momoka has the Holy Dragon inside her, so all that yang in her will be kept in balance by the yin in those ghosts!

I think this story made Momoka, who loves pandas, the happiest! (Ah, what about Ryuga?)

Actually, I like doing funny stories better than serious ones, so this story was really fun for me. I want to do another story about pandas sometime!

Touya reappeared in this story, and he officially became Ryuga's rival! Touya's voice as Yutengenyo is so creepy! I might incorporate it again soon...

Maybe he can secretly transform. Oh, I guess I can't have any more perverts in this story! (laugh)

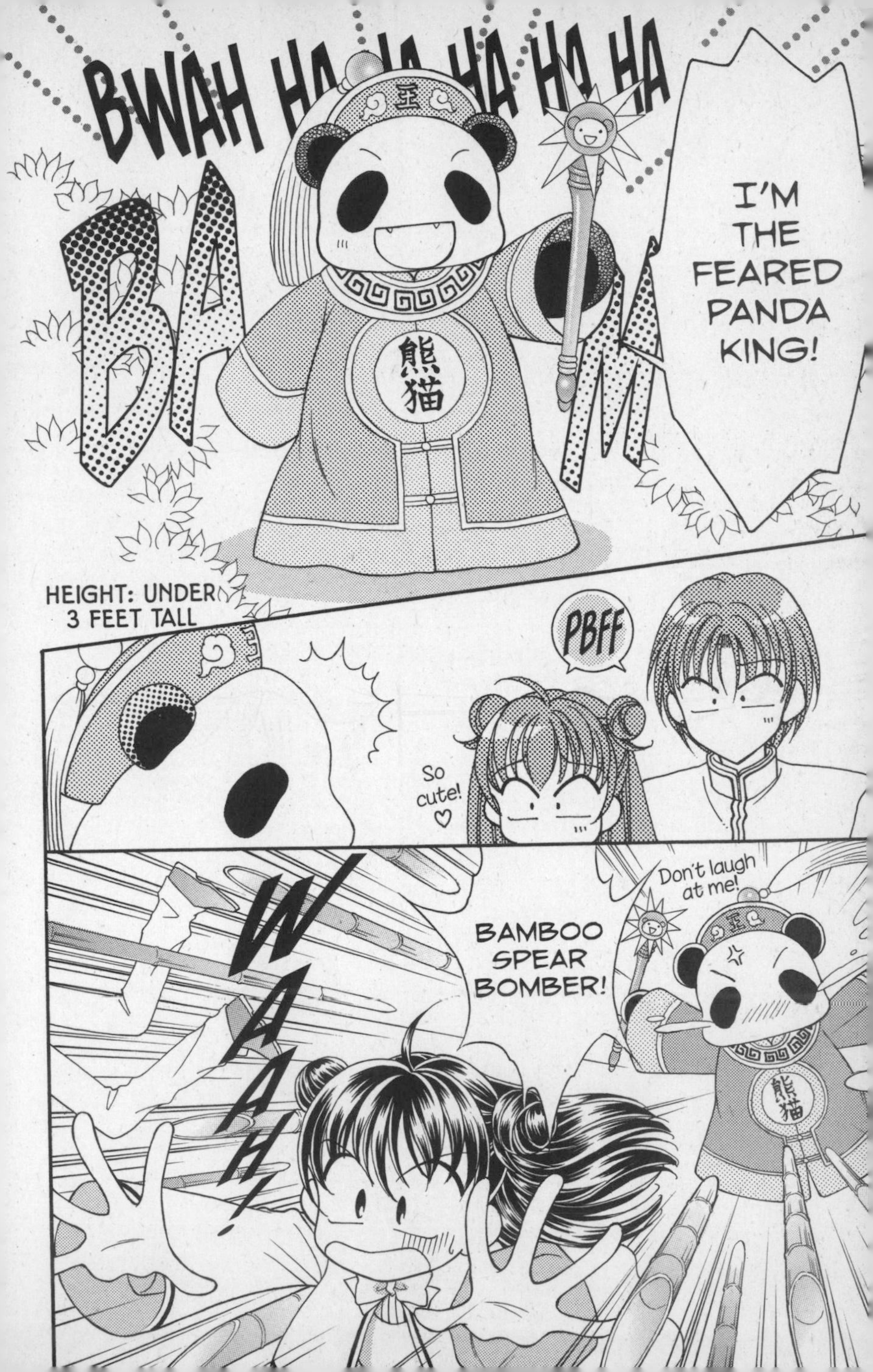
BWAH HA HA HA HA HA
I'M THE FEARED PANDA KING!
BAM
熊猫
HEIGHT: UNDER 3 FEET TALL
PBFF
So cute! ♡
Don't laugh at me!
BAMBOO SPEAR BOMBER!
WAAAH!

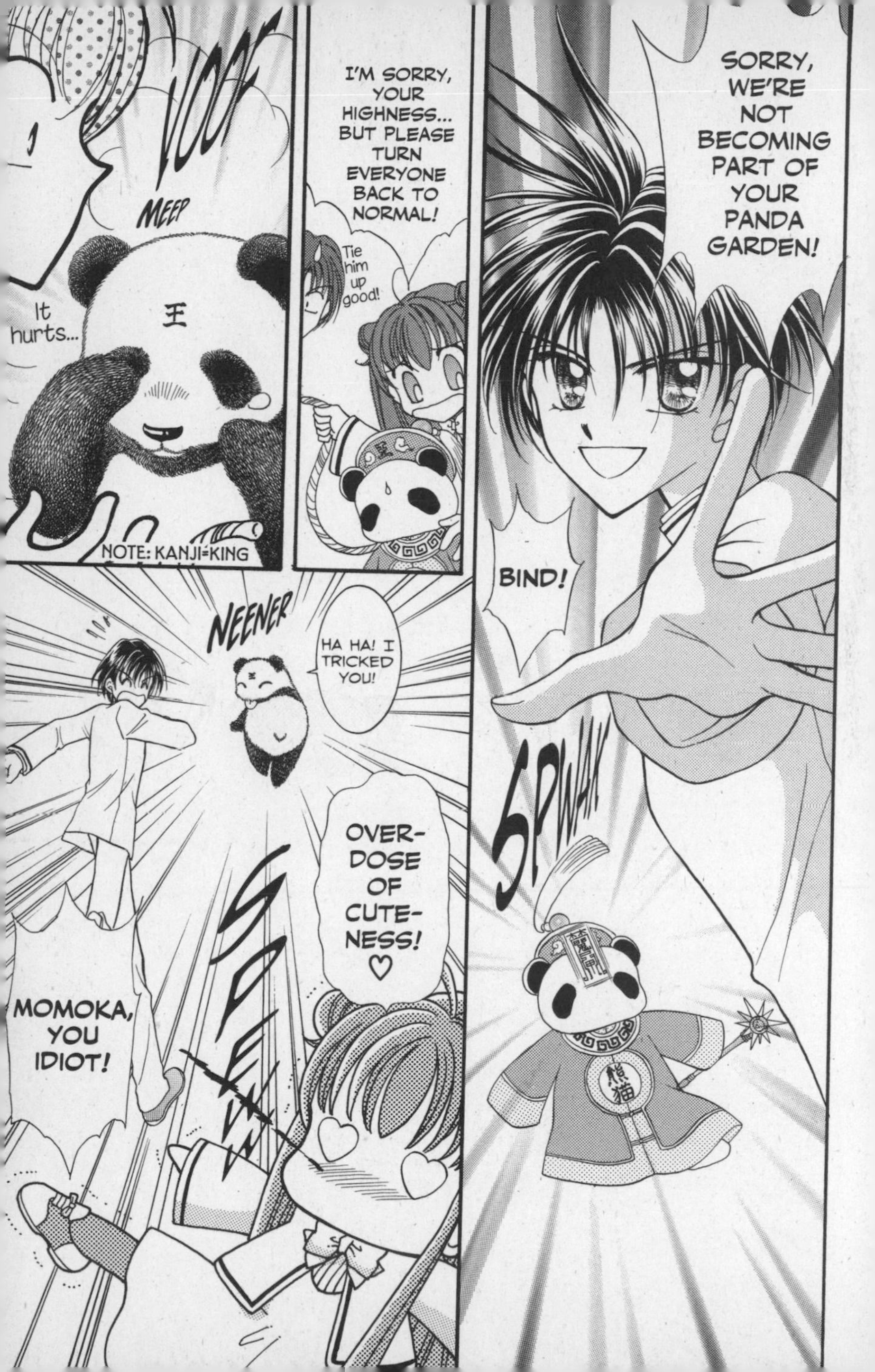
SORRY, WE'RE NOT BECOMING PART OF YOUR PANDA GARDEN!
BIND!
SPWAK
I'M SORRY, YOUR HIGHNESS... BUT PLEASE TURN EVERYONE BACK TO NORMAL!
Tie him up good!
VOOF
MEEP
It hurts...
NOTE: KANJI=KING
NEENER
HA HA! I TRICKED YOU!
OVER-DOSE OF CUTE-NESS! ♡
MOMOKA, YOU IDIOT!

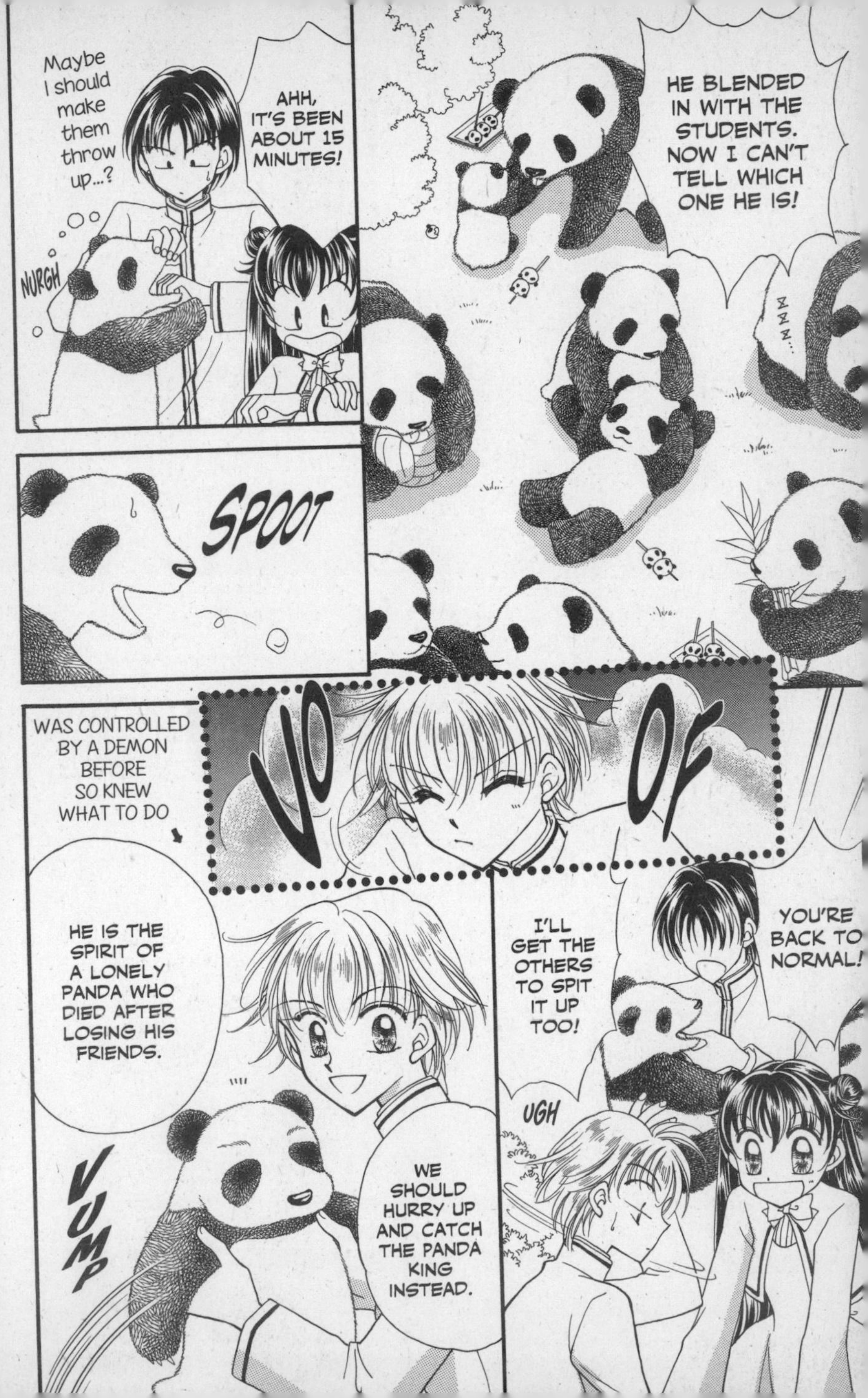
HE BLENDED IN WITH THE STUDENTS. NOW I CAN'T TELL WHICH ONE HE IS!
AHH, IT'S BEEN ABOUT 15 MINUTES!
Maybe I should make them throw up...?
NURGH
SPOOT
VOOF
WAS CONTROLLED BY A DEMON BEFORE SO KNEW WHAT TO DO
YOU'RE BACK TO NORMAL!
I'LL GET THE OTHERS TO SPIT IT UP TOO!
UGH
HE IS THE SPIRIT OF A LONELY PANDA WHO DIED AFTER LOSING HIS FRIENDS.
WE SHOULD HURRY UP AND CATCH THE PANDA KING INSTEAD.
VUMP

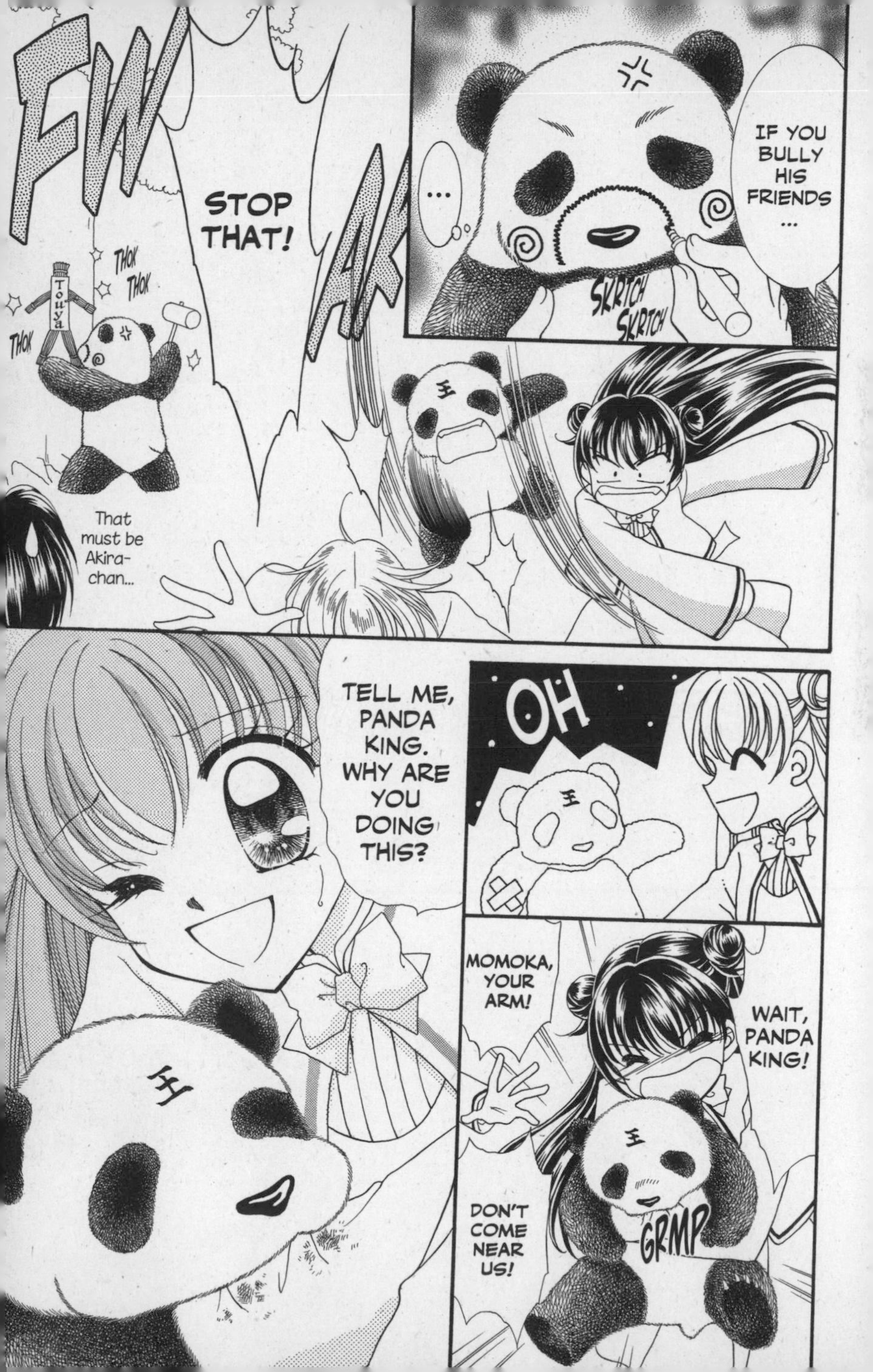
...
IF YOU BULLY HIS FRIENDS ...
SKRTCH SKRTCH
FW
AH
STOP THAT!
THOK THOK
THOK
Touya
That must be Akira-chan...
OH
WAIT, PANDA KING!
MOMOKA, YOUR ARM!
DON'T COME NEAR US!
GRMP
TELL ME, PANDA KING. WHY ARE YOU DOING THIS?

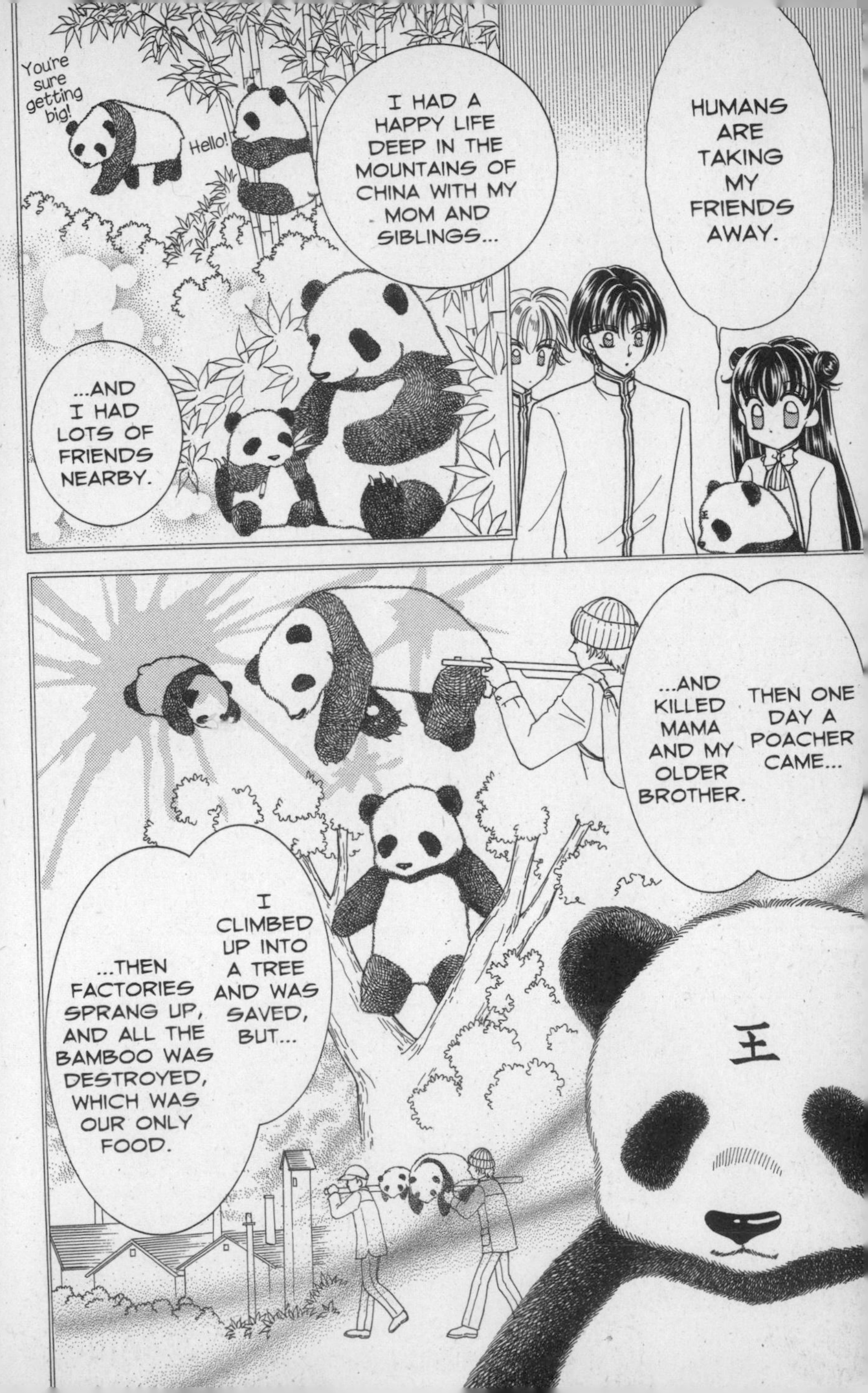
HUMANS ARE TAKING MY FRIENDS AWAY.
I HAD A HAPPY LIFE DEEP IN THE MOUNTAINS OF CHINA WITH MY MOM AND SIBLINGS...
You're sure getting big!
Hello!
...AND I HAD LOTS OF FRIENDS NEARBY.
THEN ONE DAY A POACHER CAME...
...AND KILLED MAMA AND MY OLDER BROTHER.
I CLIMBED UP INTO A TREE AND WAS SAVED, BUT...
...THEN FACTORIES SPRANG UP, AND ALL THE BAMBOO WAS DESTROYED, WHICH WAS OUR ONLY FOOD.
王

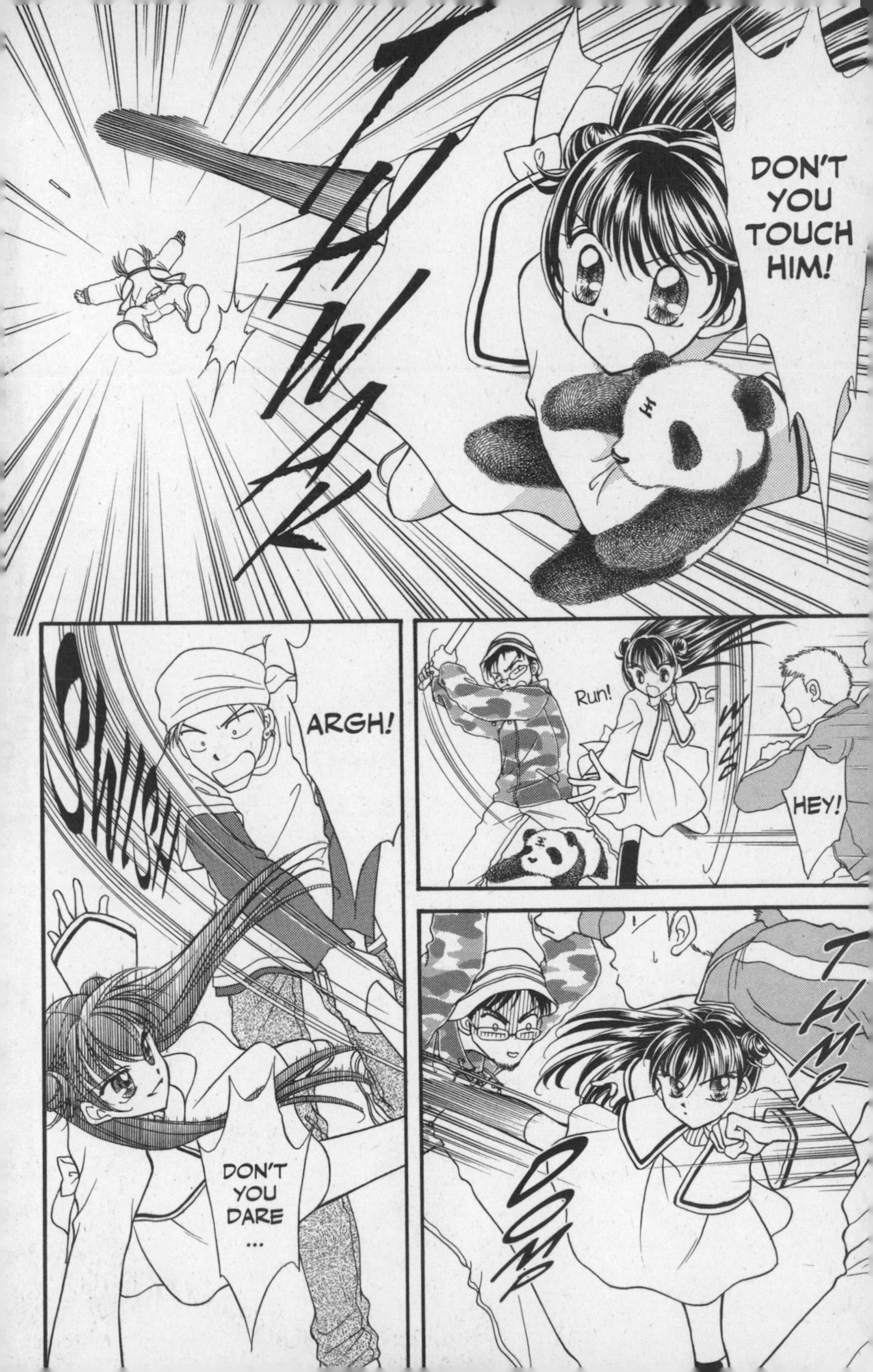
THWAK
DON'T YOU TOUCH HIM!
HEY!
Run!
THMP
ARGH!
SWISH
DON'T YOU DARE ...

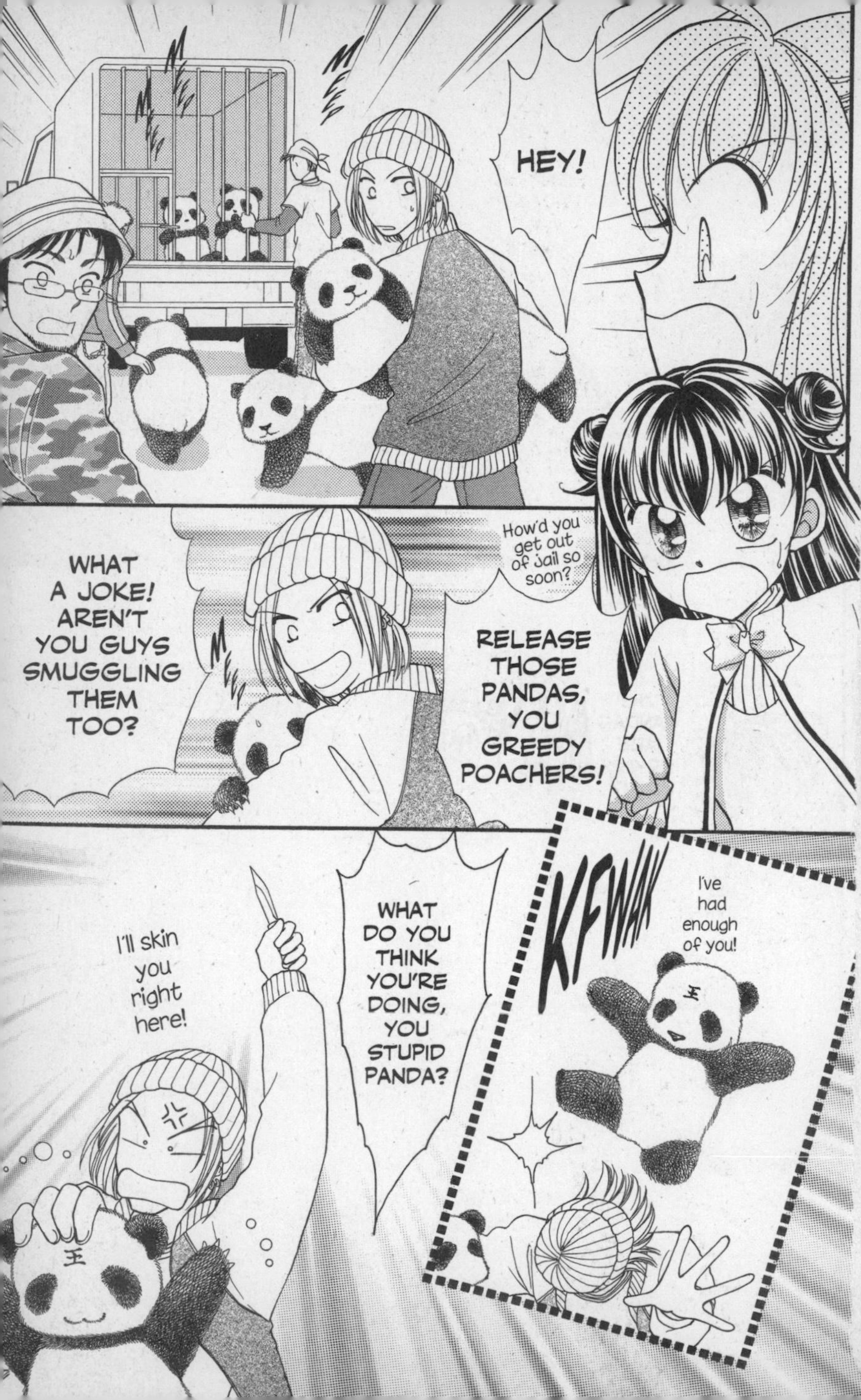
HEY!
How'd you get out of jail so soon?
RELEASE THOSE PANDAS, YOU GREEDY POACHERS!
WHAT A JOKE! AREN'T YOU GUYS SMUGGLING THEM TOO?
KFWAK
I've had enough of you!
WHAT DO YOU THINK YOU'RE DOING, YOU STUPID PANDA?
I'll skin you right here!

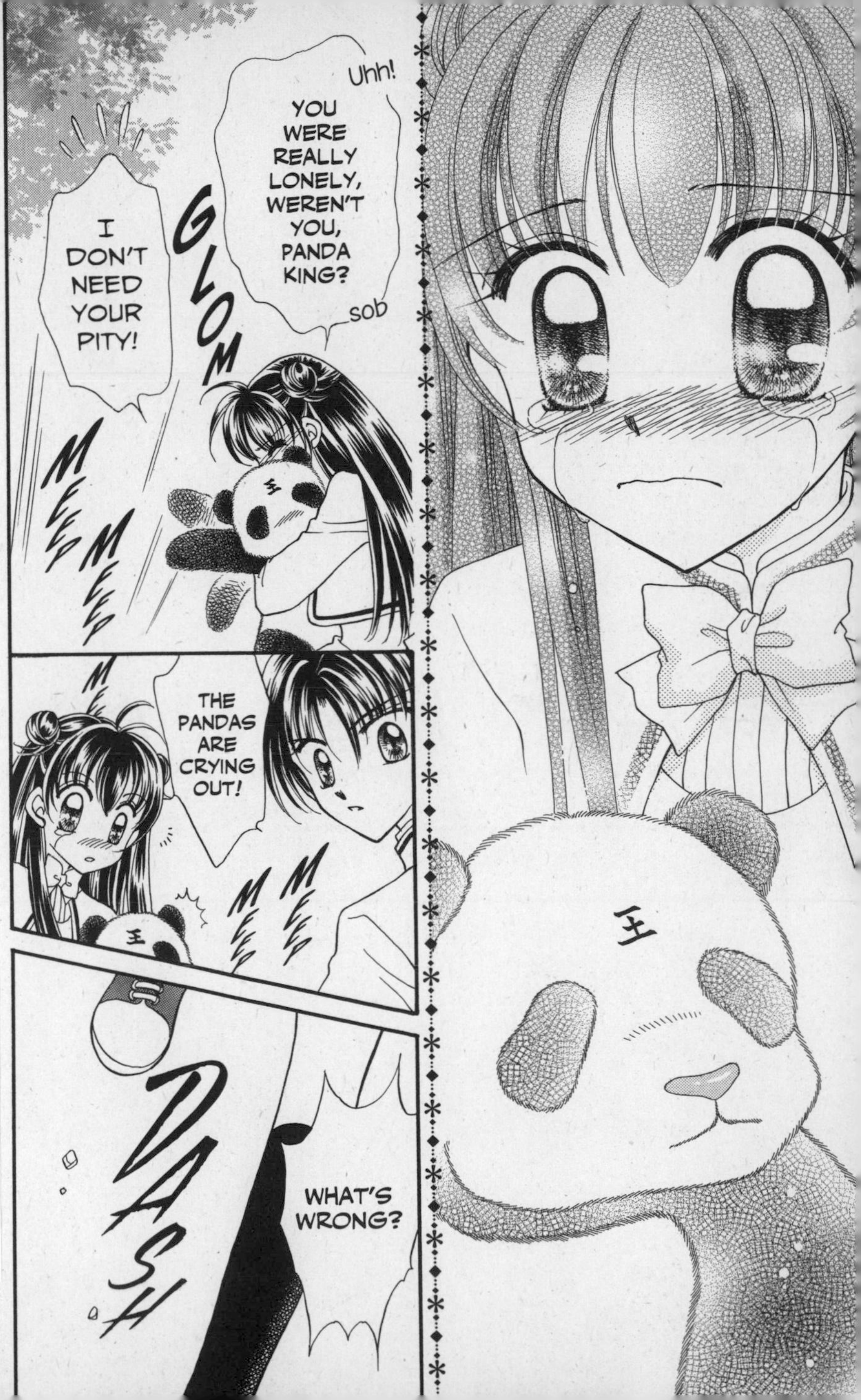
Uhh!
YOU WERE REALLY LONELY, WEREN'T YOU, PANDA KING?
sob
GLOM
I DON'T NEED YOUR PITY!
THE PANDAS ARE CRYING OUT!
WHAT'S WRONG?

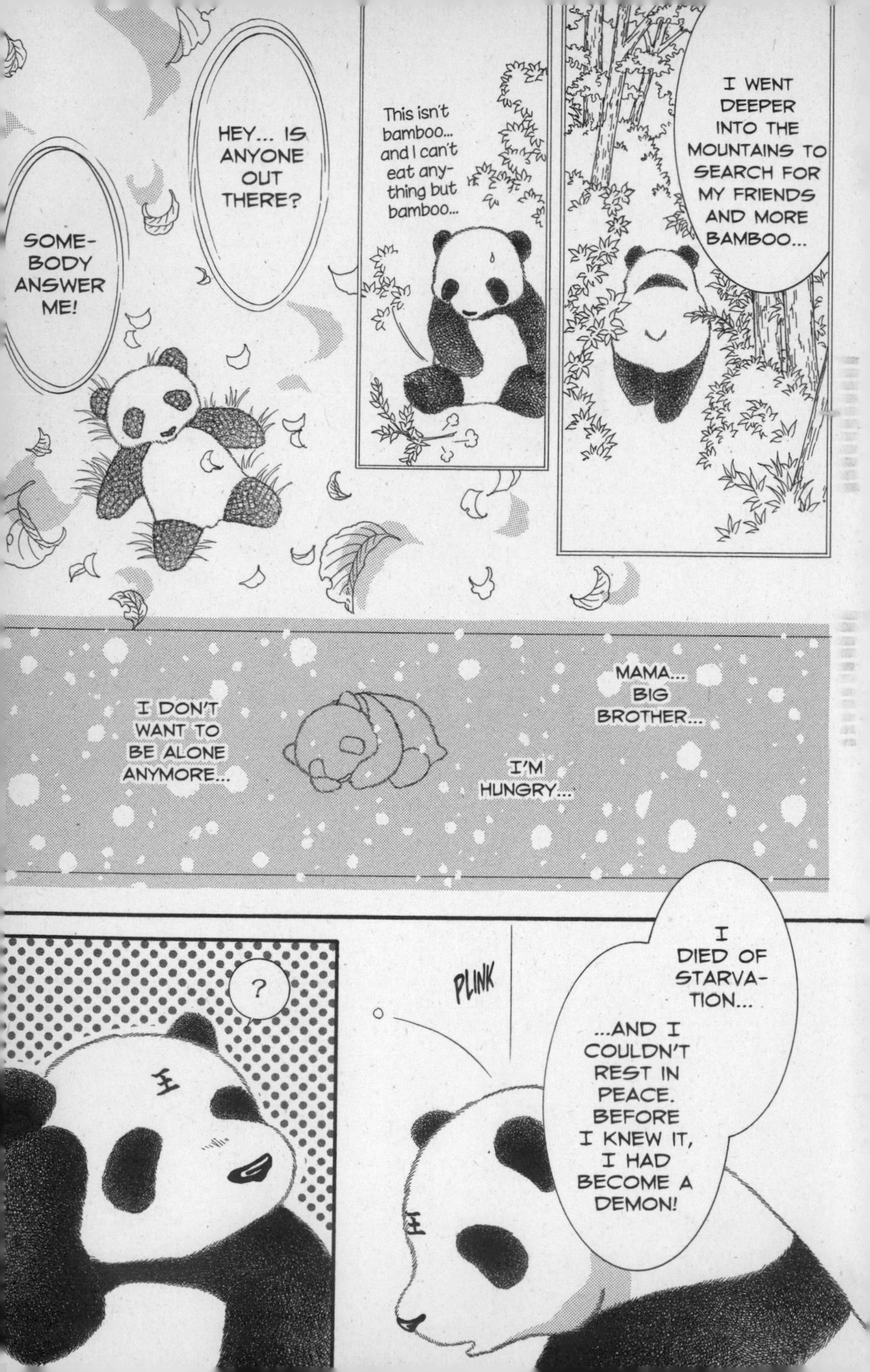
I WENT DEEPER INTO THE MOUNTAINS TO SEARCH FOR MY FRIENDS AND MORE BAMBOO...
This isn't bamboo... and I can't eat any-thing but bamboo...
HEY... IS ANYONE OUT THERE?
SOME-BODY ANSWER ME!
MAMA... BIG BROTHER...
I'M HUNGRY...
I DON'T WANT TO BE ALONE ANYMORE...
I DIED OF STARVA-TION...
...AND I COULDN'T REST IN PEACE. BEFORE I KNEW IT, I HAD BECOME A DEMON!
PLINK
?

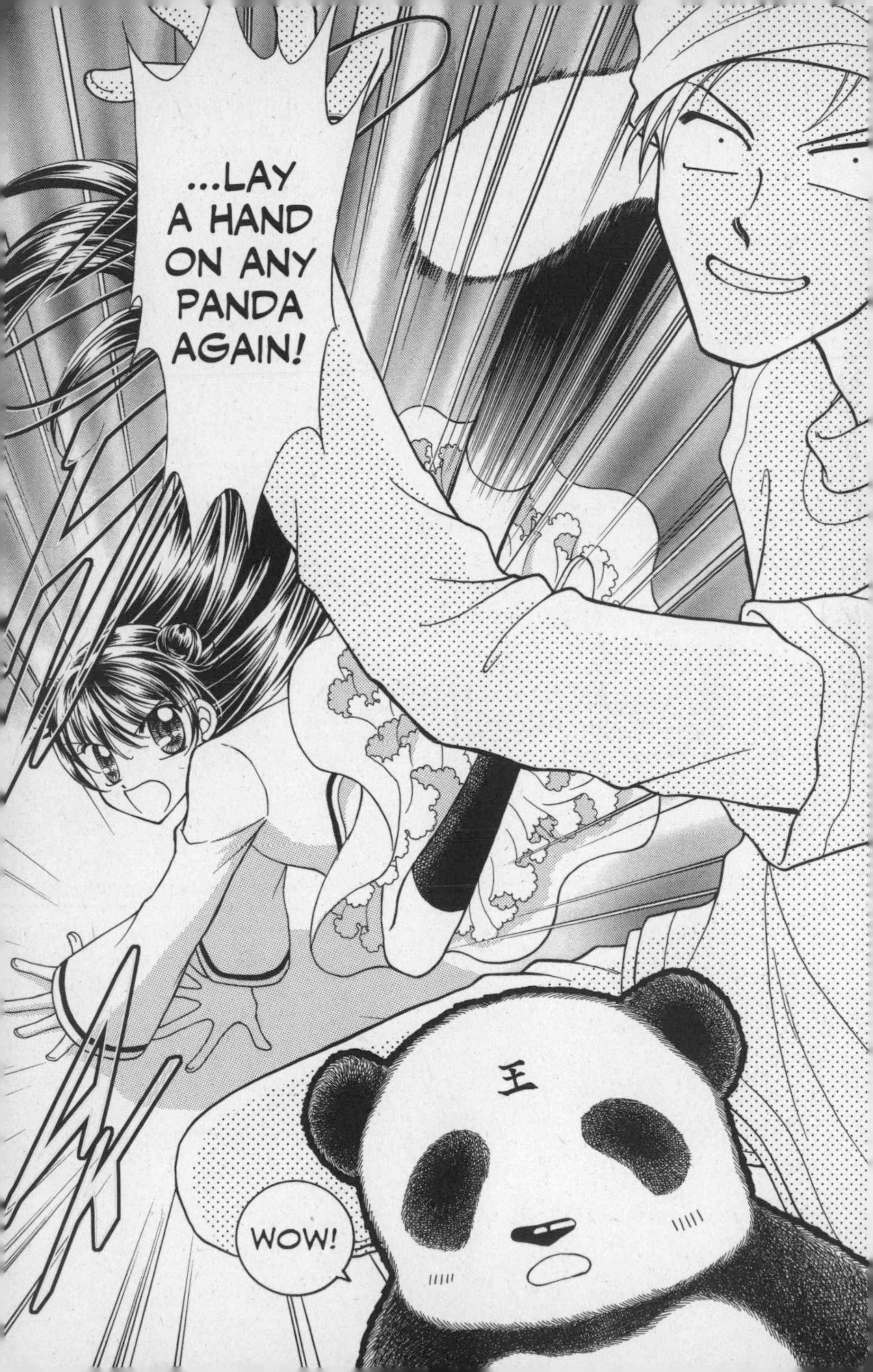
...LAY A HAND ON ANY PANDA AGAIN!
WOW!
王

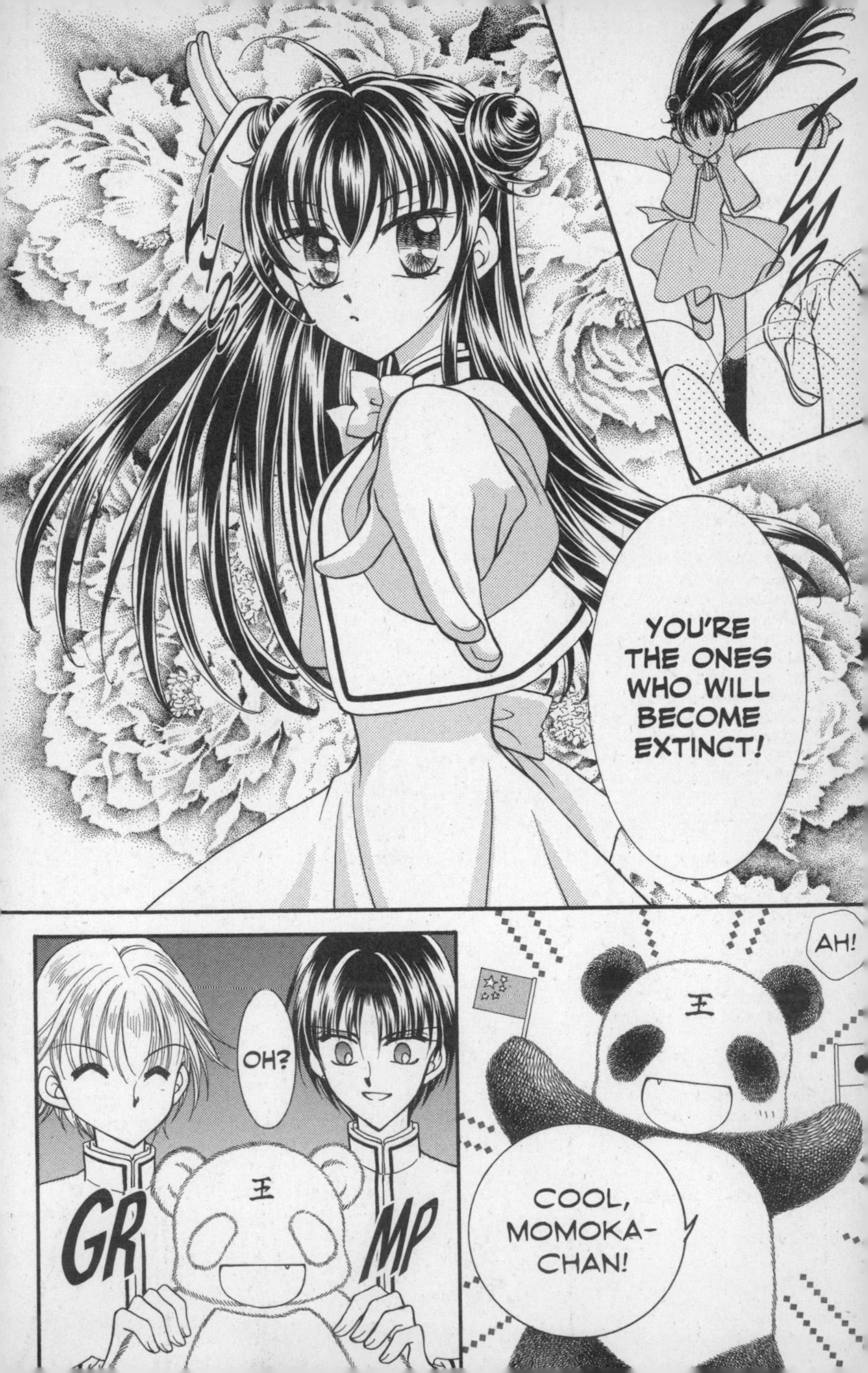
YOU'RE THE ONES WHO WILL BECOME EXTINCT!
AH!
王
COOL, MOMOKA-CHAN!
OH?
王
GRMP

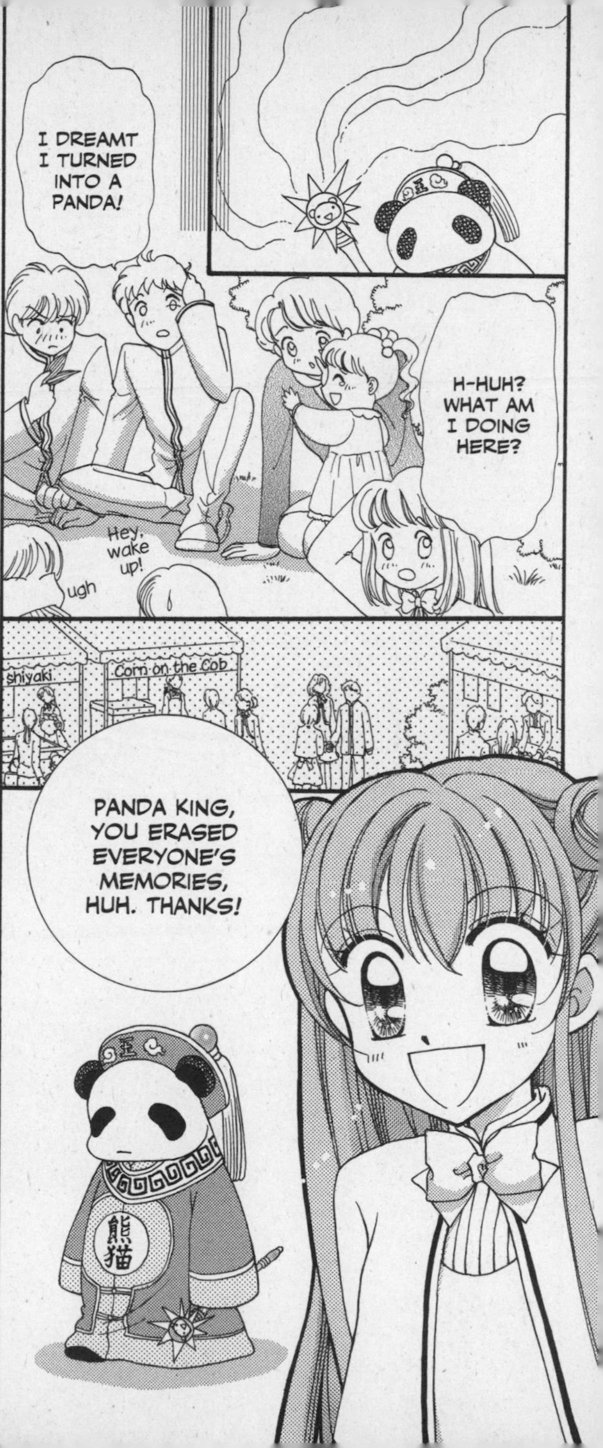
H-HUH? WHAT AM I DOING HERE?
I DREAMT I TURNED INTO A PANDA!
Hey, wake up!
ugh
Corn on the Cob
shiyaki
PANDA KING, YOU ERASED EVERYONE'S MEMORIES, HUH. THANKS!
熊猫

6

By the way, I had my assistants each draw a page.

I told them they could draw whatever they wanted, and because everyone is so enthusiastic, the pages turned out great!

The first one is "Fight, Dragon Rangers!" by Kodaka-san.

I can't say anything, but it's great! It's the Power Ranger version of *St.♥Dragon Girl!* It was so funny how everyone got into their roles. I thought Master looked so cool! And Shunran was perfect!

The part in which Ryuga and Kouryu are fighting over Red where Ryuga says, "You should be the leftover Green!" made me crack up!

Queen wrote "Kou Family Secret, Part 2." The Kou house had a power-up, huh? Now they can catch yellowtail and sea bream in the lake! I wonder if the sea king can come to my house too. Oh, I guess I'd have to have a lake though. And Touya really acts like that! And Ryuga's such a hard worker!

Speaking of Ryuga, Sasaki-san wrote "Ryuga's Secret, Part 2." I was cracking up by the fourth panel! That story has a really great impact! Ryuga's blood type is B, so he's an enthusiastic person!

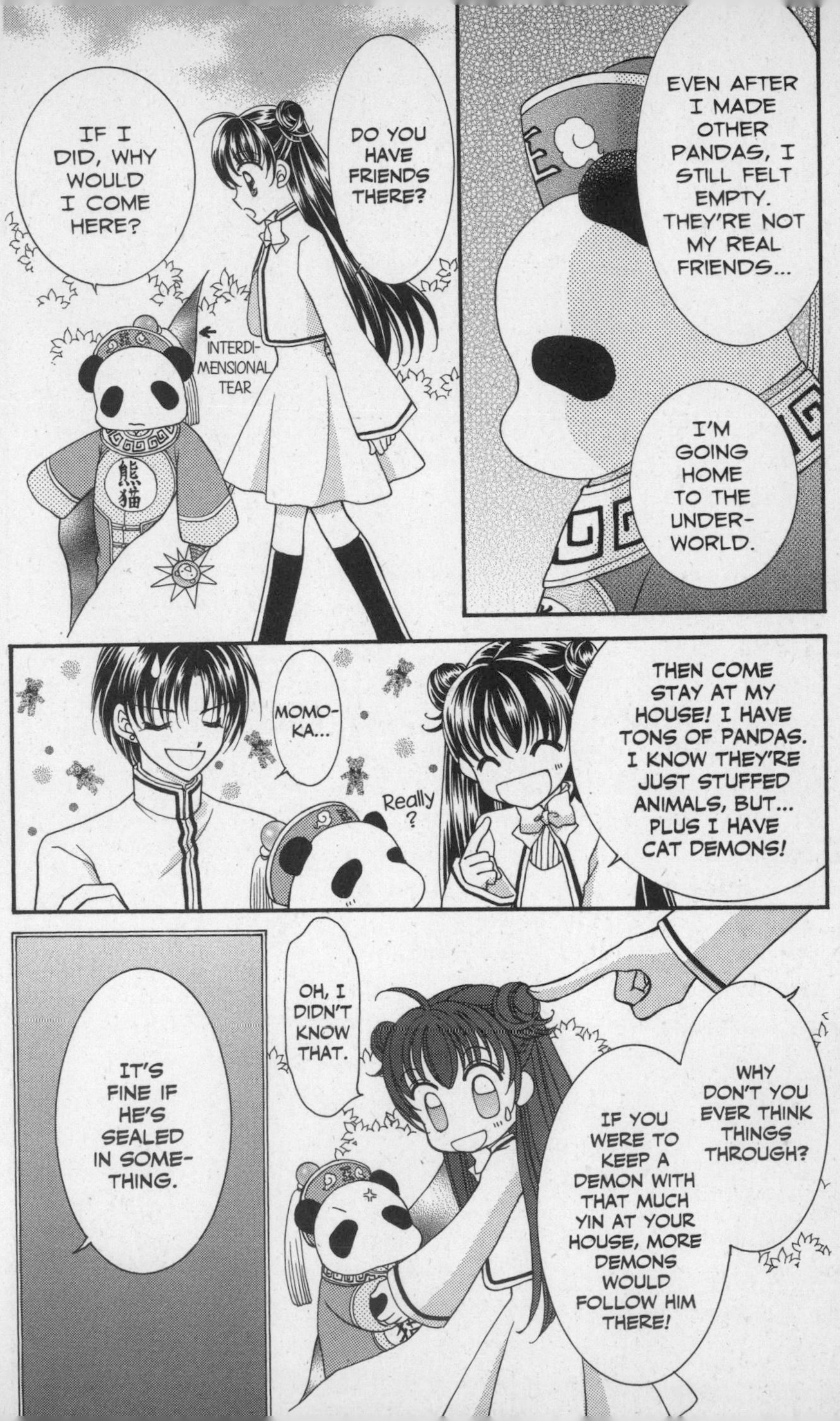
EVEN AFTER I MADE OTHER PANDAS, I STILL FELT EMPTY. THEY'RE NOT MY REAL FRIENDS...
I'M GOING HOME TO THE UNDER-WORLD.
DO YOU HAVE FRIENDS THERE?
IF I DID, WHY WOULD I COME HERE?
INTERDI-MENSIONAL TEAR
熊猫
THEN COME STAY AT MY HOUSE! I HAVE TONS OF PANDAS. I KNOW THEY'RE JUST STUFFED ANIMALS, BUT... PLUS I HAVE CAT DEMONS!
Really?
MOMO-KA...
WHY DON'T YOU EVER THINK THINGS THROUGH?
IF YOU WERE TO KEEP A DEMON WITH THAT MUCH YIN AT YOUR HOUSE, MORE DEMONS WOULD FOLLOW HIM THERE!
OH, I DIDN'T KNOW THAT.
IT'S FINE IF HE'S SEALED IN SOME-THING.

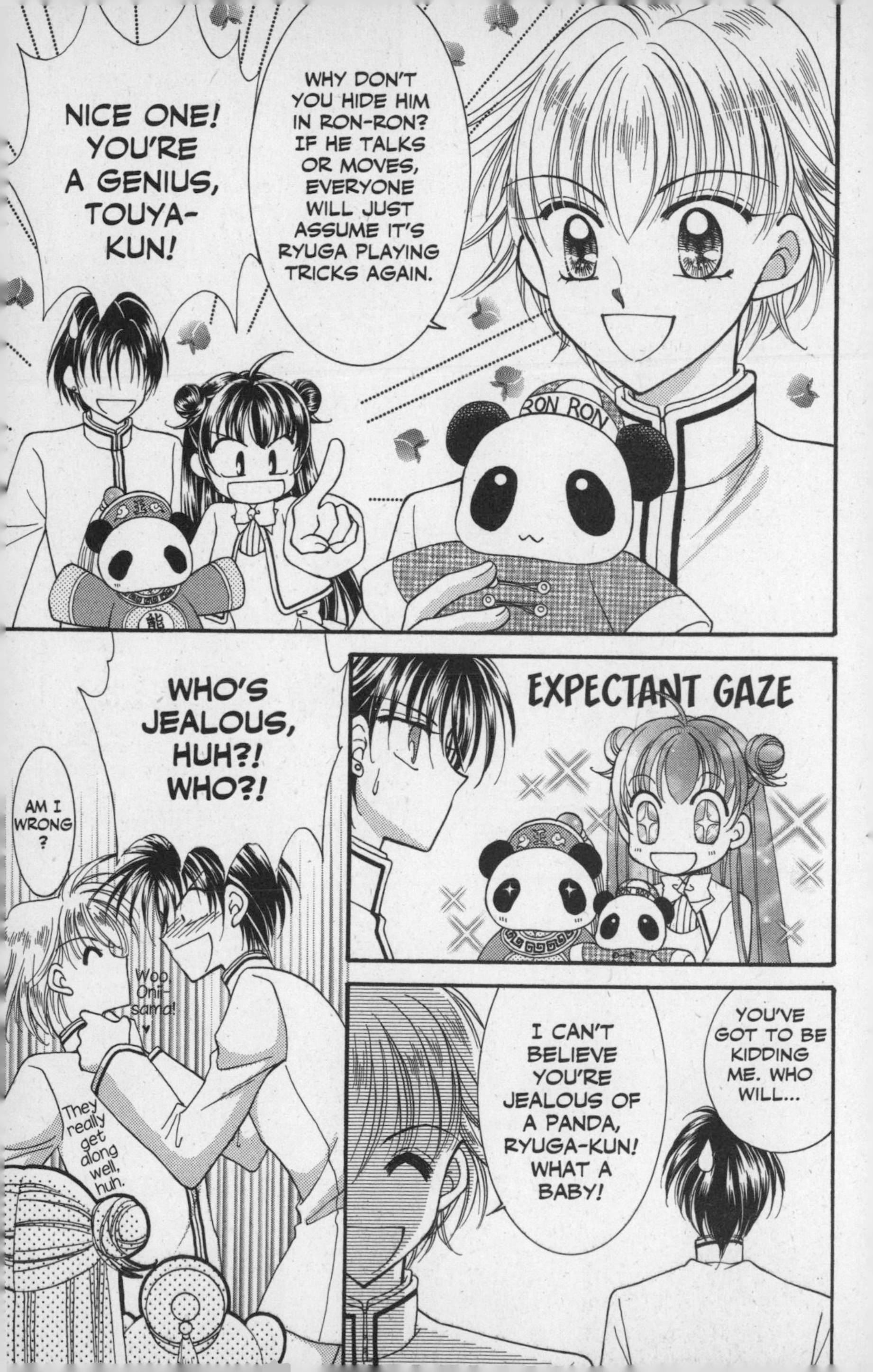
WHY DON'T YOU HIDE HIM IN RON-RON? IF HE TALKS OR MOVES, EVERYONE WILL JUST ASSUME IT'S RYUGA PLAYING TRICKS AGAIN.
NICE ONE! YOU'RE A GENIUS, TOUYA-KUN!
RON RON
EXPECTANT GAZE
YOU'VE GOT TO BE KIDDING ME. WHO WILL...
I CAN'T BELIEVE YOU'RE JEALOUS OF A PANDA, RYUGA-KUN! WHAT A BABY!
WHO'S JEALOUS, HUH?! WHO?!
AM I WRONG?
Woo, Onii-sama! ♥
They really get along well, huh.

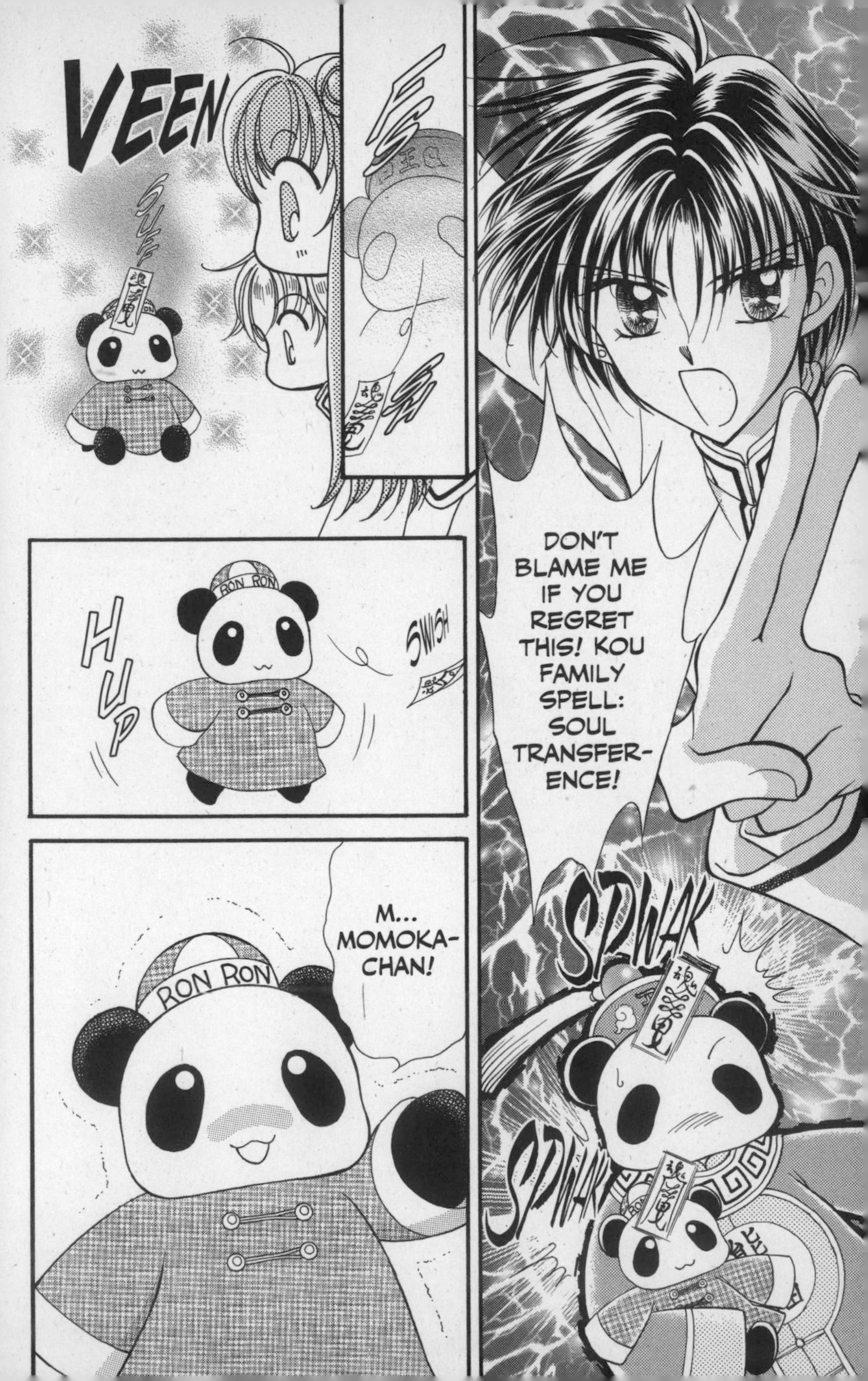
DON'T BLAME ME IF YOU REGRET THIS! KOU FAMILY SPELL: SOUL TRANSFERENCE!
SZWAK
SZWAK
VEEN
RON RON
HUP
SWISH
RON RON
M... MOMOKA-CHAN!

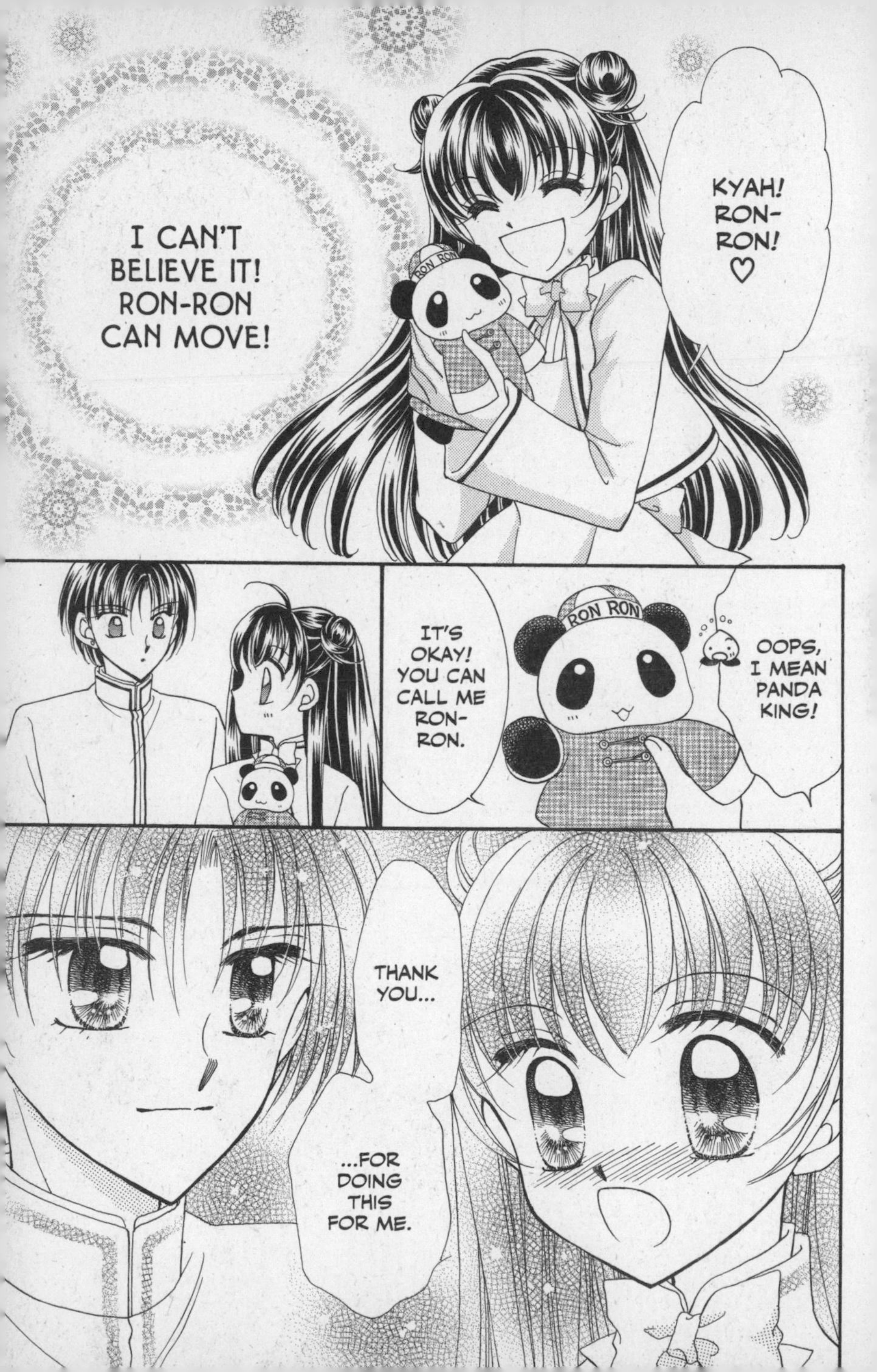
KYAH! RON-RON! ♡
I CAN'T BELIEVE IT! RON-RON CAN MOVE!
OOPS, I MEAN PANDA KING!
IT'S OKAY! YOU CAN CALL ME RON-RON.
RON RON
THANK YOU...
...FOR DOING THIS FOR ME.

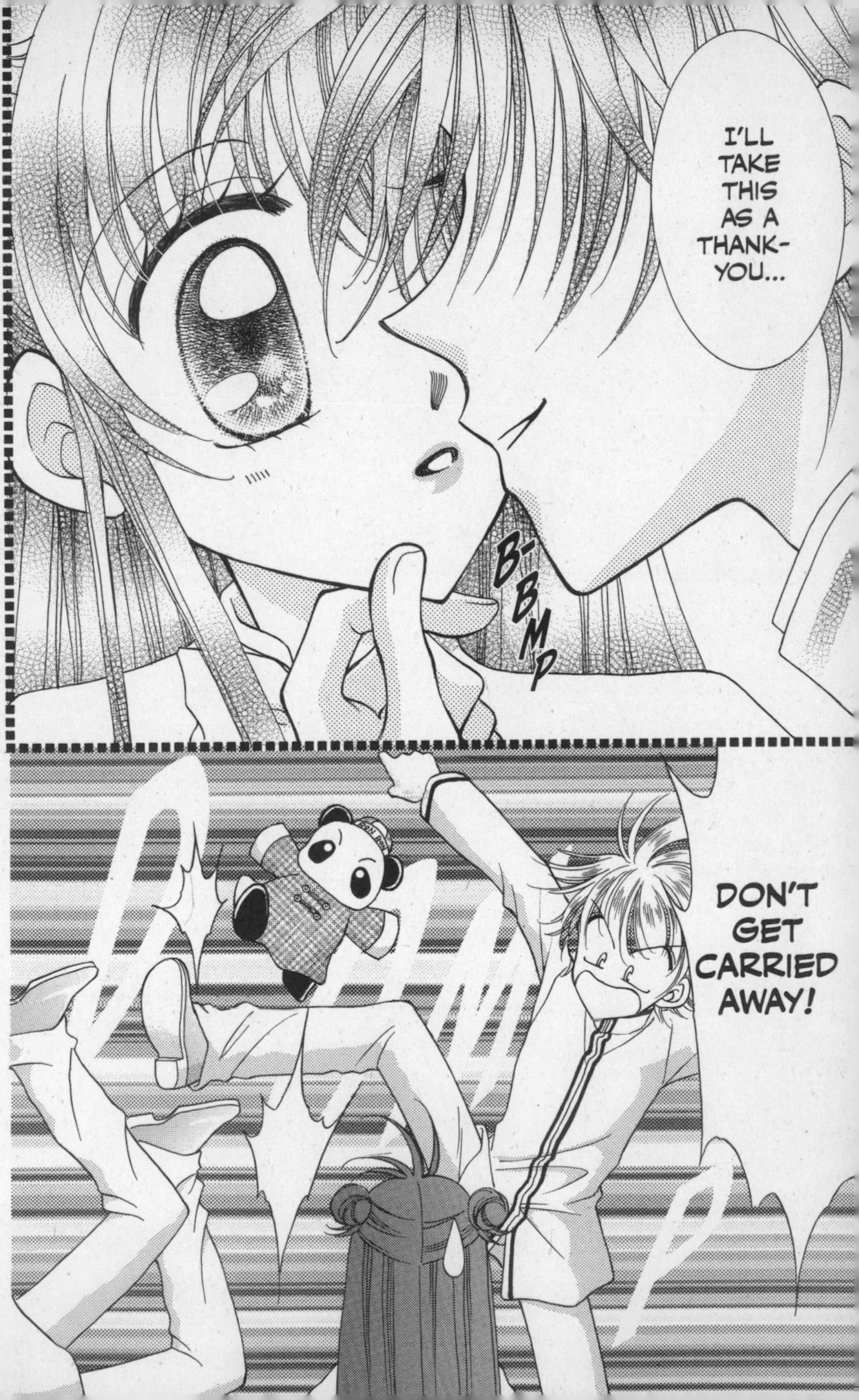
I'LL TAKE THIS AS A THANK-YOU...
B-BMP
DON'T GET CARRIED AWAY!

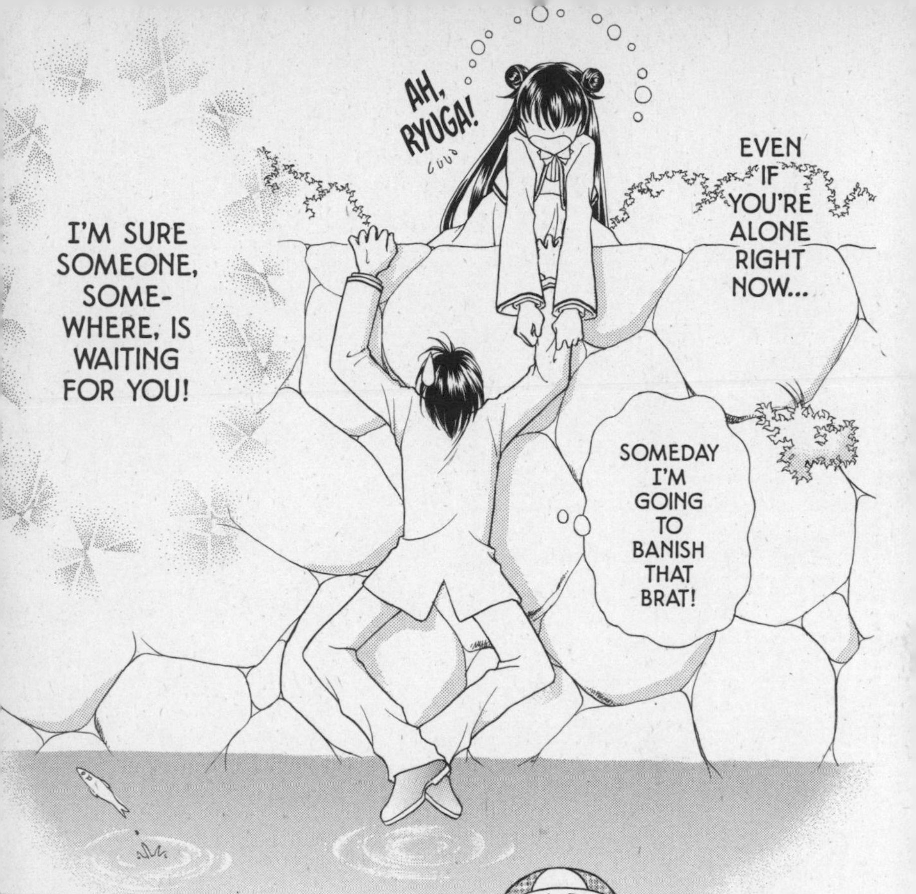
EVEN IF YOU'RE ALONE RIGHT NOW...
AH, RYUGA!
SOMEDAY I'M GOING TO BANISH THAT BRAT!
I'M SURE SOMEONE, SOME-WHERE, IS WAITING FOR YOU!

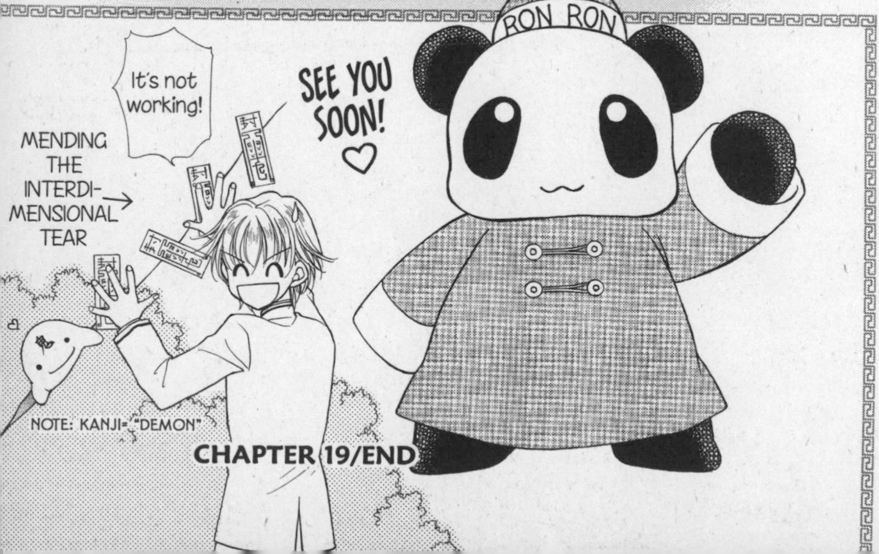
RON RON
SEE YOU SOON!
It's not working!
MENDING THE INTERDI-MENSIONAL TEAR
NOTE: KANJI= "DEMON"
CHAPTER 19/END

KOU FAMILY SECRET, PART 2

BY QUEEN

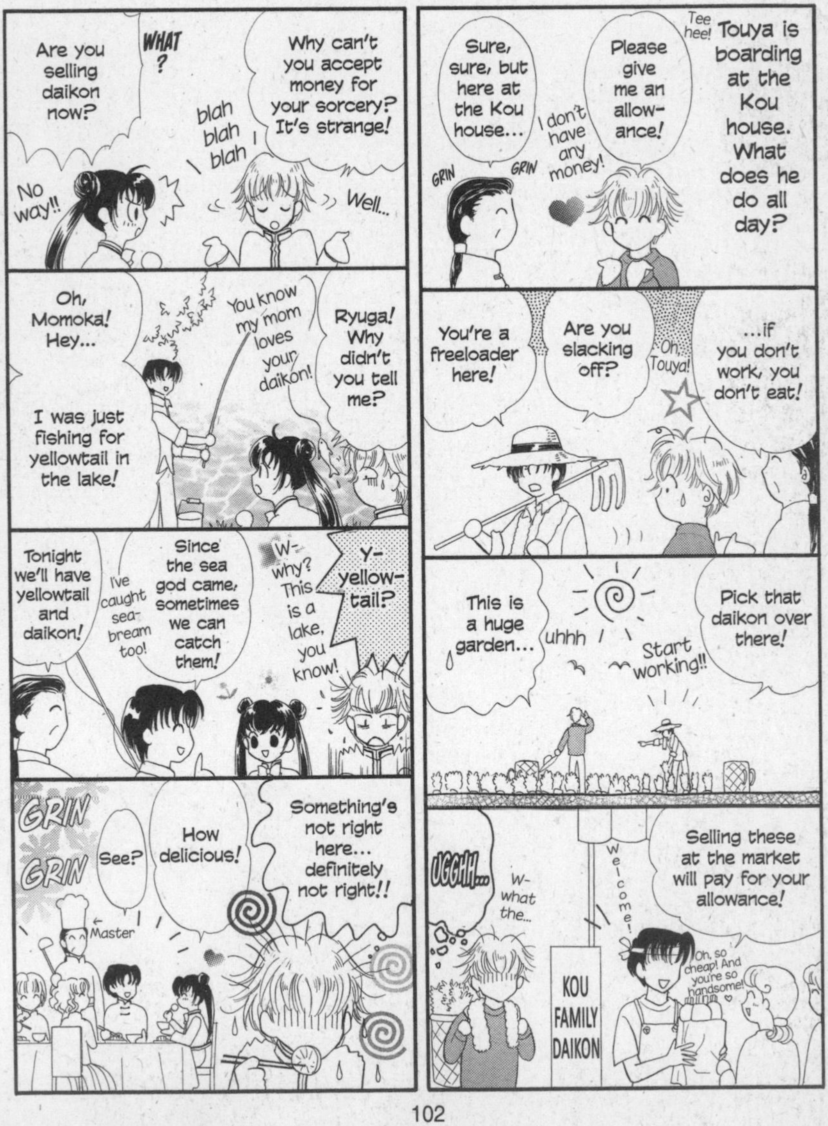
Touya is boarding at the Kou house. What does he do all day?
Tee hee!
Please give me an allowance!
I don't have any money!
Sure, sure, but here at the Kou house...
GRIN
GRIN
...if you don't work, you don't eat!
Oh, Touya!
Are you slacking off?
You're a freeloader here!
Pick that daikon over there!
Start working!!
uhhh
This is a huge garden...
Selling these at the market will pay for your allowance!
Oh, so cheap! And you're so handsome!
Welcome!
KOU FAMILY DAIKON
W-what the...
UGGHH...
Why can't you accept money for your sorcery? It's strange!
Well...
blah blah blah
WHAT?
Are you selling daikon now?
No way!!
Ryuga! Why didn't you tell me?
You know my mom loves your daikon!
Oh, Momoka! Hey...
I was just fishing for yellowtail in the lake!
Y-yellowtail?
W-why? This is a lake, you know!
Since the sea god came, sometimes we can catch them!
I've caught sea-bream too!
Tonight we'll have yellowtail and daikon!
Something's not right here... definitely not right!!
How delicious!
See?
GRIN
GRIN
Master

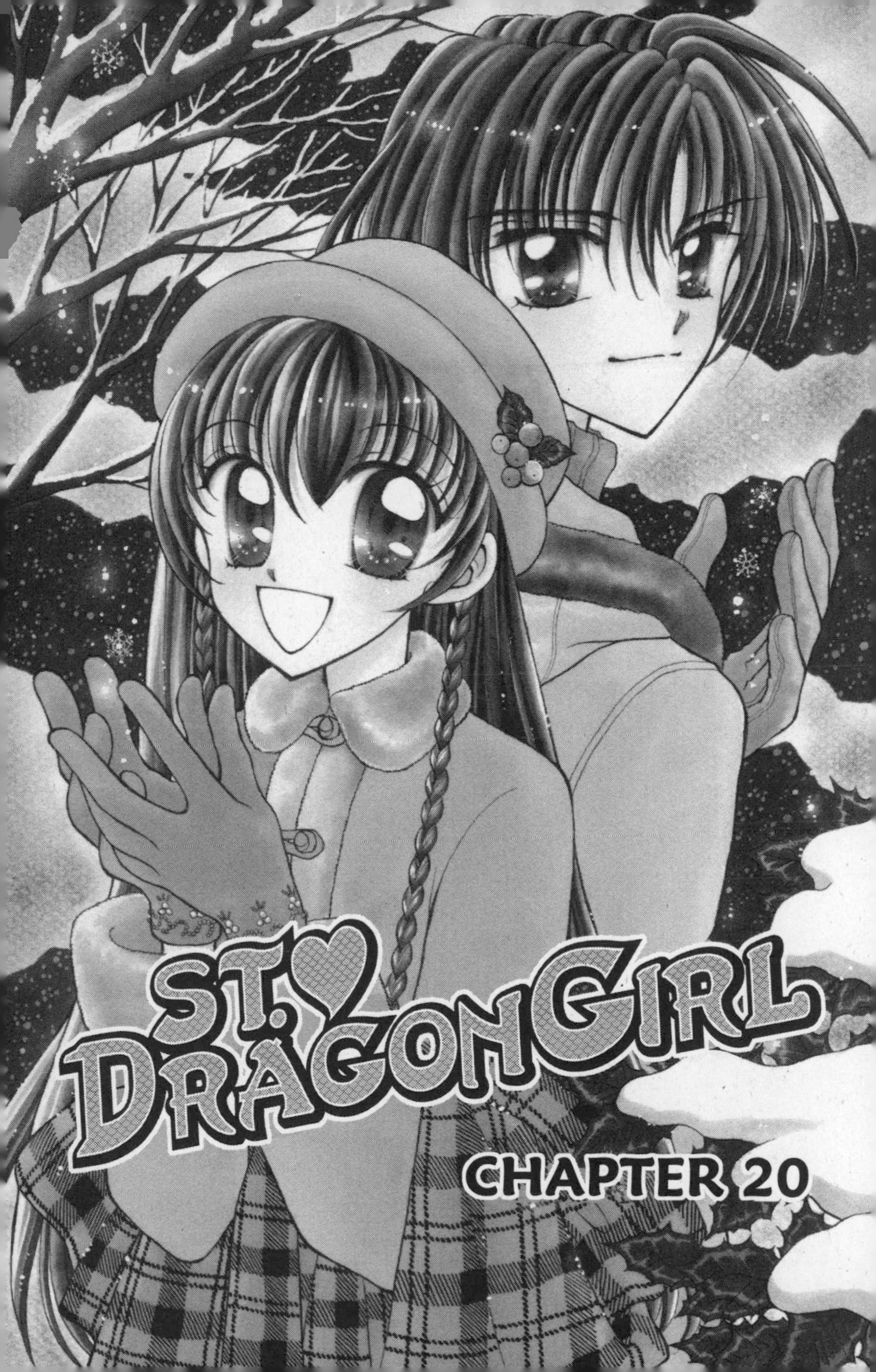
ST.♥ DRAGON GIRL
CHAPTER 20

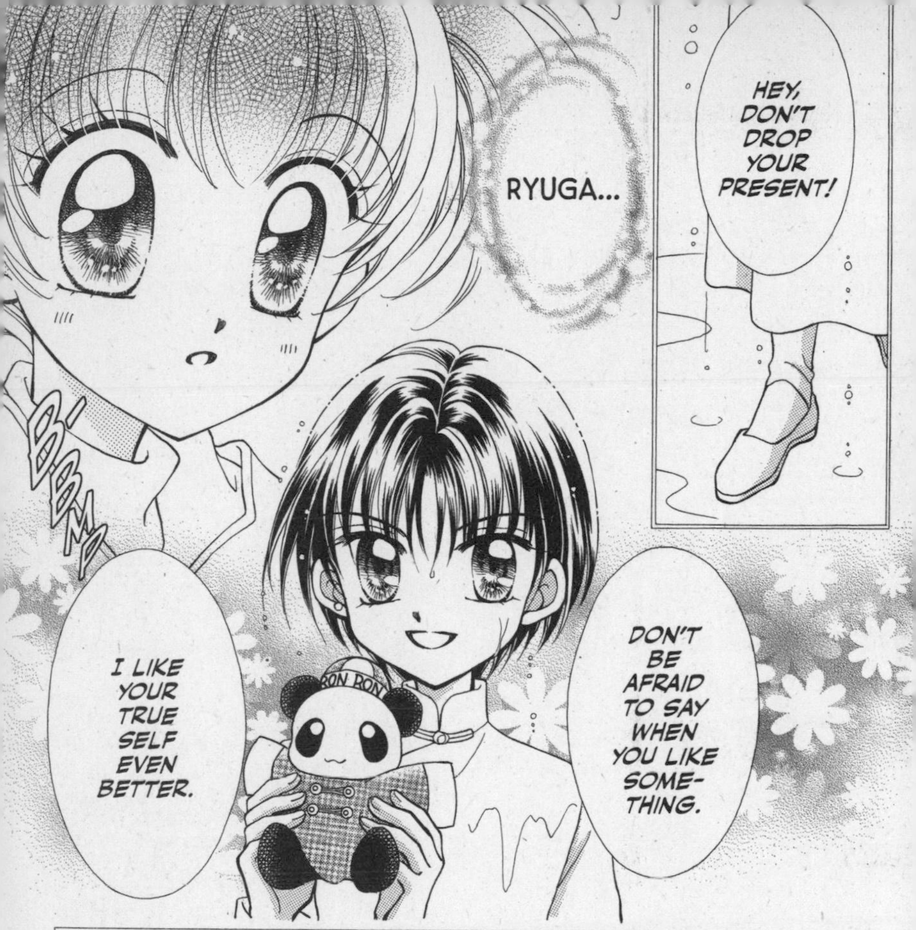
HEY, DON'T DROP YOUR PRESENT!
RYUGA...
B-BMP
DON'T BE AFRAID TO SAY WHEN YOU LIKE SOME-THING.
I LIKE YOUR TRUE SELF EVEN BETTER.
RON RON

- **I want to be a manga artist. Do I need to go to school for it?**

Hmm, I don't think it has anything to do with going to art school. I went to a junior college for art, but what I found most useful were the regular classes. Manga artists need to have a lot of knowledge about many things. It doesn't have to do with just art skill. You need to be curious and experience various things. At art school, I learned the importance of finishing something you start.

- **I can't think of a story. How do you come up with one?**

This is a difficult question. I'm the kind of person who sits at my desk and ponders it. Sometimes the idea will just come to me. The Christmas story in this volume and "Telepathic ☆ Earring" both came to me like that. However, it was hard to transfer them to paper.

For people who don't know what to write, why don't you try making a manga diary? I use the manga format to draw interesting things that happen around me. Then I show my friends. It's also a good way to convey an idea to someone easily. Also, when I think of a good character, I begin by trying to base a story around that character.

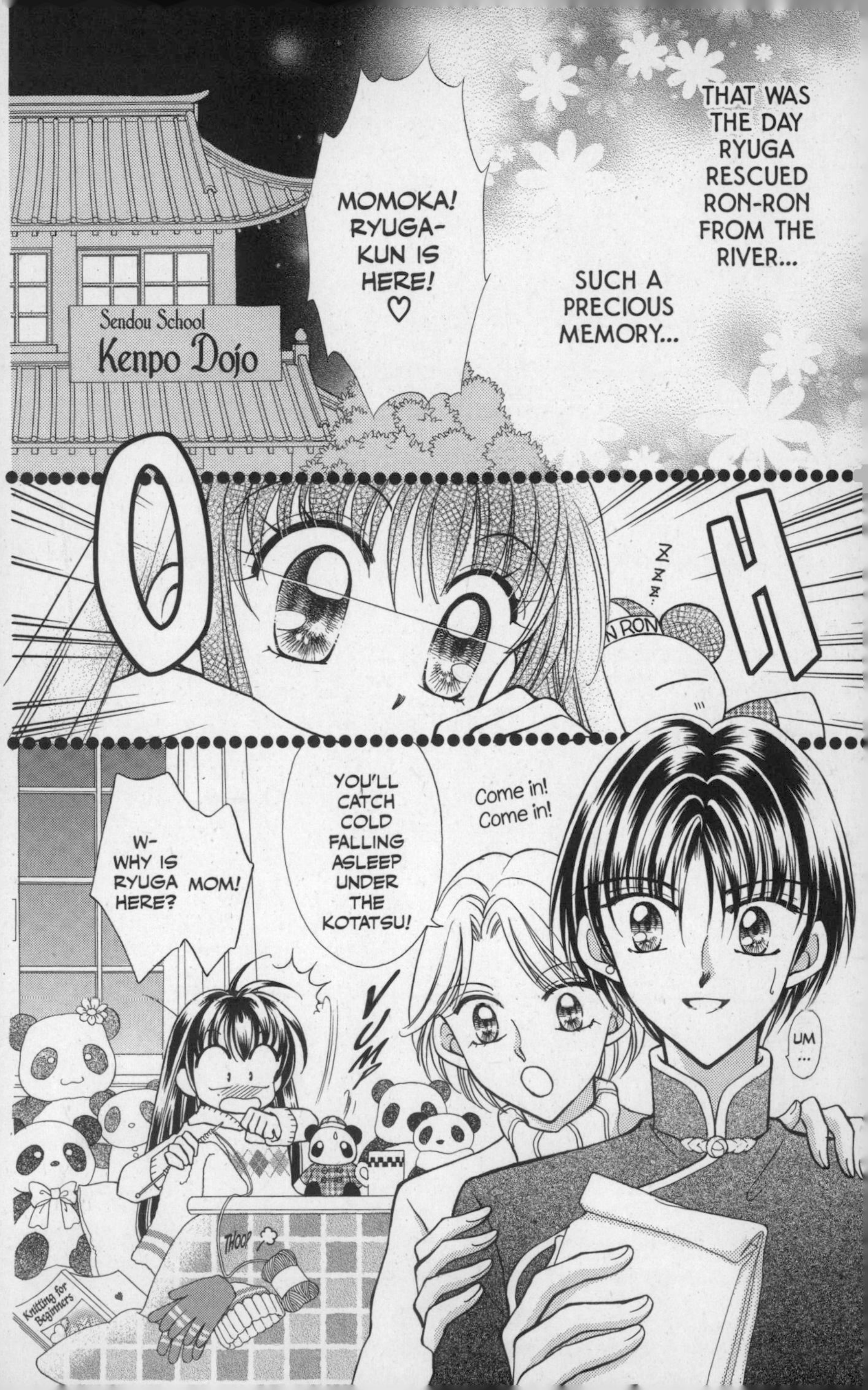

THAT WAS THE DAY RYUGA RESCUED RON-RON FROM THE RIVER...
SUCH A PRECIOUS MEMORY...
MOMOKA! RYUGA-KUN IS HERE! ♡
Sendou School
Kenpo Dojo
OH
ZZZ...
RON RON
UM...
Come in! Come in!
YOU'LL CATCH COLD FALLING ASLEEP UNDER THE KOTATSU!
MOM!
W- WHY IS RYUGA HERE?
VUM
THOOP
Knitting for Beginners

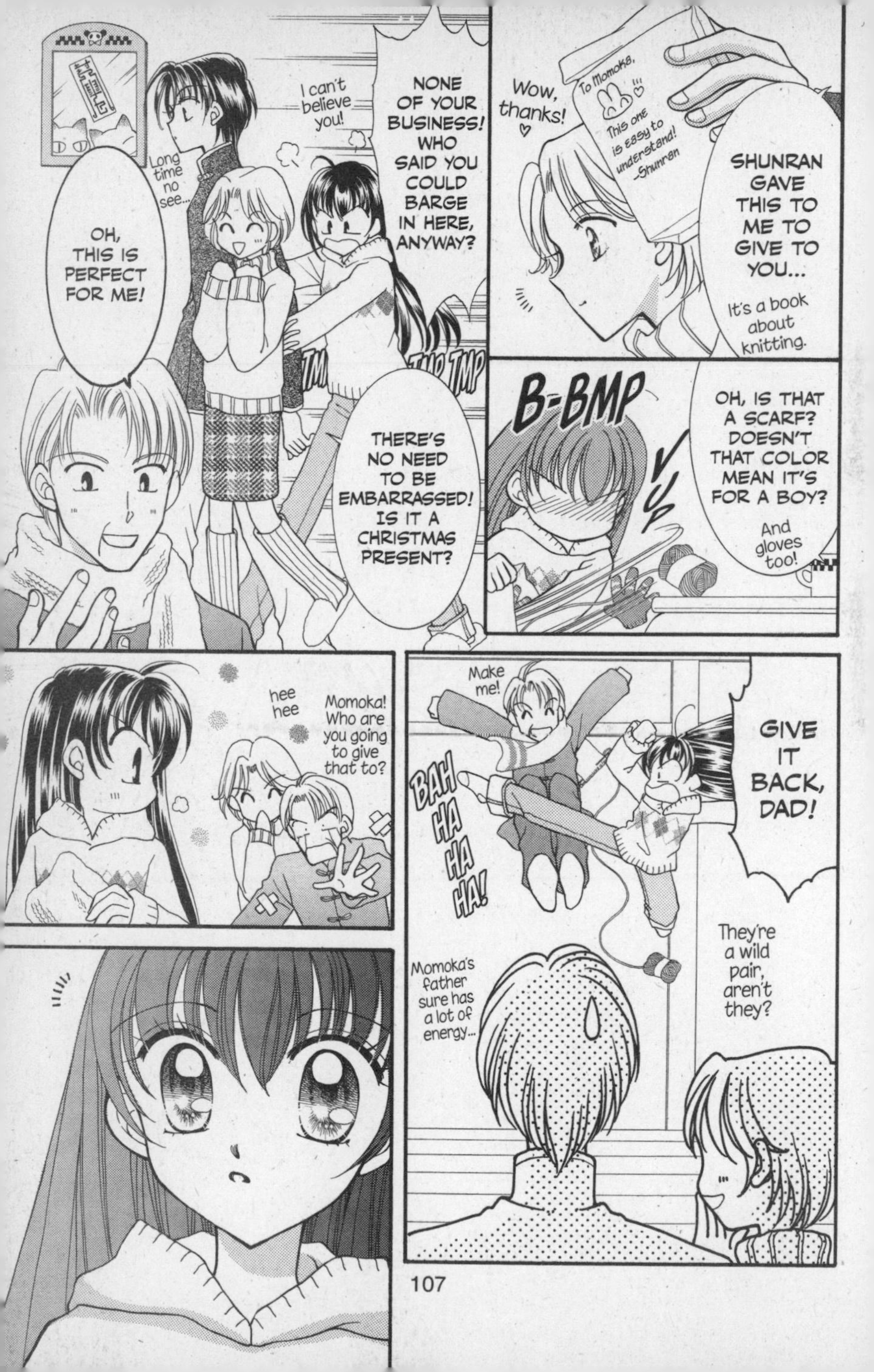
SHUNRAN GAVE THIS TO ME TO GIVE TO YOU...
It's a book about knitting.
To Momoka, This one is easy to understand! -Shunran
Wow, thanks!
OH, IS THAT A SCARF? DOESN'T THAT COLOR MEAN IT'S FOR A BOY?
And gloves too!
B-BMP
VUP
NONE OF YOUR BUSINESS! WHO SAID YOU COULD BARGE IN HERE, ANYWAY?
I can't believe you!
Long time no see...
OH, THIS IS PERFECT FOR ME!
TMP TMP
TMP
THERE'S NO NEED TO BE EMBARRASSED! IS IT A CHRISTMAS PRESENT?
GIVE IT BACK, DAD!
Make me!
BAH HA HA HA HA!
They're a wild pair, aren't they?
Momoka's father sure has a lot of energy...
Momoka! Who are you going to give that to?
hee hee

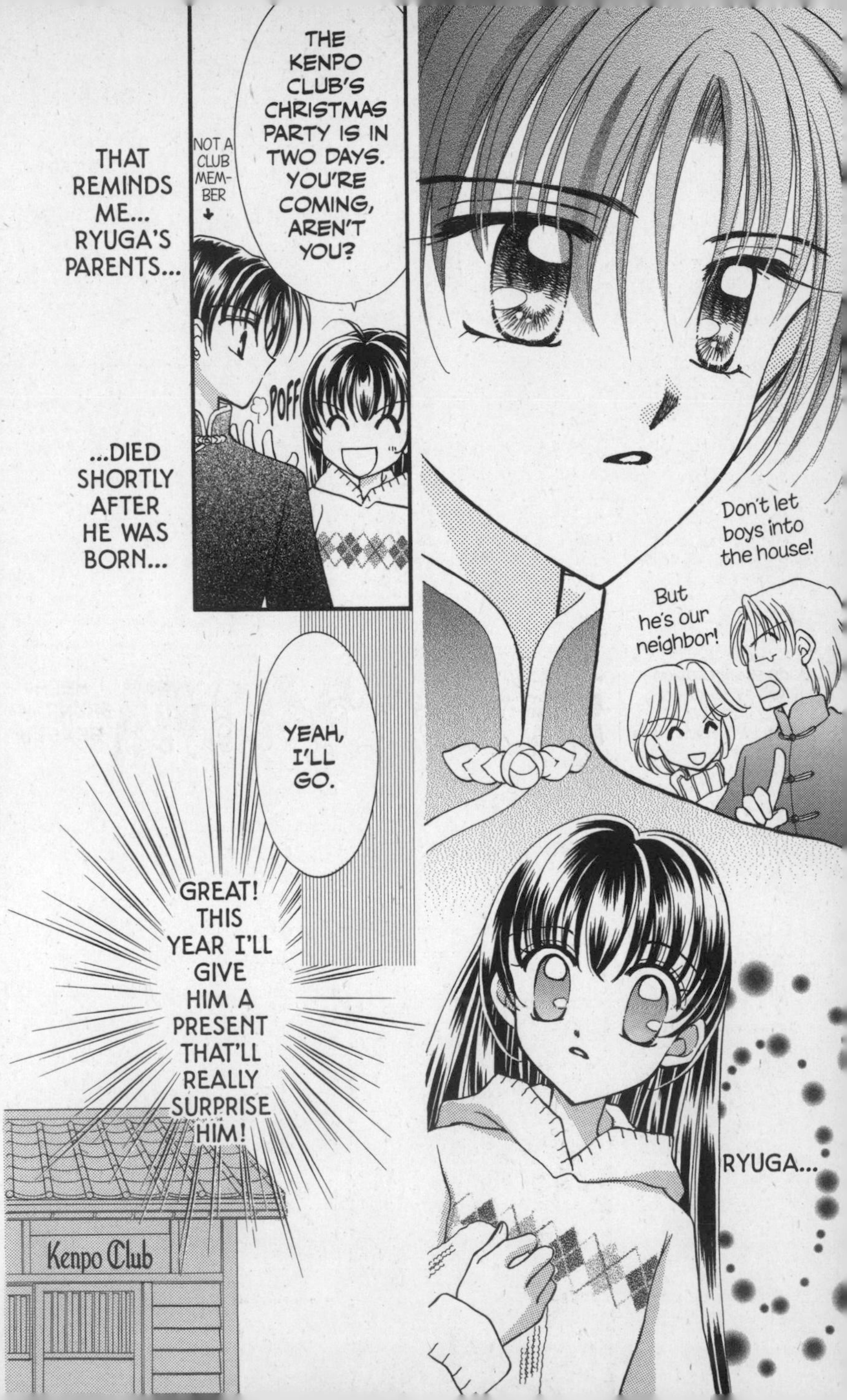
Don't let boys into the house!
But he's our neighbor!
RYUGA...
THE KENPO CLUB'S CHRISTMAS PARTY IS IN TWO DAYS. YOU'RE COMING, AREN'T YOU?
NOT A CLUB MEMBER
POFF
THAT REMINDS ME... RYUGA'S PARENTS...
...DIED SHORTLY AFTER HE WAS BORN...
YEAH, I'LL GO.
GREAT! THIS YEAR I'LL GIVE HIM A PRESENT THAT'LL REALLY SURPRISE HIM!
Kenpo Club

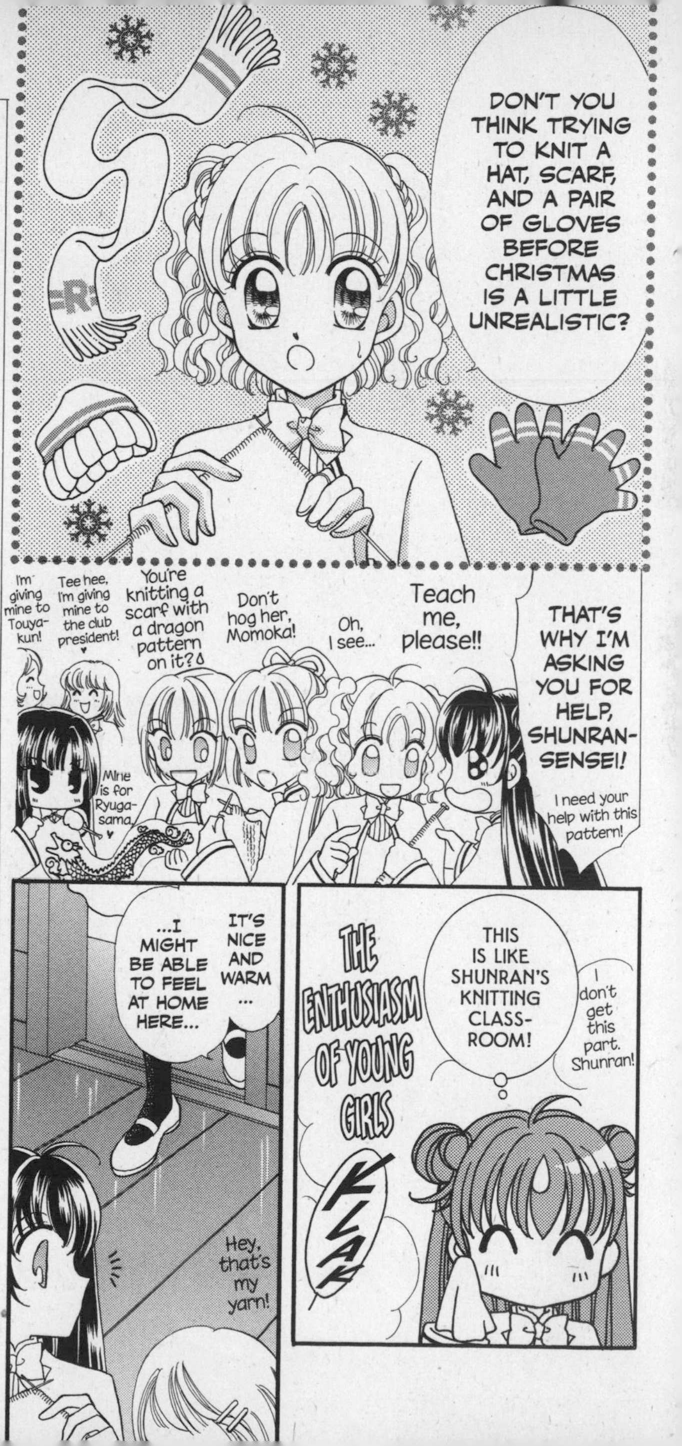
DON'T YOU THINK TRYING TO KNIT A HAT, SCARF, AND A PAIR OF GLOVES BEFORE CHRISTMAS IS A LITTLE UNREALISTIC?
THAT'S WHY I'M ASKING YOU FOR HELP, SHUNRAN-SENSEI!
I need your help with this pattern!
Teach me, please!!
Oh, I see...
Don't hog her, Momoka!
You're knitting a scarf with a dragon pattern on it?
Tee hee, I'm giving mine to the club president!
I'm giving mine to Touya-kun!
Mine is for Ryuga-sama.
THE ENTHUSIASM OF YOUNG GIRLS
THIS IS LIKE SHUNRAN'S KNITTING CLASSROOM!
I don't get this part. Shunran!
KLAK
IT'S NICE AND WARM...
...I MIGHT BE ABLE TO FEEL AT HOME HERE...
Hey, that's my yarn!

7

I'm sure Ryuga made the pockets in that story too!

The assistants' corners received a lot of great fan letters, and now the assistants have their own fans!

I'm sorry I had my assistants draw these when they were tired from deadlines. I'm really thankful.

They can draw anything! It wouldn't be an exaggeration to say that *St.♥Dragon Girl* wouldn't have been completed without them.

Not only that, but Kodaka-san is really great at drawing explosions and action scenes!

Queen is great at turning my simple clothing designs into gorgeous pieces! Sasaki-san is great at drawing buildings, and he's really fast too! He'll draw any building, no matter how high it is! (laugh)

I know we've been busy lately, but let's go do karaoke sometime soon!

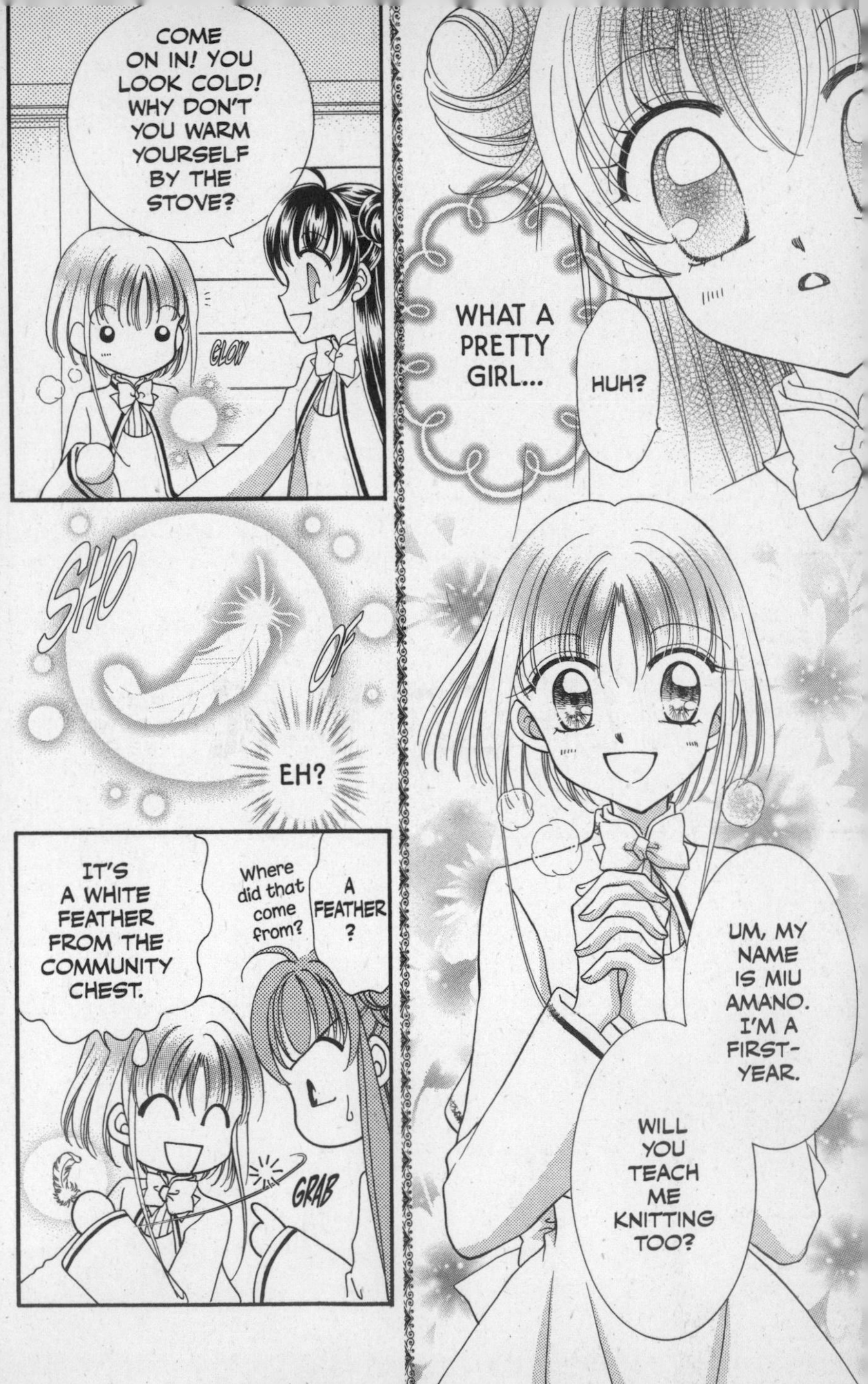
HUH?
WHAT A PRETTY GIRL...
UM, MY NAME IS MIU AMANO. I'M A FIRST-YEAR.
WILL YOU TEACH ME KNITTING TOO?
COME ON IN! YOU LOOK COLD! WHY DON'T YOU WARM YOURSELF BY THE STOVE?
GLOW
SHO
OF
EH?
A FEATHER?
Where did that come from?
IT'S A WHITE FEATHER FROM THE COMMUNITY CHEST.
GRAB

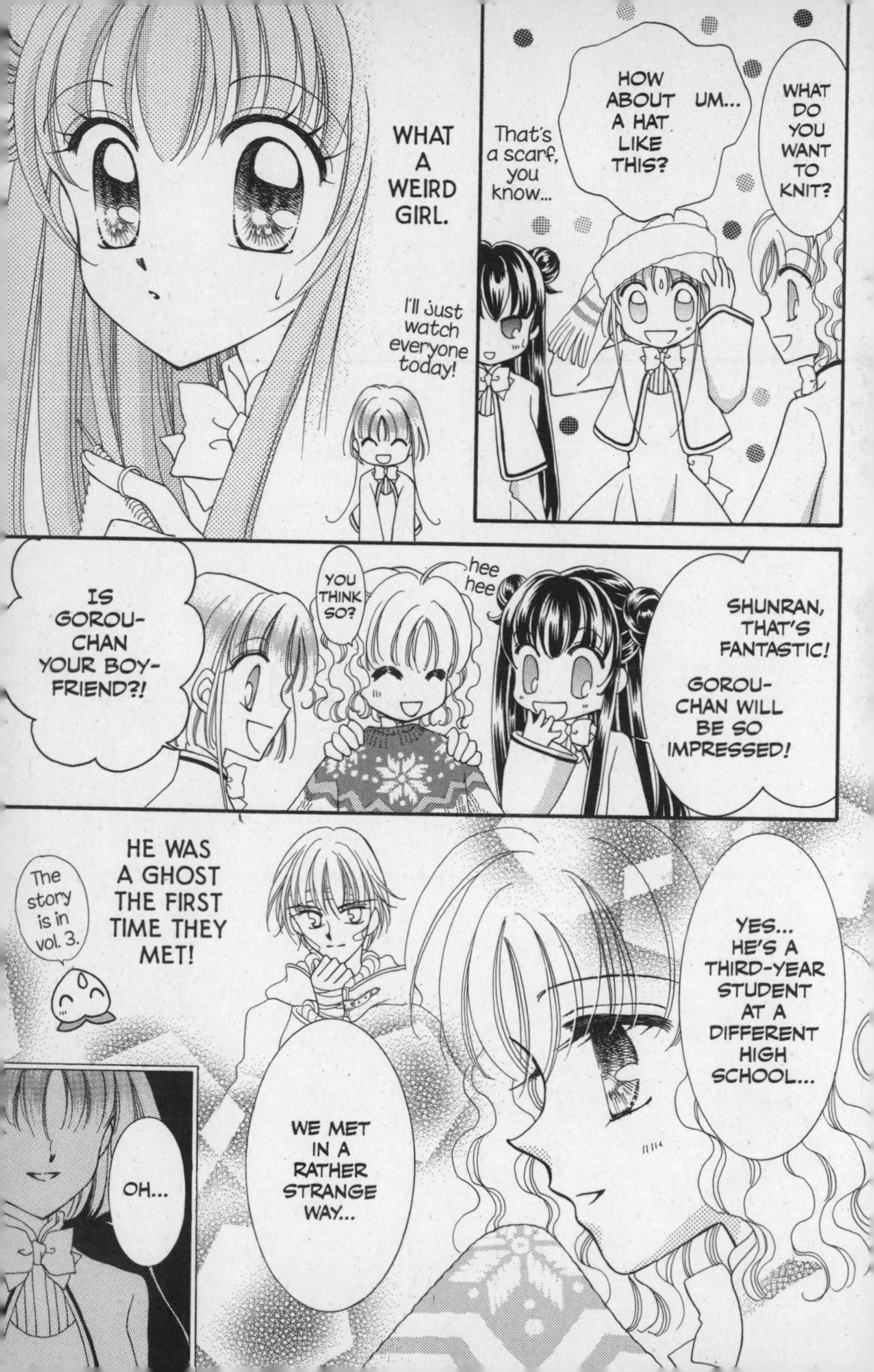
WHAT DO YOU WANT TO KNIT?
UM...
HOW ABOUT A HAT LIKE THIS?
That's a scarf, you know...
WHAT A WEIRD GIRL.
I'll just watch everyone today!
SHUNRAN, THAT'S FANTASTIC!
GOROU-CHAN WILL BE SO IMPRESSED!
hee hee
YOU THINK SO?
IS GOROU-CHAN YOUR BOY-FRIEND?!
YES... HE'S A THIRD-YEAR STUDENT AT A DIFFERENT HIGH SCHOOL...
WE MET IN A RATHER STRANGE WAY...
HE WAS A GHOST THE FIRST TIME THEY MET!
The story is in vol. 3.
OH...

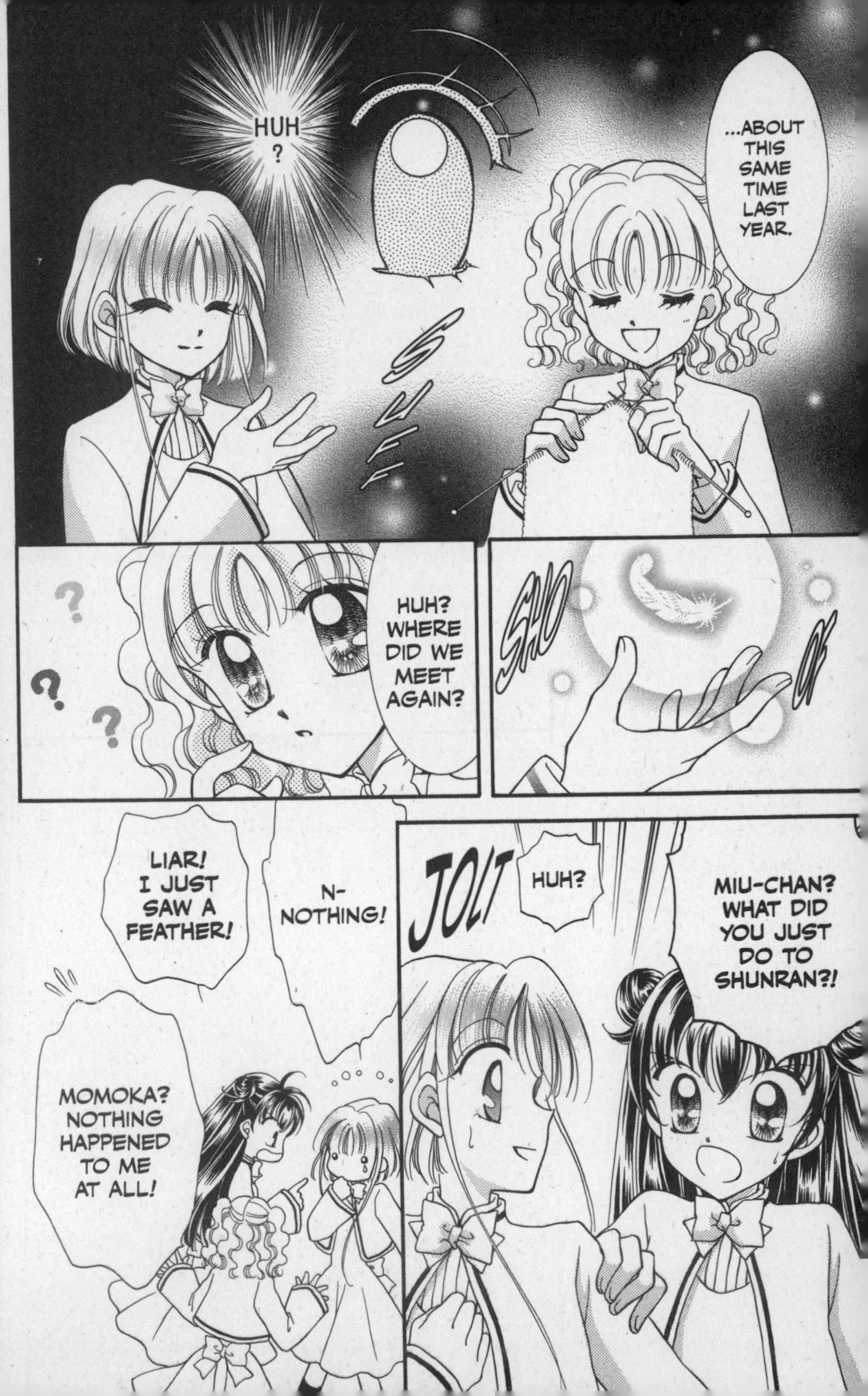
...ABOUT THIS SAME TIME LAST YEAR.
HUH ?
HUH? WHERE DID WE MEET AGAIN?
MIU-CHAN? WHAT DID YOU JUST DO TO SHUNRAN?!
HUH?
JOLT
N- NOTHING!
LIAR! I JUST SAW A FEATHER!
MOMOKA? NOTHING HAPPENED TO ME AT ALL!

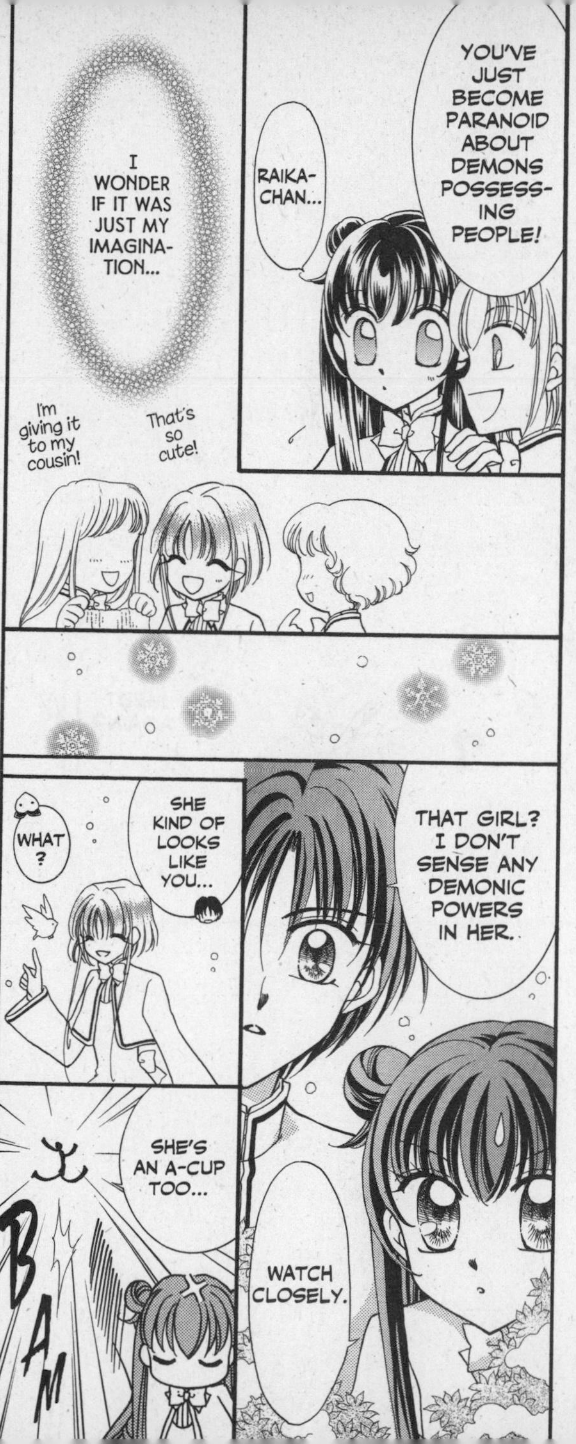
YOU'VE JUST BECOME PARANOID ABOUT DEMONS POSSESSING PEOPLE!
RAIKA-CHAN...
I WONDER IF IT WAS JUST MY IMAGINATION...
That's so cute!
I'm giving it to my cousin!
THAT GIRL? I DON'T SENSE ANY DEMONIC POWERS IN HER.
WATCH CLOSELY.
SHE KIND OF LOOKS LIKE YOU...
WHAT?
SHE'S AN A-CUP TOO...
BAM

8

A lot of people said they really loved the Christmas story in this volume.

Actually, it's my favorite story in volume 5. I love how Miu-chan is such an airhead!

A lot of people want her to appear again. But she's really a... (for those who haven't read on, I won't spoil it). If she plays too big of a role in the story, *St.♥Dragon Girl* will go in a different direction.

But I'm happy the readers liked her so much! ♡

Momoka's mom made her first appearance in this story! (Her dad has appeared a few times before.) She turned out to be more ordinary than expected. Everyone thought she was going to be stronger or something (perhaps because she's Momoka's mom).

She might look like a gentle mother at home, but away she's a strong, beautiful aesthetician! (laugh) I just didn't have enough space to write more about Mom.

However, in my mind, she does Chinese acupuncture!

I hope I get to draw her again.

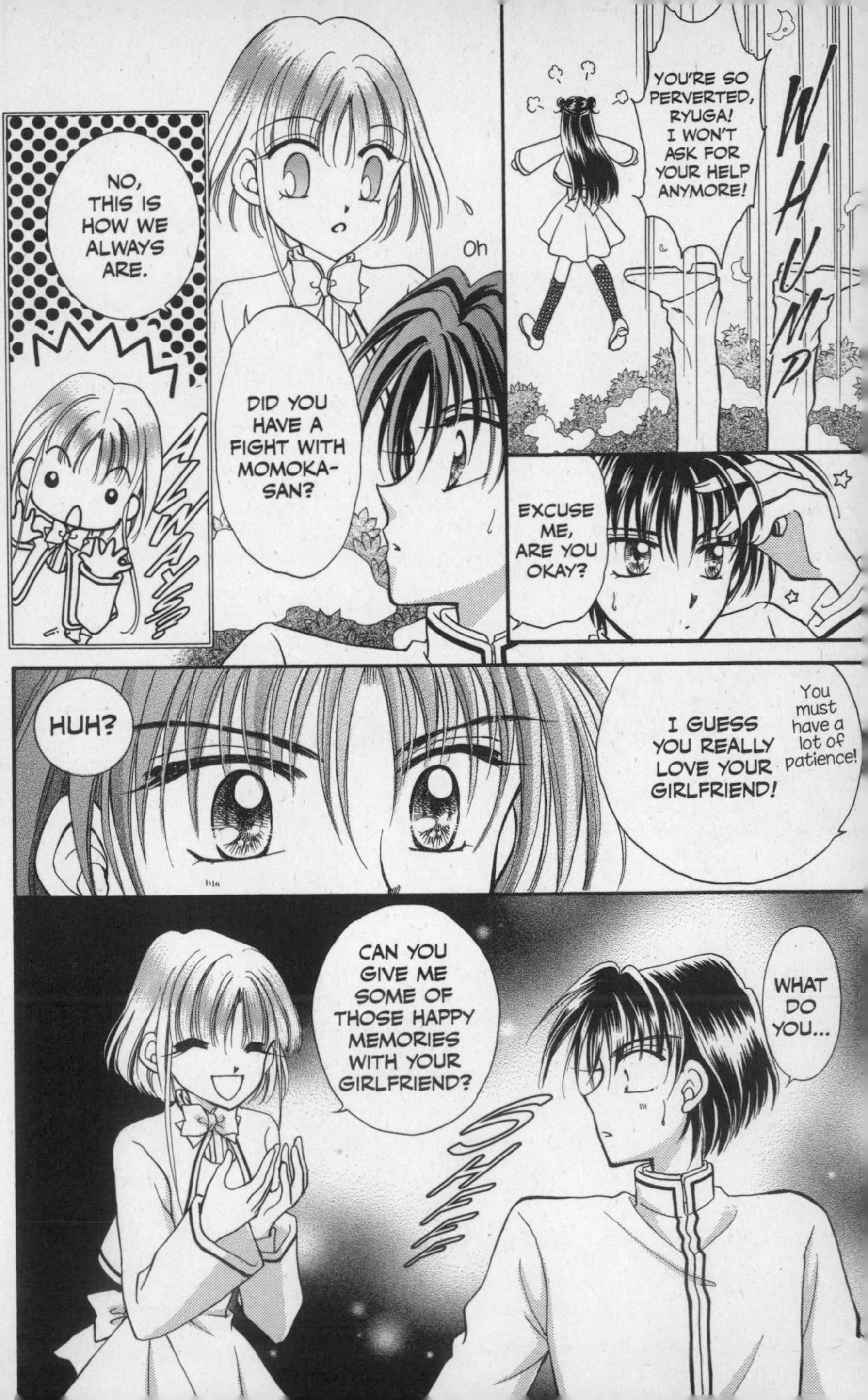
YOU'RE SO PERVERTED, RYUGA! I WON'T ASK FOR YOUR HELP ANYMORE!
WHUMD
EXCUSE ME, ARE YOU OKAY?
Oh
DID YOU HAVE A FIGHT WITH MOMOKA-SAN?
NO, THIS IS HOW WE ALWAYS ARE.
I GUESS YOU REALLY LOVE YOUR GIRLFRIEND!
You must have a lot of patience!
HUH?
WHAT DO YOU...
CAN YOU GIVE ME SOME OF THOSE HAPPY MEMORIES WITH YOUR GIRLFRIEND?

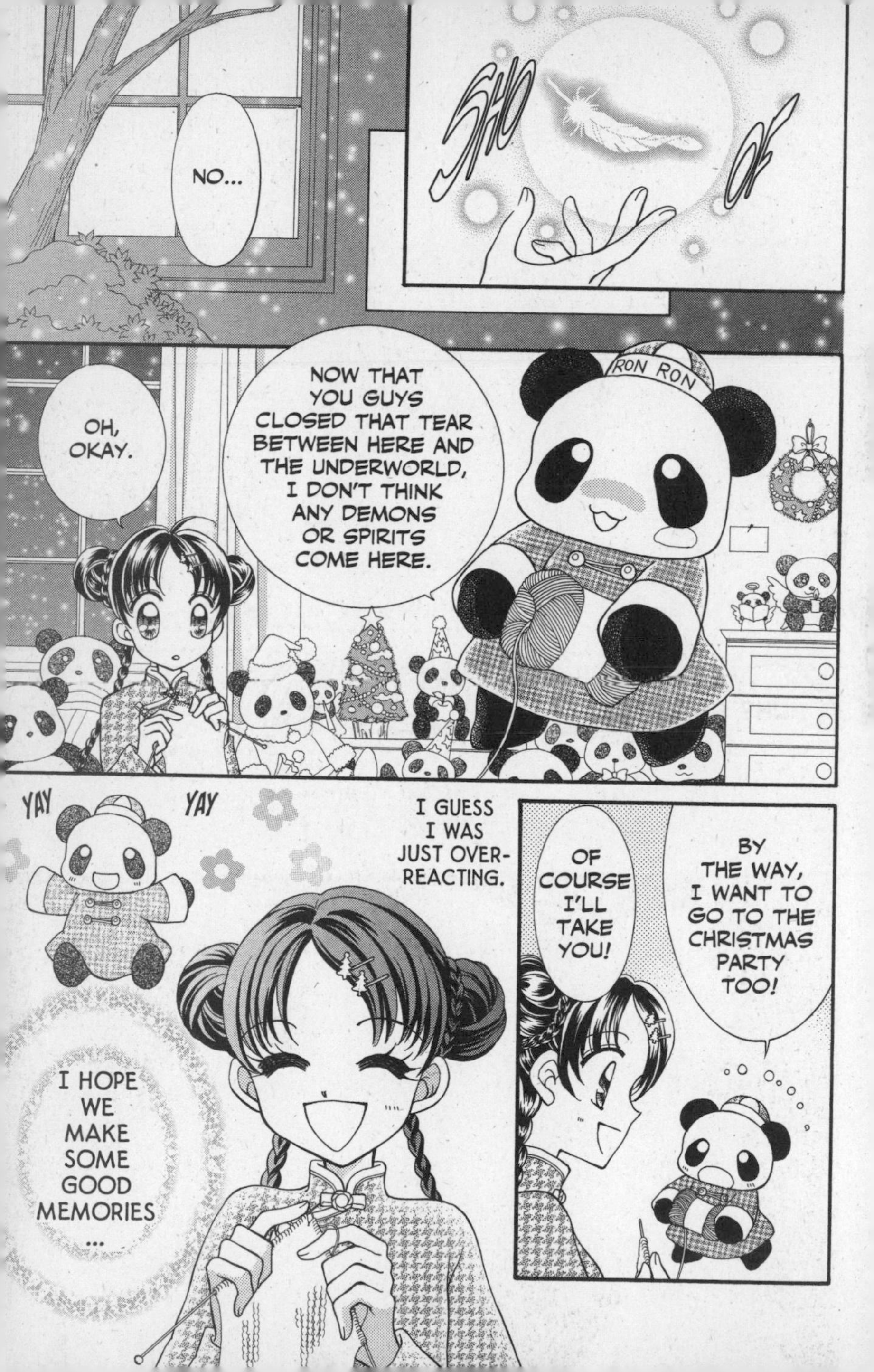

SHO
OF
NO...
RON RON
NOW THAT YOU GUYS CLOSED THAT TEAR BETWEEN HERE AND THE UNDERWORLD, I DON'T THINK ANY DEMONS OR SPIRITS COME HERE.
OH, OKAY.
BY THE WAY, I WANT TO GO TO THE CHRISTMAS PARTY TOO!
OF COURSE I'LL TAKE YOU!
I GUESS I WAS JUST OVER-REACTING.
YAY
YAY
I HOPE WE MAKE SOME GOOD MEMORIES ...

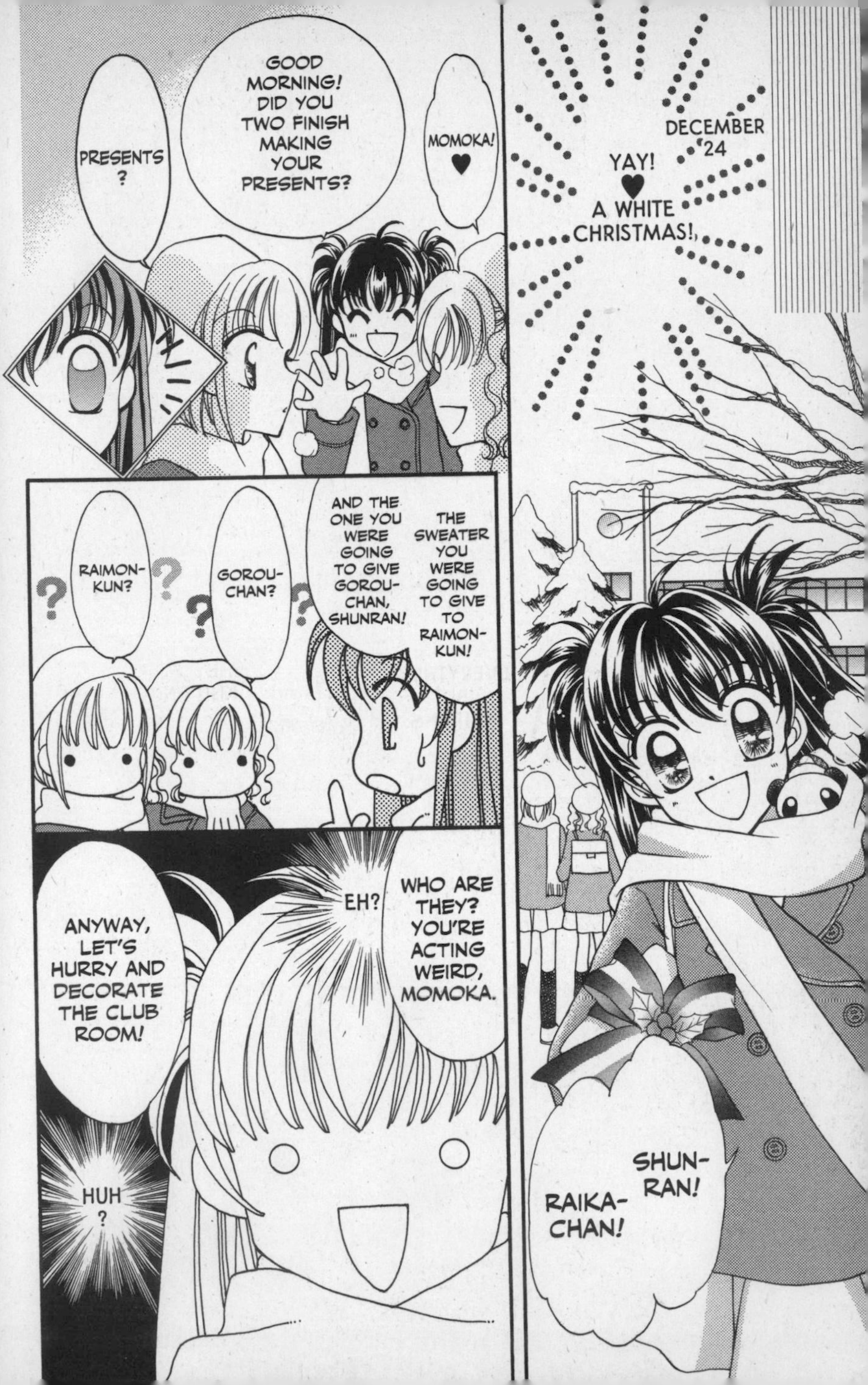
DECEMBER 24
YAY! ♥ A WHITE CHRISTMAS!
SHUN-RAN!
RAIKA-CHAN!
MOMOKA! ♥
GOOD MORNING! DID YOU TWO FINISH MAKING YOUR PRESENTS?
PRESENTS?
THE SWEATER YOU WERE GOING TO GIVE TO RAIMON-KUN!
AND THE ONE YOU WERE GOING TO GIVE GOROU-CHAN, SHUNRAN!
GOROU-CHAN?
RAIMON-KUN?
WHO ARE THEY? YOU'RE ACTING WEIRD, MOMOKA.
EH?
ANYWAY, LET'S HURRY AND DECORATE THE CLUB ROOM!
HUH?

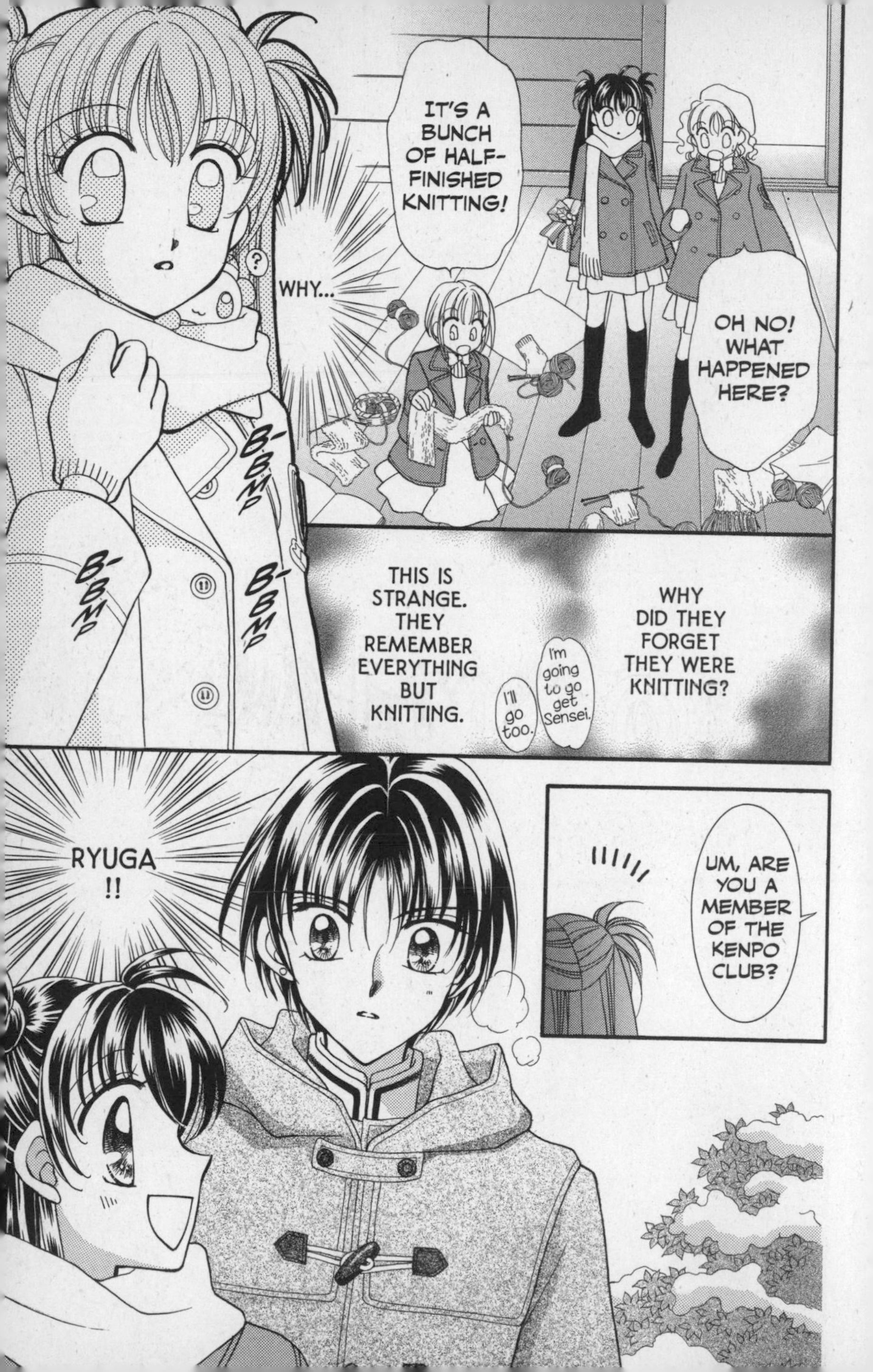
OH NO! WHAT HAPPENED HERE?
IT'S A BUNCH OF HALF-FINISHED KNITTING!
WHY DID THEY FORGET THEY WERE KNITTING?
I'm going to go get Sensei.
I'll go too.
THIS IS STRANGE. THEY REMEMBER EVERYTHING BUT KNITTING.
WHY...
?
B-BMP
B-BMP
B-BMP
UM, ARE YOU A MEMBER OF THE KENPO CLUB?
RYUGA !!

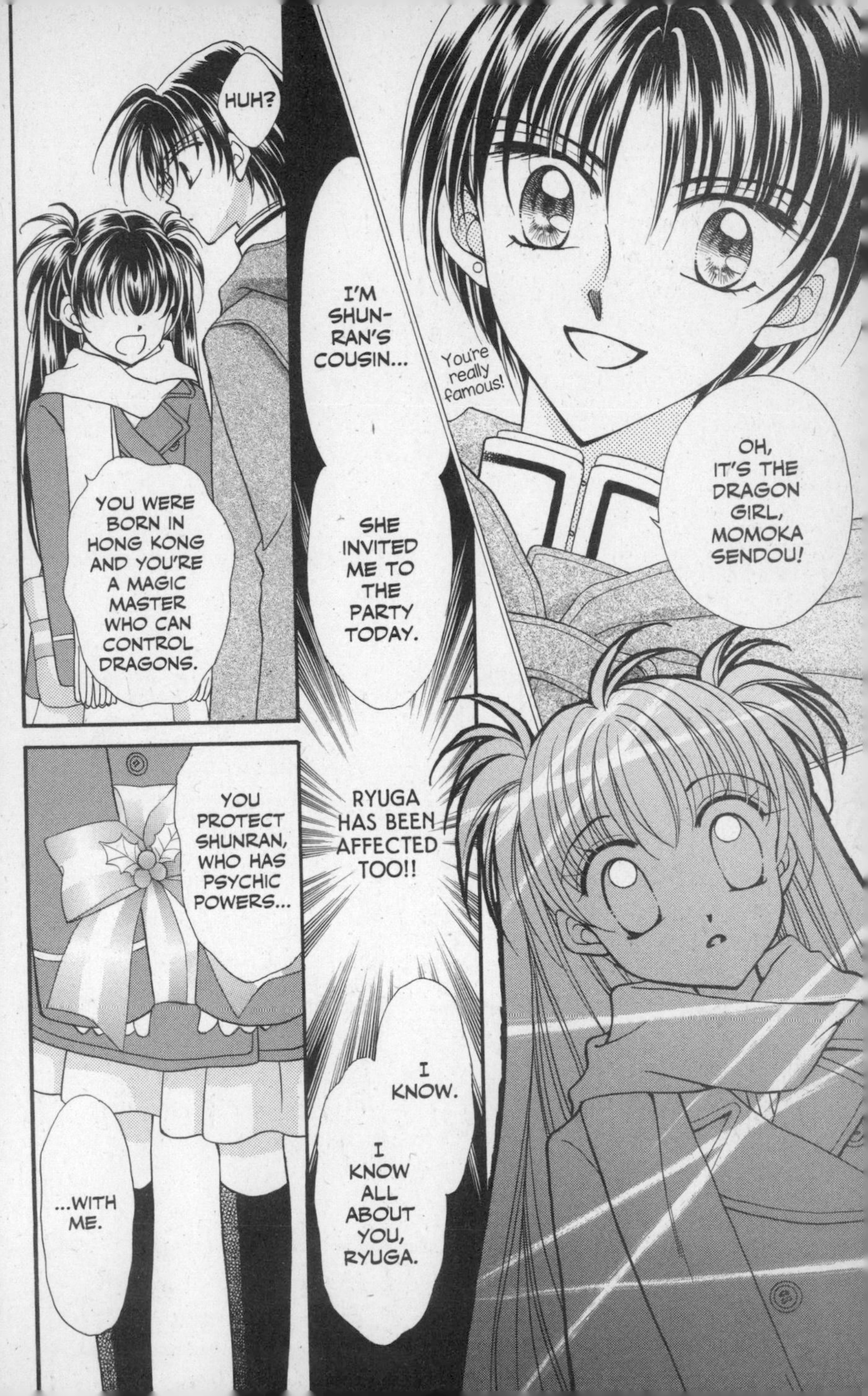
OH, IT'S THE DRAGON GIRL, MOMOKA SENDOU!
You're really famous!
I'M SHUN-RAN'S COUSIN...
SHE INVITED ME TO THE PARTY TODAY.
HUH?
YOU WERE BORN IN HONG KONG AND YOU'RE A MAGIC MASTER WHO CAN CONTROL DRAGONS.
RYUGA HAS BEEN AFFECTED TOO!!
I KNOW.
I KNOW ALL ABOUT YOU, RYUGA.
YOU PROTECT SHUNRAN, WHO HAS PSYCHIC POWERS...
...WITH ME.

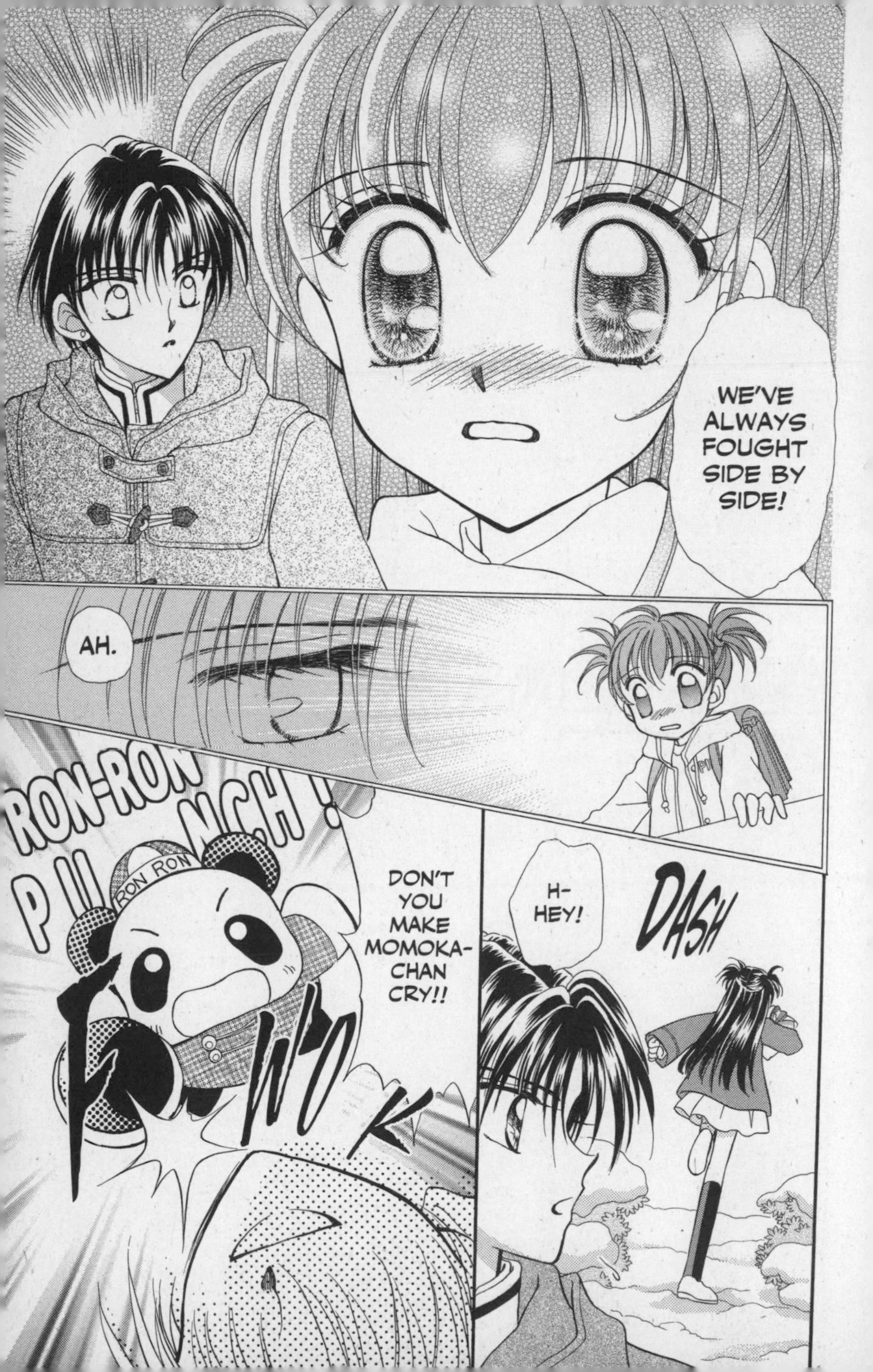
WE'VE ALWAYS FOUGHT SIDE BY SIDE!
AH.
H-HEY!
DASH
RON-RON PUNCH!
RON RON
DON'T YOU MAKE MOMOKA-CHAN CRY!!
FWOK

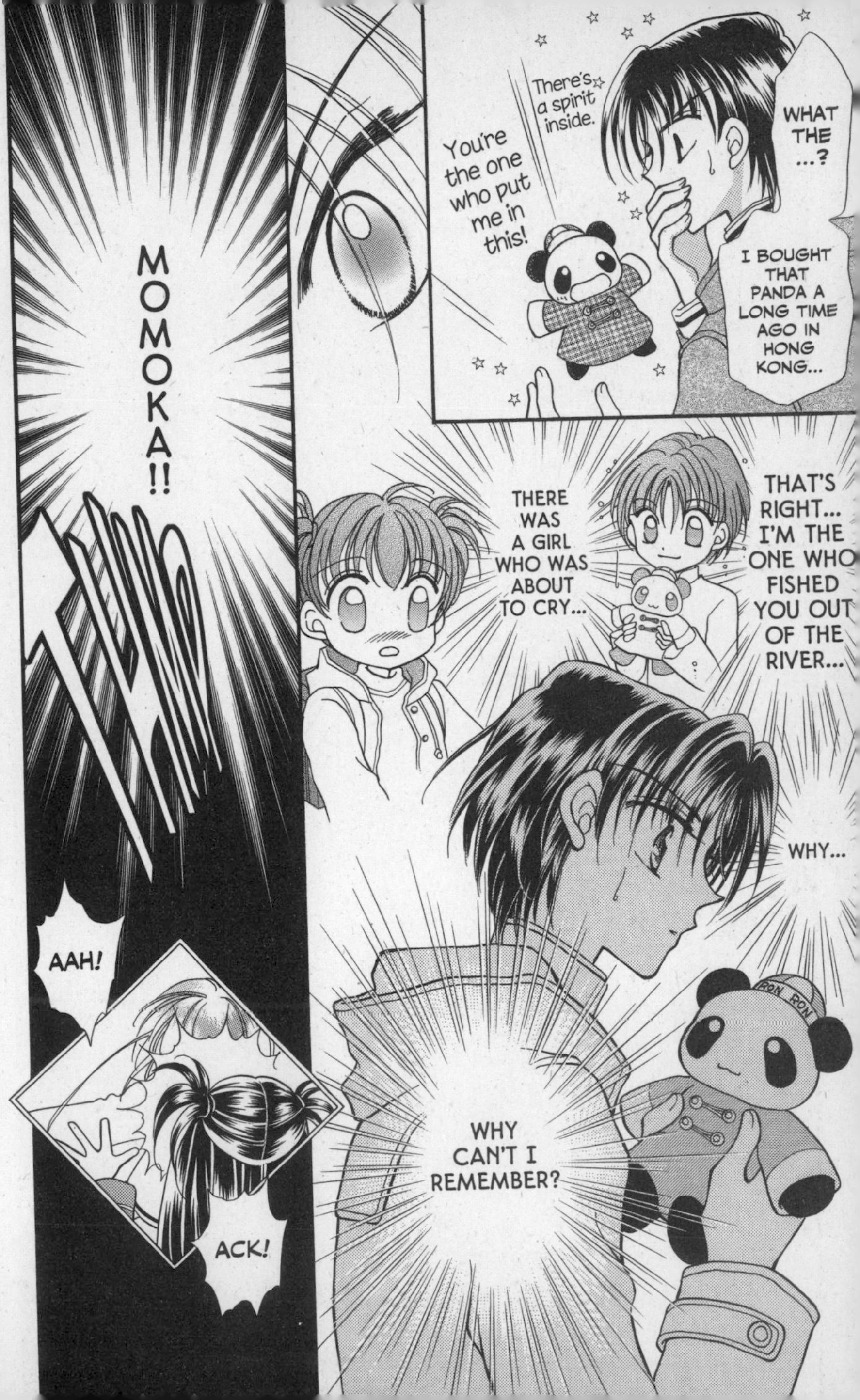
WHAT THE ...?
I BOUGHT THAT PANDA A LONG TIME AGO IN HONG KONG...
There's a spirit inside.
You're the one who put me in this!
THAT'S RIGHT... I'M THE ONE WHO FISHED YOU OUT OF THE RIVER...
THERE WAS A GIRL WHO WAS ABOUT TO CRY...
WHY...
WHY CAN'T I REMEMBER?
MOMOKA!!
AAH!
ACK!

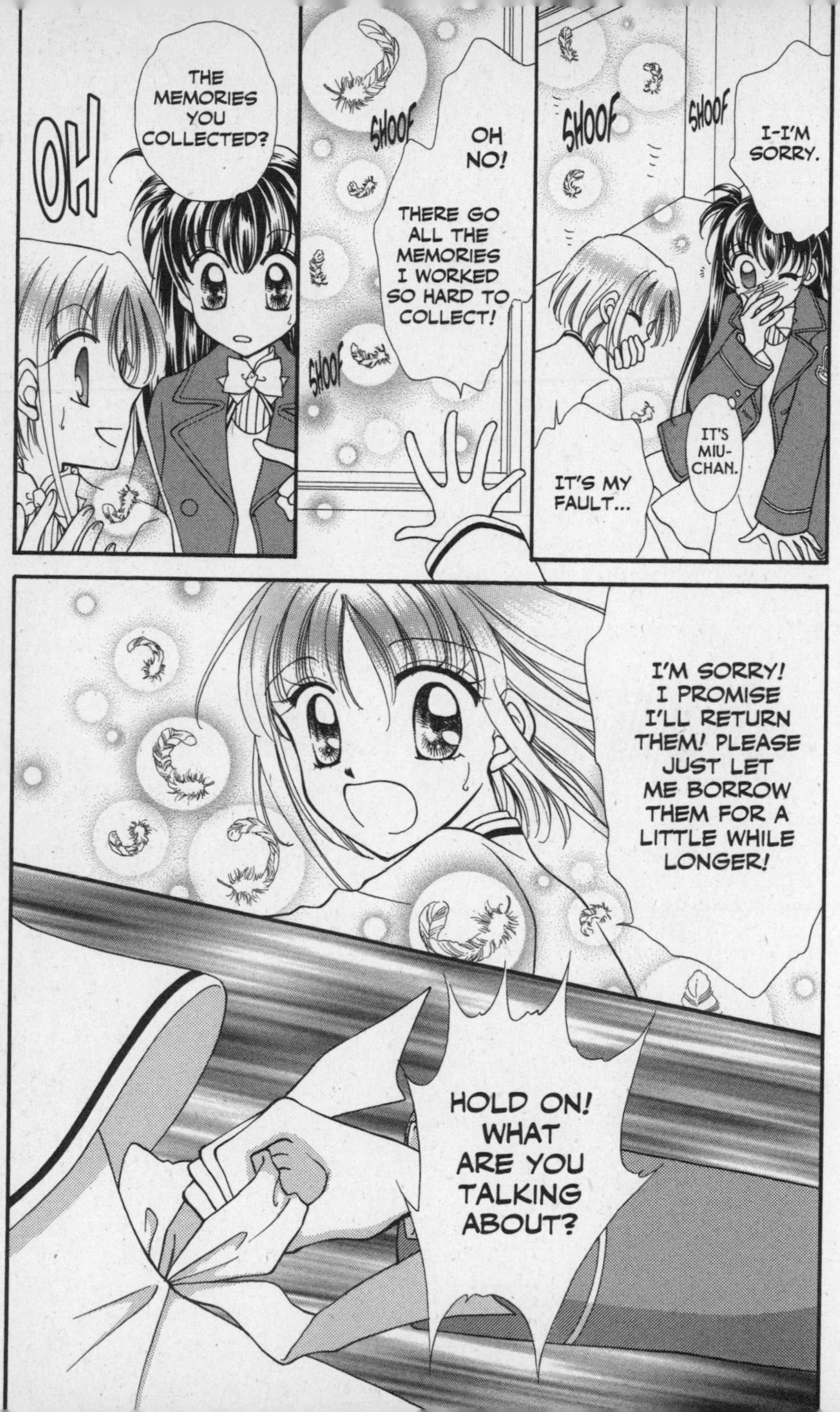
I-I'M SORRY.
SHOOF
SHOOF
IT'S MIU-CHAN.
IT'S MY FAULT...
OH NO!
SHOOF
THERE GO ALL THE MEMORIES I WORKED SO HARD TO COLLECT!
SHOOF
THE MEMORIES YOU COLLECTED?
OH
I'M SORRY! I PROMISE I'LL RETURN THEM! PLEASE JUST LET ME BORROW THEM FOR A LITTLE WHILE LONGER!
HOLD ON! WHAT ARE YOU TALKING ABOUT?

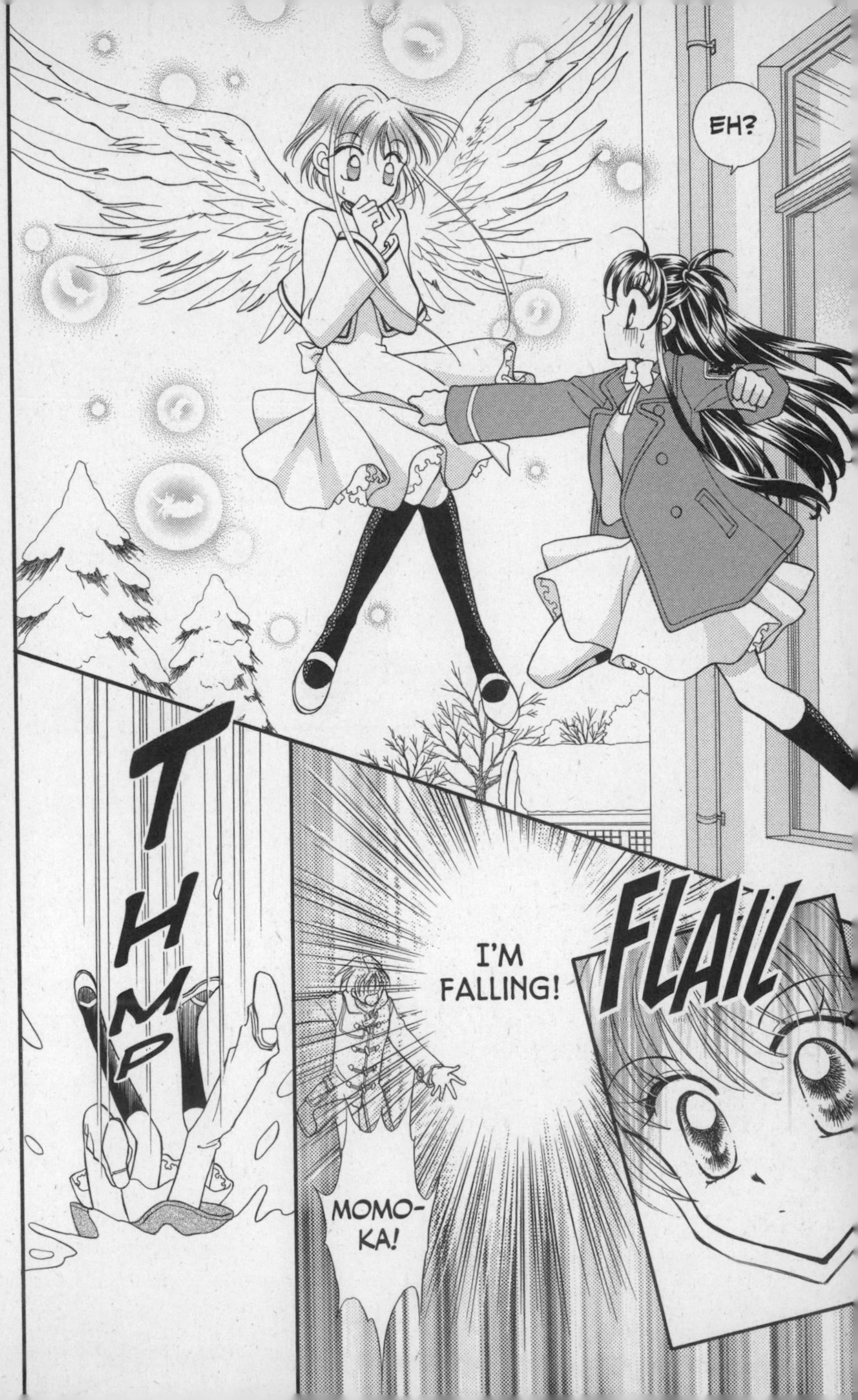
EH?
FLAIL
I'M FALLING!
MOMO-KA!
THMP

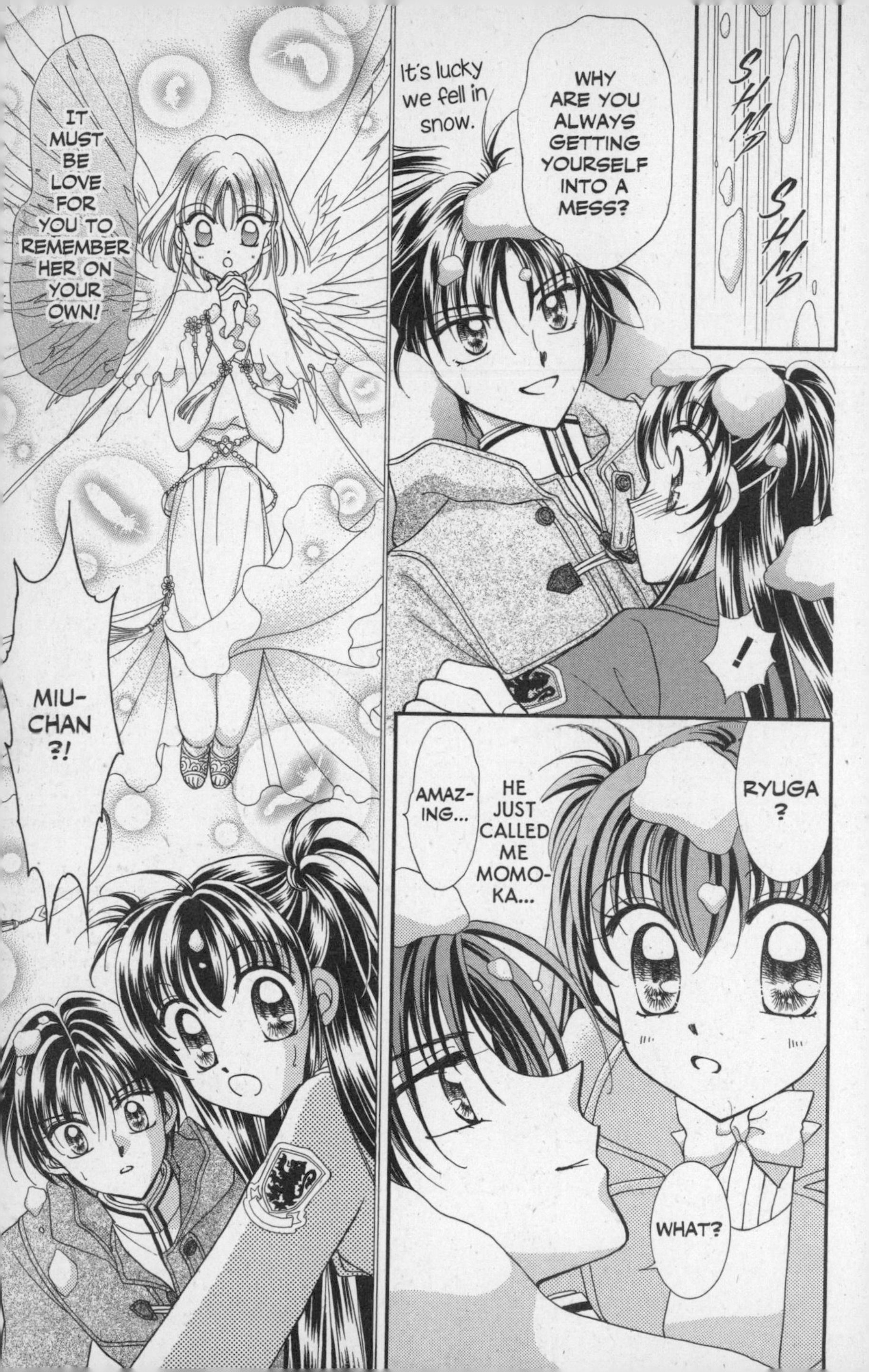
SHMP SHMP
WHY ARE YOU ALWAYS GETTING YOURSELF INTO A MESS?
It's lucky we fell in snow.
!
RYUGA?
HE JUST CALLED ME MOMOKA...
AMAZING...
WHAT?
IT MUST BE LOVE FOR YOU TO REMEMBER HER ON YOUR OWN!
MIU-CHAN?!

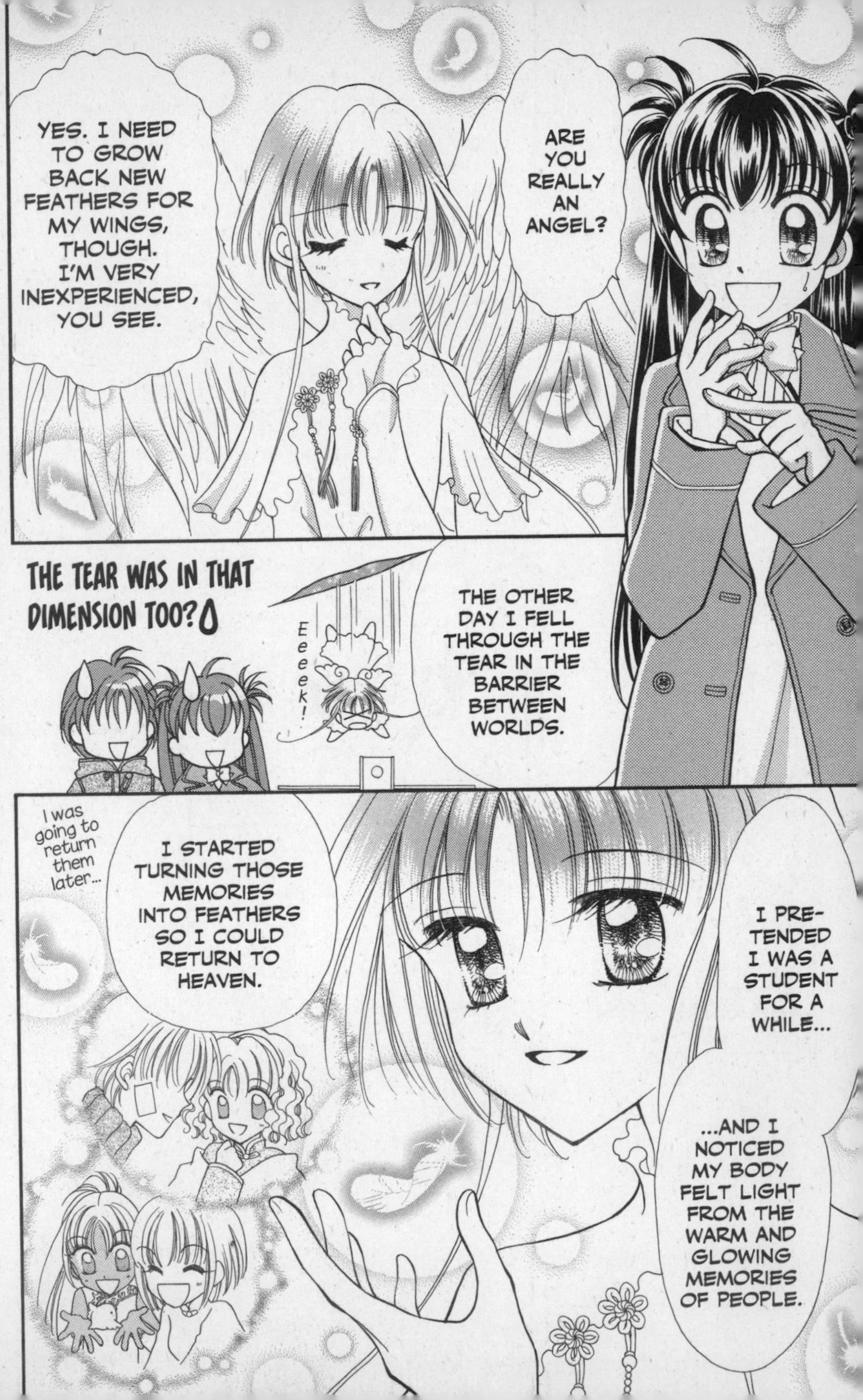
ARE YOU REALLY AN ANGEL?
YES. I NEED TO GROW BACK NEW FEATHERS FOR MY WINGS, THOUGH. I'M VERY INEXPERIENCED, YOU SEE.
THE OTHER DAY I FELL THROUGH THE TEAR IN THE BARRIER BETWEEN WORLDS.
Eeeek!
THE TEAR WAS IN THAT DIMENSION TOO?
I PRE-TENDED I WAS A STUDENT FOR A WHILE...
...AND I NOTICED MY BODY FELT LIGHT FROM THE WARM AND GLOWING MEMORIES OF PEOPLE.
I STARTED TURNING THOSE MEMORIES INTO FEATHERS SO I COULD RETURN TO HEAVEN.
I was going to return them later...

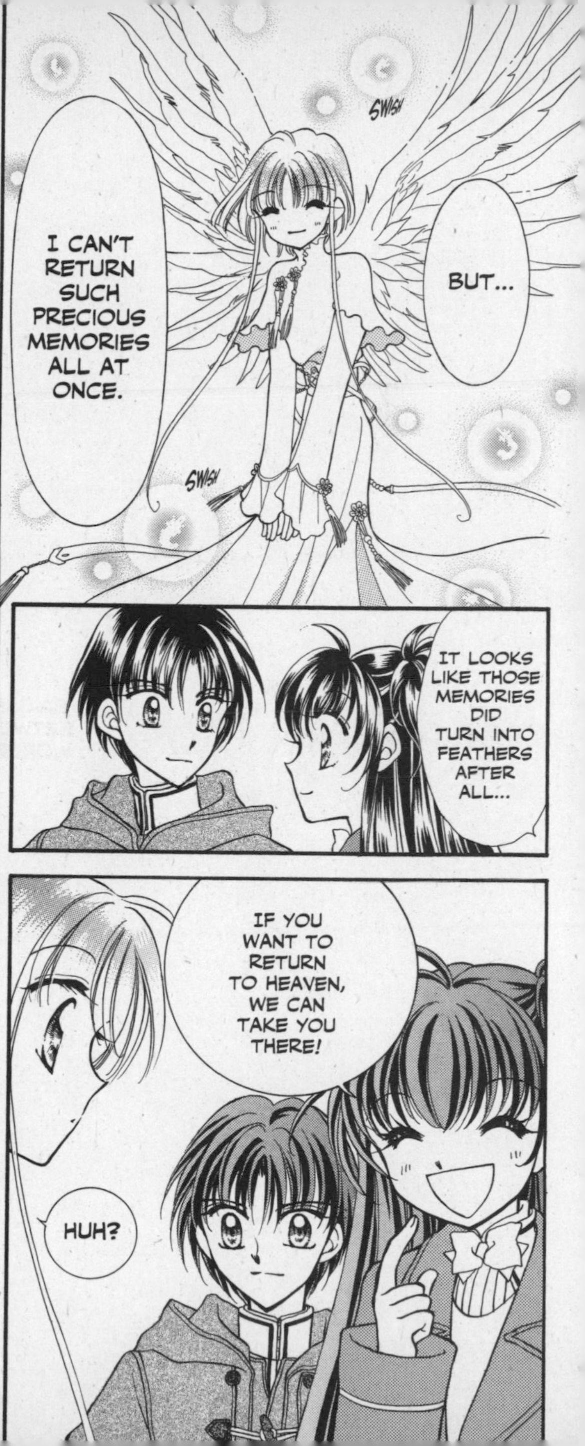
SWISH
BUT...
I CAN'T RETURN SUCH PRECIOUS MEMORIES ALL AT ONCE.
SWISH
IT LOOKS LIKE THOSE MEMORIES DID TURN INTO FEATHERS AFTER ALL...
IF YOU WANT TO RETURN TO HEAVEN, WE CAN TAKE YOU THERE!
HUH?

9

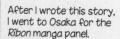

After I wrote this story, I went to Osaka for the *Ribon* manga panel.

For the panel, an editor first chooses several individuals who will contribute ideas, and then we discuss troubles and concerns regarding our work. The editors and people in charge address our issues. It's a bit like a manga class.

I went with Yuki Kobayashi. I met her once at the Fukuoka panel, but it had been a while, so I was really nervous.

There were about 12 contributors there, and everyone was really enthusiastic. Maybe it was because of the atmosphere in Osaka. But talking with everyone was really fun. We drew so much that my hands got stiff! (laugh)

Before I debuted, I was called to a panel in Tokyo. The teachers that time were Yoshizumi-sensei, Yazawa-sensei, and Tanigawa-sensei. There were about 30 contributors there. We all got to ask questions, and my heart was pounding as the mic was being passed to me. I'm bad at knowing where to divide the panels, so I asked them about that.

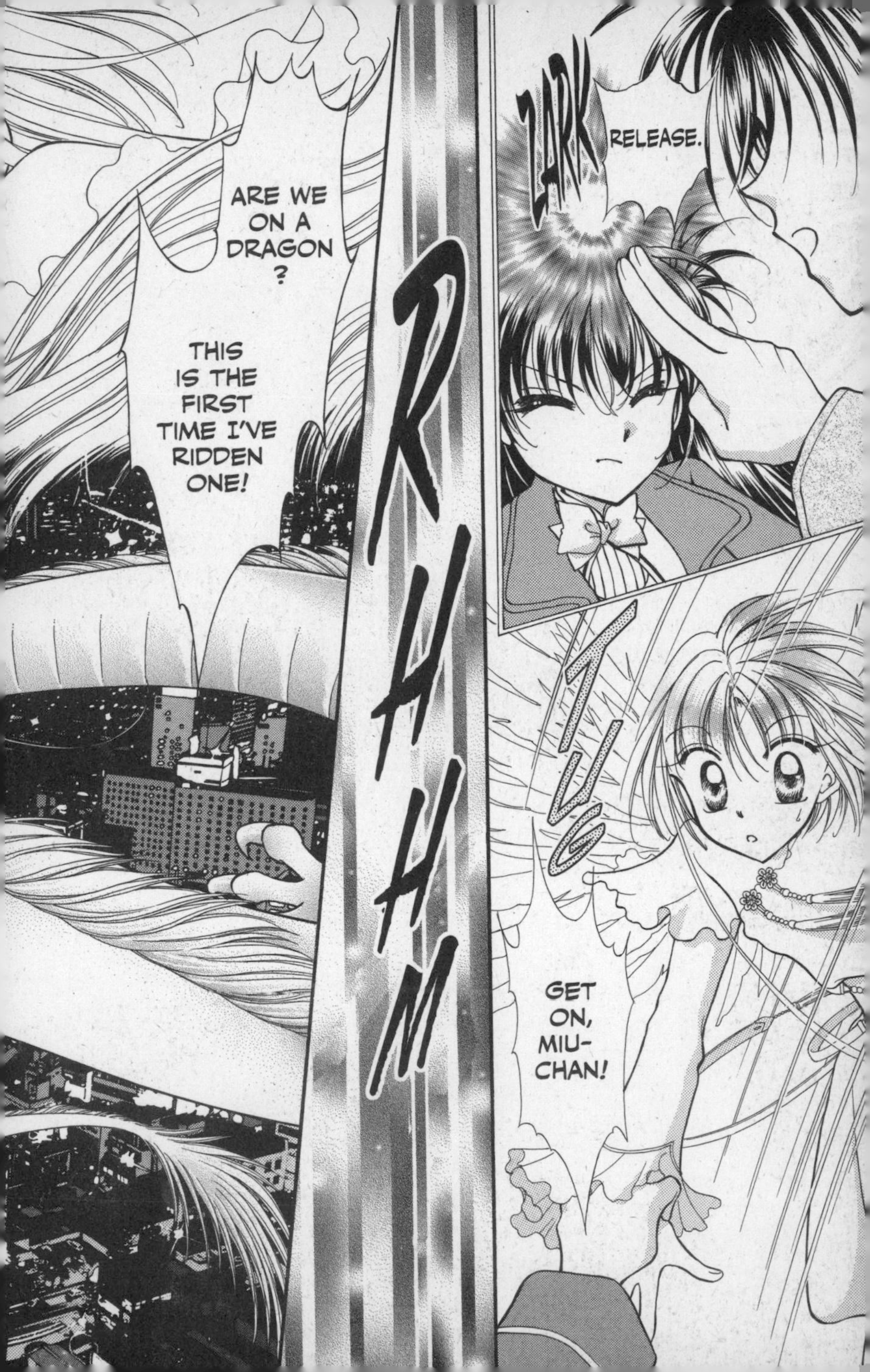
ZARK
RELEASE.
GET ON, MIU-CHAN!
RHHHM
ARE WE ON A DRAGON?
THIS IS THE FIRST TIME I'VE RIDDEN ONE!

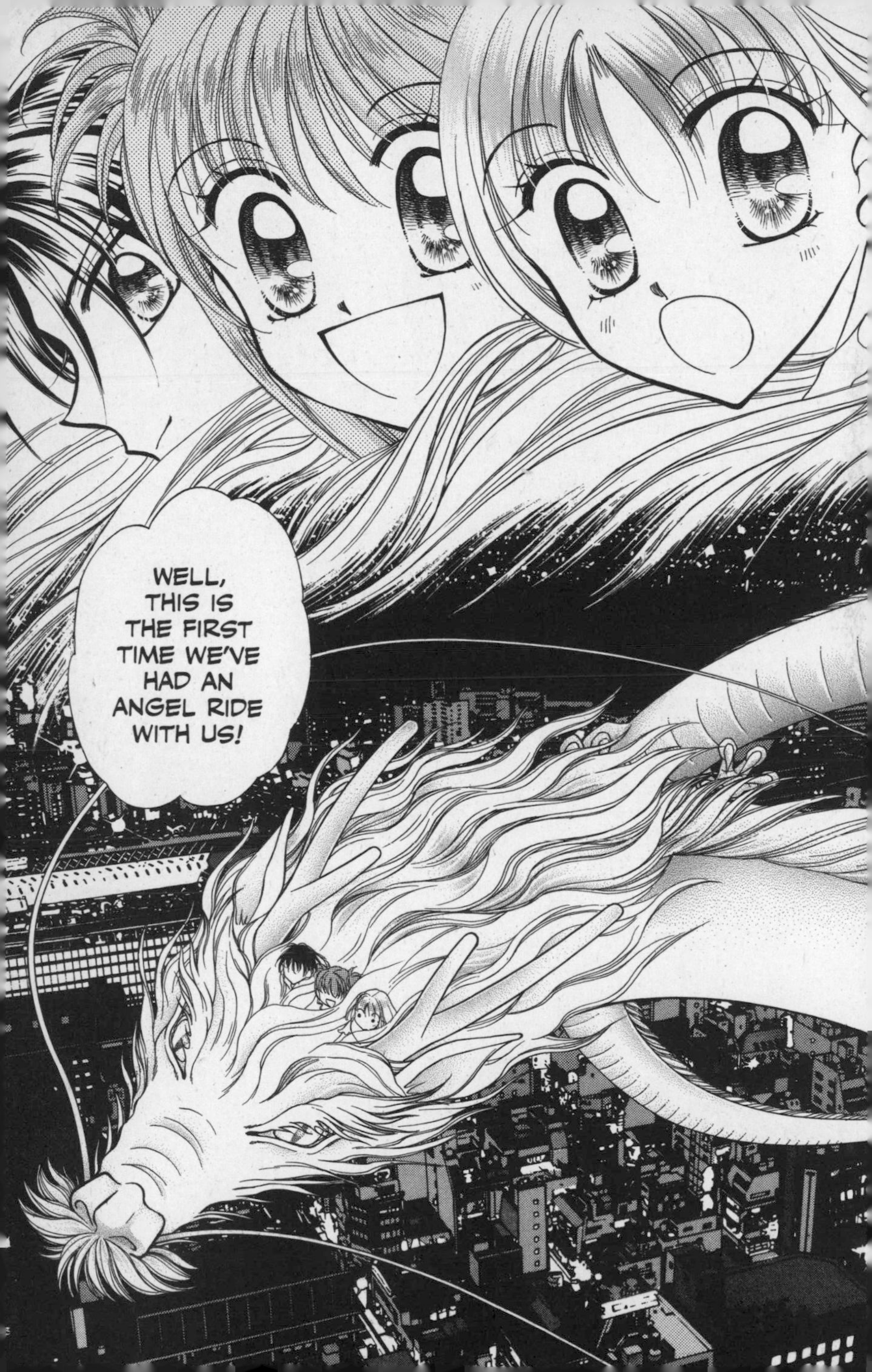
WELL, THIS IS THE FIRST TIME WE'VE HAD AN ANGEL RIDE WITH US!

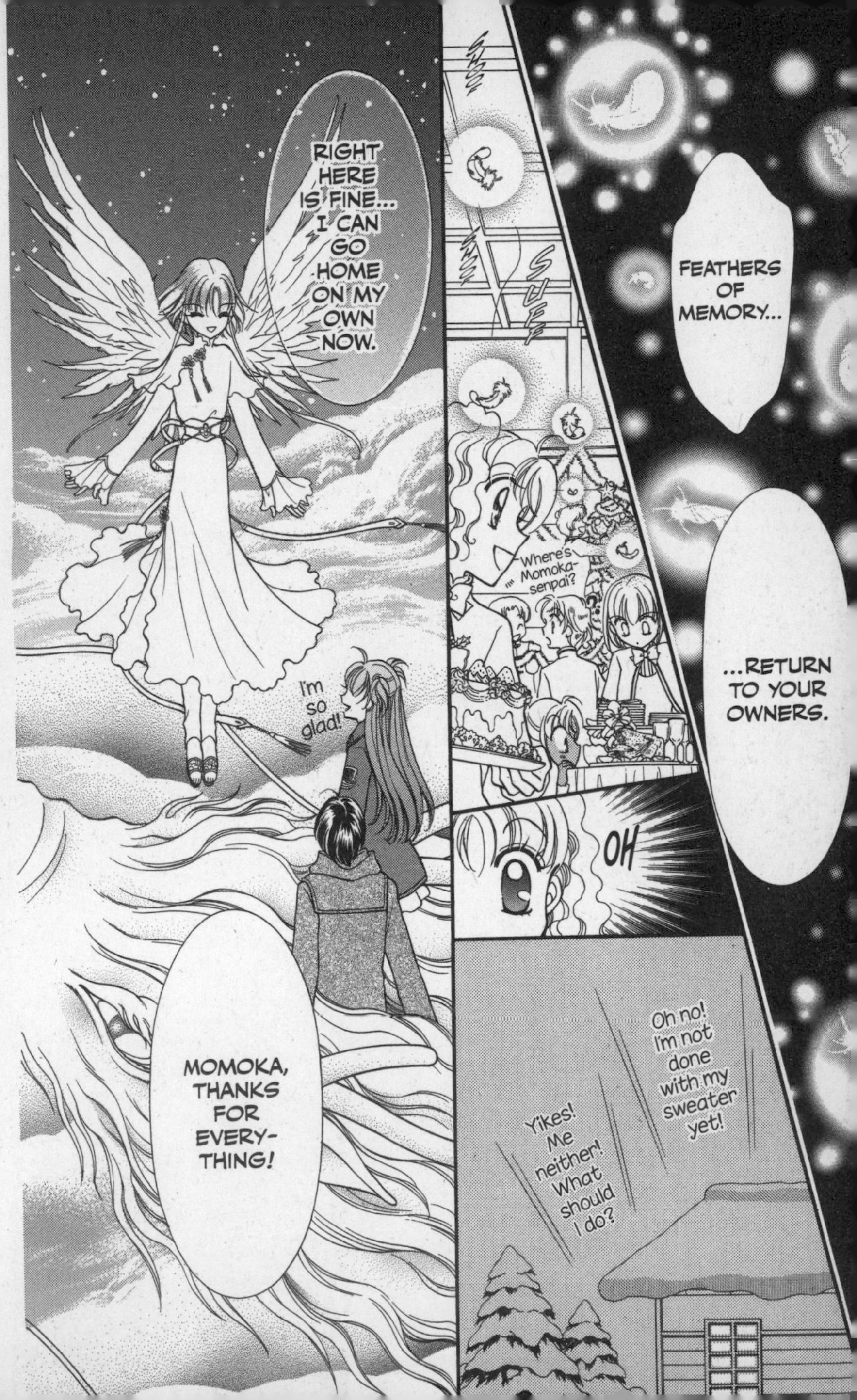
FEATHERS OF MEMORY...
...RETURN TO YOUR OWNERS.
SHOO
SHOO
SUFF
Where's Momoka-senpai?
OH
Oh no! I'm not done with my sweater yet!
Yikes! Me neither! What should I do?
RIGHT HERE IS FINE... I CAN GO HOME ON MY OWN NOW.
I'm so glad!
MOMOKA, THANKS FOR EVERY-THING!

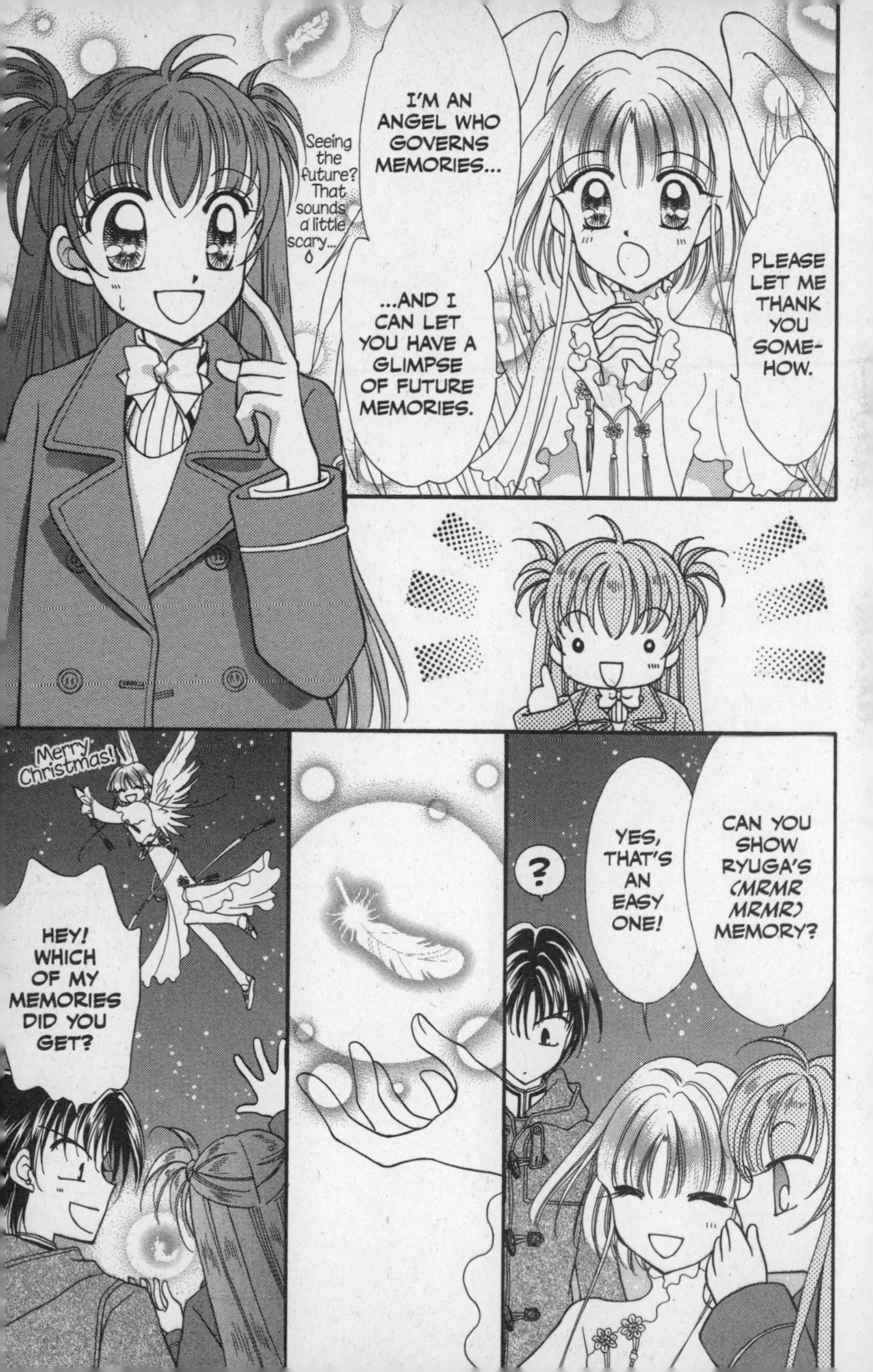
PLEASE LET ME THANK YOU SOMEHOW.
I'M AN ANGEL WHO GOVERNS MEMORIES...
...AND I CAN LET YOU HAVE A GLIMPSE OF FUTURE MEMORIES.
Seeing the future? That sounds a little scary...
CAN YOU SHOW RYUGA'S (MRMR MRMR) MEMORY?
YES, THAT'S AN EASY ONE!
?
Merry Christmas!
HEY! WHICH OF MY MEMORIES DID YOU GET?

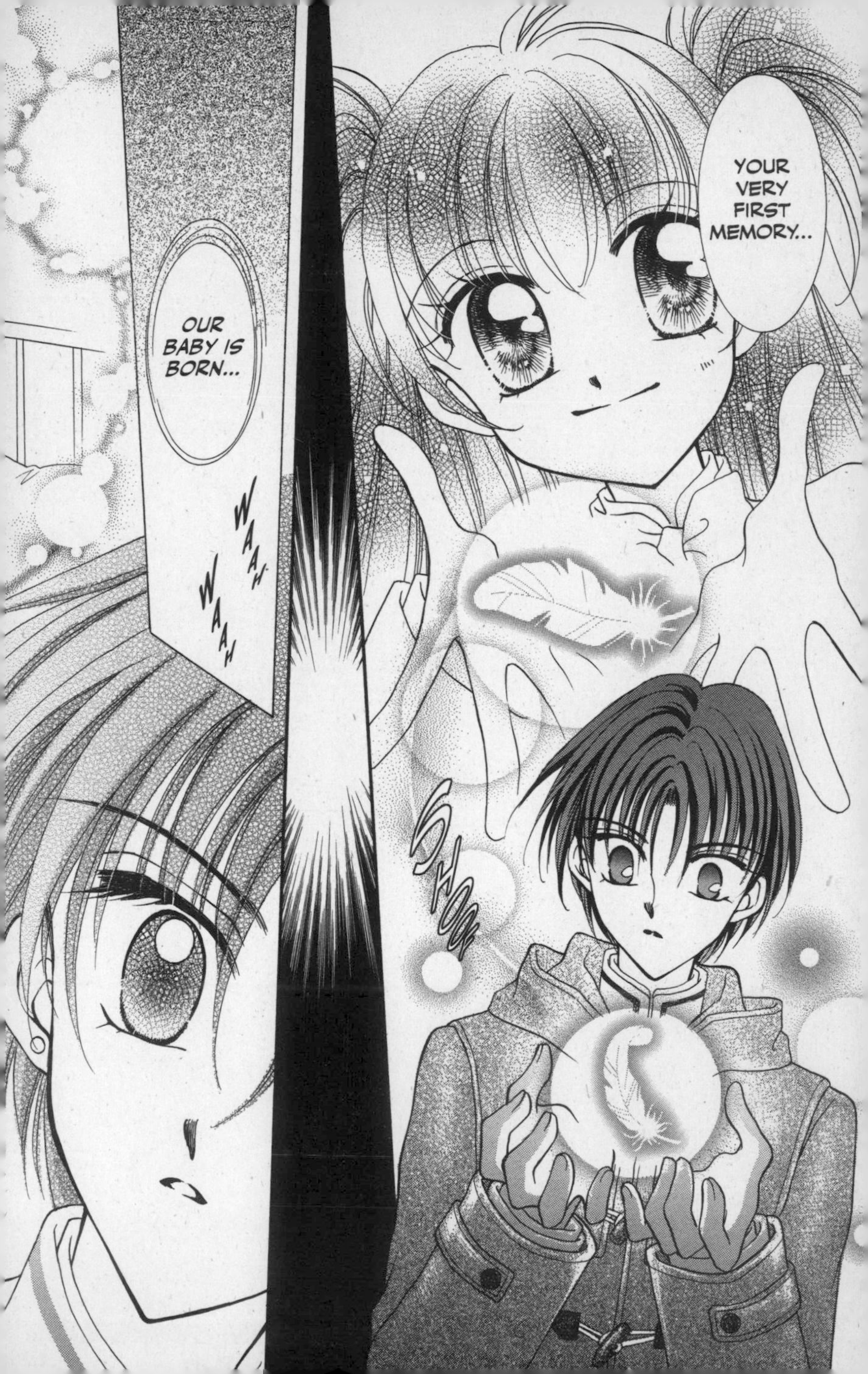
YOUR VERY FIRST MEMORY...
OUR BABY IS BORN...
WAAAH
WAAAH

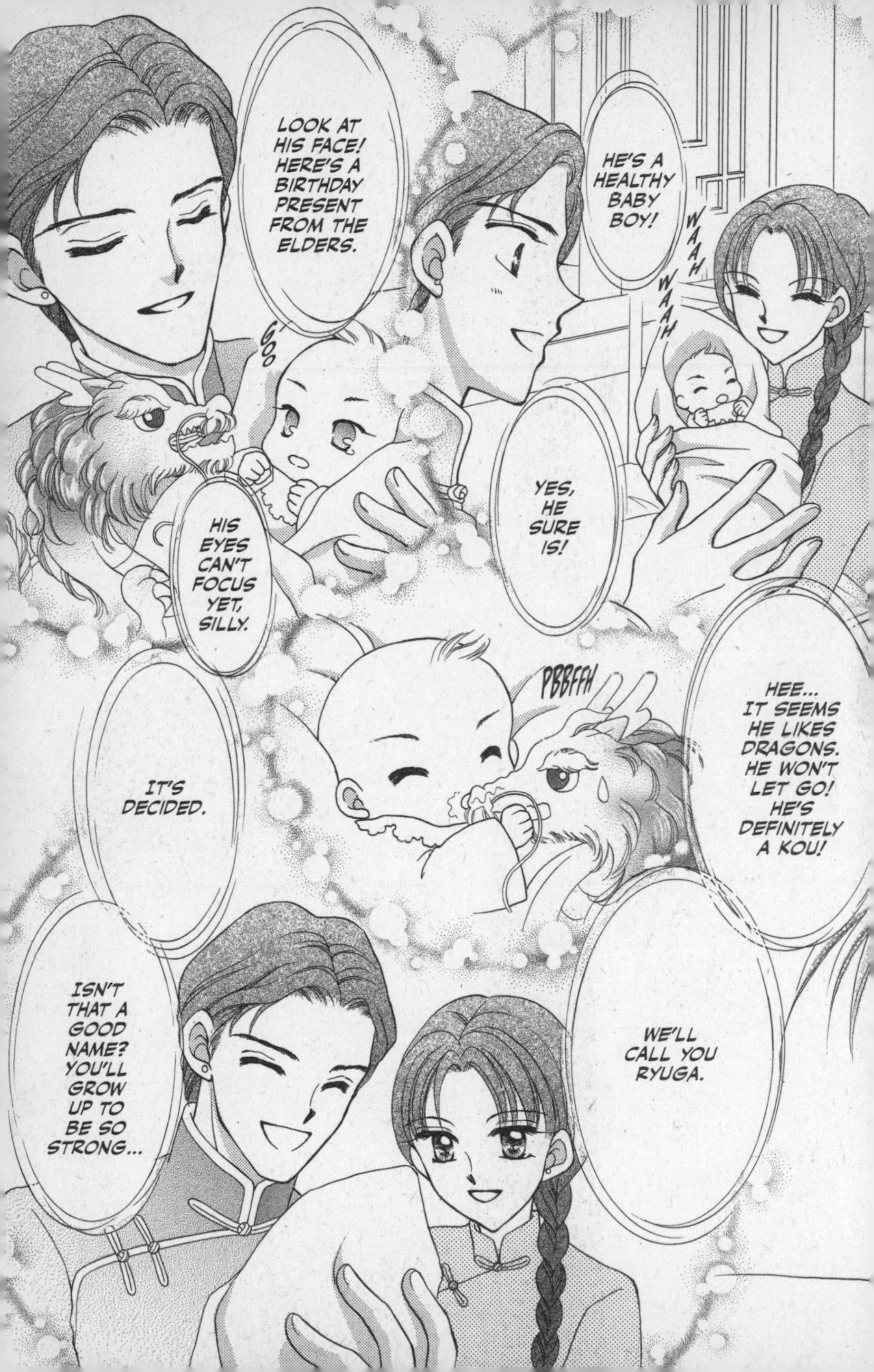
HE'S A HEALTHY BABY BOY!
WAAH WAAH
YES, HE SURE IS!
LOOK AT HIS FACE! HERE'S A BIRTHDAY PRESENT FROM THE ELDERS.
GOO
HIS EYES CAN'T FOCUS YET, SILLY.
PBBFFH
HEE... IT SEEMS HE LIKES DRAGONS. HE WON'T LET GO! HE'S DEFINITELY A KOU!
IT'S DECIDED.
WE'LL CALL YOU RYUGA.
ISN'T THAT A GOOD NAME? YOU'LL GROW UP TO BE SO STRONG...

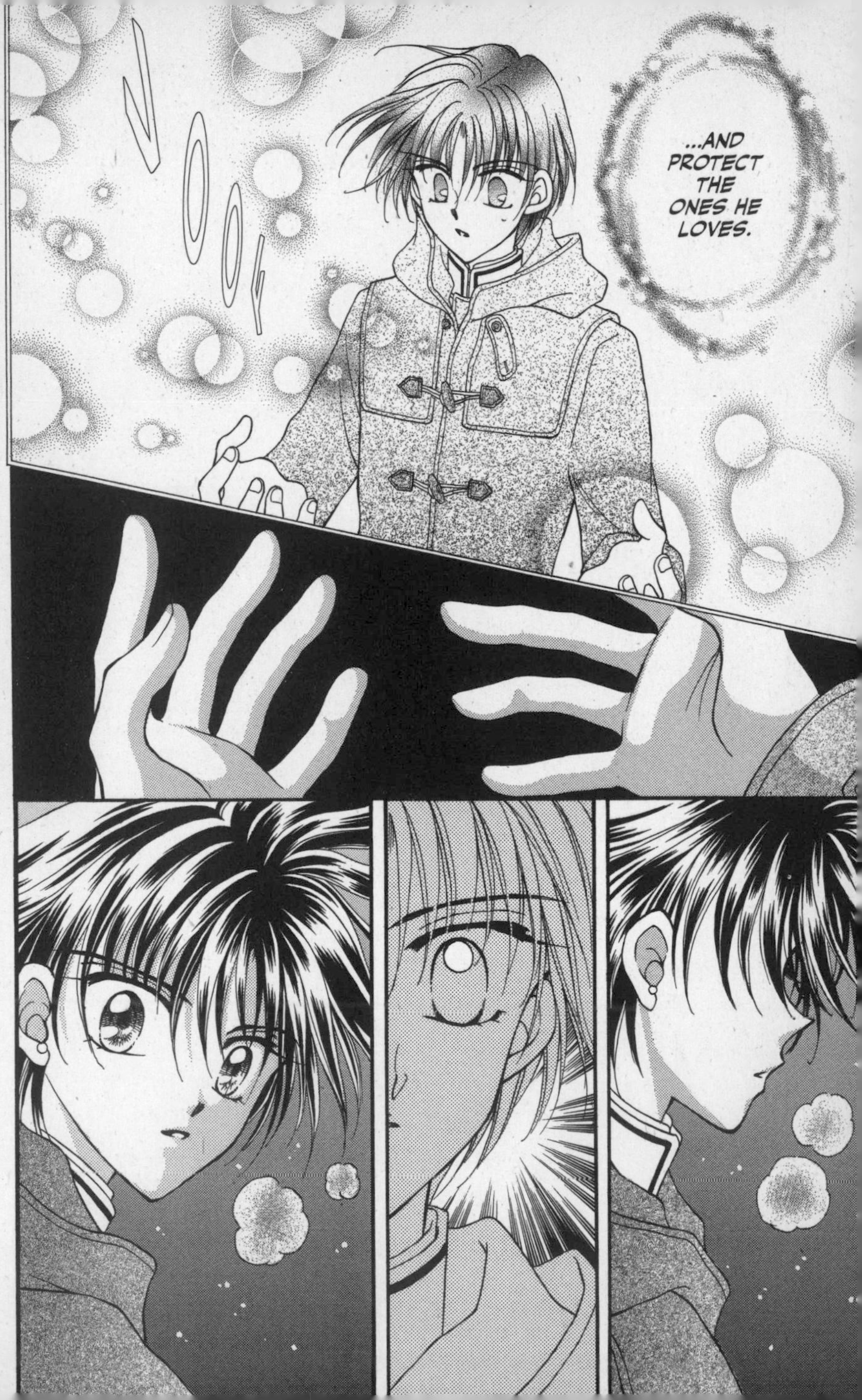
...AND PROTECT THE ONES HE LOVES.

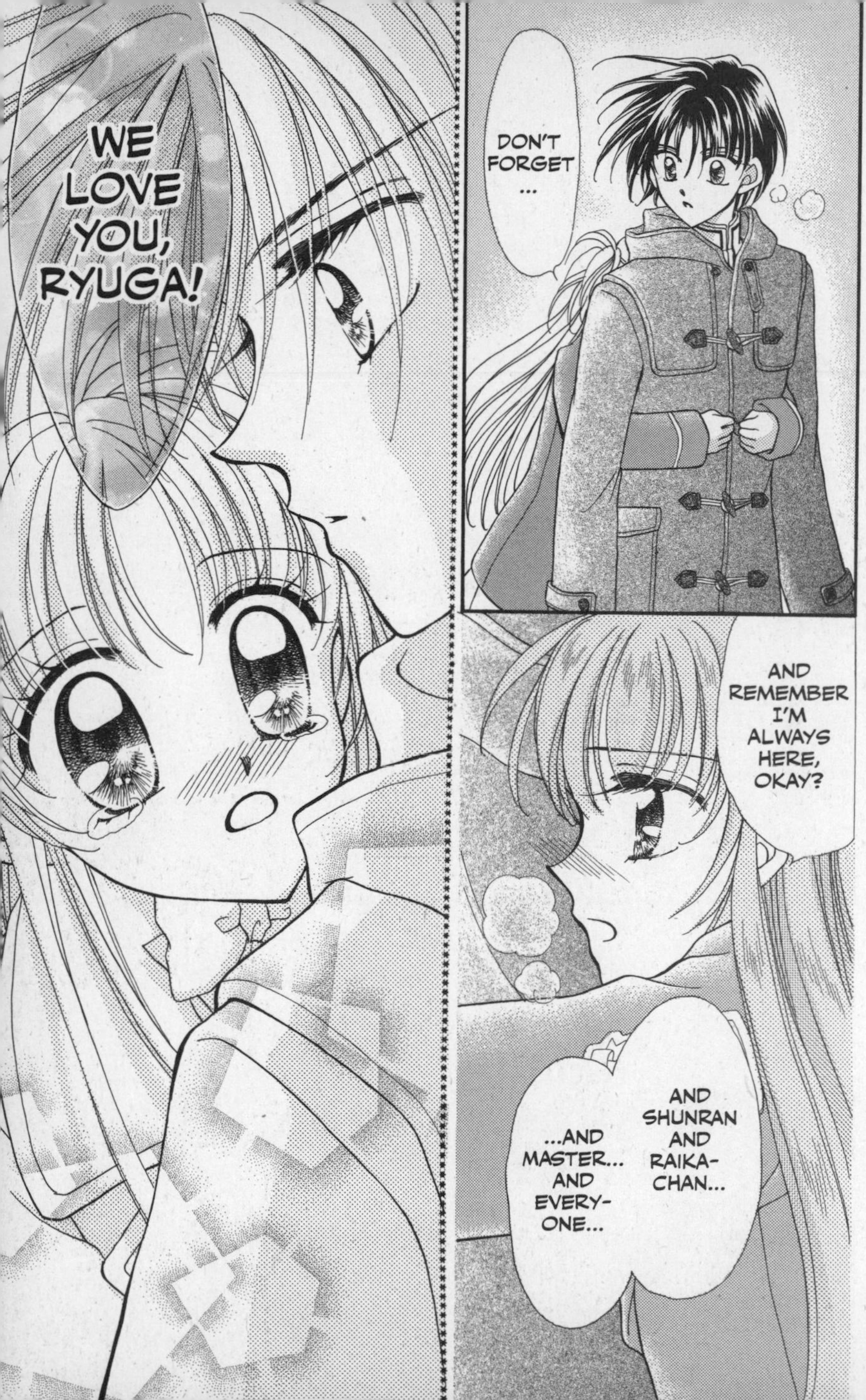
DON'T FORGET ...
AND REMEMBER I'M ALWAYS HERE, OKAY?
AND SHUNRAN AND RAIKA-CHAN...
...AND MASTER... AND EVERY-ONE...
WE LOVE YOU, RYUGA!

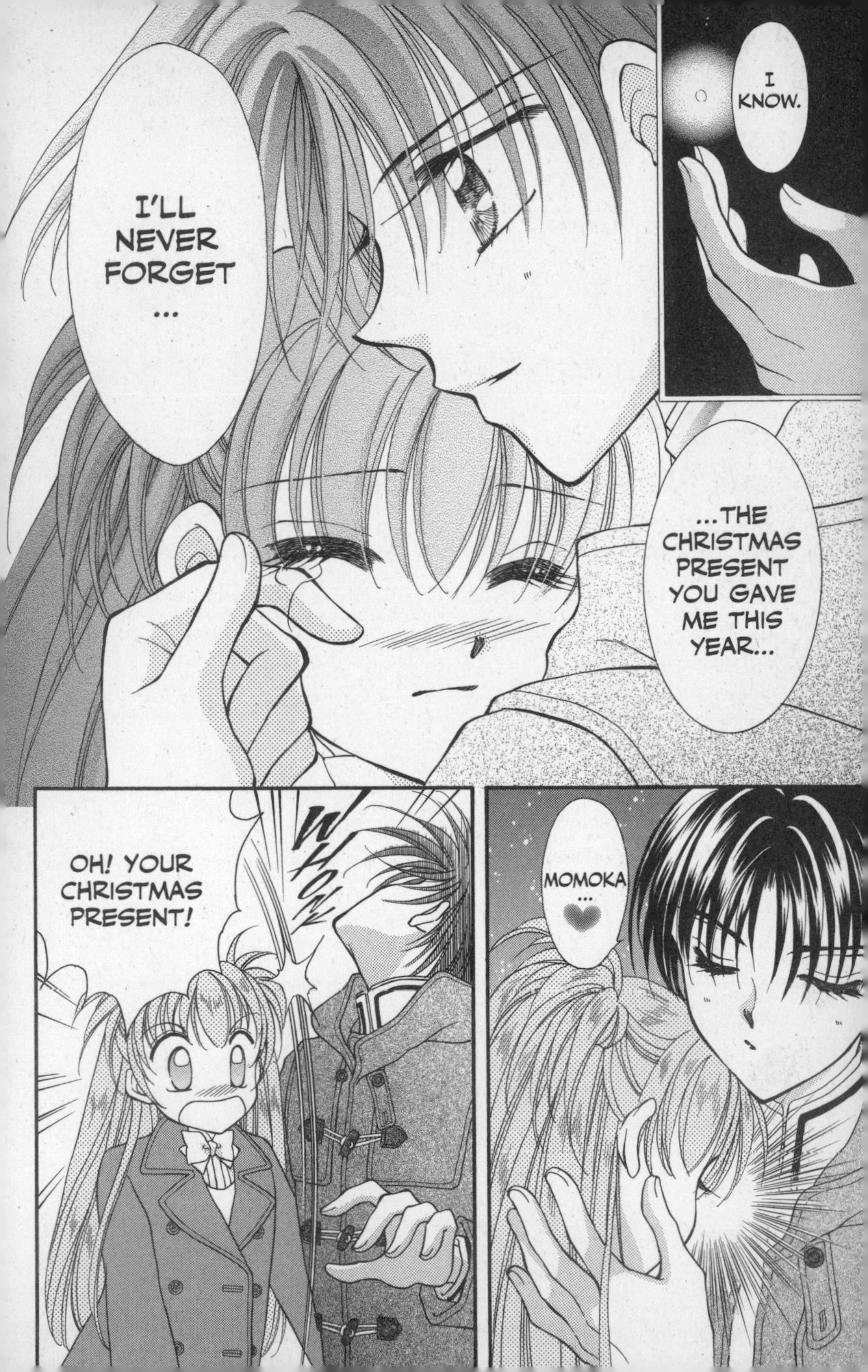
I KNOW.
I'LL NEVER FORGET ...
...THE CHRISTMAS PRESENT YOU GAVE ME THIS YEAR...
MOMOKA ... ♥
OH! YOUR CHRISTMAS PRESENT!
WHOMP

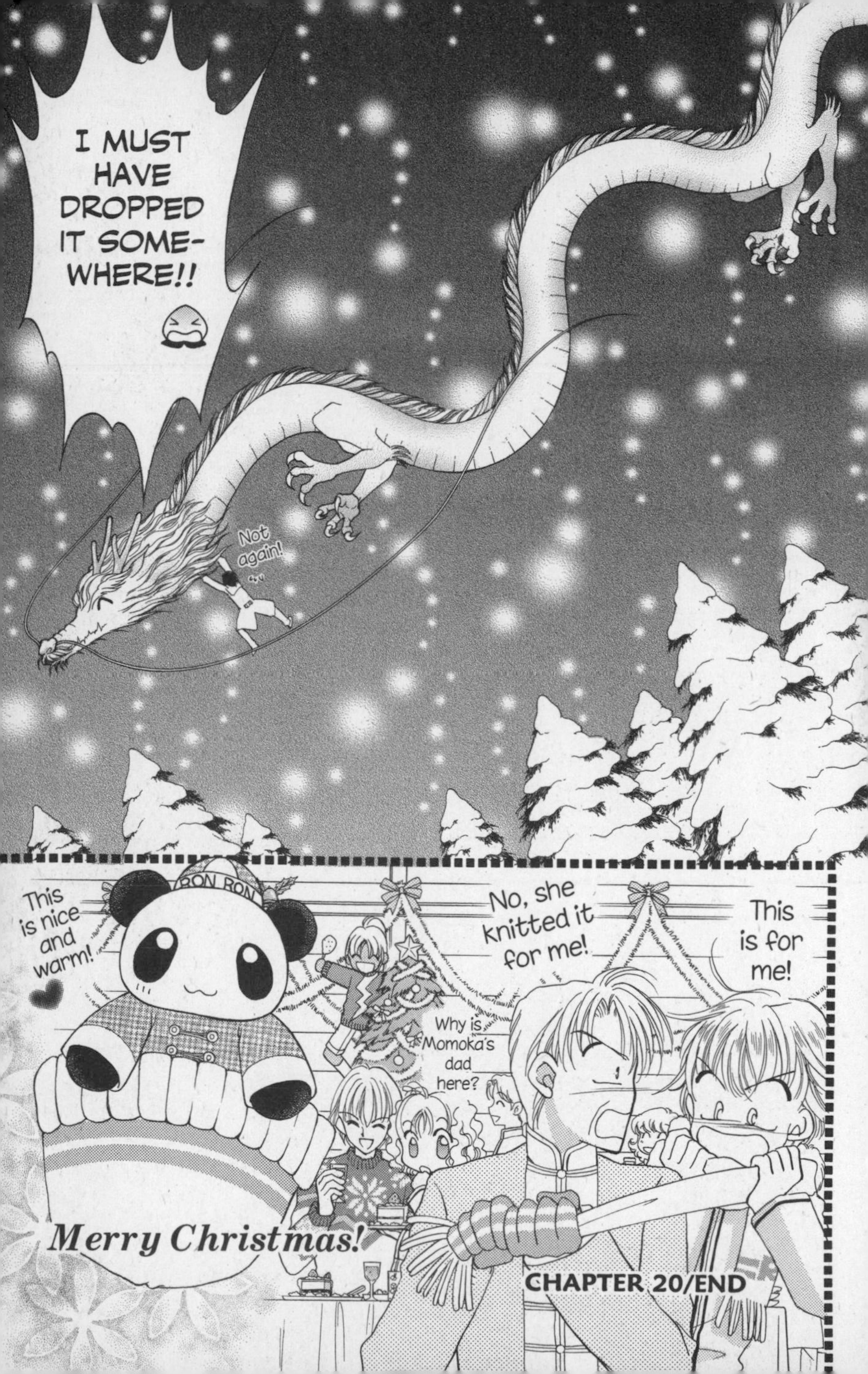
I MUST HAVE DROPPED IT SOME-WHERE!!
Not again!
This is for me!
No, she knitted it for me!
Why is Momoka's dad here?
RON RON
This is nice and warm!
Merry Christmas!
CHAPTER 20/END

RYUGA'S SECRET, PART 2

BY SASAKI

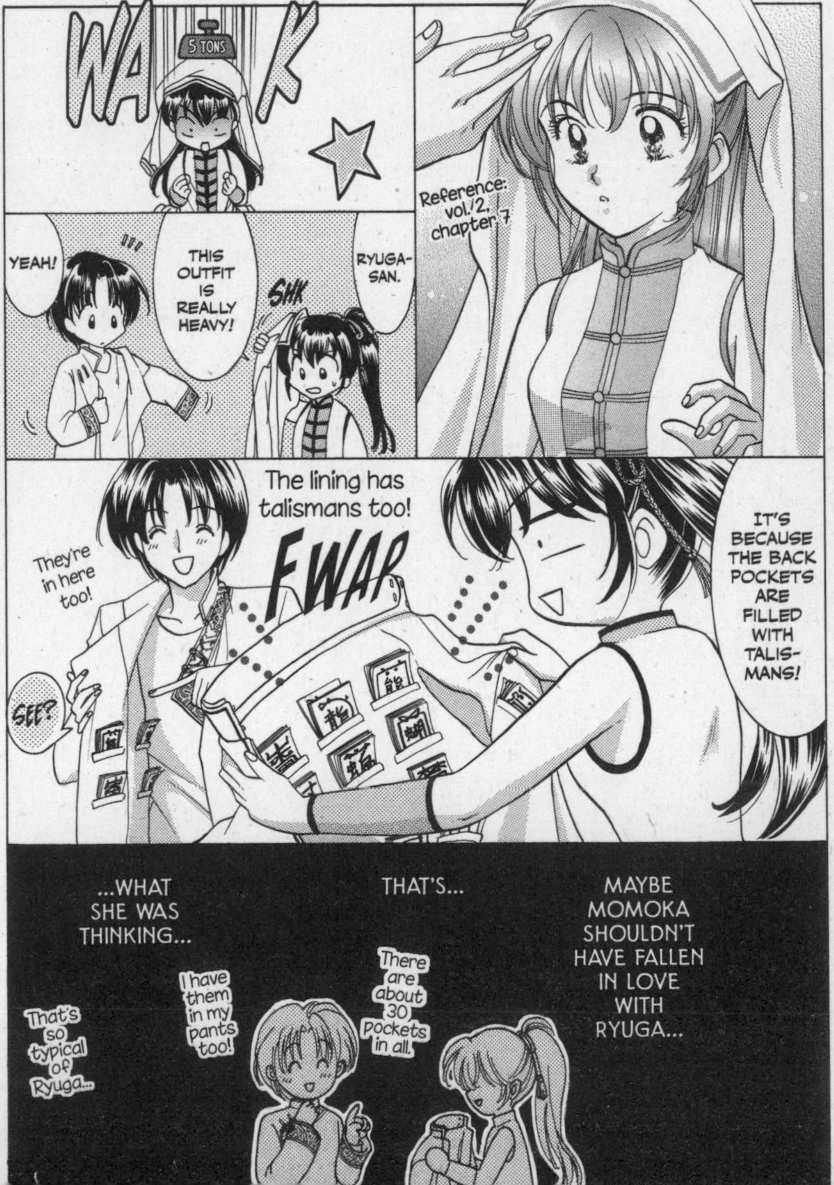

Reference: vol. 2, chapter 7
WA K
5 TONS
RYUGA-SAN.
SHK
THIS OUTFIT IS REALLY HEAVY!
YEAH!
IT'S BECAUSE THE BACK POCKETS ARE FILLED WITH TALIS-MANS!
The lining has talismans too!
FWAP
They're in here too!
SEE?
MAYBE MOMOKA SHOULDN'T HAVE FALLEN IN LOVE WITH RYUGA...
THAT'S...
...WHAT SHE WAS THINKING...
There are about 30 pockets in all.
I have them in my pants too!
That's so typical of Ryuga...

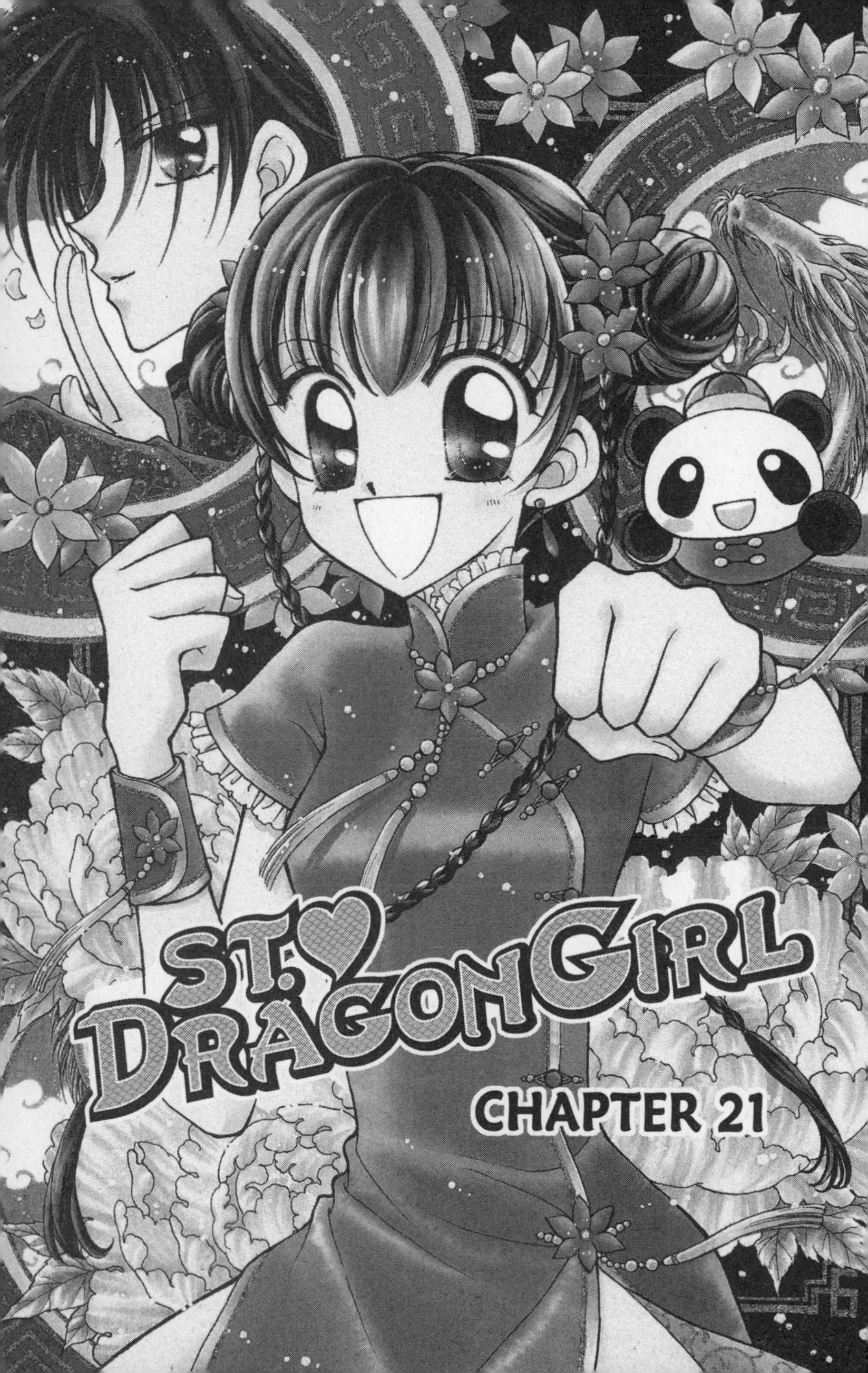
ST.♥DRAGON GIRL
CHAPTER 21

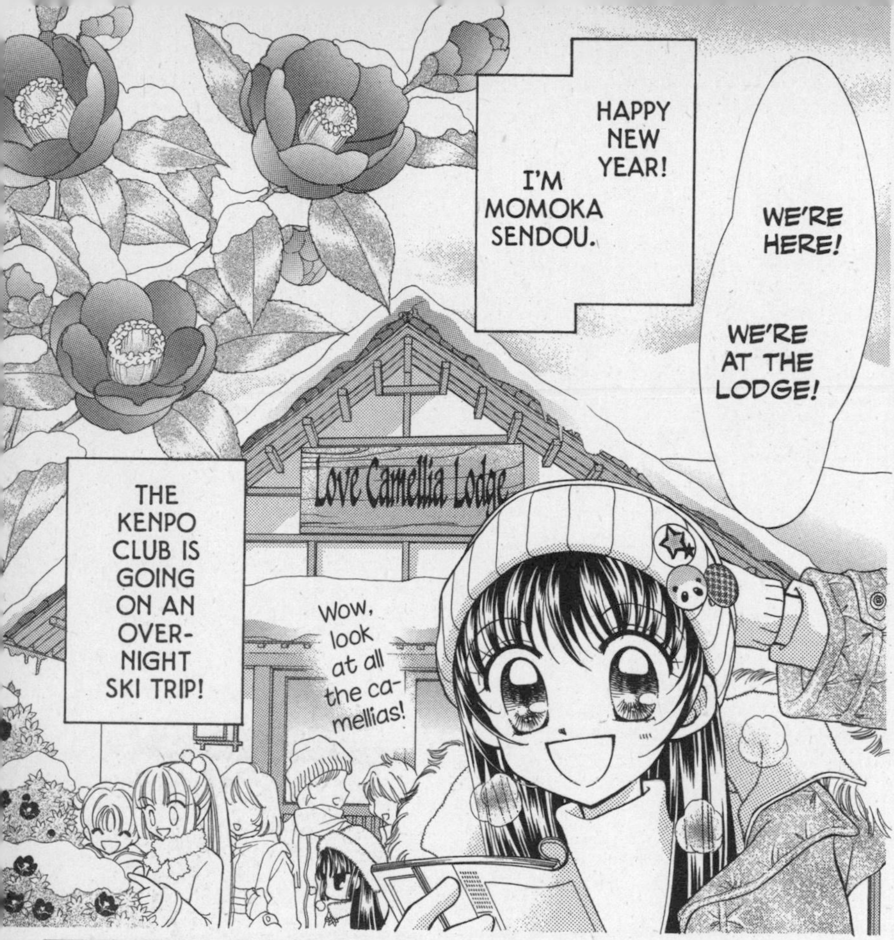
WE'RE HERE!
WE'RE AT THE LODGE!
HAPPY NEW YEAR!
I'M MOMOKA SENDOU.
Love Camellia Lodge
THE KENPO CLUB IS GOING ON AN OVERNIGHT SKI TRIP!
Wow, look at all the camellias!

- **What is screentone? Where can you buy it?**

Screentone is kind of like a big sticker, and it's used for patterns on clothes or shadows on objects. You cut it out and then paste it over and over again on your drawing. For example, there is screentone in the panel above on the camellia petals, leaves, and the sign on the inn. Also, the shadow on the snow and Momoka's clothes are all done by using screentone.

There are a lot of kinds, and new ones are always being developed, so I'm not sure how many exist in total. You can use them in all different ways. (Besides just sticking them on...)

For example, for clouds you can use a cutter and shade them little by little. Also you can layer them to create a sense of depth. This can be used to portray a sunrise or sunset. There are endless possibilities for its use. You can find it at large art supply stores in Japan. You can also get it via mail order. However, if you can find it locally, that's great.

I buy mine at a big art supply store in Shinjuku called TOO. The store also sells color ink, manuscript paper, and inking pens. I use a Zebra G inking pen.

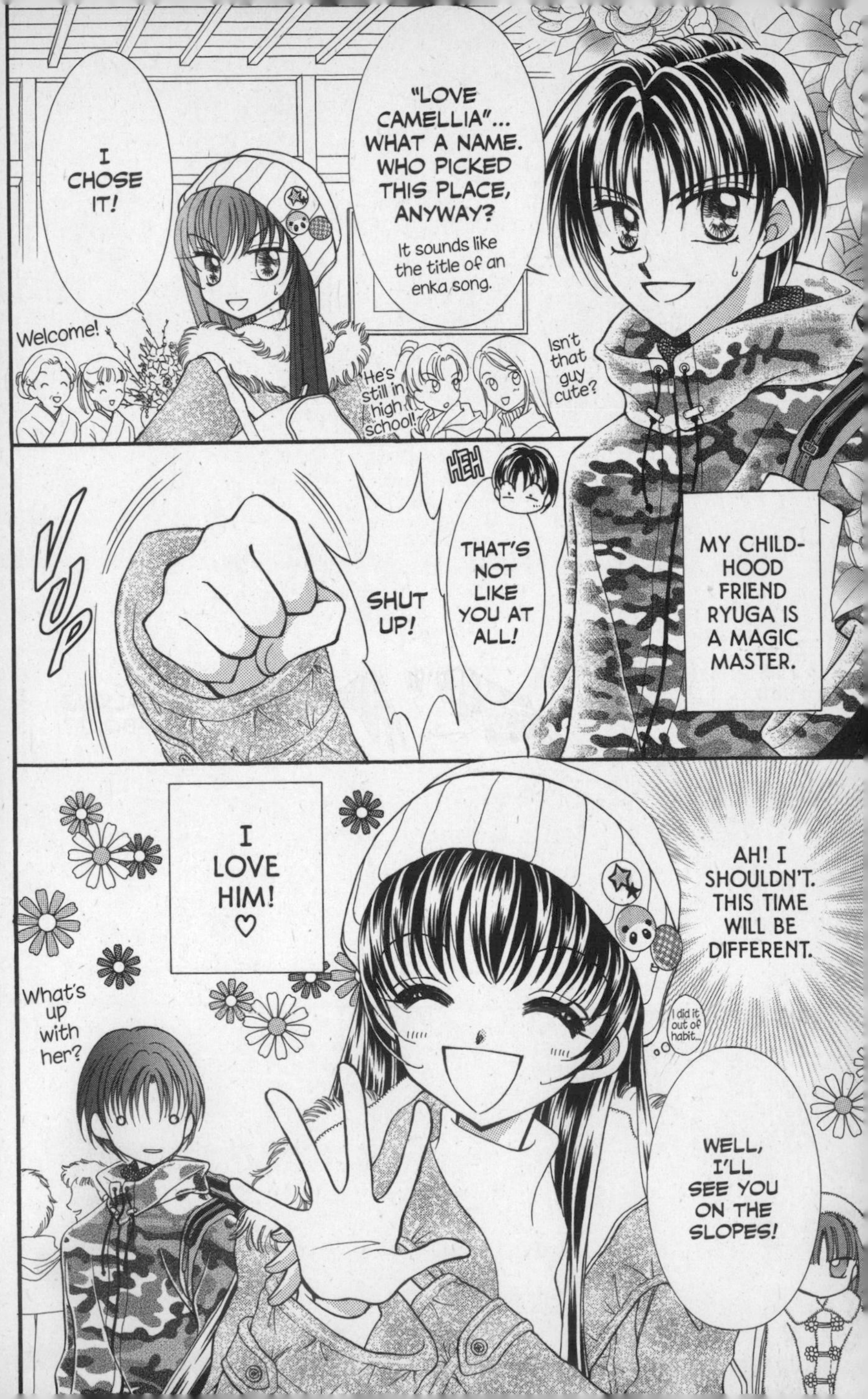
"LOVE CAMELLIA"... WHAT A NAME. WHO PICKED THIS PLACE, ANYWAY?
It sounds like the title of an enka song.
MY CHILD-HOOD FRIEND RYUGA IS A MAGIC MASTER.
Isn't that guy cute?
He's still in high school!
I CHOSE IT!
Welcome!
HEH
THAT'S NOT LIKE YOU AT ALL!
SHUT UP!
VUUP
AH! I SHOULDN'T. THIS TIME WILL BE DIFFERENT.
I did it out of habit...
I LOVE HIM! ♡
WELL, I'LL SEE YOU ON THE SLOPES!
What's up with her?

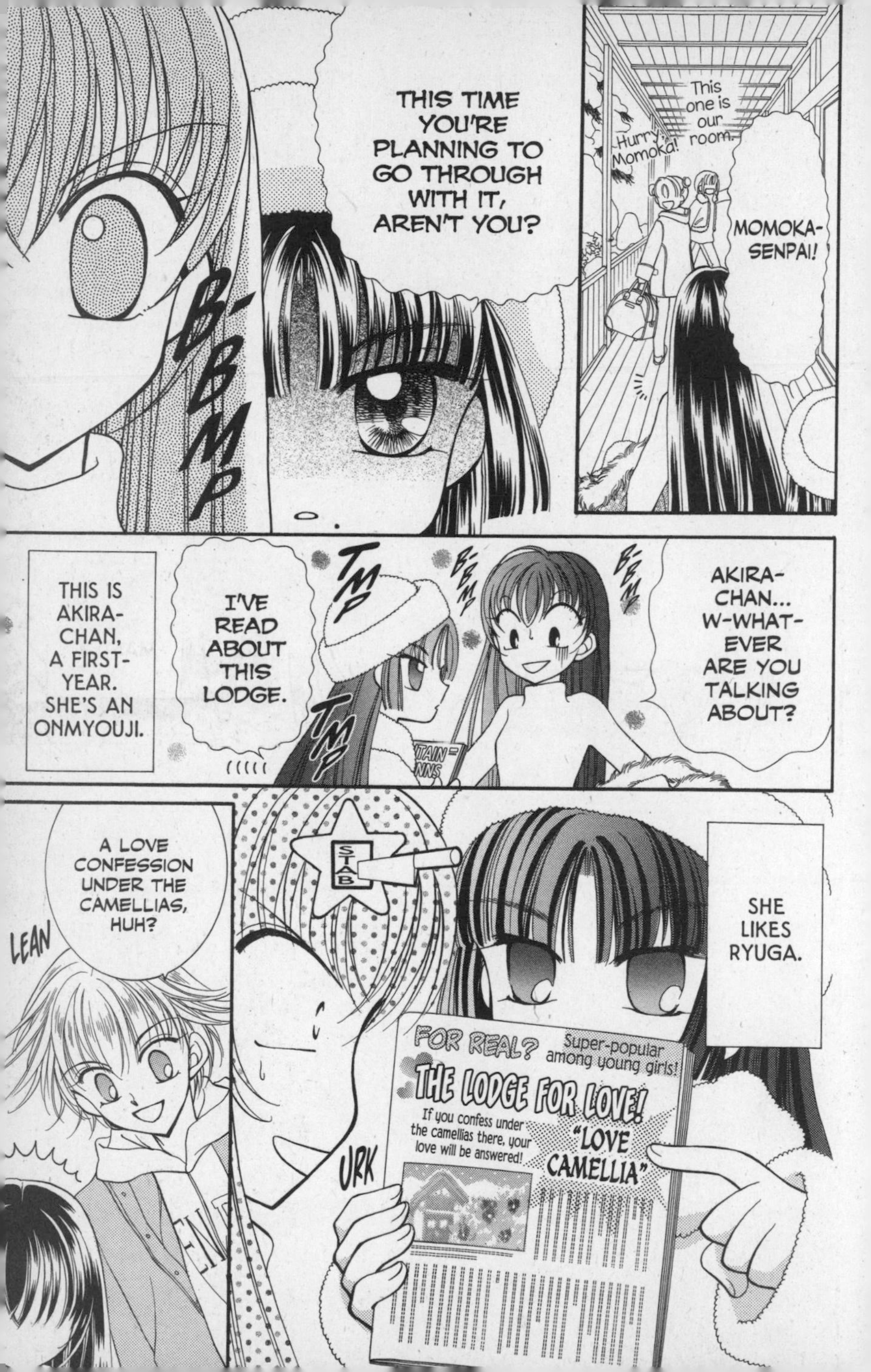

This one is our room.
Hurry Momoka!
MOMOKA-SENPAI!
THIS TIME YOU'RE PLANNING TO GO THROUGH WITH IT, AREN'T YOU?
B-BMP
AKIRA-CHAN... W-WHATEVER ARE YOU TALKING ABOUT?
B-BMP
B-BMP
TMP
TMP
I'VE READ ABOUT THIS LODGE.
THIS IS AKIRA-CHAN, A FIRST-YEAR. SHE'S AN ONMYOUJI.
SHE LIKES RYUGA.
STAB
FOR REAL? Super-popular among young girls!
THE LODGE FOR LOVE!
If you confess under the camellias there, your love will be answered!
"LOVE CAMELLIA"
URK
A LOVE CONFESSION UNDER THE CAMELLIAS, HUH?
LEAN

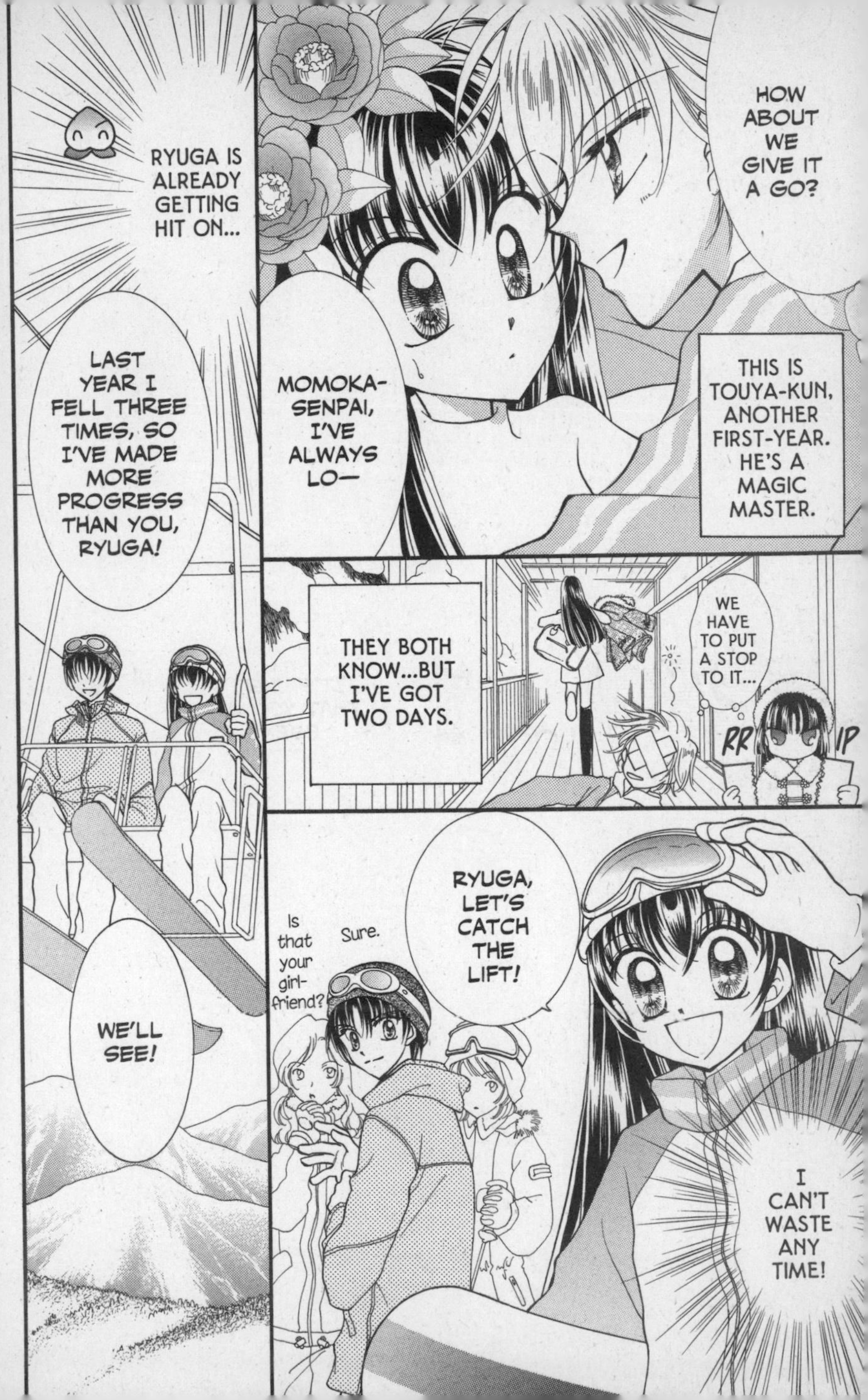
HOW ABOUT WE GIVE IT A GO?
THIS IS TOUYA-KUN, ANOTHER FIRST-YEAR. HE'S A MAGIC MASTER.
MOMOKA-SENPAI, I'VE ALWAYS LO—
WE HAVE TO PUT A STOP TO IT...
RRIP
THEY BOTH KNOW...BUT I'VE GOT TWO DAYS.
I CAN'T WASTE ANY TIME!
RYUGA, LET'S CATCH THE LIFT!
Sure.
Is that your girlfriend?
RYUGA IS ALREADY GETTING HIT ON...
LAST YEAR I FELL THREE TIMES, SO I'VE MADE MORE PROGRESS THAN YOU, RYUGA!
WE'LL SEE!

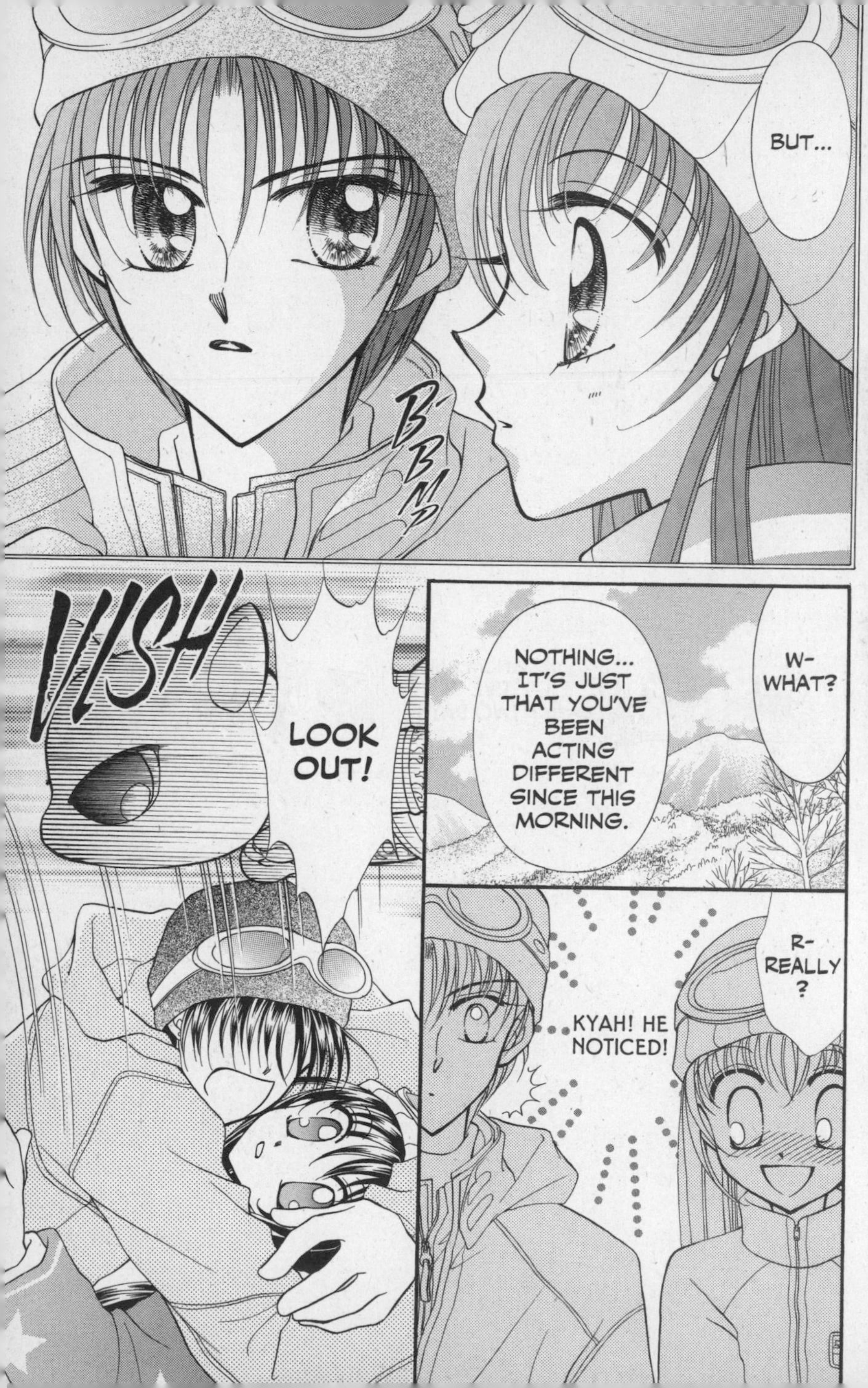
BUT...
B-BMP
W-WHAT?
NOTHING... IT'S JUST THAT YOU'VE BEEN ACTING DIFFERENT SINCE THIS MORNING.
R-REALLY?
KYAH! HE NOTICED!
VISH
LOOK OUT!

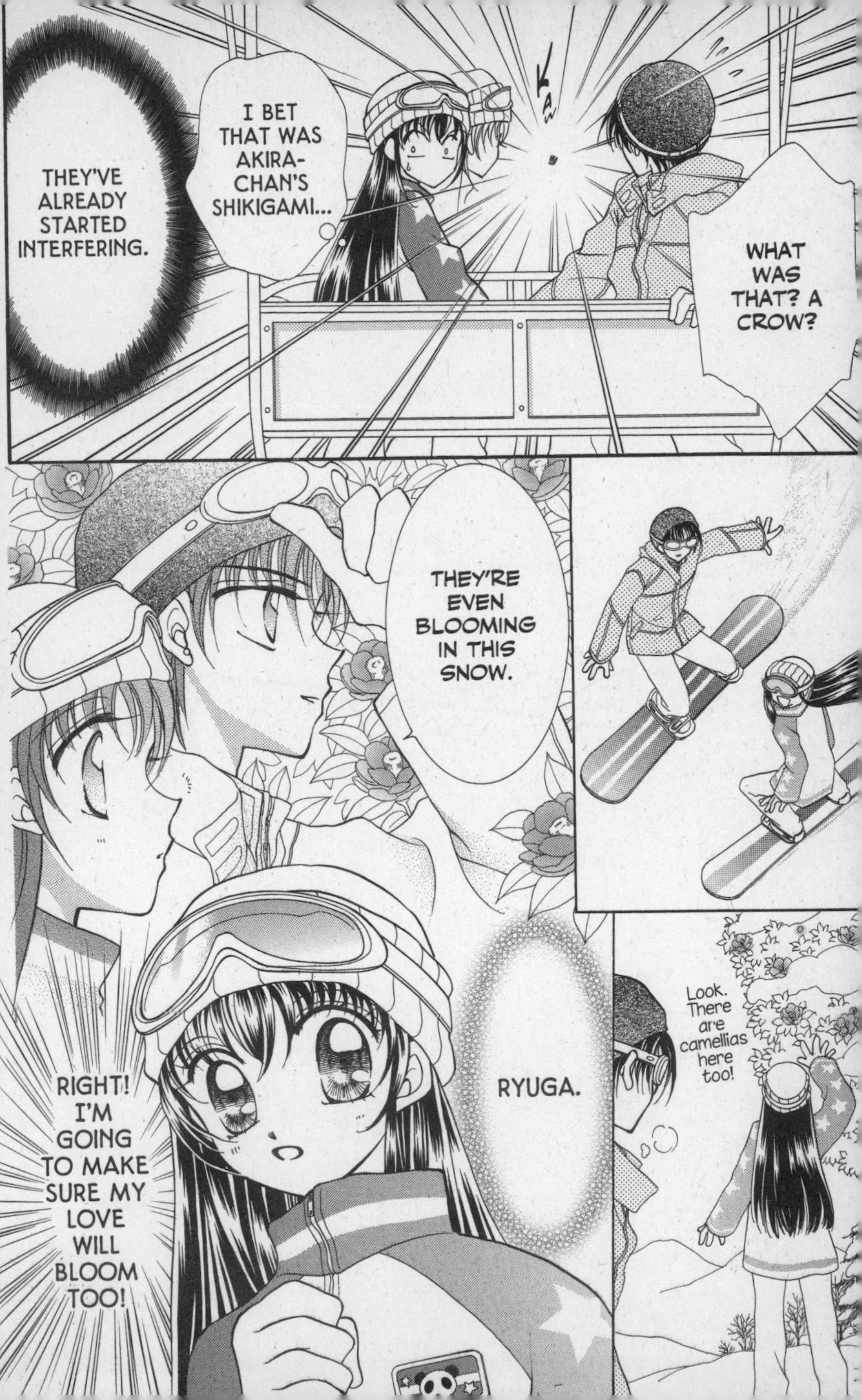
KAW
WHAT WAS THAT? A CROW?
I BET THAT WAS AKIRA-CHAN'S SHIKIGAMI...
THEY'VE ALREADY STARTED INTERFERING.
Look. There are camellias here too!
THEY'RE EVEN BLOOMING IN THIS SNOW.
RYUGA.
RIGHT! I'M GOING TO MAKE SURE MY LOVE WILL BLOOM TOO!

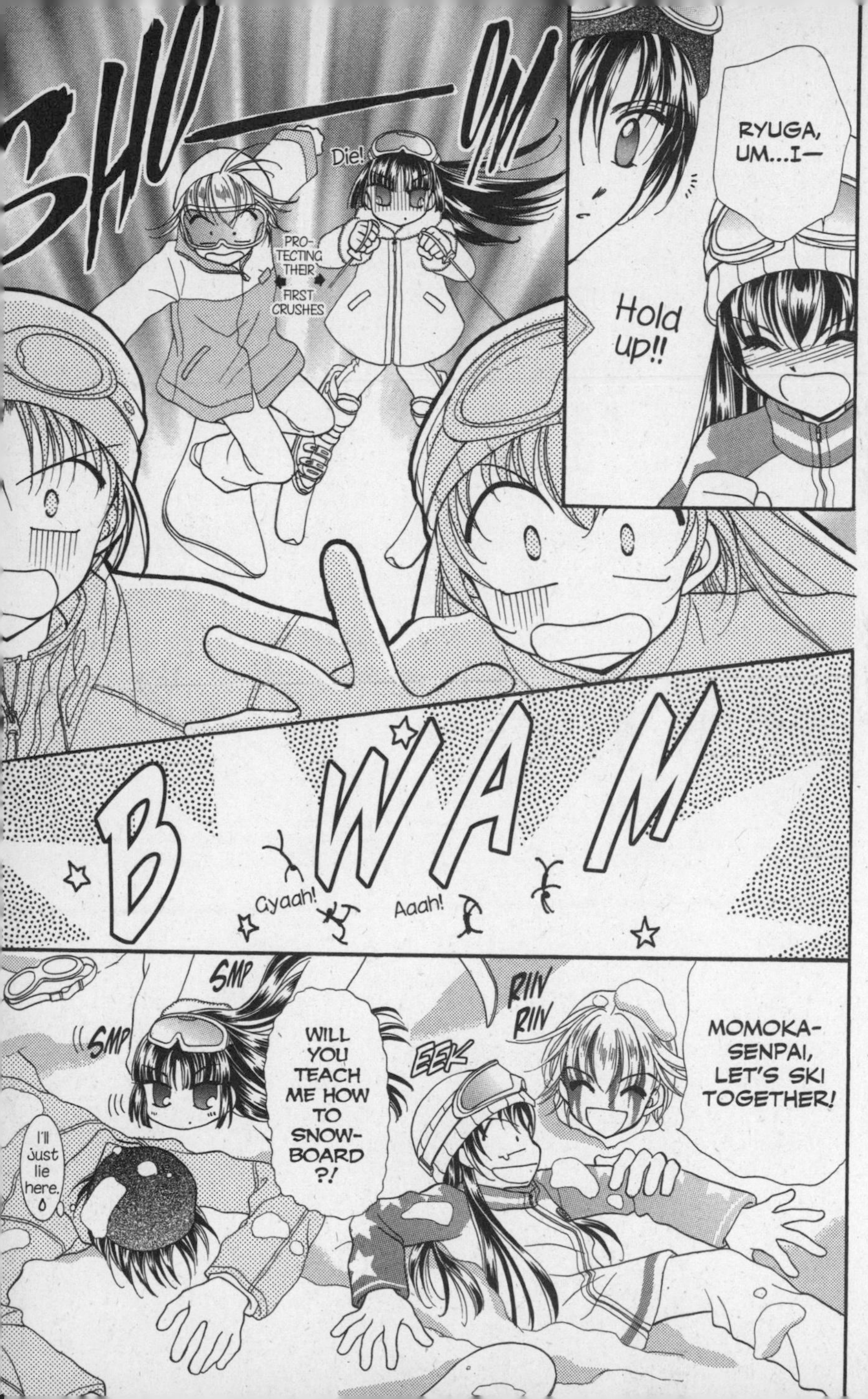
RYUGA, UM...I—
Hold up!!
SHU—OM
Die!
PRO-TECTING THEIR FIRST CRUSHES
BWAM
Aaah!
Gyaah!
MOMOKA-SENPAI, LET'S SKI TOGETHER!
RIIV RIIV
EEK
WILL YOU TEACH ME HOW TO SNOW-BOARD?!
SMP
SMP
I'll just lie here.

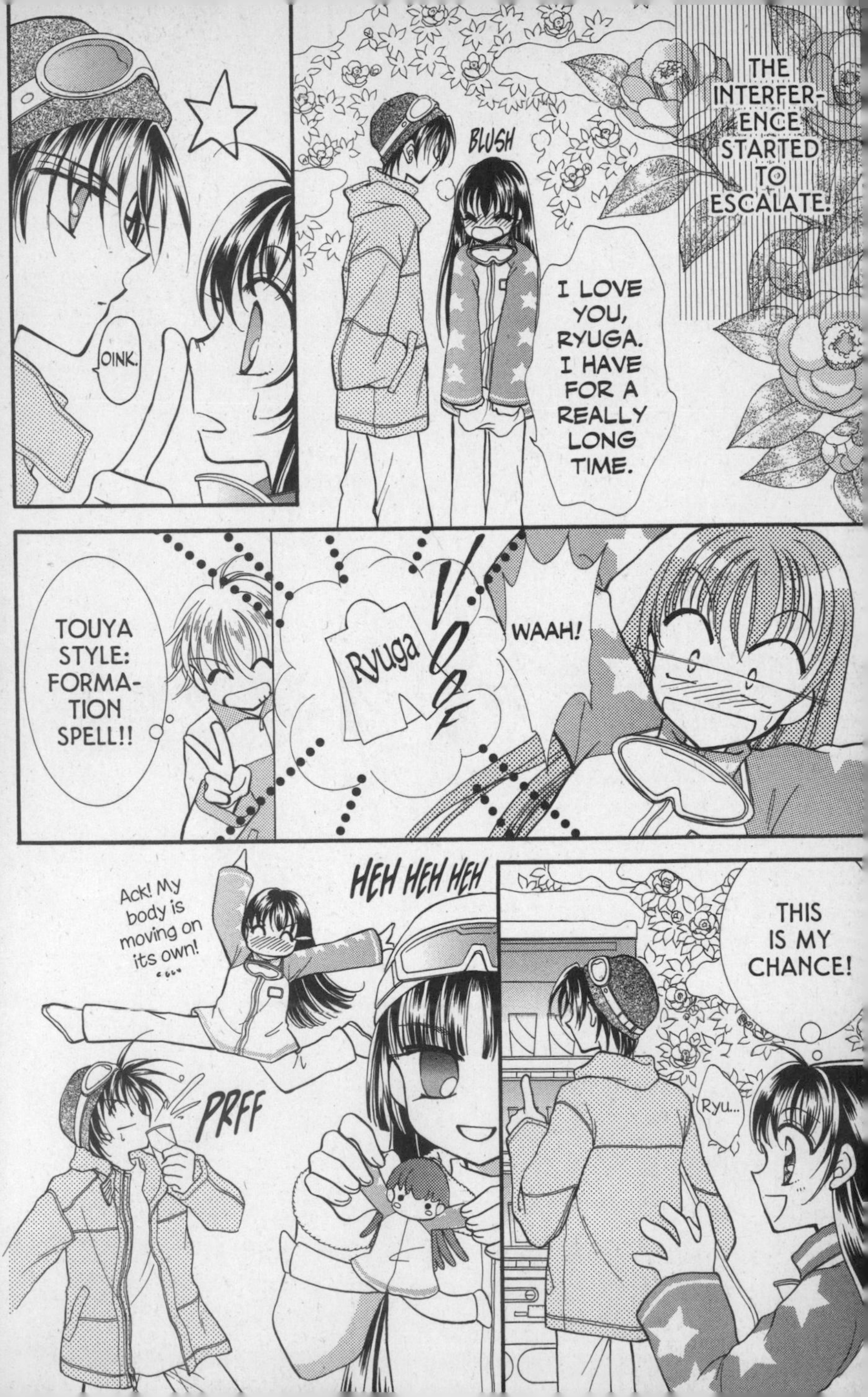
THE INTERFERENCE STARTED TO ESCALATE.
BLUSH
I LOVE YOU, RYUGA. I HAVE FOR A REALLY LONG TIME.
OINK.
WAAH!
Ryuga
TOUYA STYLE: FORMATION SPELL!!
THIS IS MY CHANCE!
Ryu...
HEH HEH HEH
Ack! My body is moving on its own!
PRFF

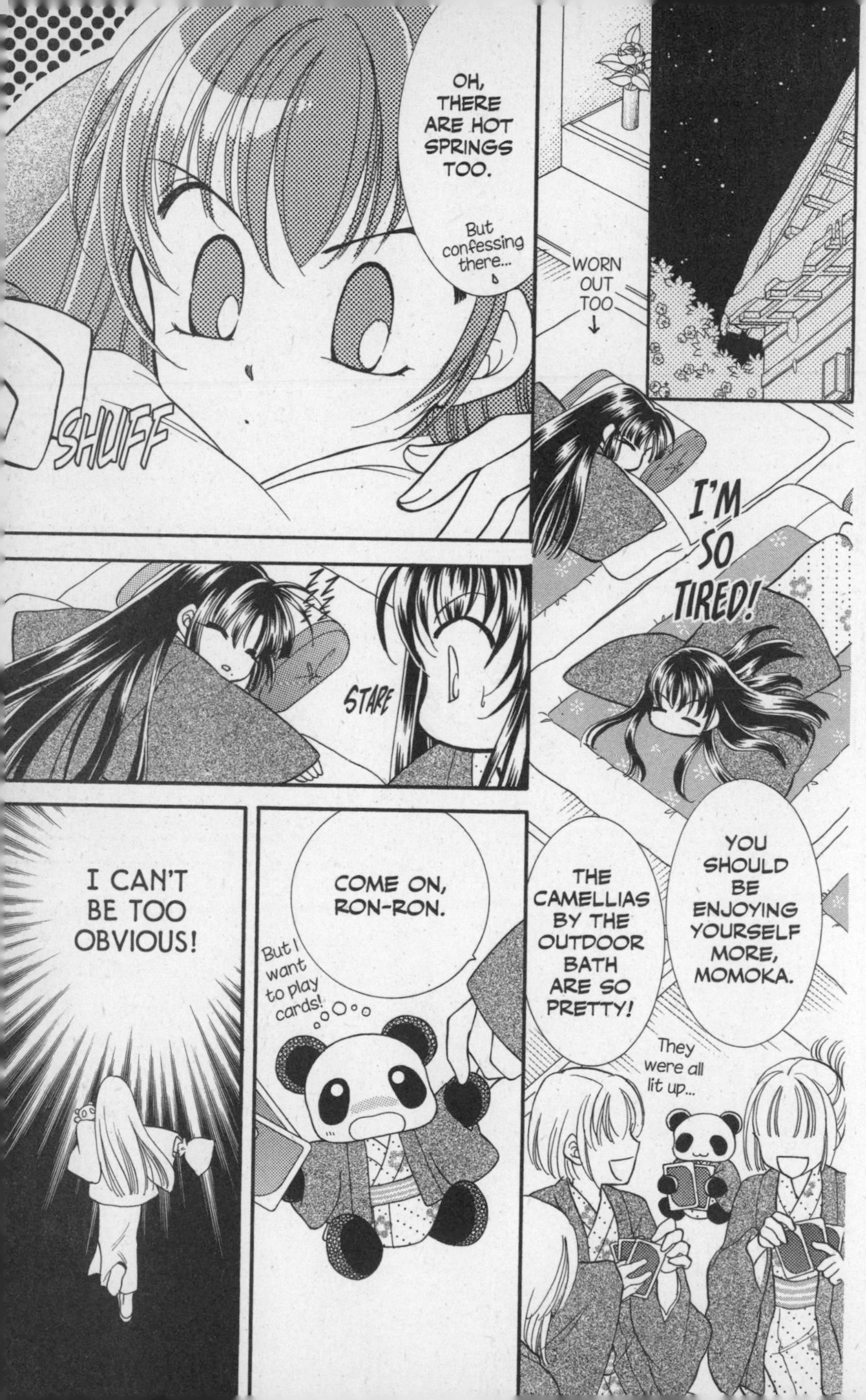
WORN OUT TOO
OH, THERE ARE HOT SPRINGS TOO.
But confessing there...
SHUFF
I'M SO TIRED!
STARE
YOU SHOULD BE ENJOYING YOURSELF MORE, MOMOKA.
THE CAMELLIAS BY THE OUTDOOR BATH ARE SO PRETTY!
They were all lit up...
COME ON, RON-RON.
But I want to play cards!
I CAN'T BE TOO OBVIOUS!

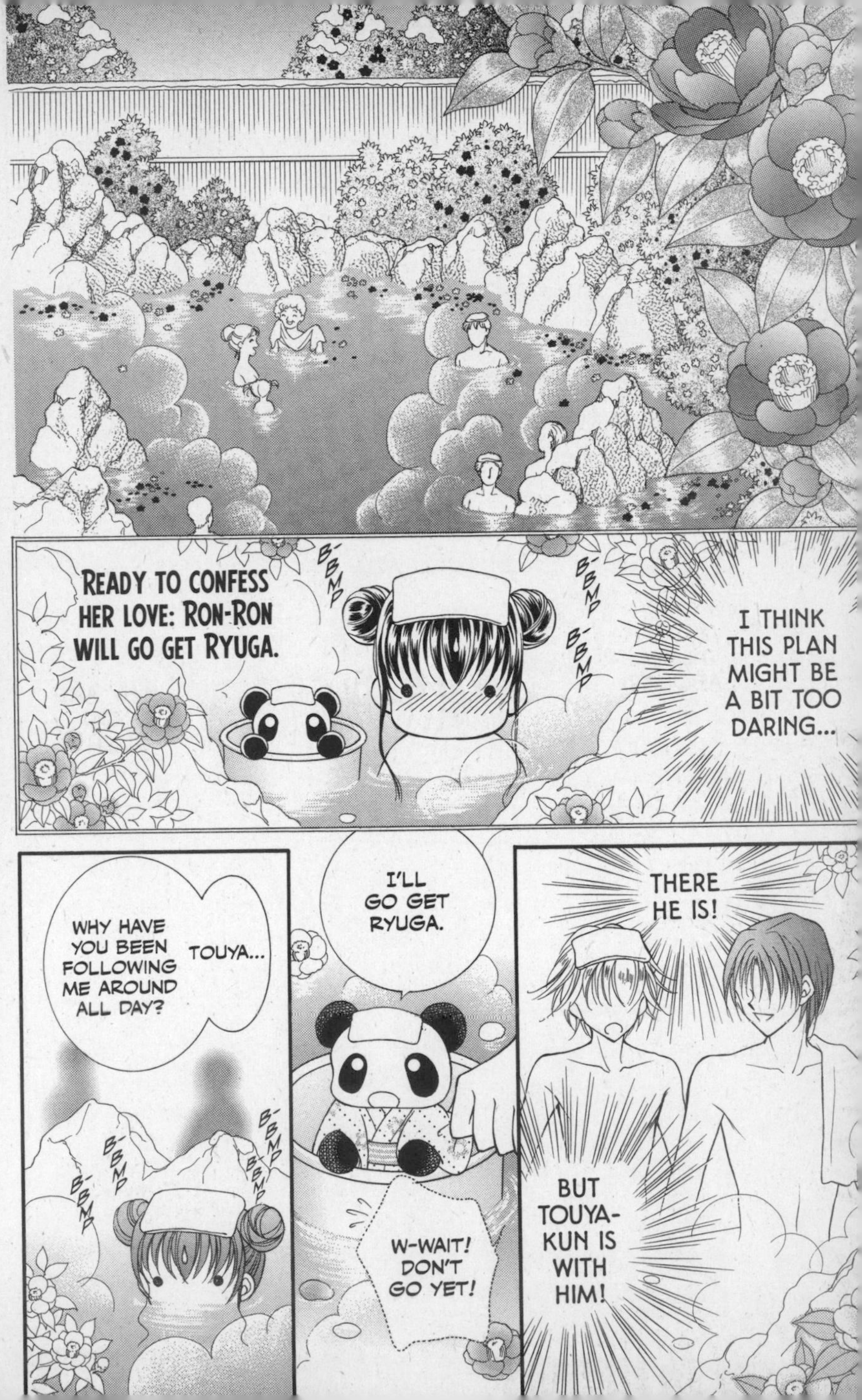
I THINK THIS PLAN MIGHT BE A BIT TOO DARING...
B-BMP B-BMP
B-BMP
READY TO CONFESS HER LOVE: RON-RON WILL GO GET RYUGA.
THERE HE IS!
BUT TOUYA-KUN IS WITH HIM!
I'LL GO GET RYUGA.
W-WAIT! DON'T GO YET!
TOUYA...
WHY HAVE YOU BEEN FOLLOWING ME AROUND ALL DAY?
B-BMP B-BMP
B-BMP

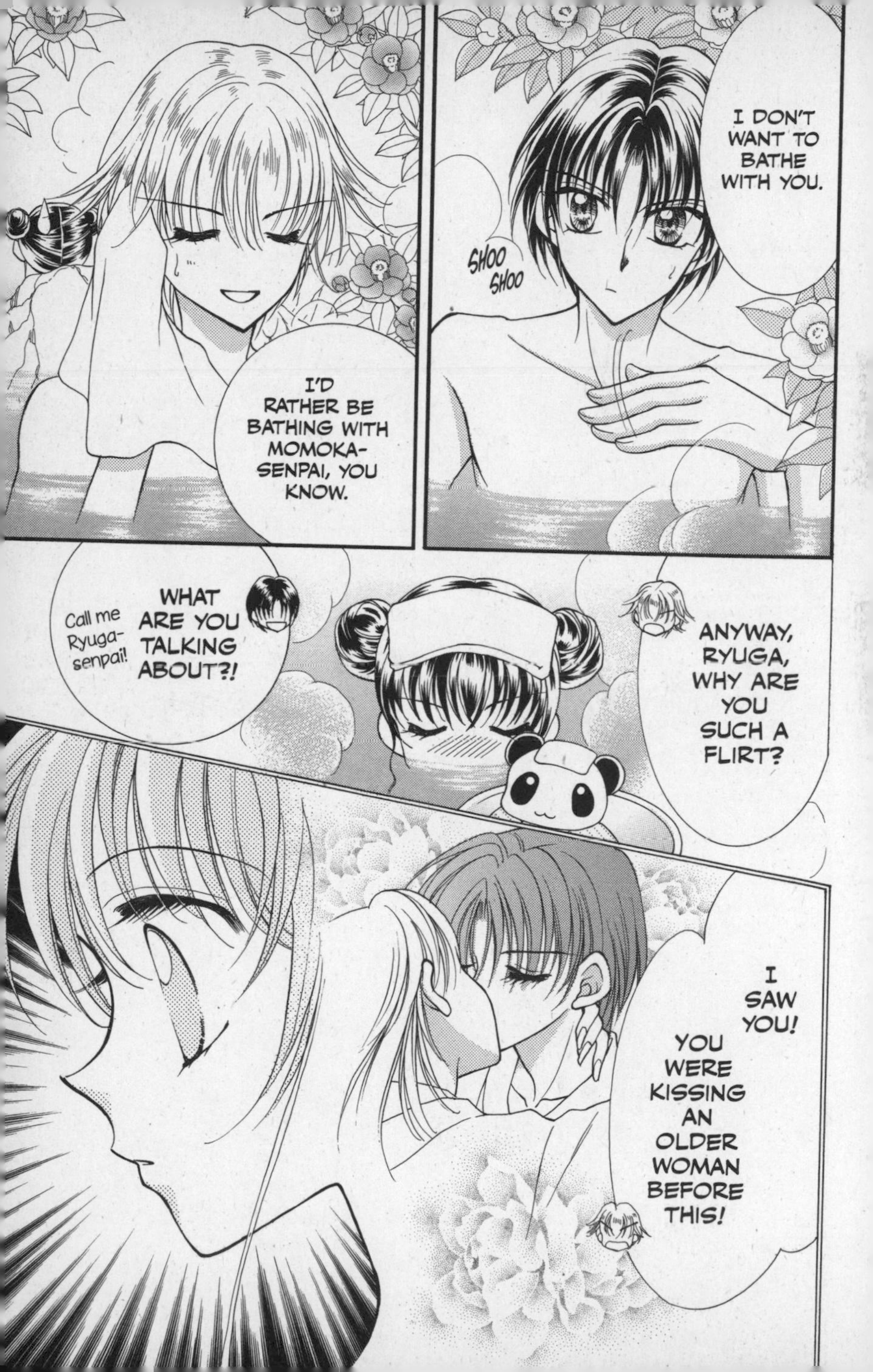
I DON'T WANT TO BATHE WITH YOU.
SHOO SHOO
I'D RATHER BE BATHING WITH MOMOKA-SENPAI, YOU KNOW.
ANYWAY, RYUGA, WHY ARE YOU SUCH A FLIRT?
WHAT ARE YOU TALKING ABOUT?!
Call me Ryuga-senpai!
I SAW YOU!
YOU WERE KISSING AN OLDER WOMAN BEFORE THIS!

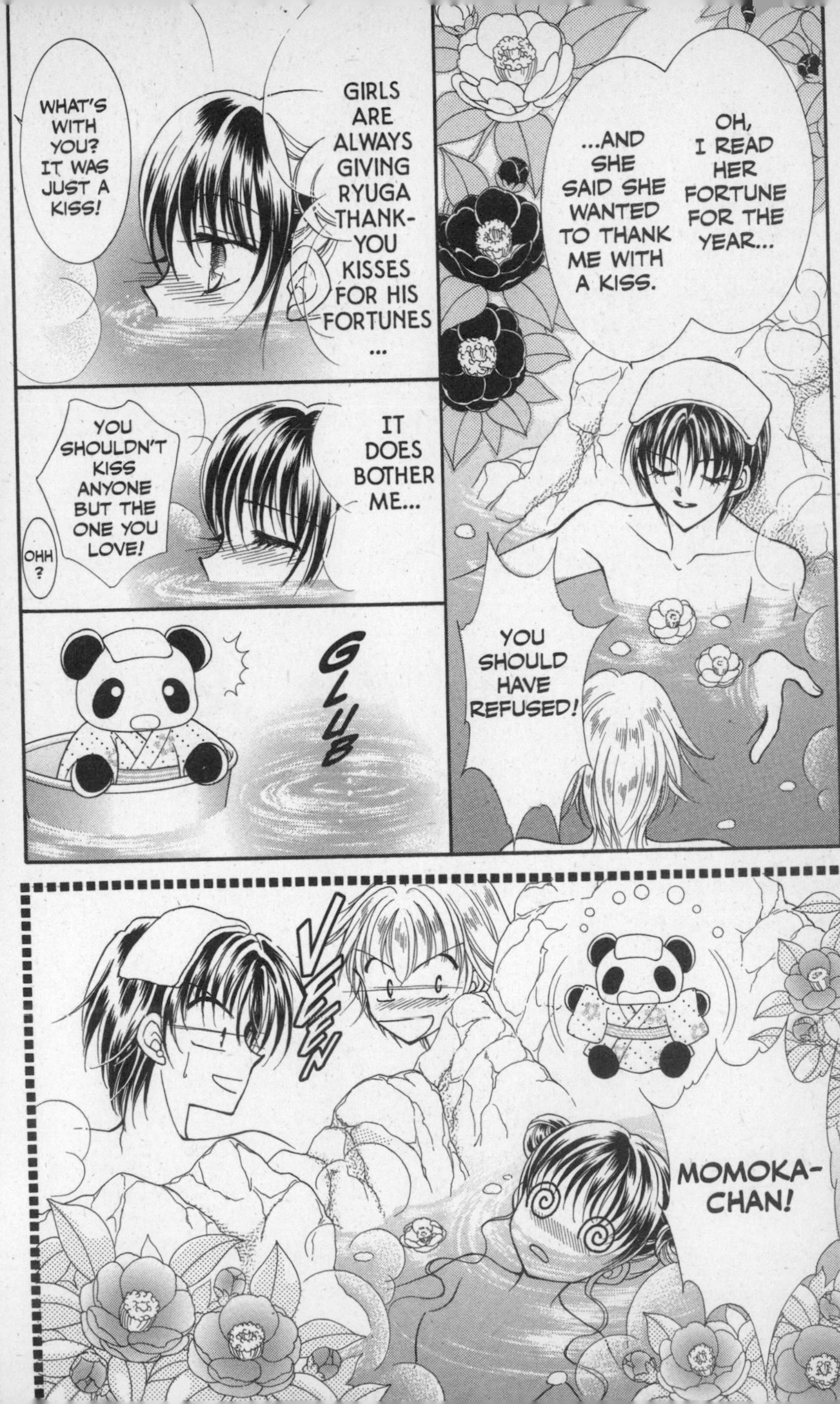
OH, I READ HER FORTUNE FOR THE YEAR...
...AND SHE SAID SHE WANTED TO THANK ME WITH A KISS.
YOU SHOULD HAVE REFUSED!
GIRLS ARE ALWAYS GIVING RYUGA THANK-YOU KISSES FOR HIS FORTUNES ...
WHAT'S WITH YOU? IT WAS JUST A KISS!
IT DOES BOTHER ME...
YOU SHOULDN'T KISS ANYONE BUT THE ONE YOU LOVE!
OHH?
GLUB
MOMOKA-CHAN!

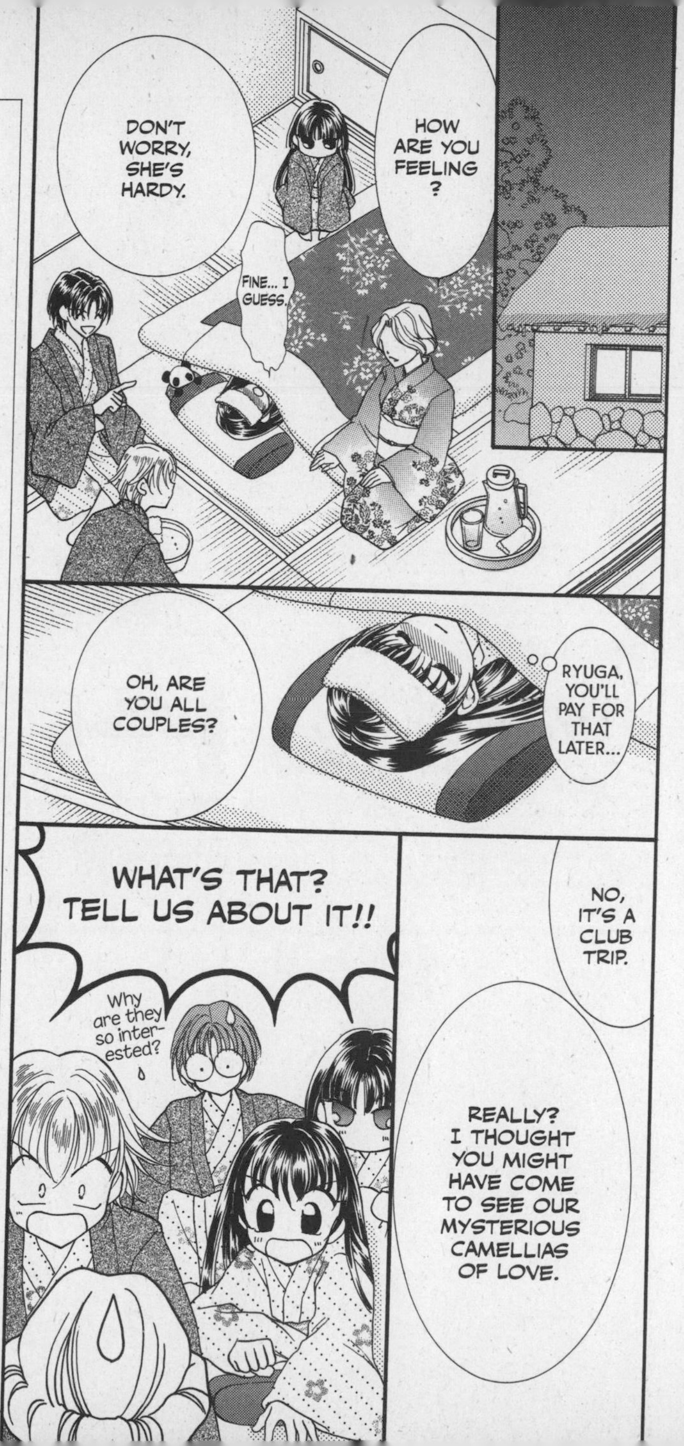
HOW ARE YOU FEELING?
FINE... I GUESS.
DON'T WORRY, SHE'S HARDY.
RYUGA, YOU'LL PAY FOR THAT LATER...
OH, ARE YOU ALL COUPLES?
NO, IT'S A CLUB TRIP.
REALLY? I THOUGHT YOU MIGHT HAVE COME TO SEE OUR MYSTERIOUS CAMELLIAS OF LOVE.
WHAT'S THAT? TELL US ABOUT IT!!
Why are they so interested?

10

I wonder if it was a dumb question. At least Yazawa-sensei answered it very politely, and I was really impressed.

I have really enjoyed being a contributor, but this time I was a "sensei."

No matter who comes to the screening, I hope all the contributors will try their best!

I know it's depressing when you've worked so hard on manga but haven't debuted yet.

But don't give up! Give your all to every piece you draw—you'll grow as an artist, and the editors will definitely notice!

Aim for the stars! Aim for *Ribon*!

That's a *Ribon* star!

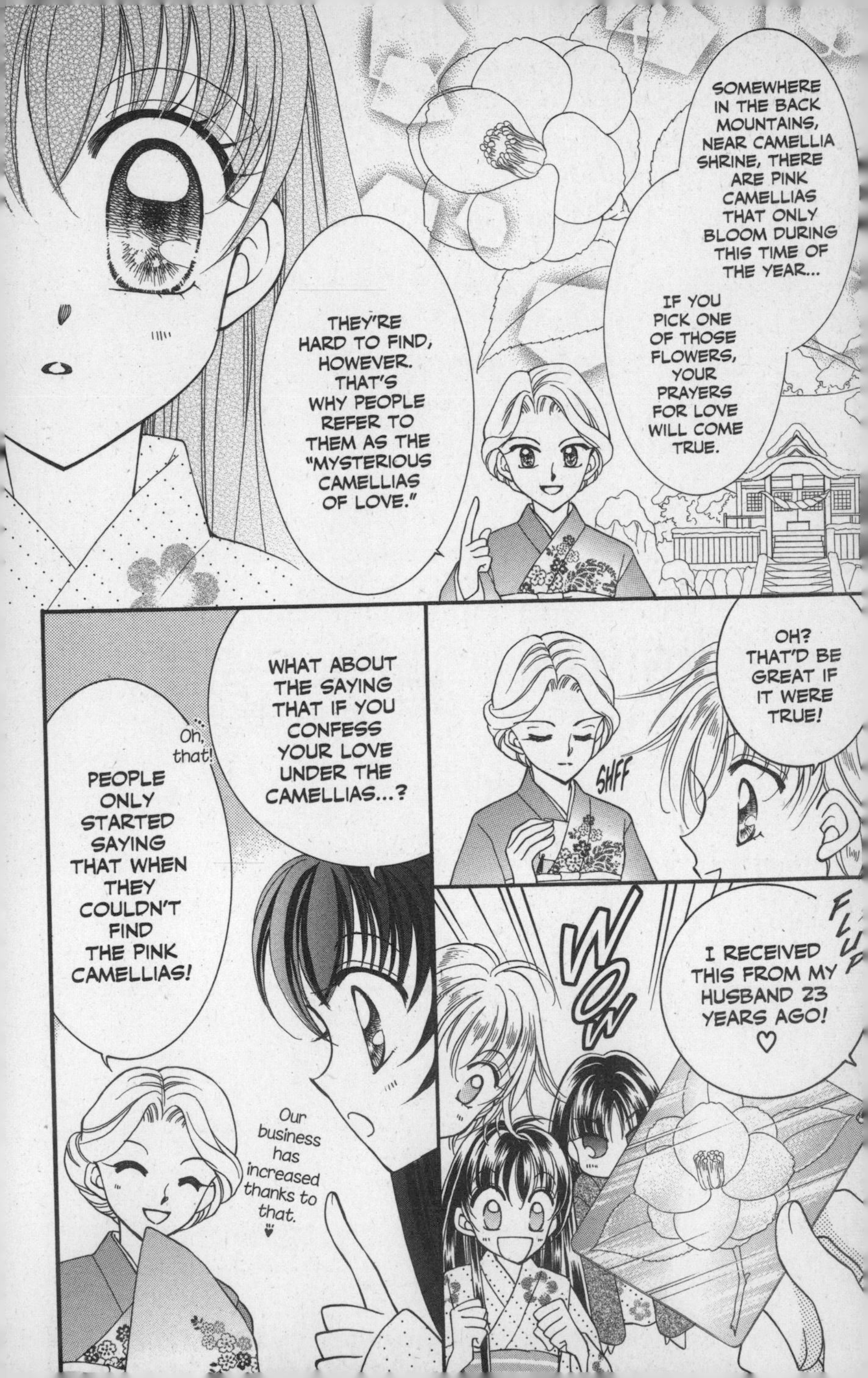
SOMEWHERE IN THE BACK MOUNTAINS, NEAR CAMELLIA SHRINE, THERE ARE PINK CAMELLIAS THAT ONLY BLOOM DURING THIS TIME OF THE YEAR...
IF YOU PICK ONE OF THOSE FLOWERS, YOUR PRAYERS FOR LOVE WILL COME TRUE.
THEY'RE HARD TO FIND, HOWEVER. THAT'S WHY PEOPLE REFER TO THEM AS THE "MYSTERIOUS CAMELLIAS OF LOVE."
OH? THAT'D BE GREAT IF IT WERE TRUE!
SHFF
FLUP
WOW
I RECEIVED THIS FROM MY HUSBAND 23 YEARS AGO! ♡
WHAT ABOUT THE SAYING THAT IF YOU CONFESS YOUR LOVE UNDER THE CAMELLIAS...?
Oh, that!
PEOPLE ONLY STARTED SAYING THAT WHEN THEY COULDN'T FIND THE PINK CAMELLIAS!
Our business has increased thanks to that.

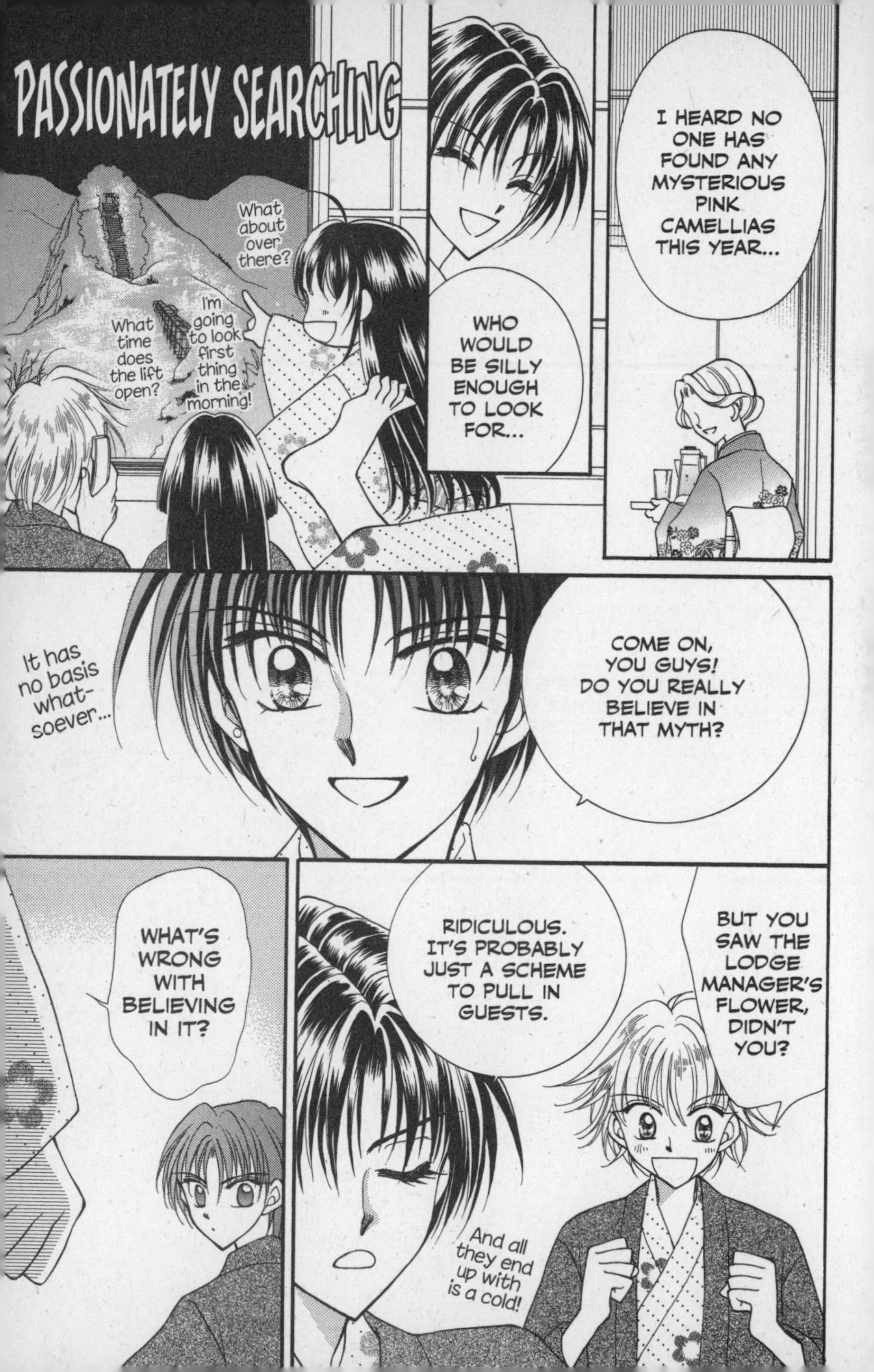
PASSIONATELY SEARCHING
I HEARD NO ONE HAS FOUND ANY MYSTERIOUS PINK CAMELLIAS THIS YEAR...
WHO WOULD BE SILLY ENOUGH TO LOOK FOR...
What about over there?
I'm going to look first thing in the morning!
What time does the lift open?
COME ON, YOU GUYS! DO YOU REALLY BELIEVE IN THAT MYTH?
It has no basis whatsoever...
BUT YOU SAW THE LODGE MANAGER'S FLOWER, DIDN'T YOU?
RIDICULOUS. IT'S PROBABLY JUST A SCHEME TO PULL IN GUESTS.
And all they end up with is a cold!
WHAT'S WRONG WITH BELIEVING IN IT?

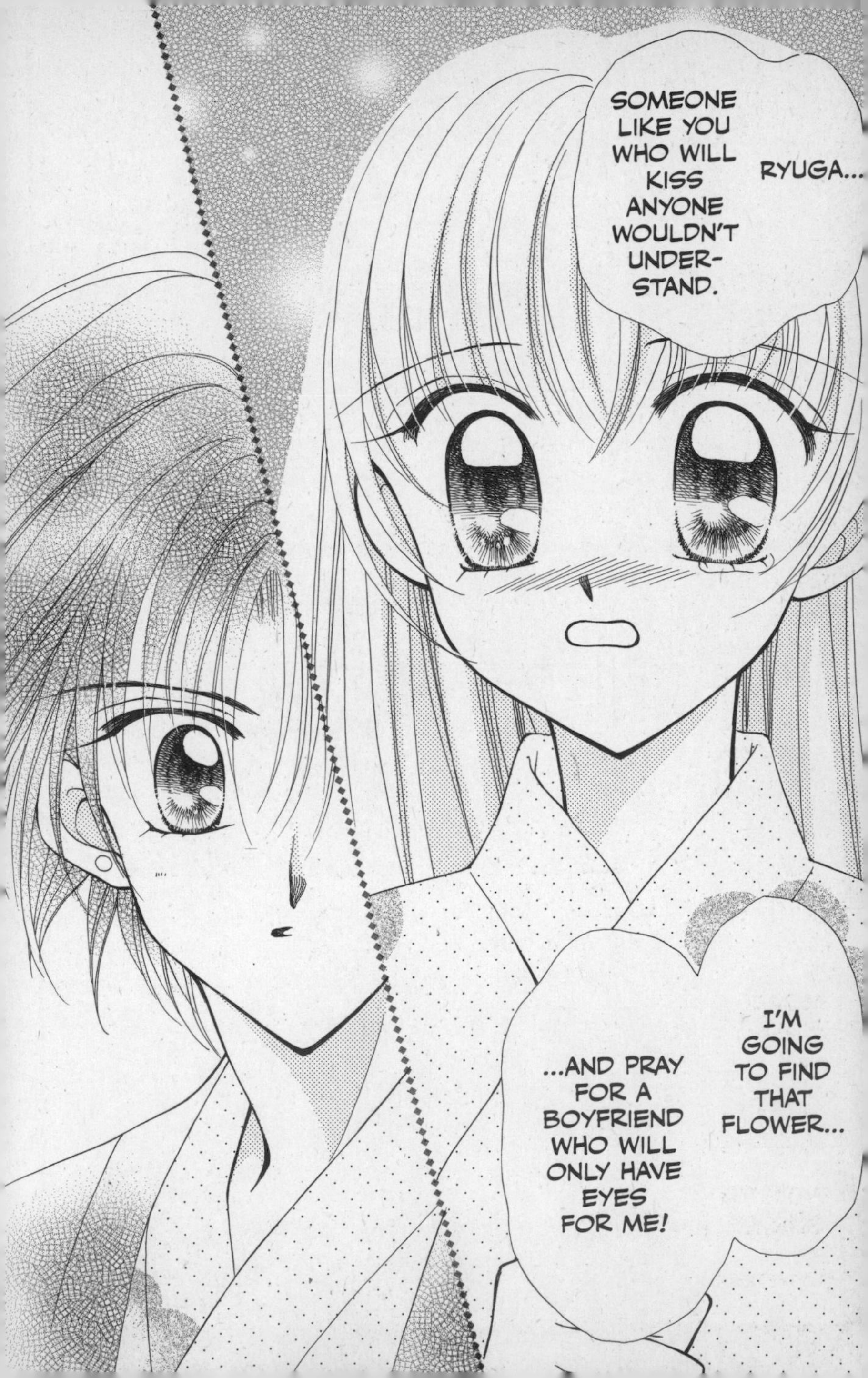
RYUGA...
SOMEONE LIKE YOU WHO WILL KISS ANYONE WOULDN'T UNDER-STAND.
I'M GOING TO FIND THAT FLOWER...
...AND PRAY FOR A BOYFRIEND WHO WILL ONLY HAVE EYES FOR ME!

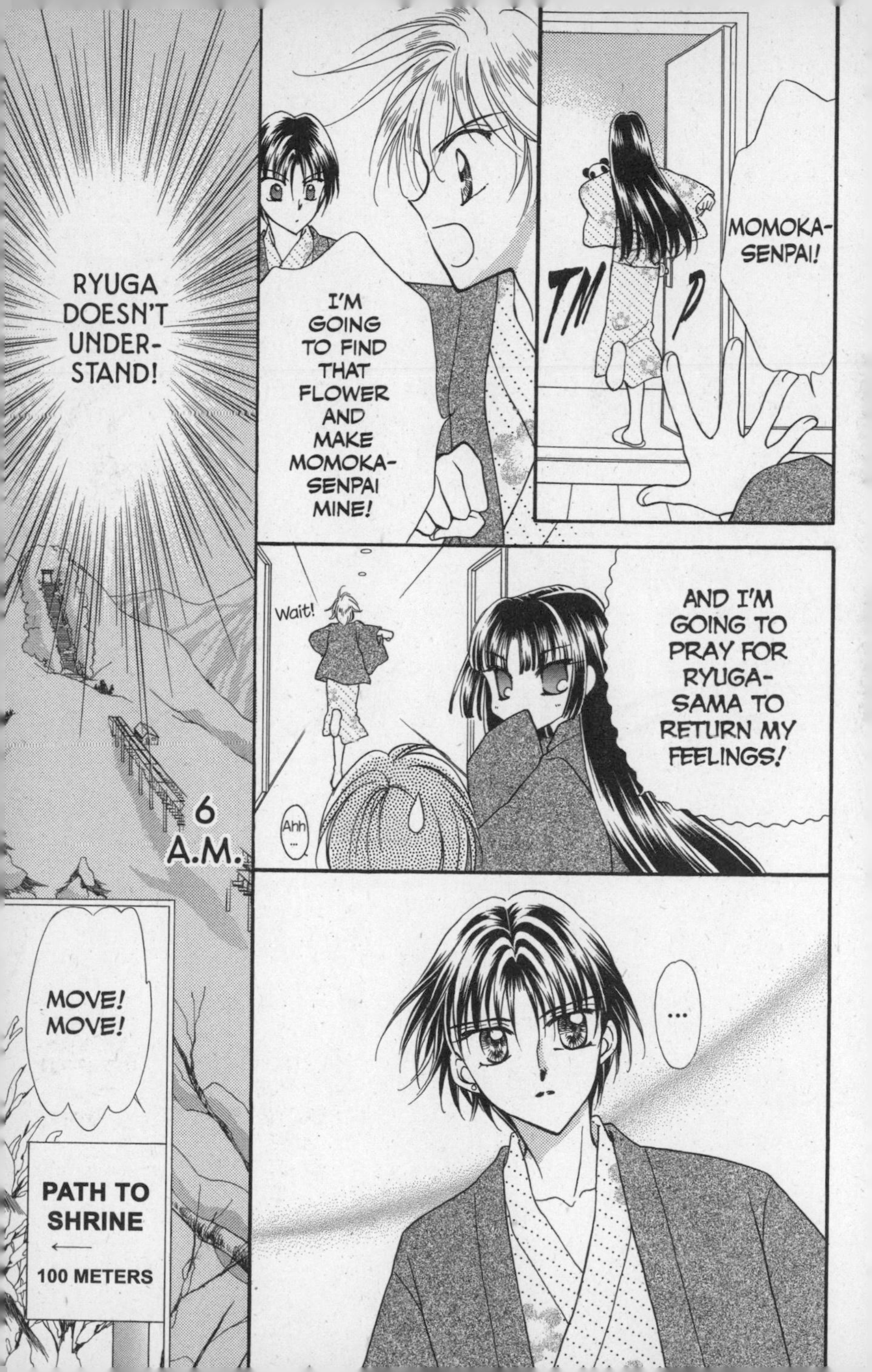

MOMOKA-SENPAI!
TMP
I'M GOING TO FIND THAT FLOWER AND MAKE MOMOKA-SENPAI MINE!
AND I'M GOING TO PRAY FOR RYUGA-SAMA TO RETURN MY FEELINGS!
Wait!
Ahh...
...
RYUGA DOESN'T UNDER-STAND!
6 A.M.
MOVE! MOVE!
PATH TO SHRINE
←
100 METERS

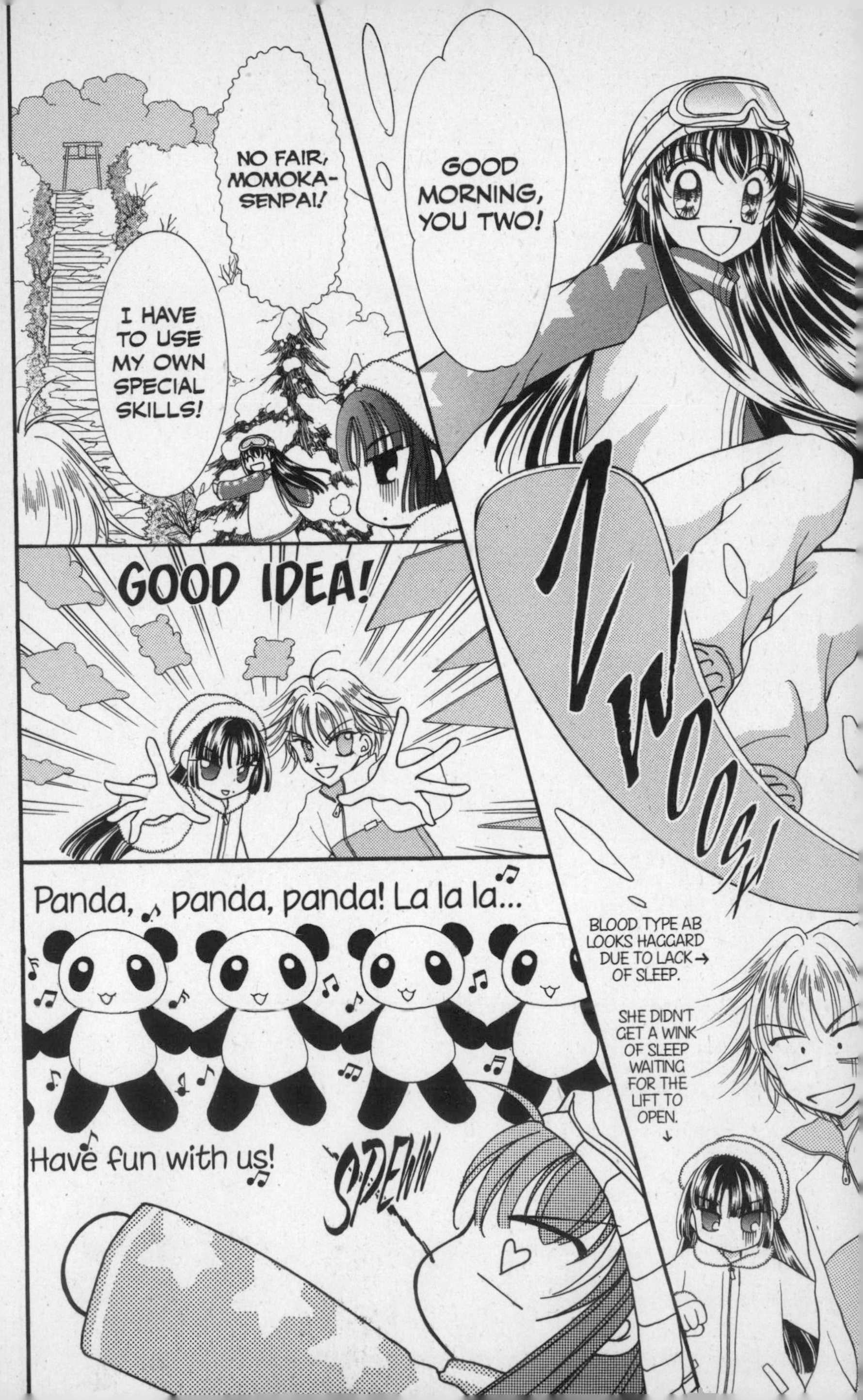
GOOD MORNING, YOU TWO!
WHOOSH
NO FAIR, MOMOKA-SENPAI!
I HAVE TO USE MY OWN SPECIAL SKILLS!
GOOD IDEA!
BLOOD TYPE AB LOOKS HAGGARD DUE TO LACK OF SLEEP. →
SHE DIDN'T GET A WINK OF SLEEP WAITING FOR THE LIFT TO OPEN. ↓
Panda, panda, panda! La la la...
Have fun with us!

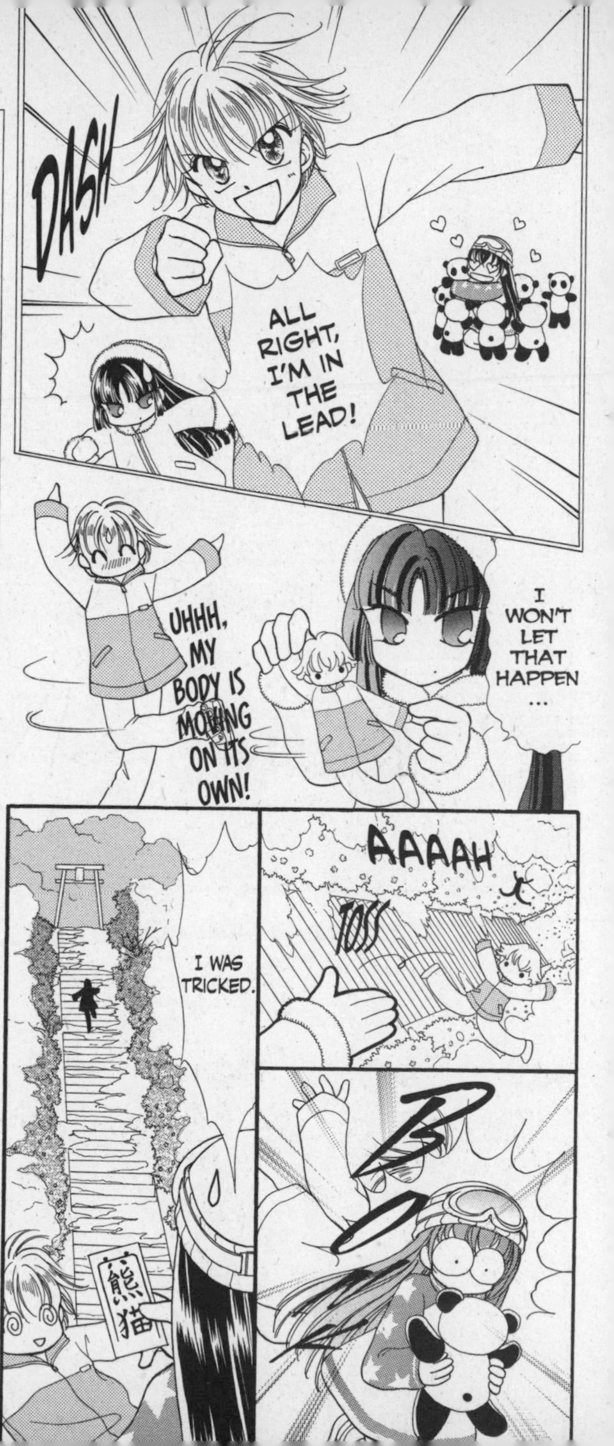
DASH
ALL RIGHT, I'M IN THE LEAD!
I WON'T LET THAT HAPPEN...
UHHH, MY BODY IS MOVING ON ITS OWN!
AAAAH
TOSS
I WAS TRICKED.
熊猫

11

I couldn't think of the "Love Camellia" name for a while, and on top of that, I had to draw a lodge, hot springs, and camellias! It took up a lot of time.

I usually don't pull an all-nighter before my deadlines. (At any rate, I can't do them!) This time, however, I really didn't sleep at all. Even when the assistants came, I was still nervous!

A snowy mountain and hot springs were new locations for *St. ♥ Dragon Girl*, so it was refreshing!

I had planned to have a camellia fairy or something similar appear, but the story became too complicated. Instead, it ended up as a story about love and fortunes.

Well, as long as you feel like going on a trip to a hot springs after reading this story, I'm satisfied.

Everyone thought Ron-Ron was really cute ♥ in his yukata in this chapter. Someone asked if Momoka made it. But no, she didn't! Panda King can still use magic, so he conjured it up himself! The magic words were "Lovely Ron-Ron Metamorphosis!" When you want to dress up, try it out! (Just kidding!)

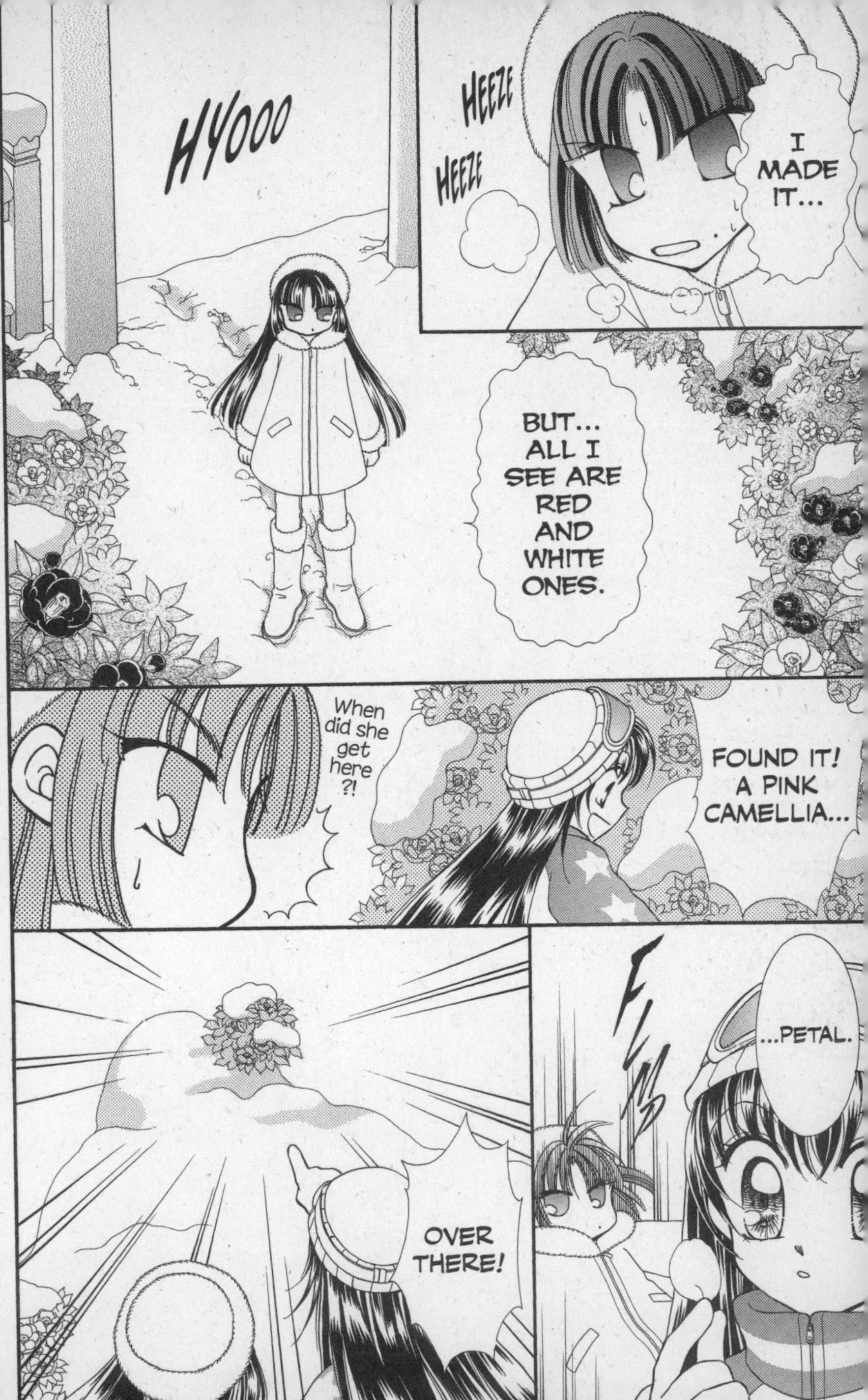
HEEZE
HEEZE
I MADE IT...
BUT... ALL I SEE ARE RED AND WHITE ONES.
HYOOO
FOUND IT! A PINK CAMELLIA...
When did she get here?!
FLING
...PETAL.
OVER THERE!

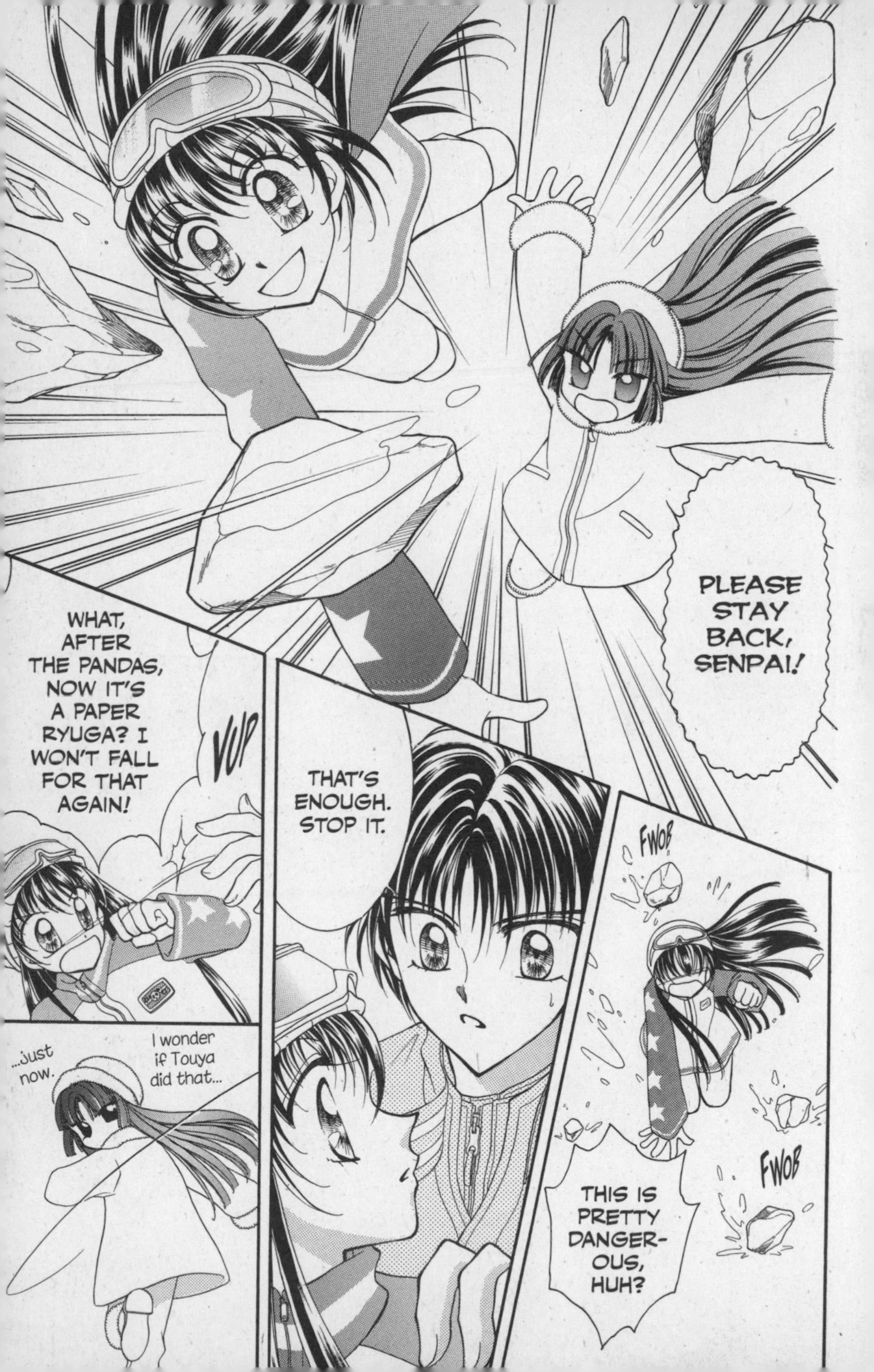
PLEASE STAY BACK, SENPAI!
FWOB
FWOB
THIS IS PRETTY DANGER-OUS, HUH?
THAT'S ENOUGH. STOP IT.
WHAT, AFTER THE PANDAS, NOW IT'S A PAPER RYUGA? I WON'T FALL FOR THAT AGAIN!
VUP
I wonder if Touya did that...
...just now.

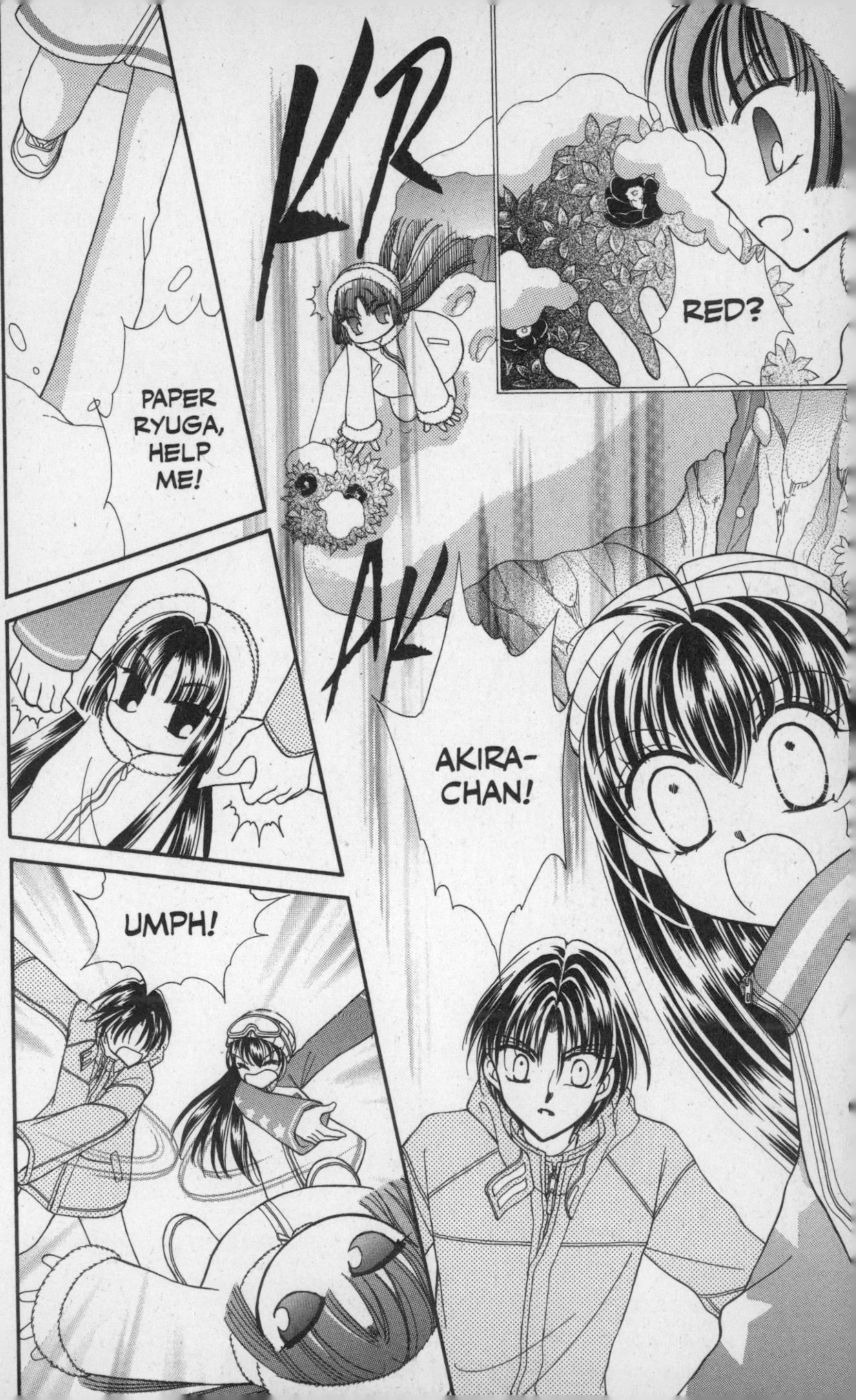
RED?
KRAK
AKIRA-CHAN!
PAPER RYUGA, HELP ME!
UMPH!

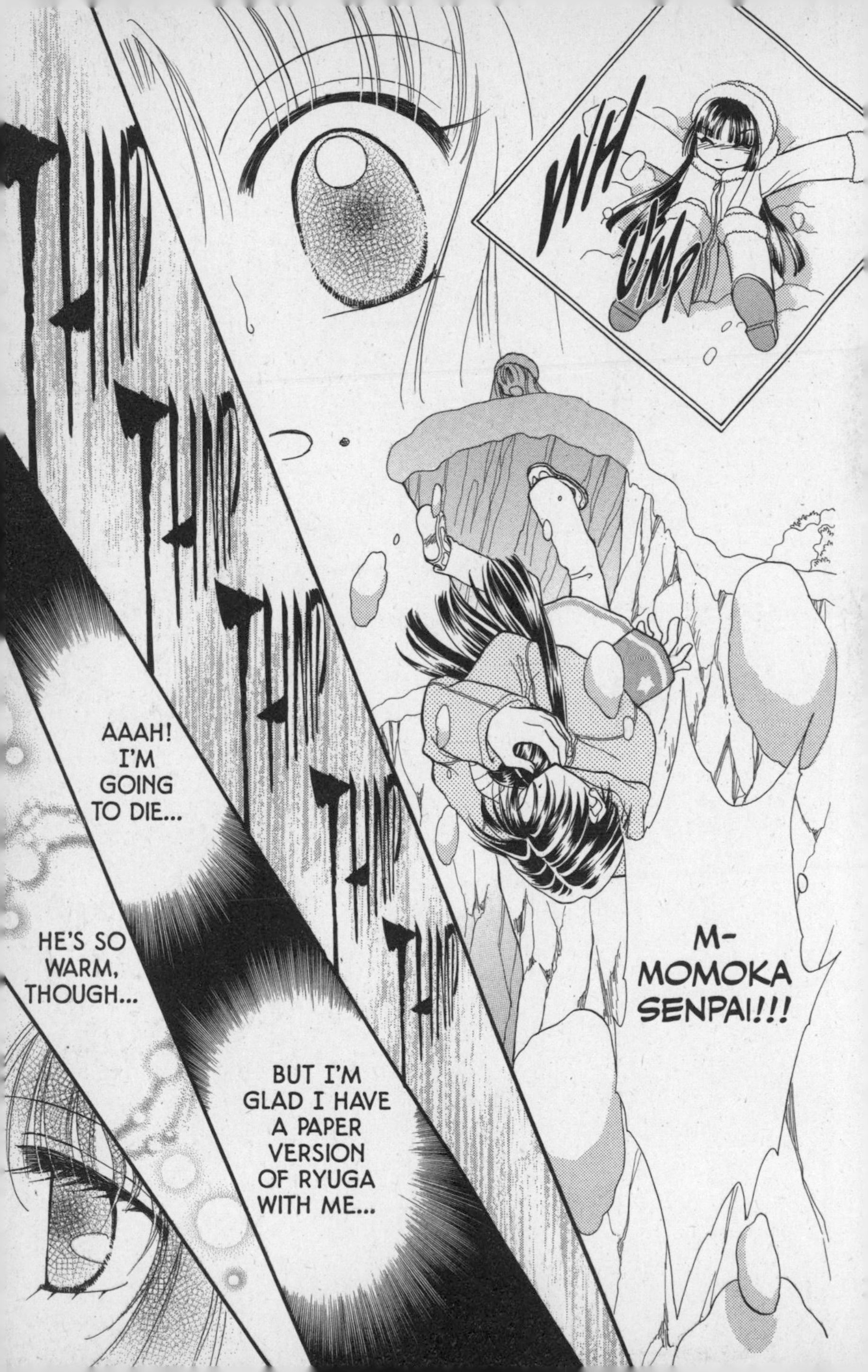
WHUMP
M-MOMOKA SENPAI!!!
THUMP THUMP THUMP THUMP THUMP
AAAH! I'M GOING TO DIE...
HE'S SO WARM, THOUGH...
BUT I'M GLAD I HAVE A PAPER VERSION OF RYUGA WITH ME...

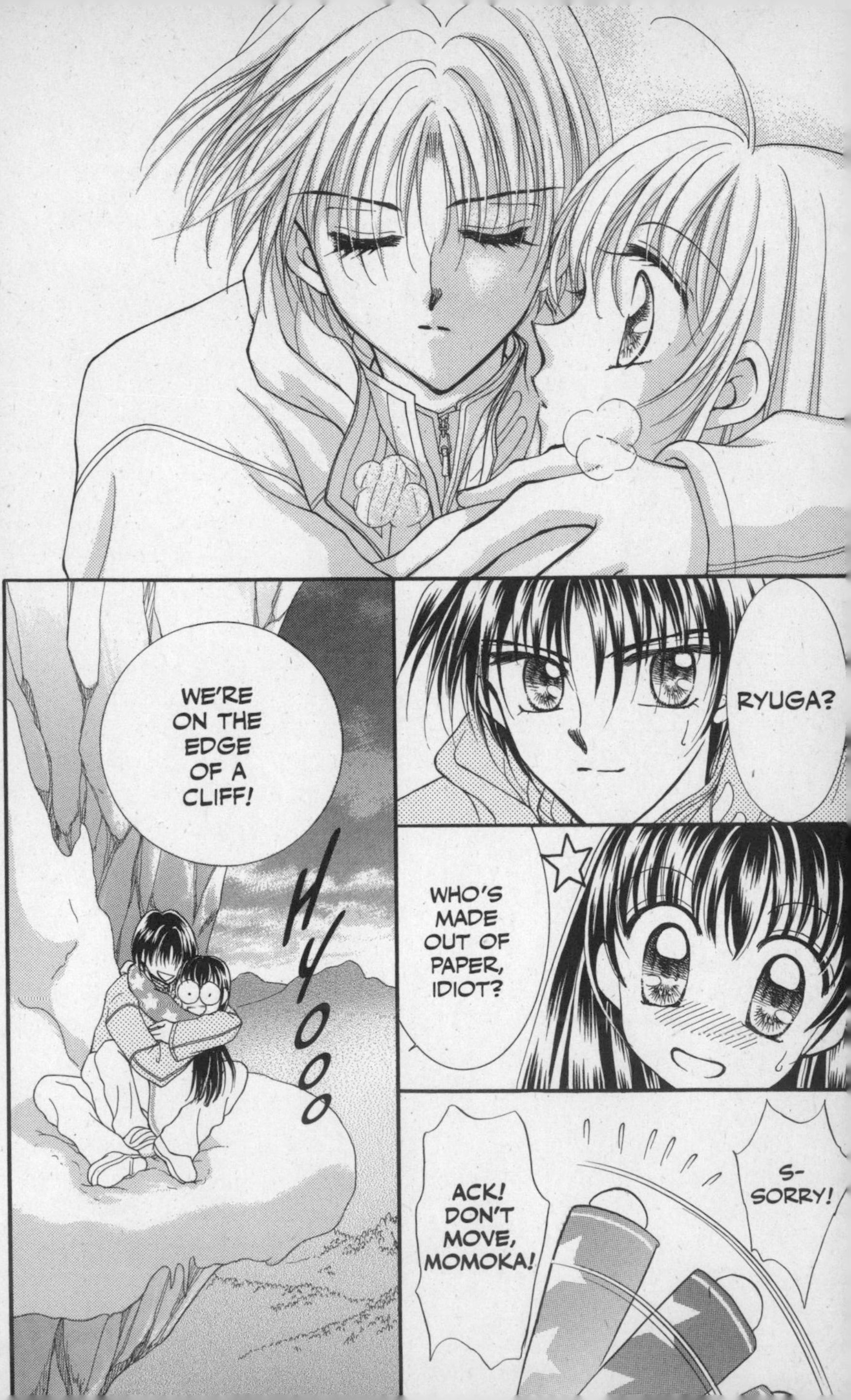
RYUGA?
WHO'S MADE OUT OF PAPER, IDIOT?
S-SORRY!
ACK! DON'T MOVE, MOMOKA!
WE'RE ON THE EDGE OF A CLIFF!
HYUOOO

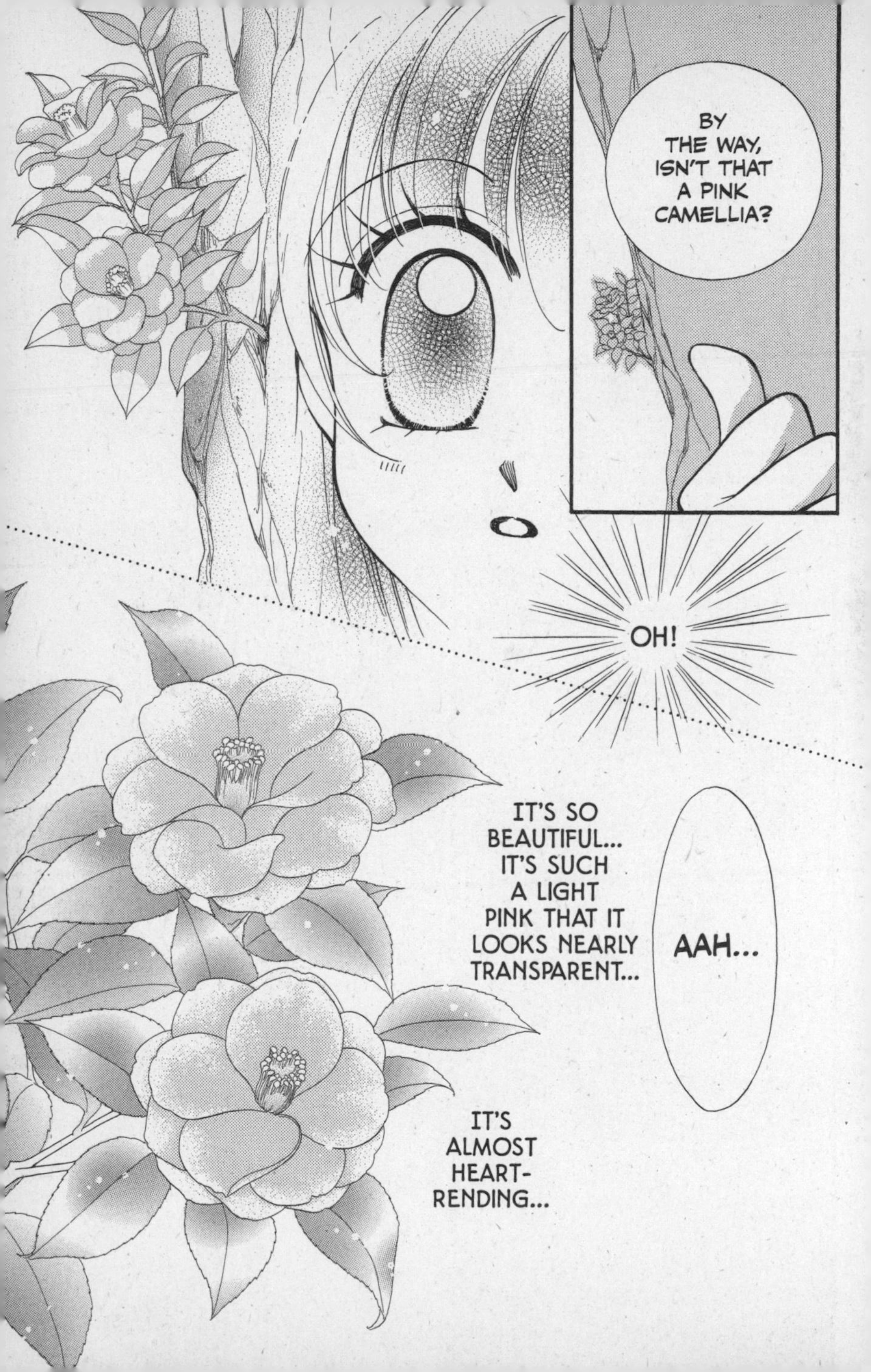
BY THE WAY, ISN'T THAT A PINK CAMELLIA?
OH!
AAH...
IT'S SO BEAUTIFUL... IT'S SUCH A LIGHT PINK THAT IT LOOKS NEARLY TRANSPARENT...
IT'S ALMOST HEART-RENDING...

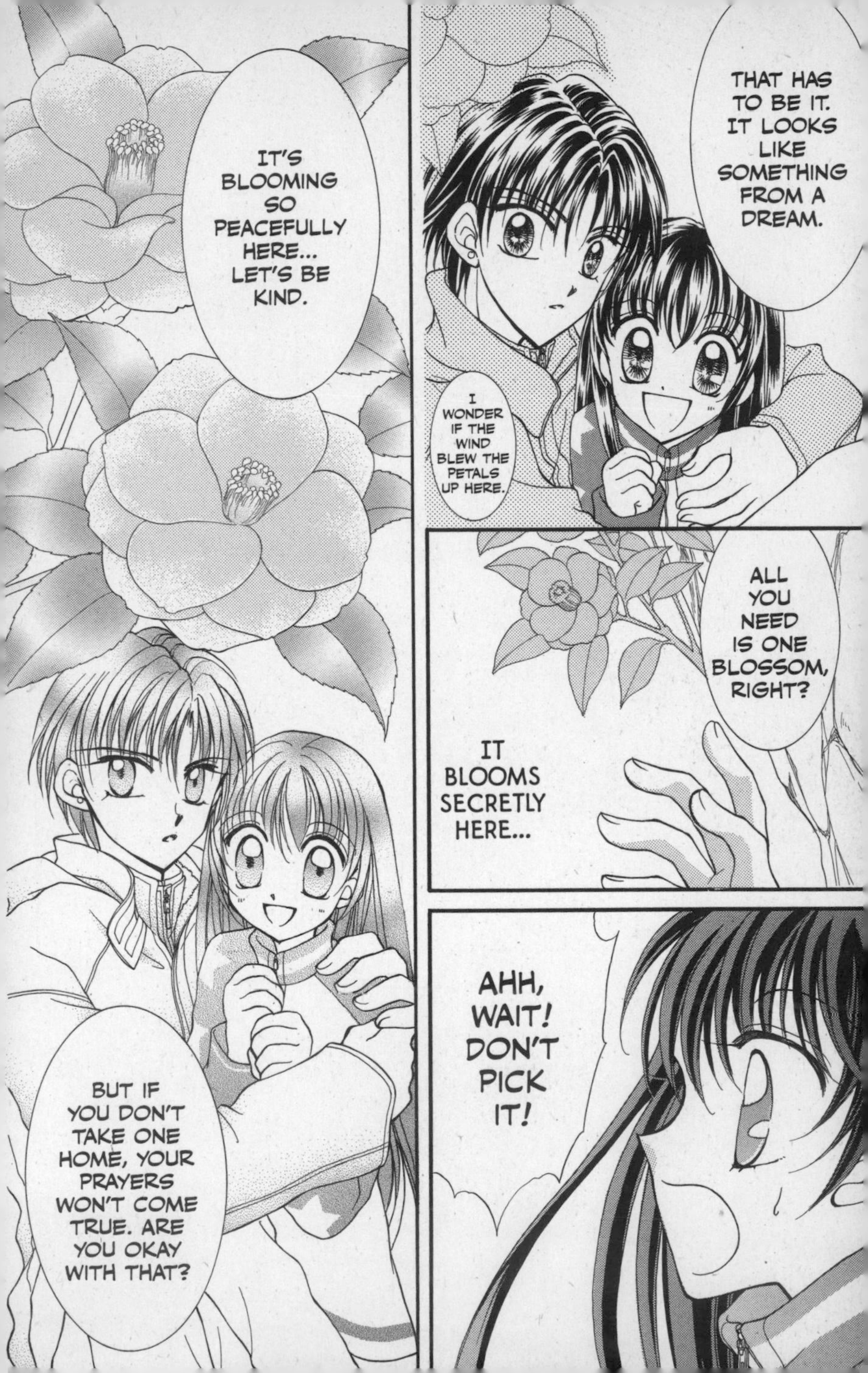
THAT HAS TO BE IT. IT LOOKS LIKE SOMETHING FROM A DREAM.
I WONDER IF THE WIND BLEW THE PETALS UP HERE.
ALL YOU NEED IS ONE BLOSSOM, RIGHT?
IT BLOOMS SECRETLY HERE...
AHH, WAIT! DON'T PICK IT!
IT'S BLOOMING SO PEACEFULLY HERE... LET'S BE KIND.
BUT IF YOU DON'T TAKE ONE HOME, YOUR PRAYERS WON'T COME TRUE. ARE YOU OKAY WITH THAT?

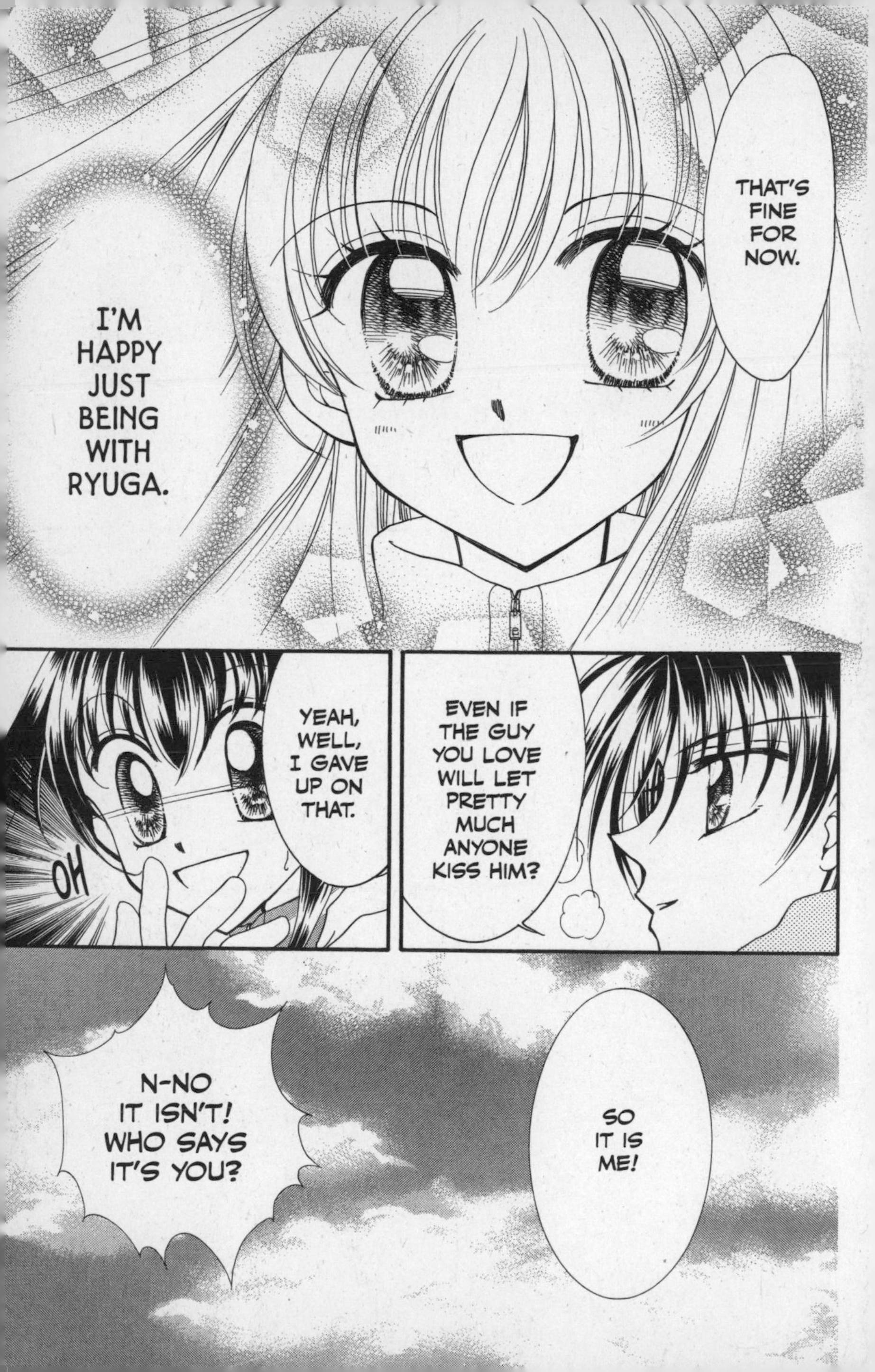
THAT'S FINE FOR NOW.
I'M HAPPY JUST BEING WITH RYUGA.
EVEN IF THE GUY YOU LOVE WILL LET PRETTY MUCH ANYONE KISS HIM?
YEAH, WELL, I GAVE UP ON THAT.
OH
SO IT IS ME!
N-NO IT ISN'T! WHO SAYS IT'S YOU?

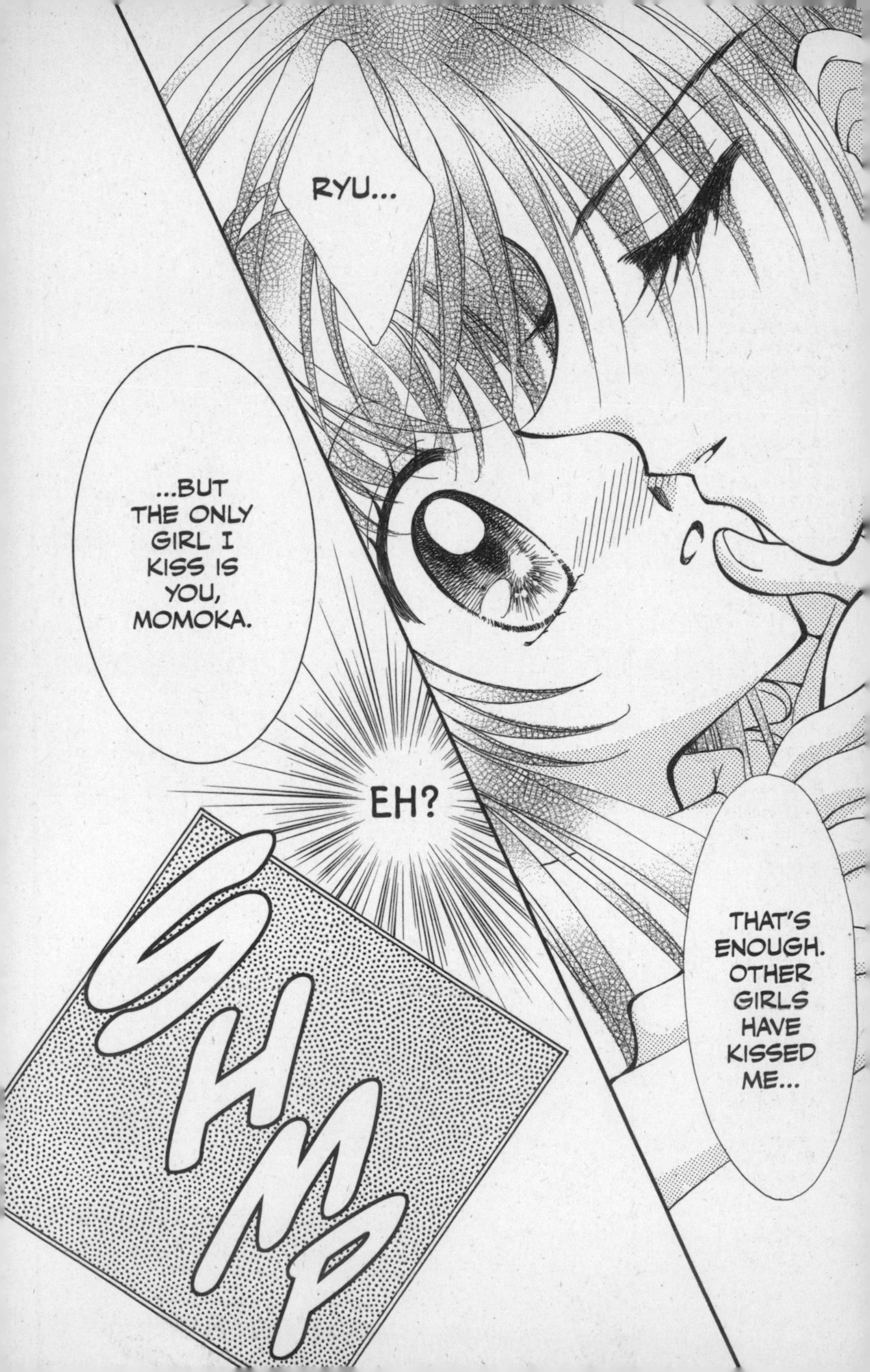
RYU...
THAT'S ENOUGH. OTHER GIRLS HAVE KISSED ME...
...BUT THE ONLY GIRL I KISS IS YOU, MOMOKA.
EH?

12

This is the last sidebar. I'm going off on a tangent, but "The Seven Mysteries of the School Special" appeared in a special summer issue of *Ribon*.

Everyone was so energetic when they were in the first grade! (laugh) Ryuga and Shunran had just come to Japan, and Shunran's Japanese wasn't very good yet. I wonder if Master taught Ryuga?

I always get requests to draw the time Ryuga and Momoka first met. If I have a chance, I will!

If you want to read other stories about them or see any specific demons, let me know!

Thanks for reading up until this point! Please enjoy the bonus story. I'll see you again in volume 6!

SPECIAL THANKS

Kotaka-san
Hiromasa-san
Sasaki-san
Masako-san
Hajime-san
Sanjouba-san
Matsuo-san
Kikue-san
Yukari-san

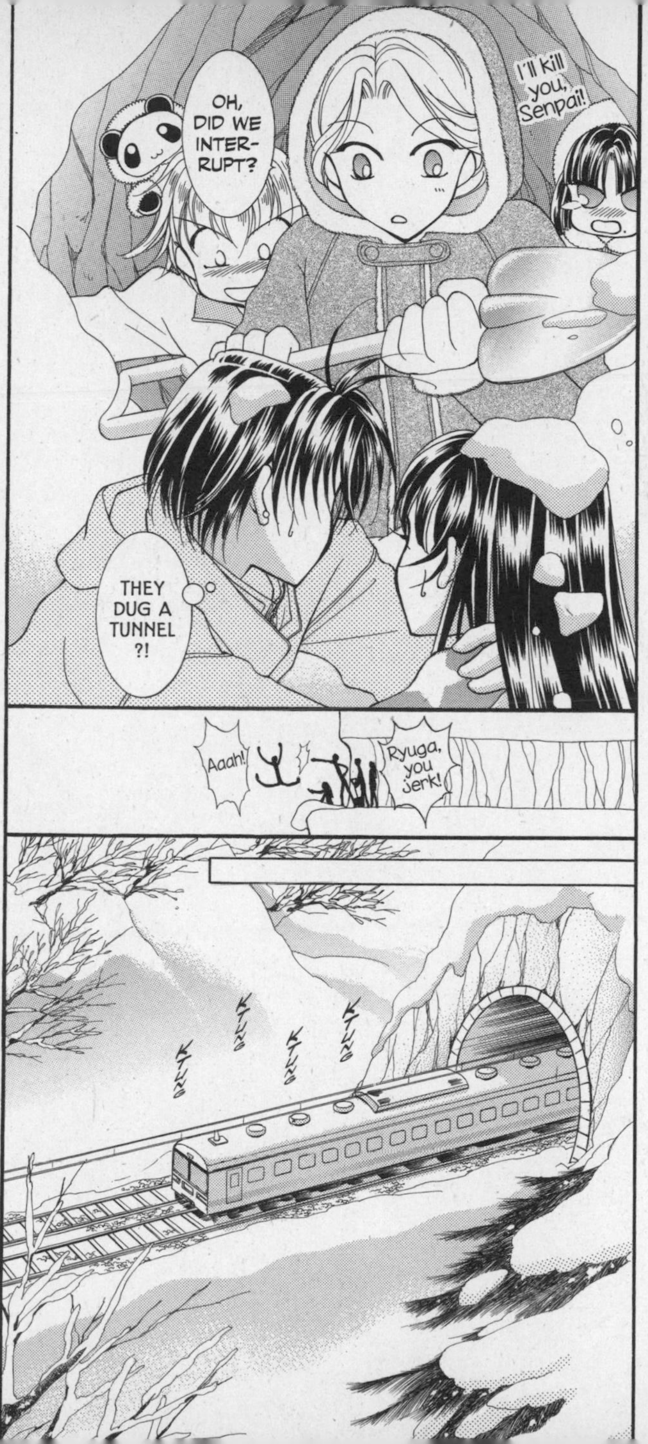
I'll kill you, Senpai!
OH, DID WE INTERRUPT?
THEY DUG A TUNNEL?!
Ryuga, you jerk!
Aaah!
KTUNG
KTUNG
KTUNG
KTUNG

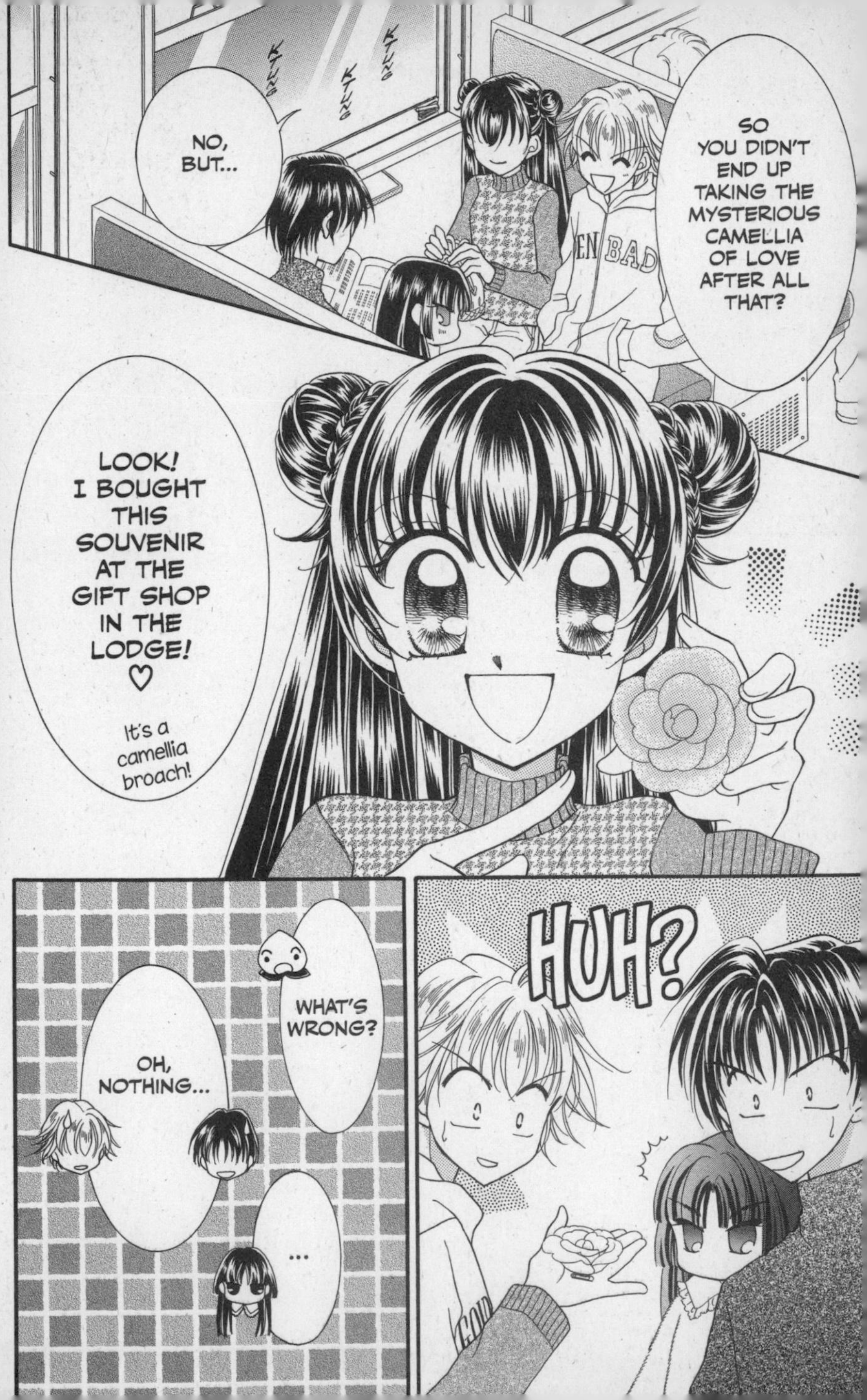
SO YOU DIDN'T END UP TAKING THE MYSTERIOUS CAMELLIA OF LOVE AFTER ALL THAT?
KTING KTING
NO, BUT...
LOOK! I BOUGHT THIS SOUVENIR AT THE GIFT SHOP IN THE LODGE! ♡
It's a camellia broach!
HUH?
WHAT'S WRONG?
OH, NOTHING...
...

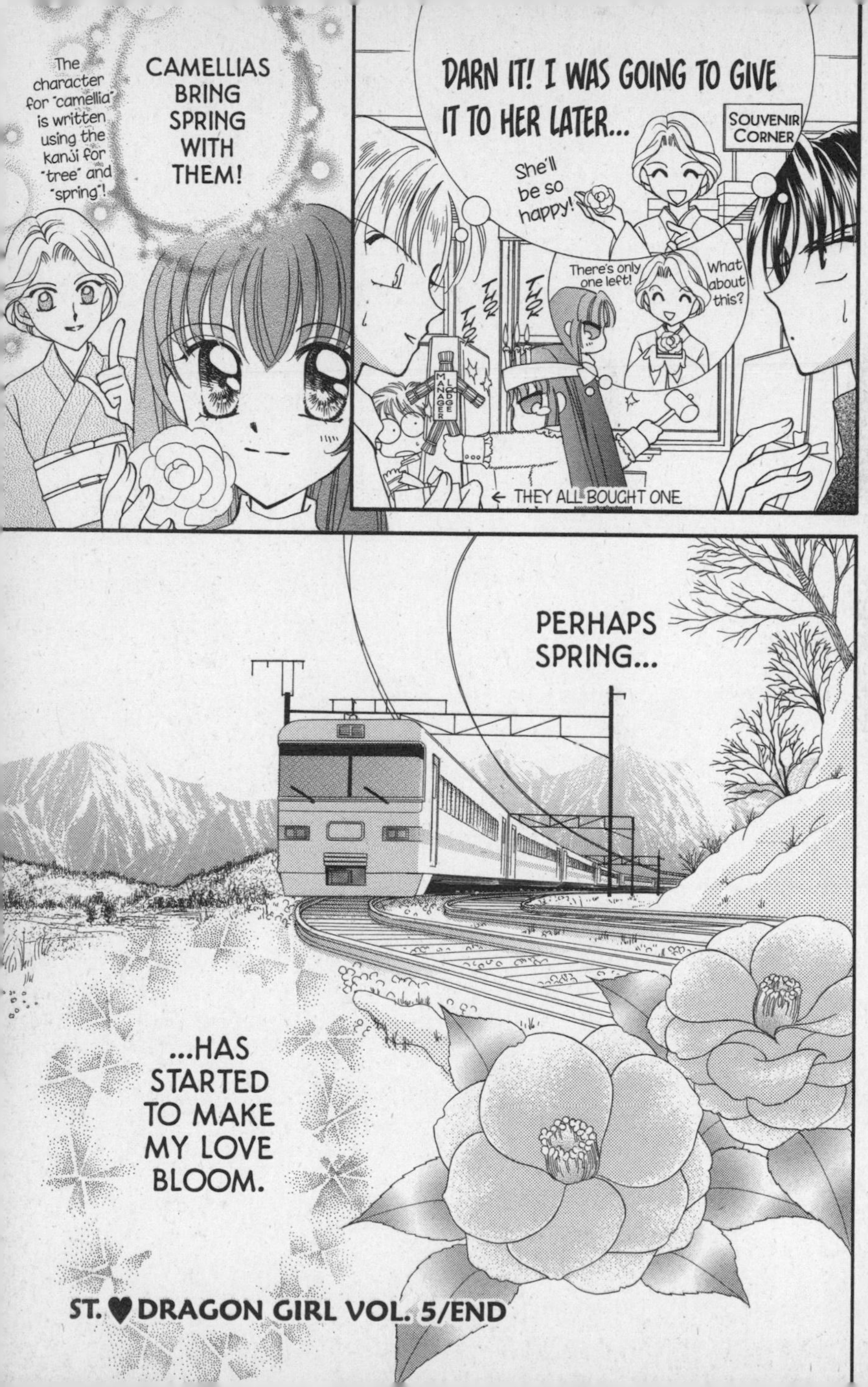
DARN IT! I WAS GOING TO GIVE IT TO HER LATER...
SOUVENIR CORNER
She'll be so happy!
What about this?
There's only one left!
THOK THOK
THOK
LODGE MANAGER
← THEY ALL BOUGHT ONE
CAMELLIAS BRING SPRING WITH THEM!
The character for "camellia" is written using the kanji for "tree" and "spring"!
PERHAPS SPRING...
...HAS STARTED TO MAKE MY LOVE BLOOM.
ST. ♥ DRAGON GIRL VOL. 5/END

St. ♥ Dragon Girl Fan Art

Megan Eden

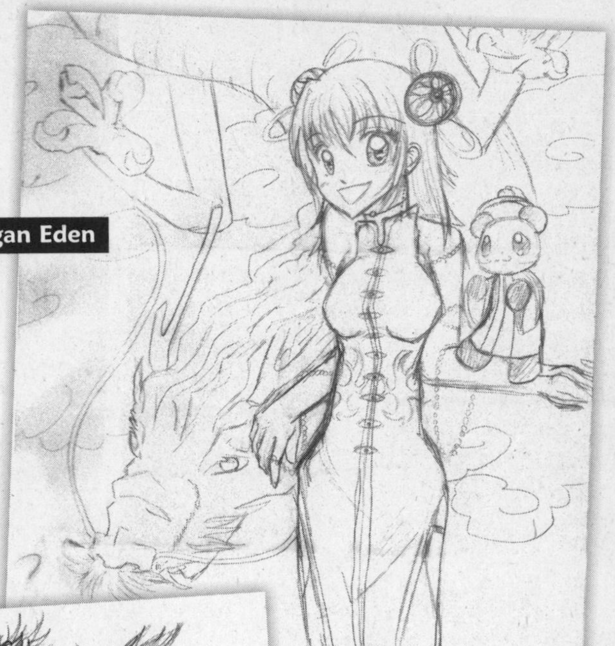

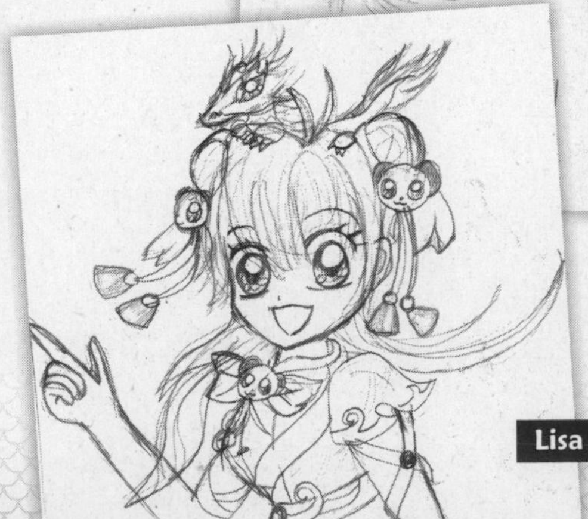

Lisa Nguyen

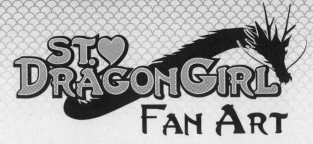

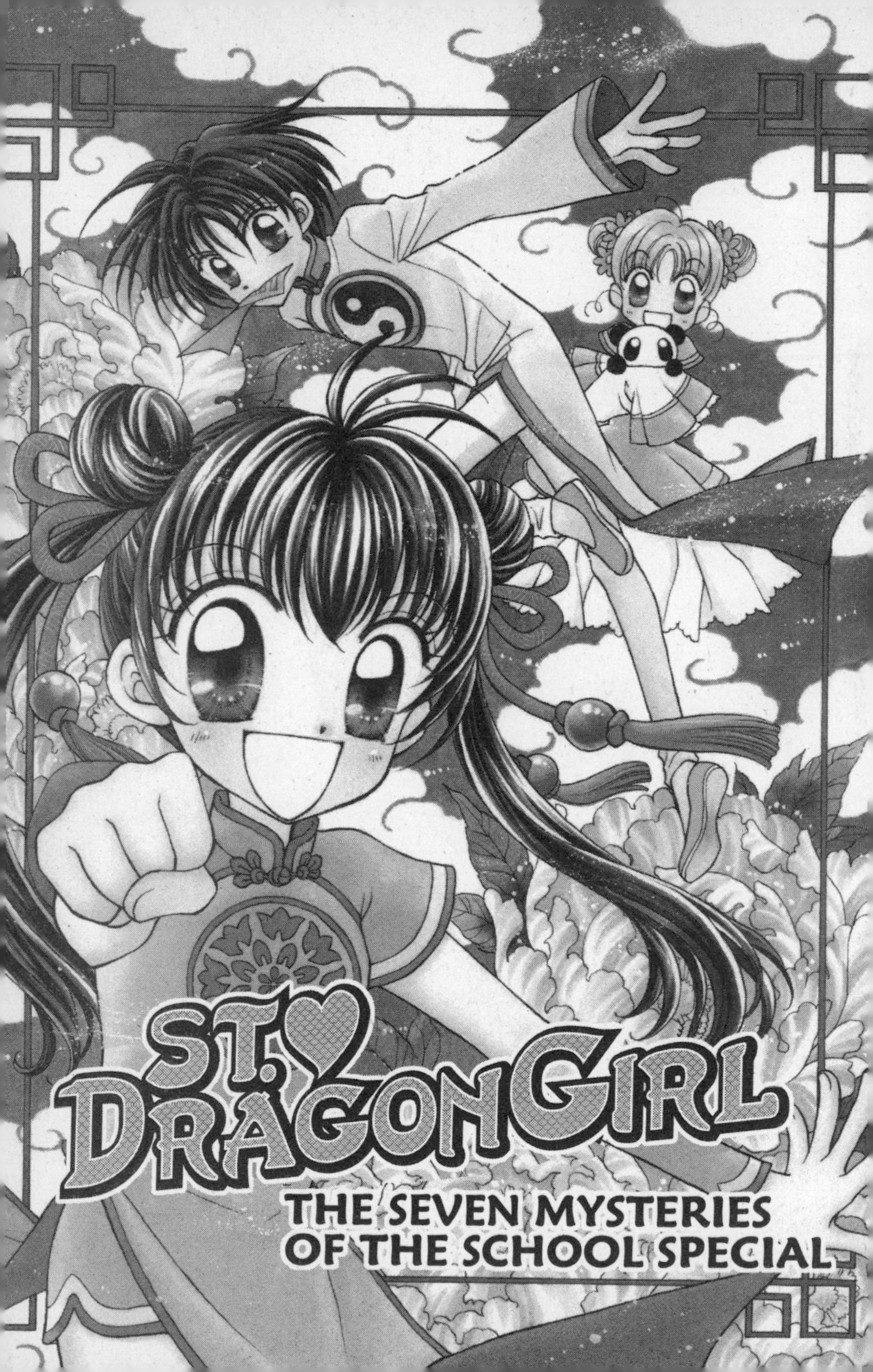
ST. DRAGON GIRL
THE SEVEN MYSTERIES
OF THE SCHOOL SPECIAL

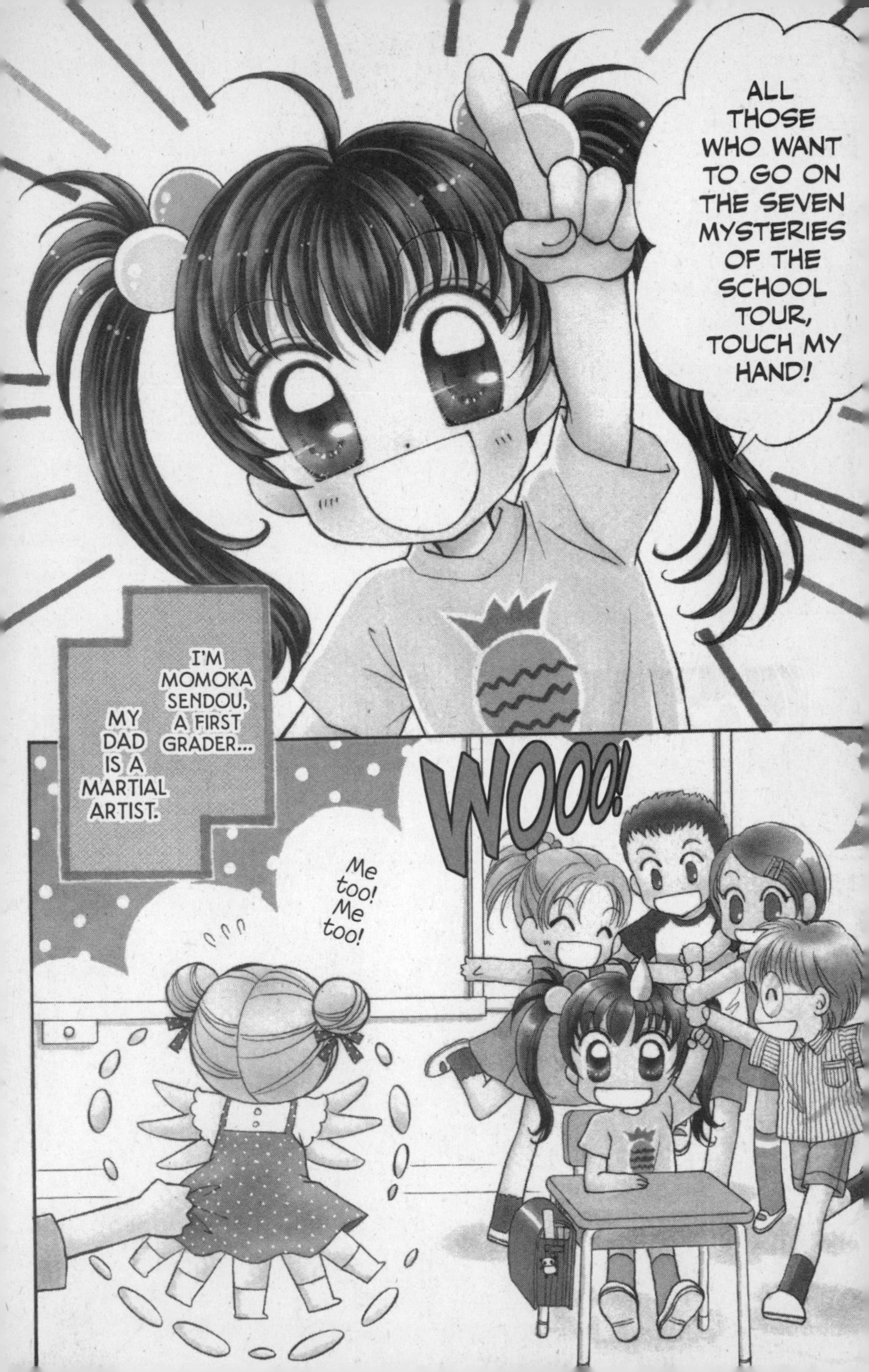
ALL THOSE WHO WANT TO GO ON THE SEVEN MYSTERIES OF THE SCHOOL TOUR, TOUCH MY HAND!
I'M MOMOKA SENDOU, A FIRST GRADER...
MY DAD IS A MARTIAL ARTIST.
WOOO!
Me too! Me too!

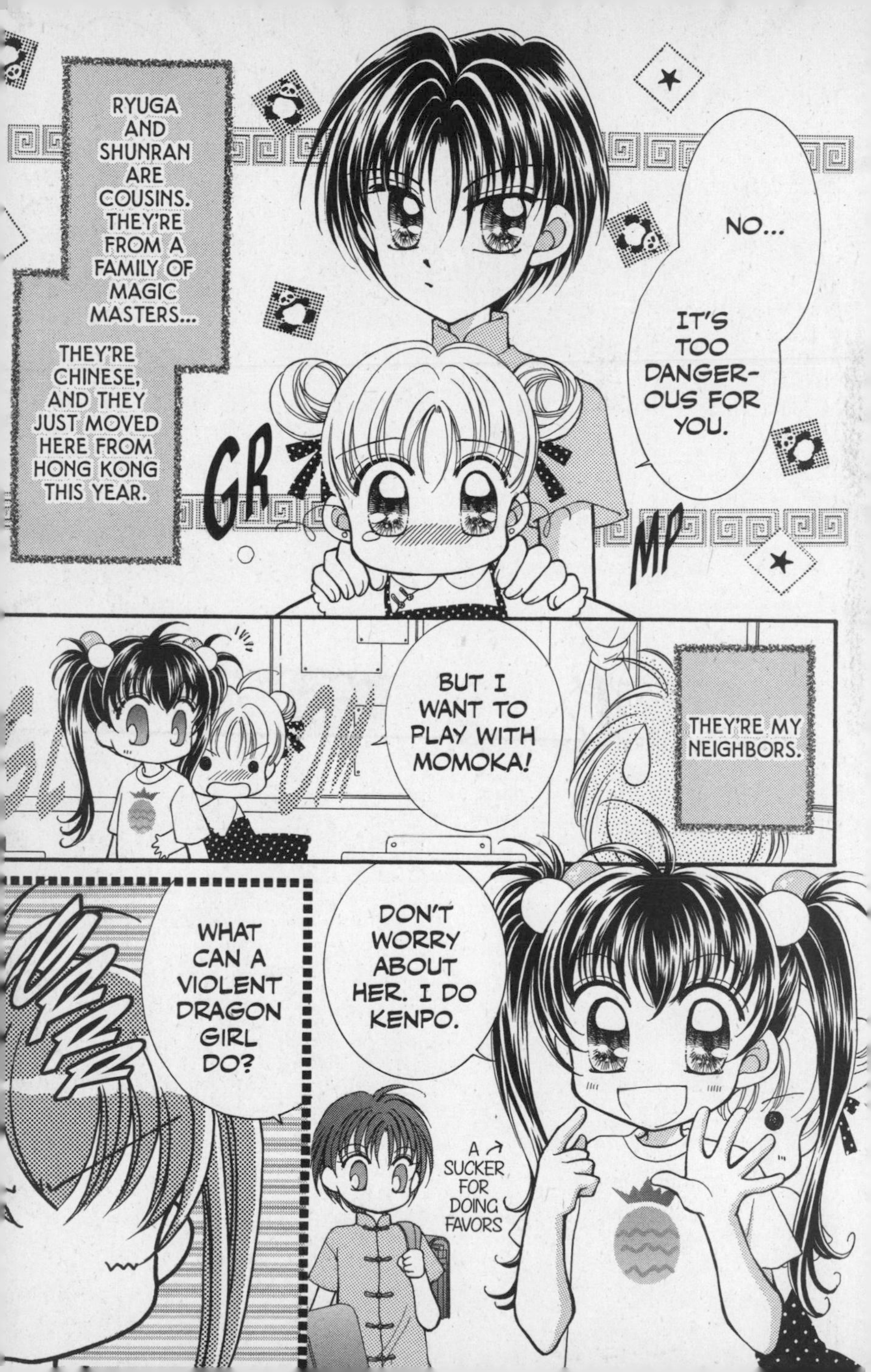
NO...
IT'S TOO DANGER-OUS FOR YOU.
RYUGA AND SHUNRAN ARE COUSINS. THEY'RE FROM A FAMILY OF MAGIC MASTERS...
THEY'RE CHINESE, AND THEY JUST MOVED HERE FROM HONG KONG THIS YEAR.
GR
MP
THEY'RE MY NEIGHBORS.
BUT I WANT TO PLAY WITH MOMOKA!
DON'T WORRY ABOUT HER. I DO KENPO.
A SUCKER FOR DOING FAVORS
WHAT CAN A VIOLENT DRAGON GIRL DO?

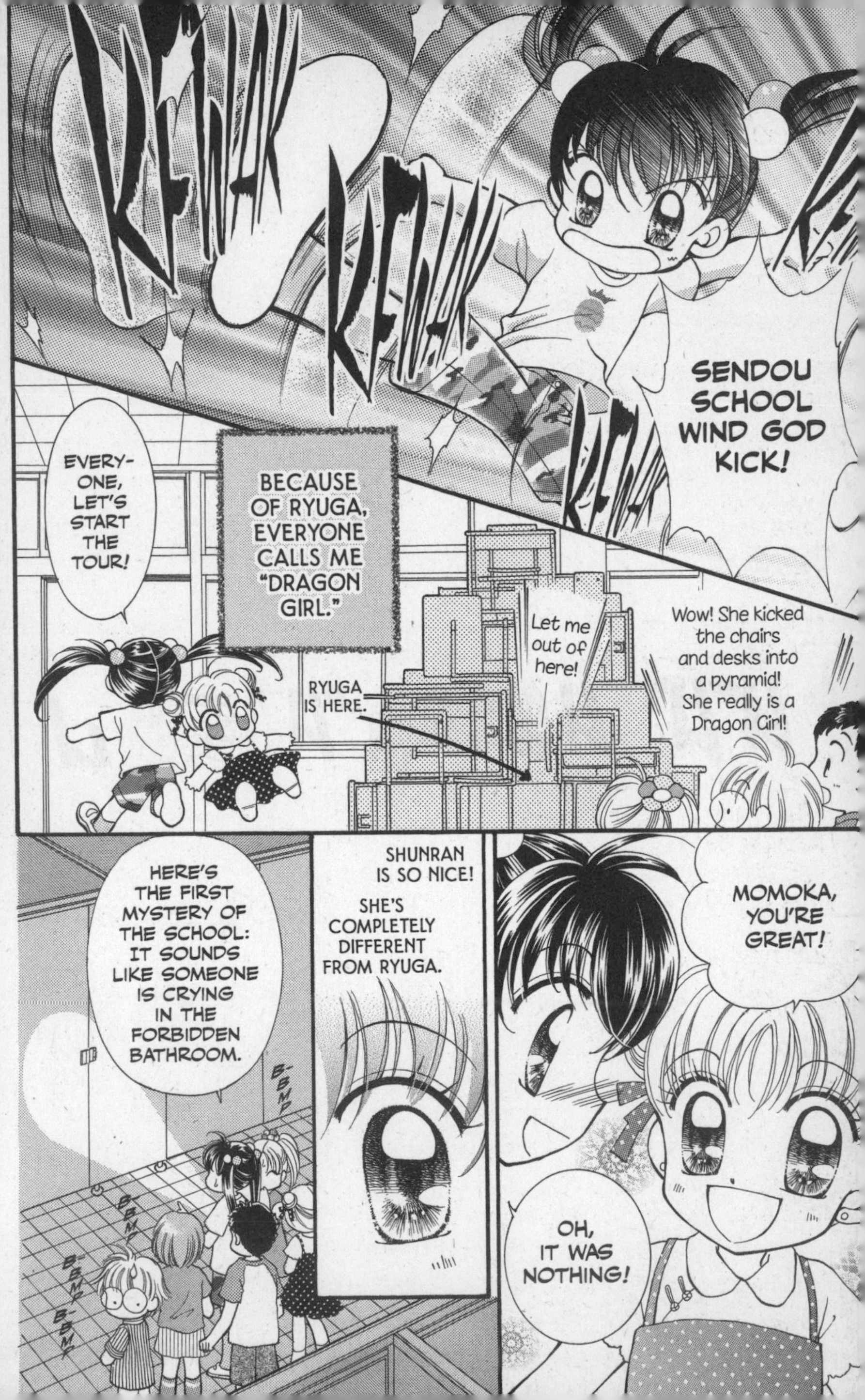
KFWAK
KFWAK
SENDOU SCHOOL WIND GOD KICK!
Wow! She kicked the chairs and desks into a pyramid! She really is a Dragon Girl!
Let me out of here!
RYUGA IS HERE.
BECAUSE OF RYUGA, EVERYONE CALLS ME "DRAGON GIRL."
EVERY-ONE, LET'S START THE TOUR!
MOMOKA, YOU'RE GREAT!
OH, IT WAS NOTHING!
SHUNRAN IS SO NICE!
SHE'S COMPLETELY DIFFERENT FROM RYUGA.
HERE'S THE FIRST MYSTERY OF THE SCHOOL: IT SOUNDS LIKE SOMEONE IS CRYING IN THE FORBIDDEN BATHROOM.
B-BMP
B-BMP
B-BMP
B-BMP

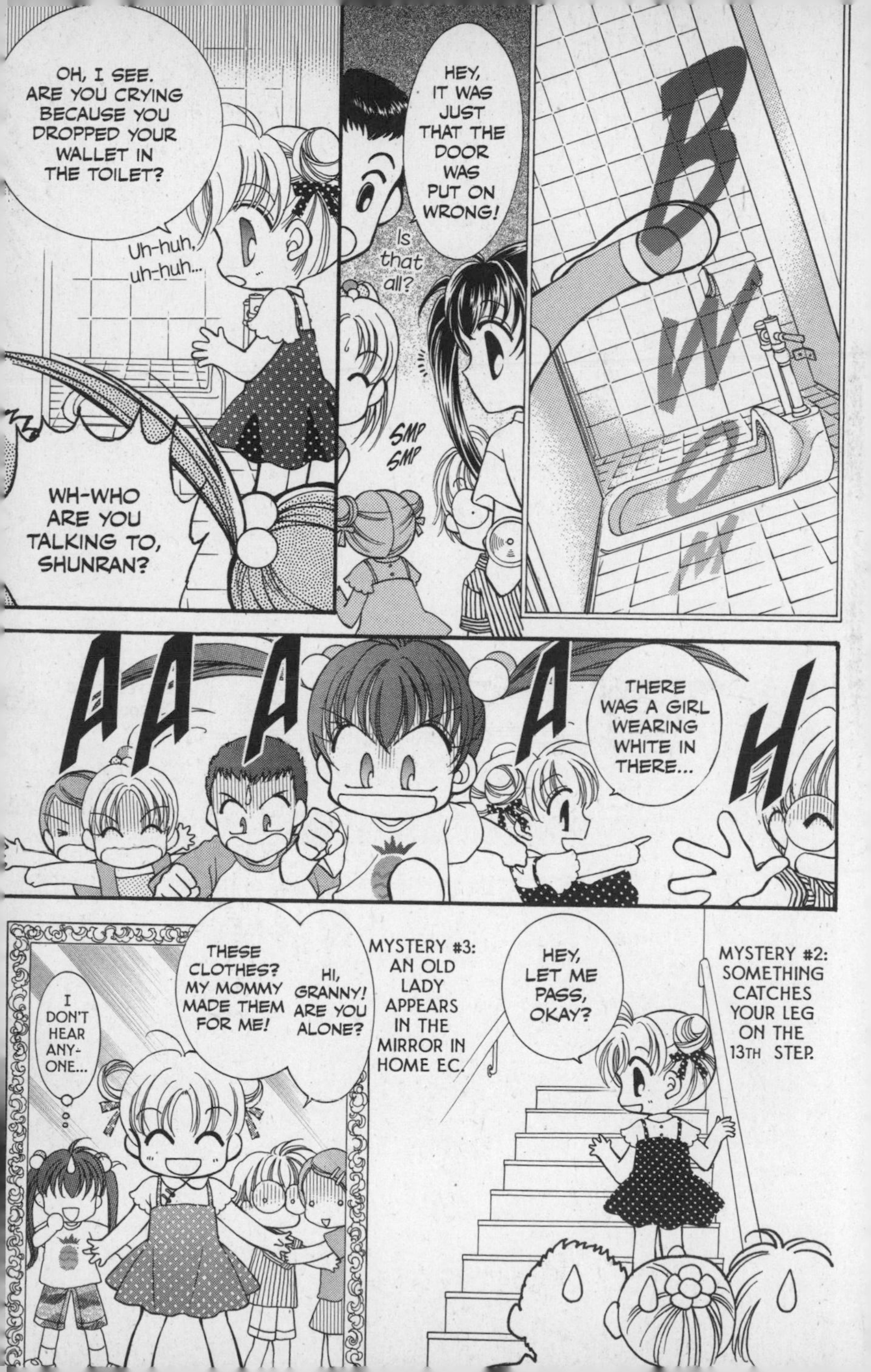
BWOM
HEY, IT WAS JUST THAT THE DOOR WAS PUT ON WRONG!
Is that all?
SMP SMP
OH, I SEE. ARE YOU CRYING BECAUSE YOU DROPPED YOUR WALLET IN THE TOILET?
Uh-huh, uh-huh...
WH-WHO ARE YOU TALKING TO, SHUNRAN?
THERE WAS A GIRL WEARING WHITE IN THERE...
AAAAH
MYSTERY #2: SOMETHING CATCHES YOUR LEG ON THE 13TH STEP.
HEY, LET ME PASS, OKAY?
MYSTERY #3: AN OLD LADY APPEARS IN THE MIRROR IN HOME EC.
HI, GRANNY! ARE YOU ALONE?
THESE CLOTHES? MY MOMMY MADE THEM FOR ME!
I DON'T HEAR ANY-ONE...

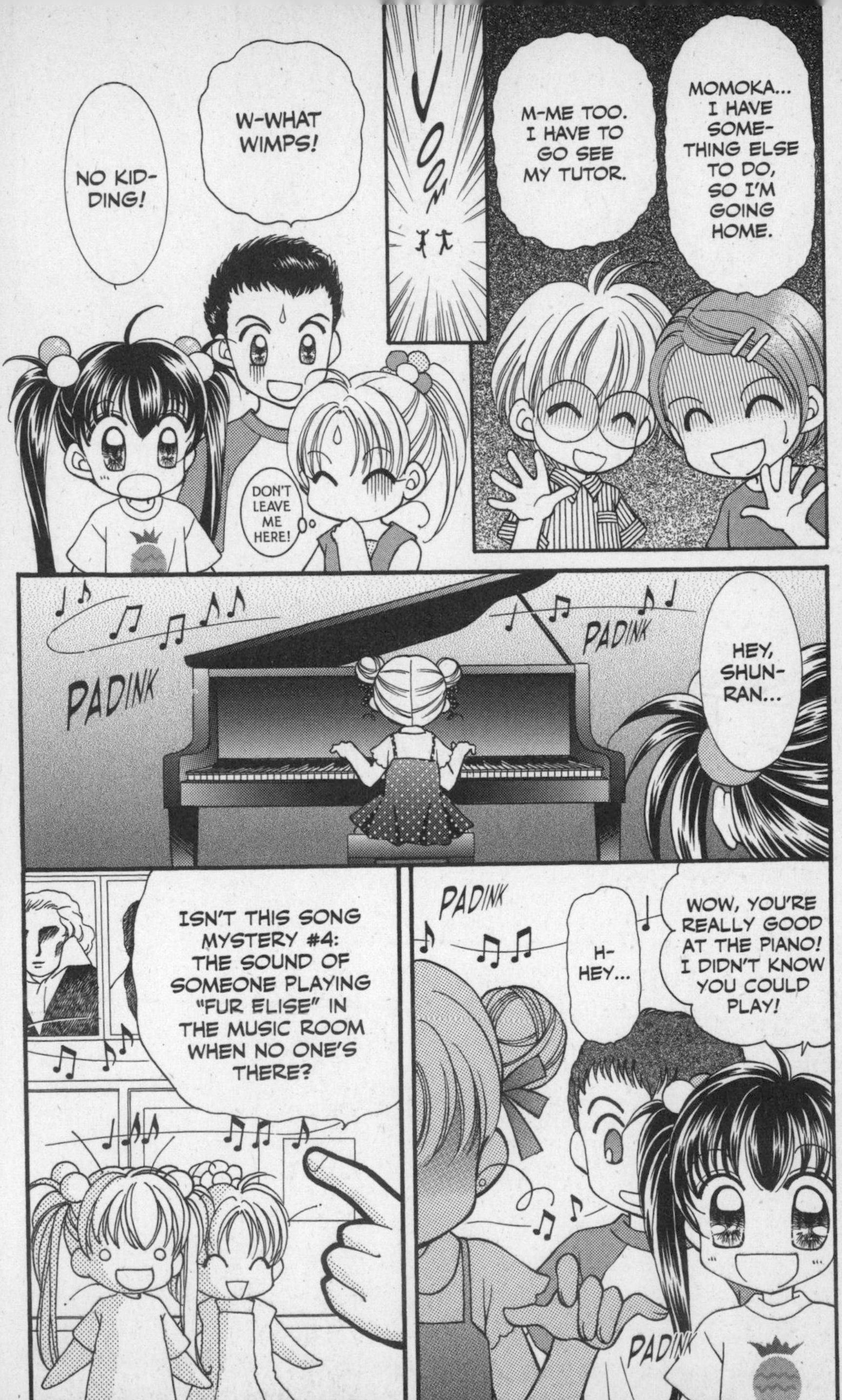
MOMOKA... I HAVE SOME-THING ELSE TO DO, SO I'M GOING HOME.
M-ME TOO. I HAVE TO GO SEE MY TUTOR.
VOOM
W-WHAT WIMPS!
NO KID-DING!
DON'T LEAVE ME HERE!
HEY, SHUN-RAN...
PADINK
PADINK
WOW, YOU'RE REALLY GOOD AT THE PIANO! I DIDN'T KNOW YOU COULD PLAY!
H-HEY...
PADINK
PADINK
ISN'T THIS SONG MYSTERY #4: THE SOUND OF SOMEONE PLAYING "FUR ELISE" IN THE MUSIC ROOM WHEN NO ONE'S THERE?

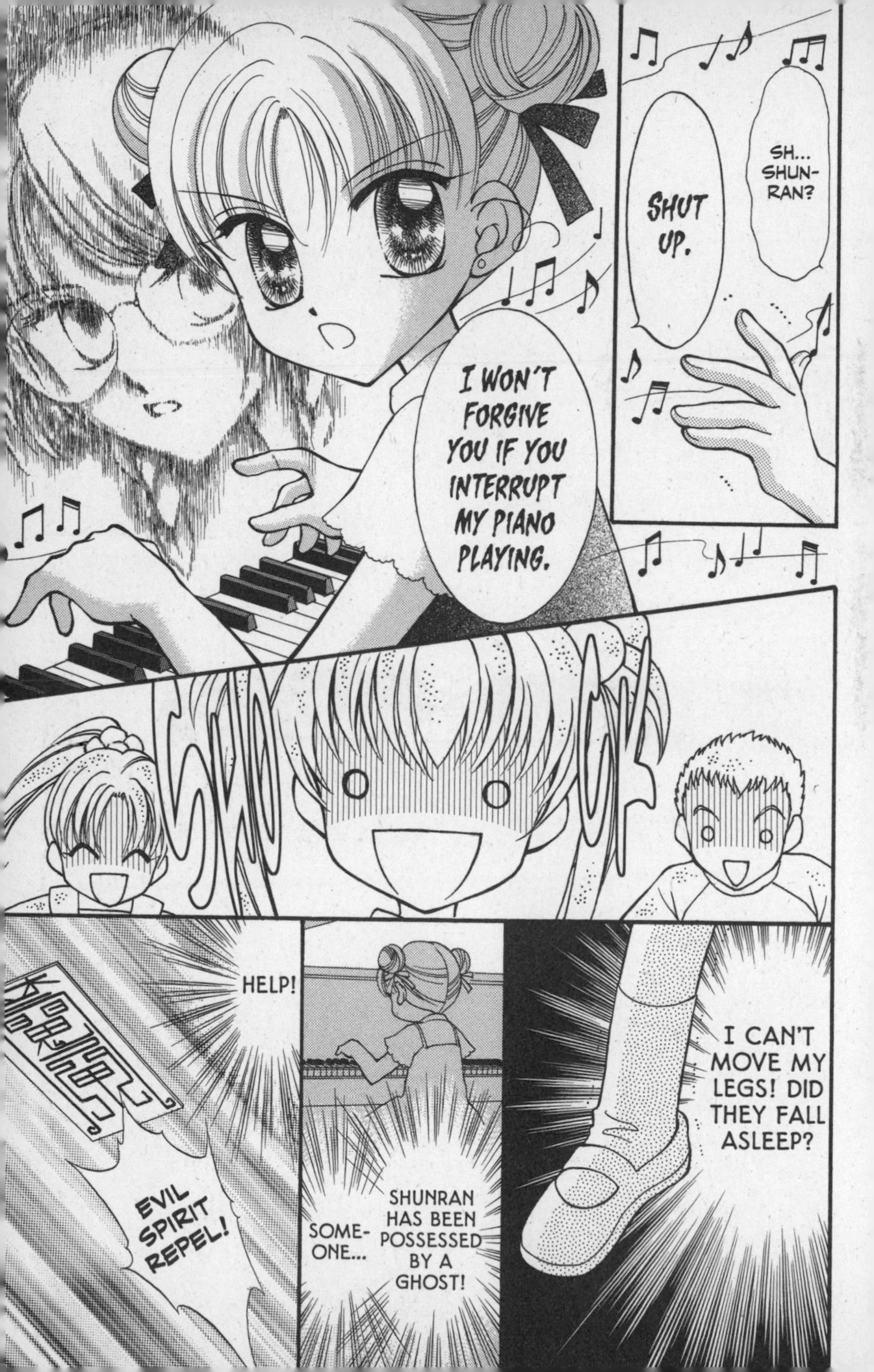

SH... SHUN-RAN?
SHUT UP.
I WON'T FORGIVE YOU IF YOU INTERRUPT MY PIANO PLAYING.
I CAN'T MOVE MY LEGS! DID THEY FALL ASLEEP?
SHUNRAN HAS BEEN POSSESSED BY A GHOST!
SOME-ONE...
HELP!
EVIL SPIRIT REPEL!

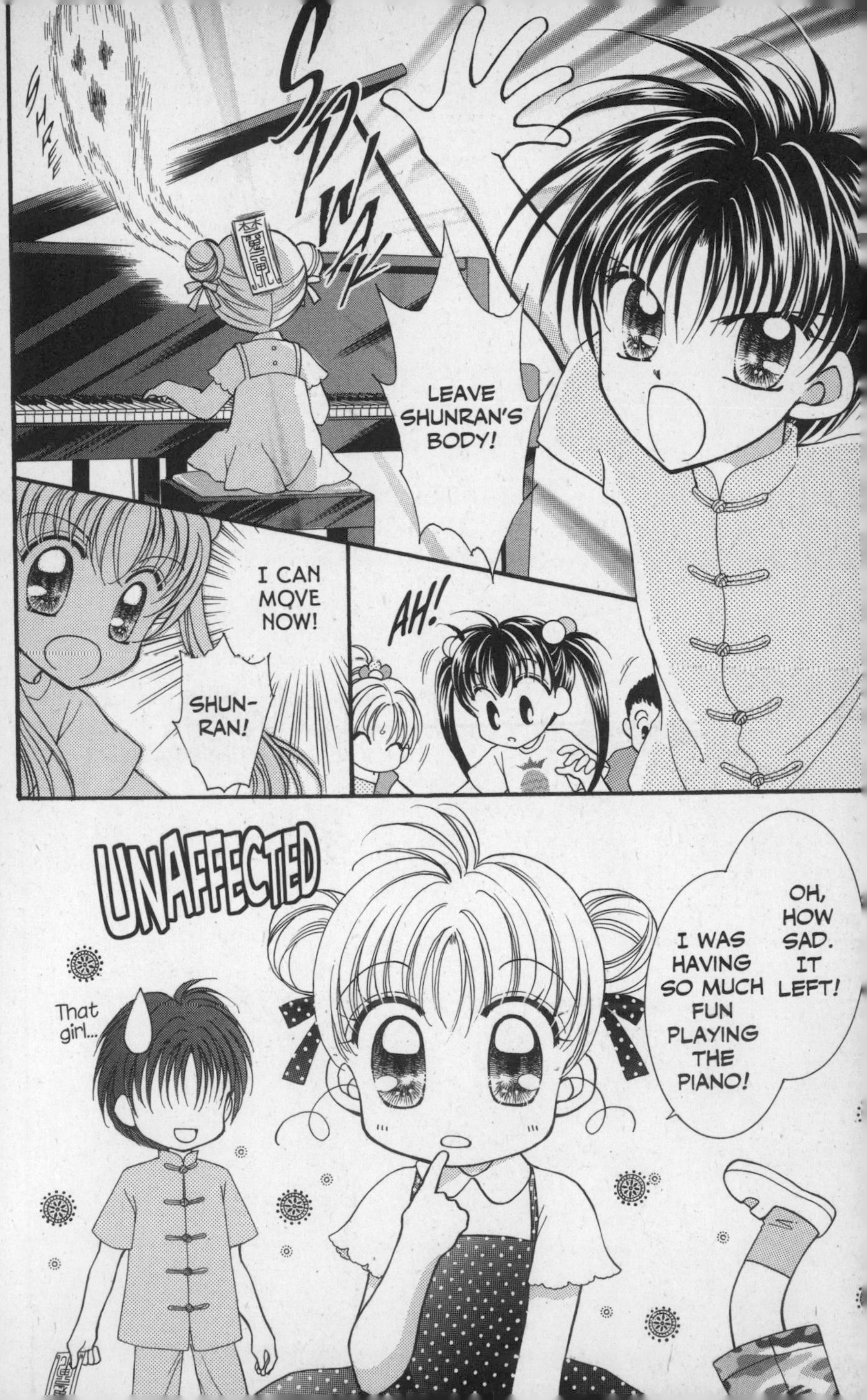

SHWAK
LEAVE SHUNRAN'S BODY!
SHWEE
AH!
I CAN MOVE NOW!
SHUN-RAN!
OH, HOW SAD. IT LEFT!
I WAS HAVING SO MUCH FUN PLAYING THE PIANO!
UNAFFECTED
That girl...

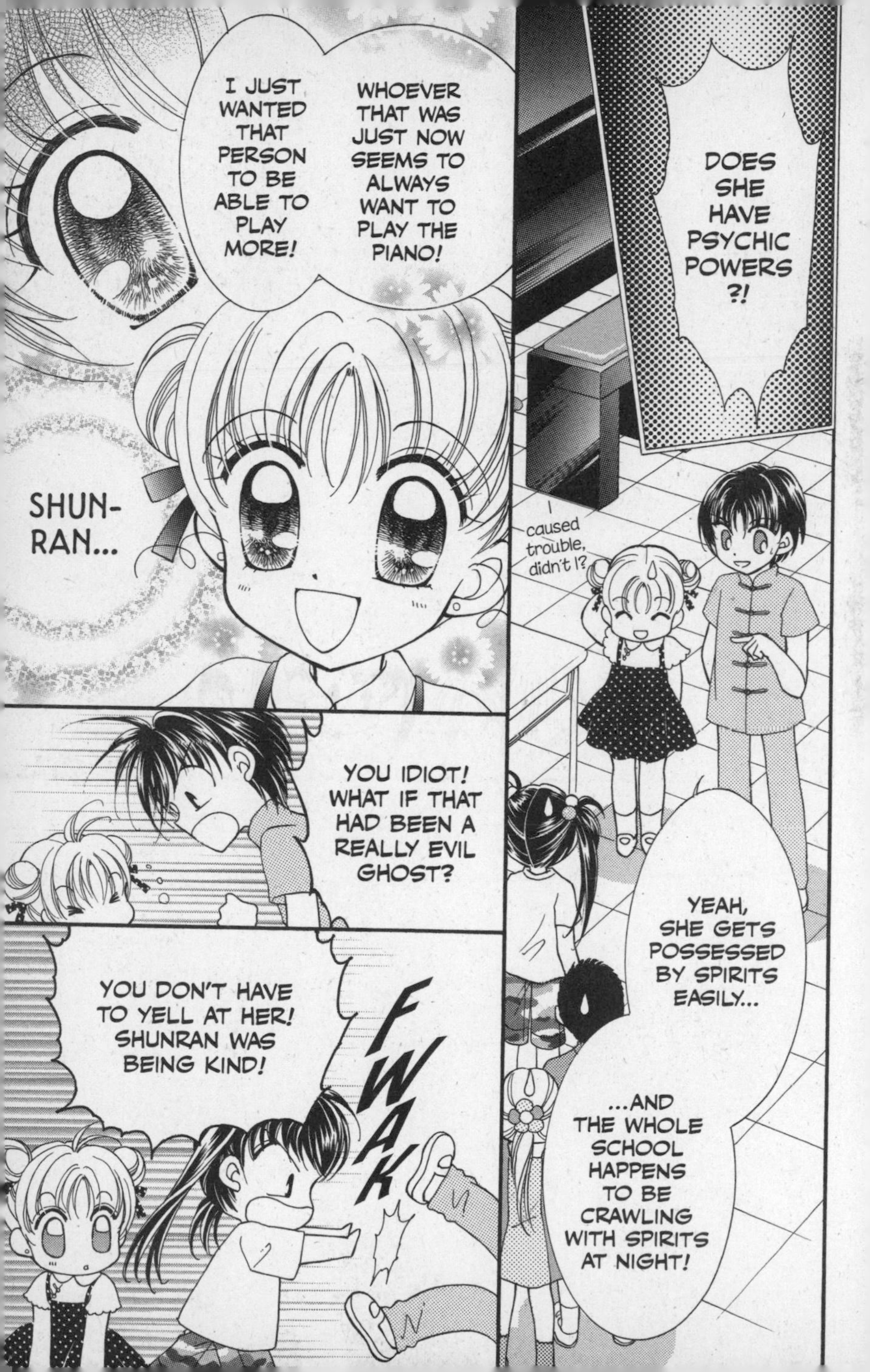
DOES SHE HAVE PSYCHIC POWERS?!
I caused trouble, didn't I?
YEAH, SHE GETS POSSESSED BY SPIRITS EASILY...
...AND THE WHOLE SCHOOL HAPPENS TO BE CRAWLING WITH SPIRITS AT NIGHT!
WHOEVER THAT WAS JUST NOW SEEMS TO ALWAYS WANT TO PLAY THE PIANO!
I JUST WANTED THAT PERSON TO BE ABLE TO PLAY MORE!
SHUN-RAN...
YOU IDIOT! WHAT IF THAT HAD BEEN A REALLY EVIL GHOST?
FWAK
YOU DON'T HAVE TO YELL AT HER! SHUNRAN WAS BEING KIND!

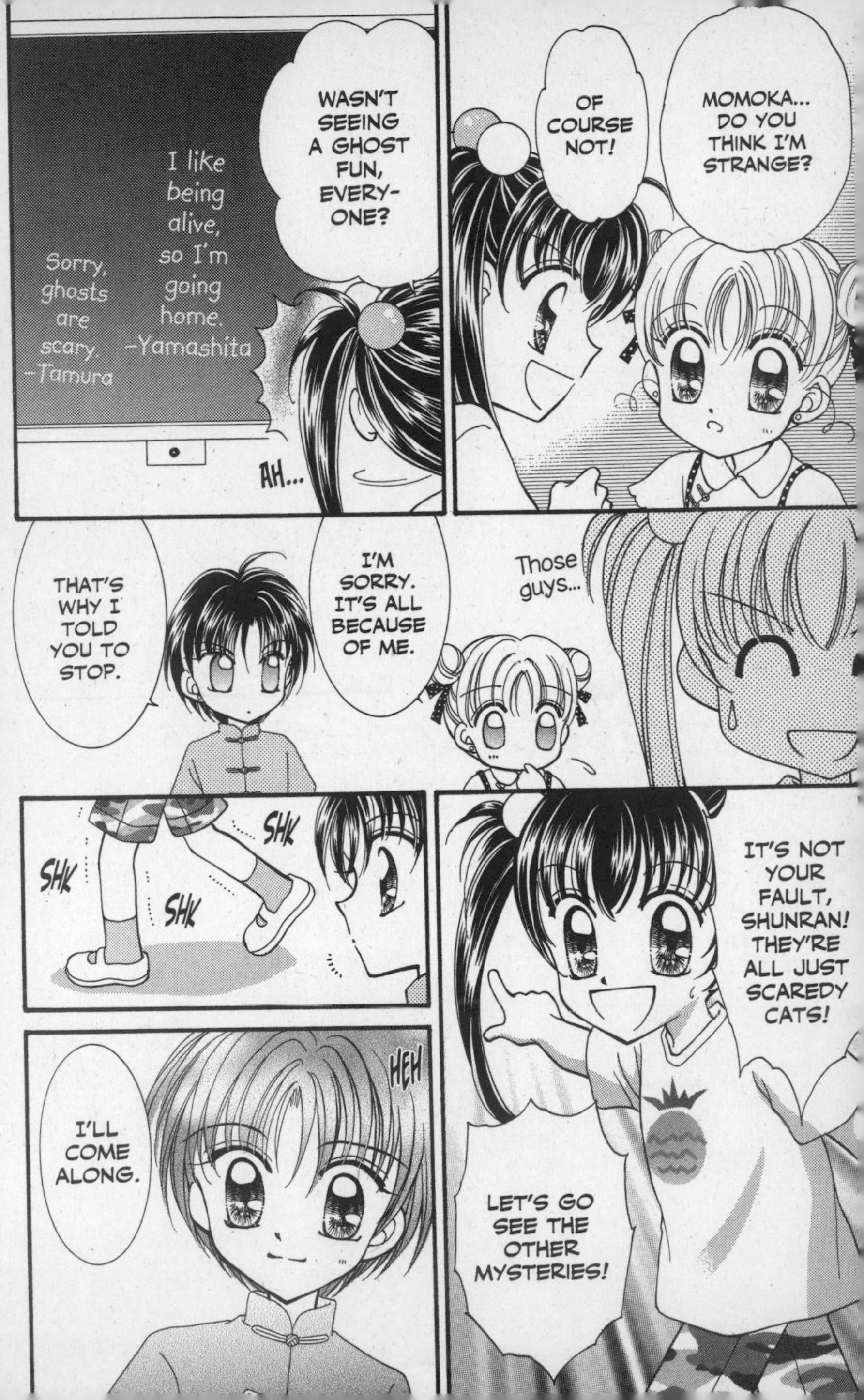
MOMOKA... DO YOU THINK I'M STRANGE?
OF COURSE NOT!
WASN'T SEEING A GHOST FUN, EVERYONE?
I like being alive, so I'm going home. -Yamashita
Sorry, ghosts are scary. -Tamura
AH...
Those guys...
I'M SORRY. IT'S ALL BECAUSE OF ME.
THAT'S WHY I TOLD YOU TO STOP.
IT'S NOT YOUR FAULT, SHUNRAN! THEY'RE ALL JUST SCAREDY CATS!
LET'S GO SEE THE OTHER MYSTERIES!
SHK
SHK
SHK
HEH
I'LL COME ALONG.

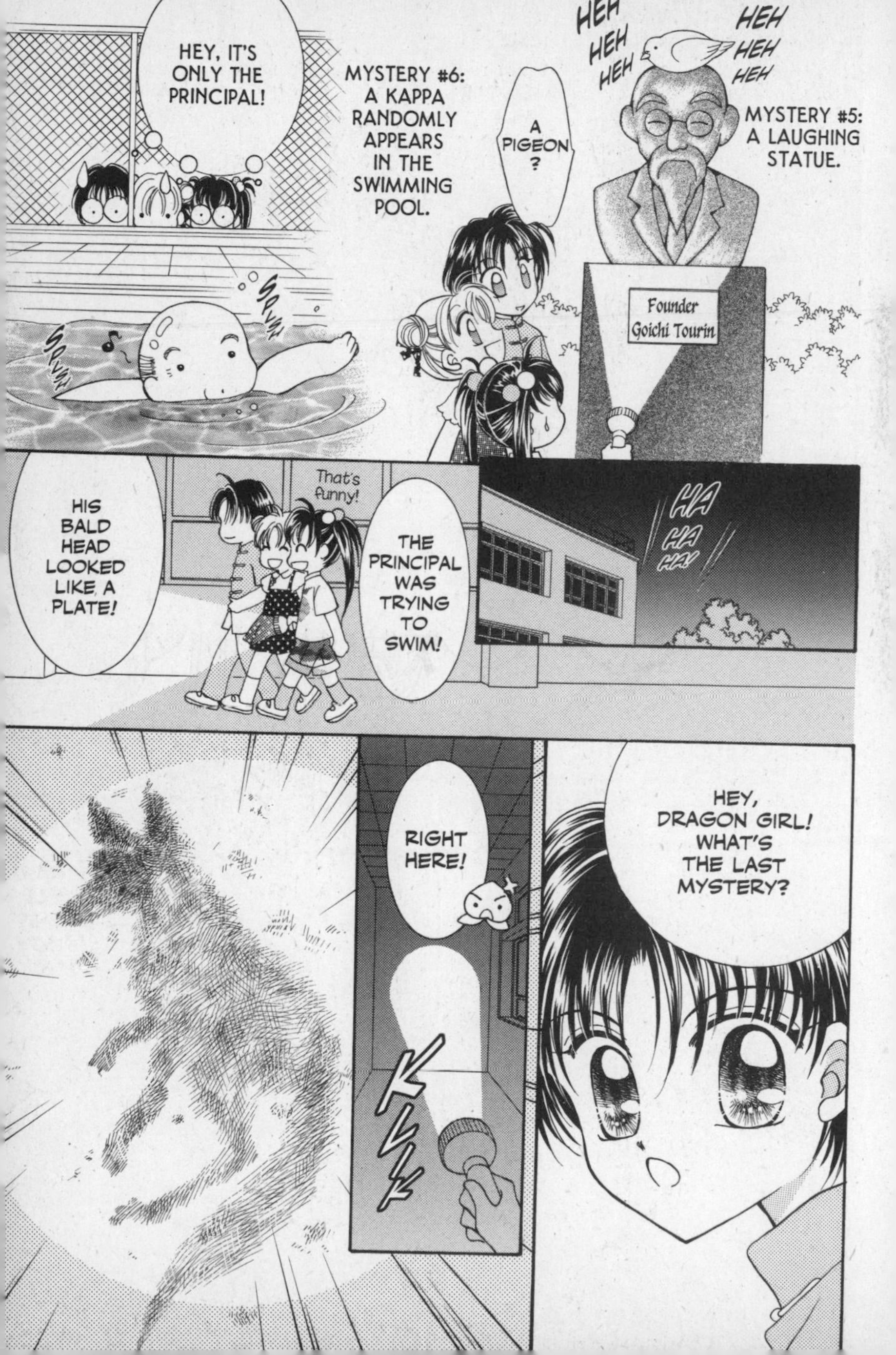
HEH HEH HEH
HEH HEH HEH
MYSTERY #5: A LAUGHING STATUE.
Founder Goichi Tourin
A PIGEON ?
MYSTERY #6: A KAPPA RANDOMLY APPEARS IN THE SWIMMING POOL.
HEY, IT'S ONLY THE PRINCIPAL!
HA HA HA!
THE PRINCIPAL WAS TRYING TO SWIM!
That's funny!
HIS BALD HEAD LOOKED LIKE A PLATE!
HEY, DRAGON GIRL! WHAT'S THE LAST MYSTERY?
RIGHT HERE!

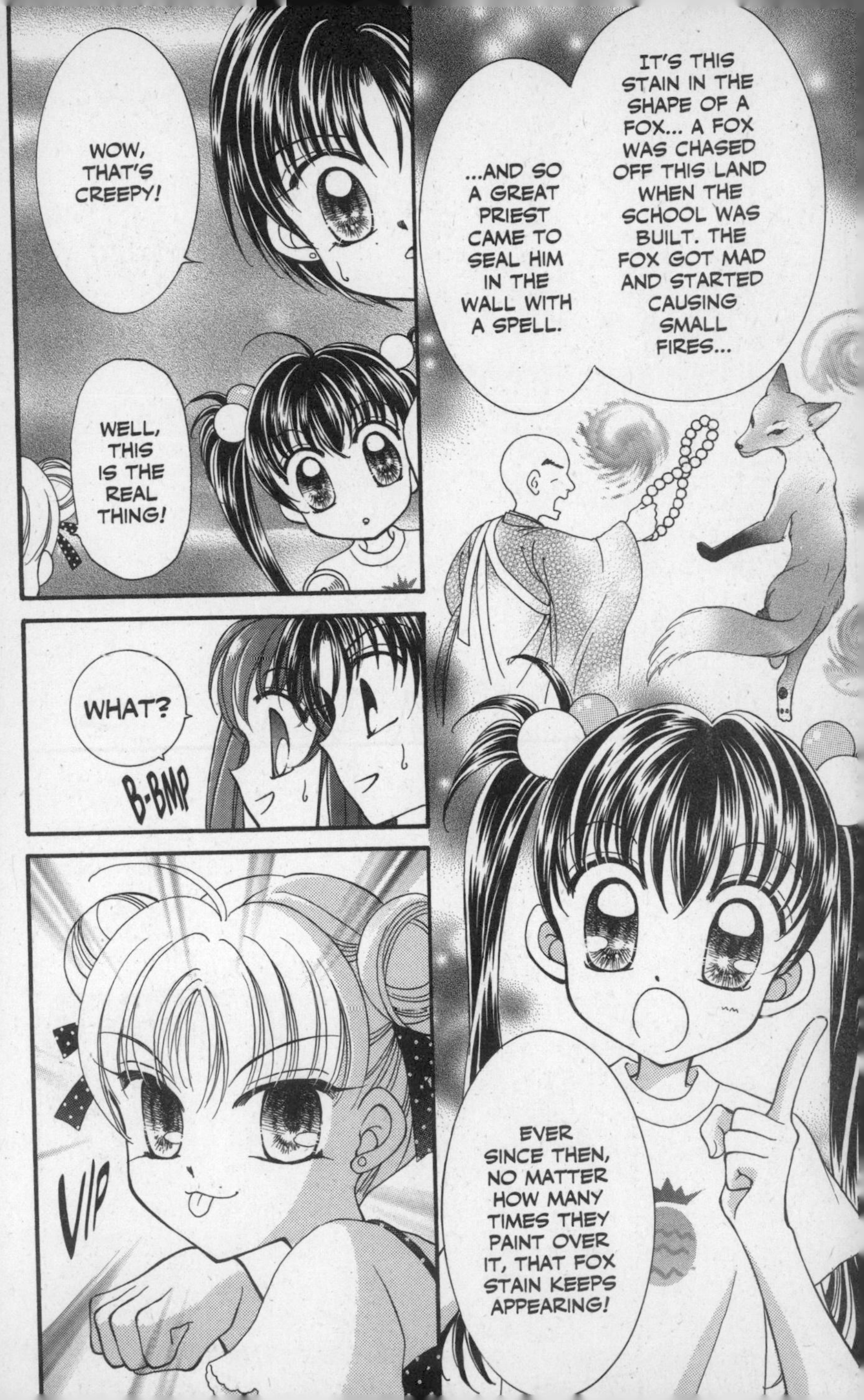
IT'S THIS STAIN IN THE SHAPE OF A FOX... A FOX WAS CHASED OFF THIS LAND WHEN THE SCHOOL WAS BUILT. THE FOX GOT MAD AND STARTED CAUSING SMALL FIRES...
...AND SO A GREAT PRIEST CAME TO SEAL HIM IN THE WALL WITH A SPELL.
EVER SINCE THEN, NO MATTER HOW MANY TIMES THEY PAINT OVER IT, THAT FOX STAIN KEEPS APPEARING!
WOW, THAT'S CREEPY!
WELL, THIS IS THE REAL THING!
WHAT?
B-BMP
VIP

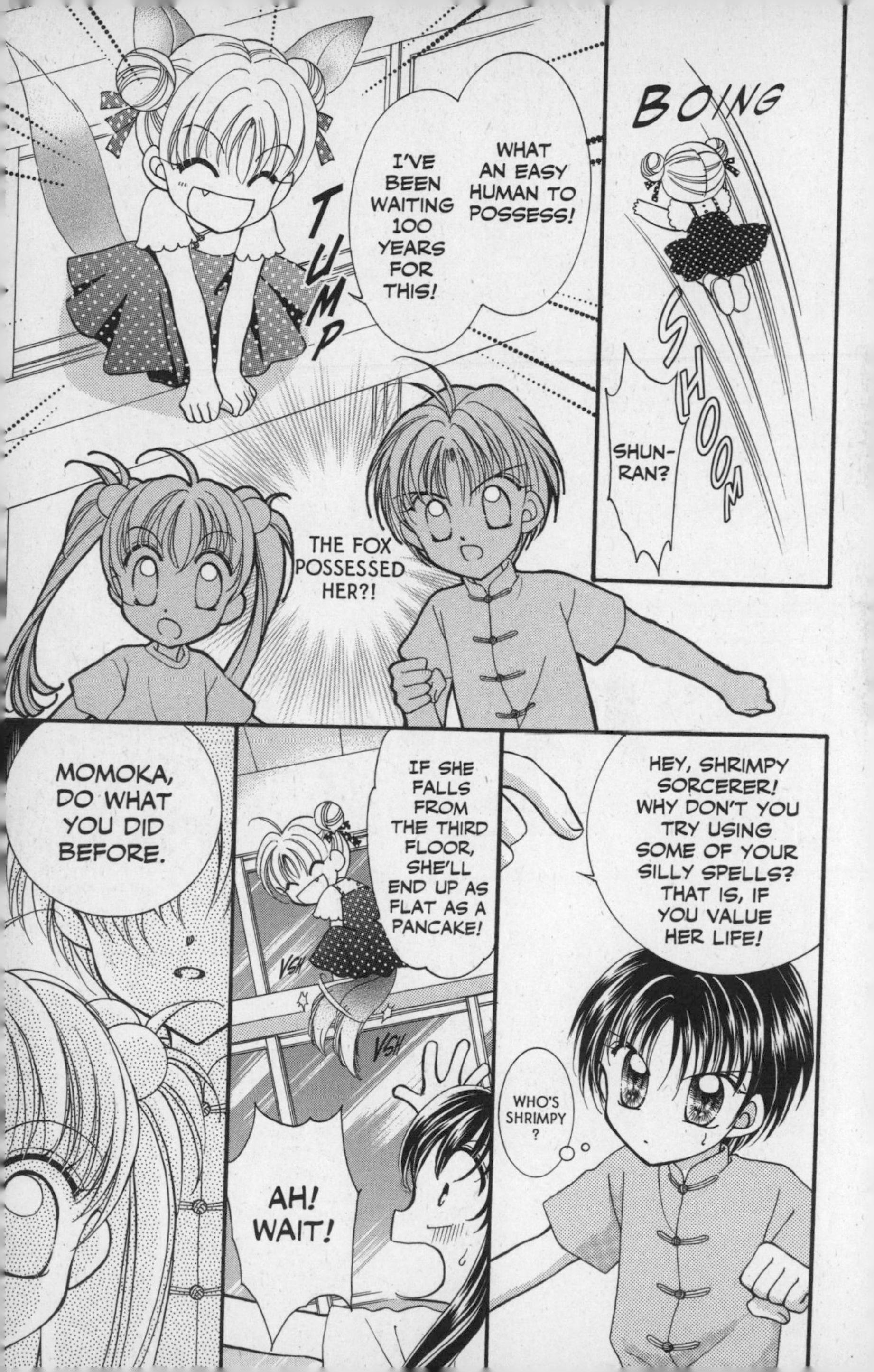
BOING
SHOOM
SHUN-RAN?
TUMP
WHAT AN EASY HUMAN TO POSSESS!
I'VE BEEN WAITING 100 YEARS FOR THIS!
THE FOX POSSESSED HER?!
HEY, SHRIMPY SORCERER! WHY DON'T YOU TRY USING SOME OF YOUR SILLY SPELLS? THAT IS, IF YOU VALUE HER LIFE!
WHO'S SHRIMPY?
IF SHE FALLS FROM THE THIRD FLOOR, SHE'LL END UP AS FLAT AS A PANCAKE!
VSH
VSH
AH! WAIT!
MOMOKA, DO WHAT YOU DID BEFORE.

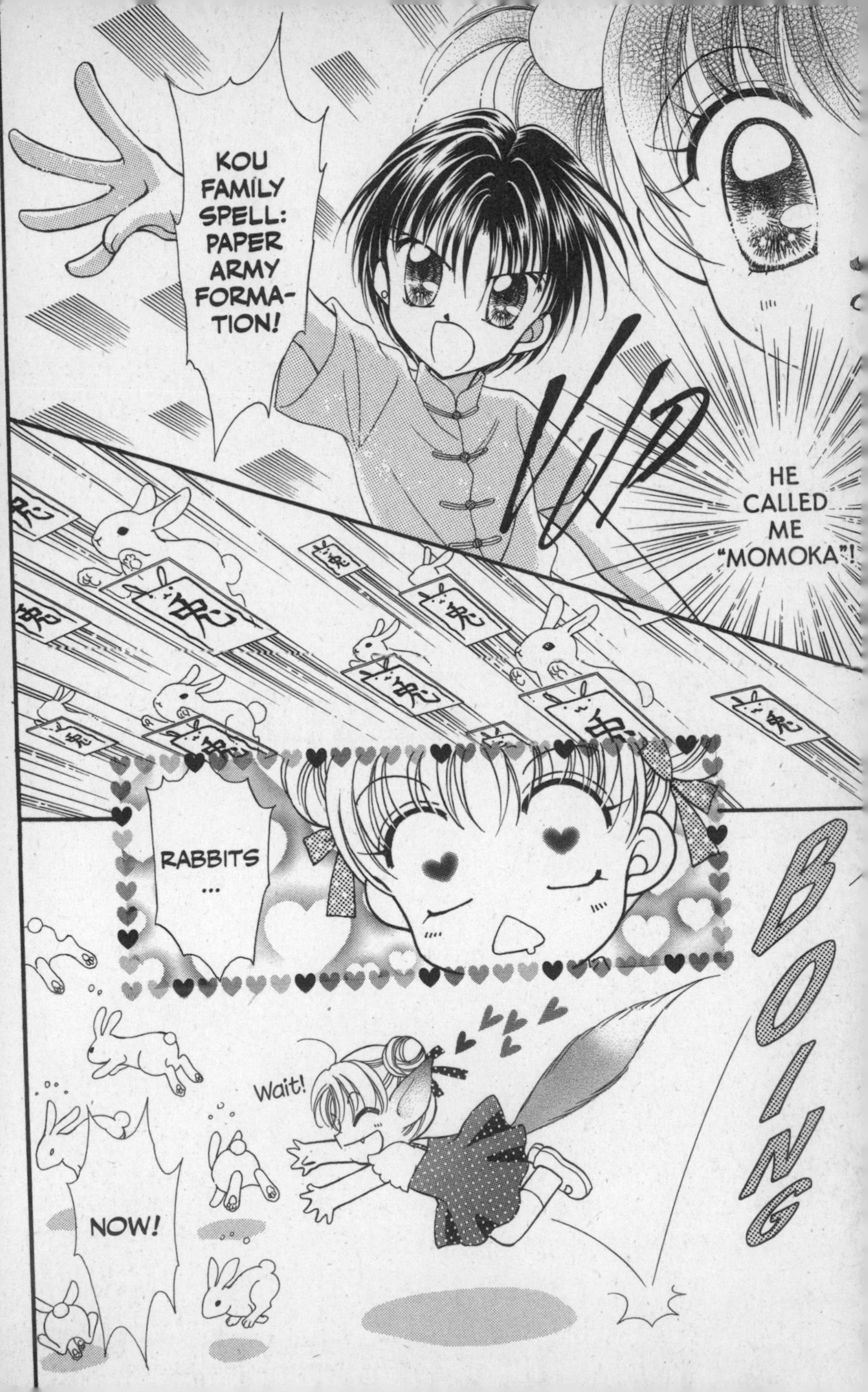

HE CALLED ME "MOMOKA"!
KOU FAMILY SPELL: PAPER ARMY FORMATION!
RABBITS ...
BOING
Wait!
NOW!

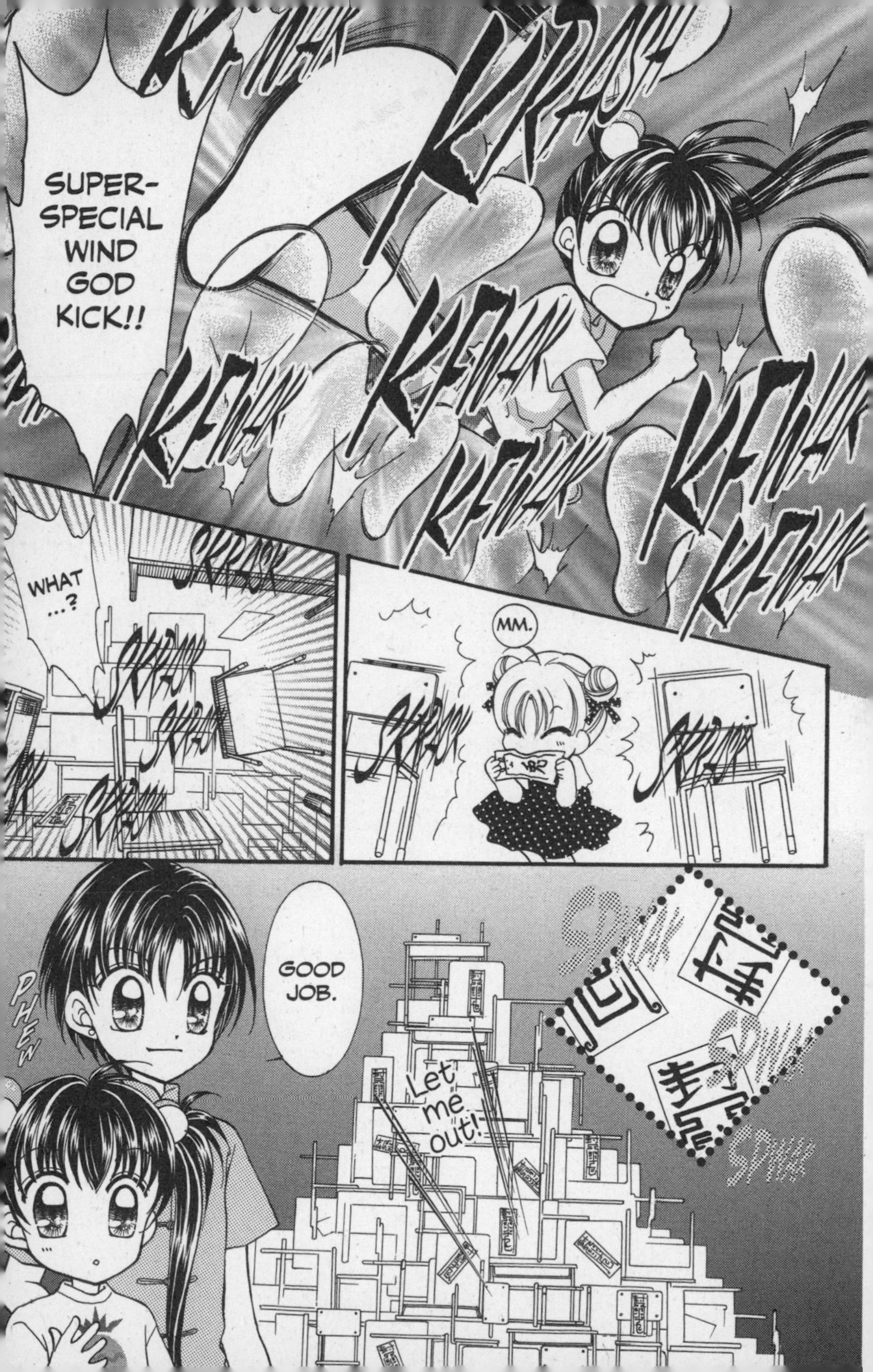
SUPER-SPECIAL WIND GOD KICK!!
MM.
WHAT ...?
GOOD JOB.
PHEW
...
Let me out!

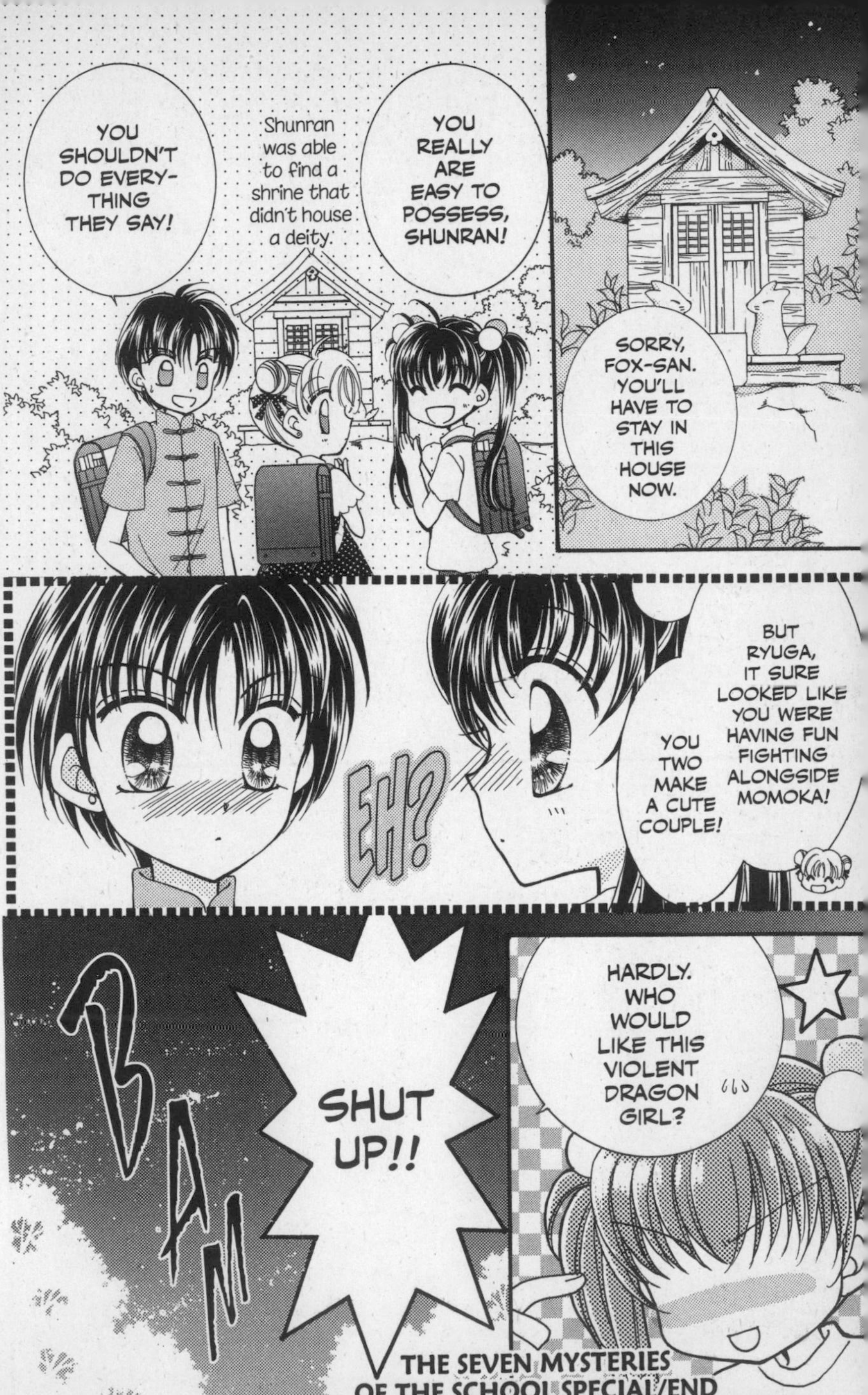
SORRY, FOX-SAN. YOU'LL HAVE TO STAY IN THIS HOUSE NOW.
YOU REALLY ARE EASY TO POSSESS, SHUNRAN!
Shunran was able to find a shrine that didn't house a deity.
YOU SHOULDN'T DO EVERY-THING THEY SAY!
BUT RYUGA, IT SURE LOOKED LIKE YOU WERE HAVING FUN FIGHTING ALONGSIDE MOMOKA!
YOU TWO MAKE A CUTE COUPLE!
EH?
HARDLY. WHO WOULD LIKE THIS VIOLENT DRAGON GIRL?
SHUT UP!!
BAM

THE SEVEN MYSTERIES OF THE SCHOOL SPECIAL/END

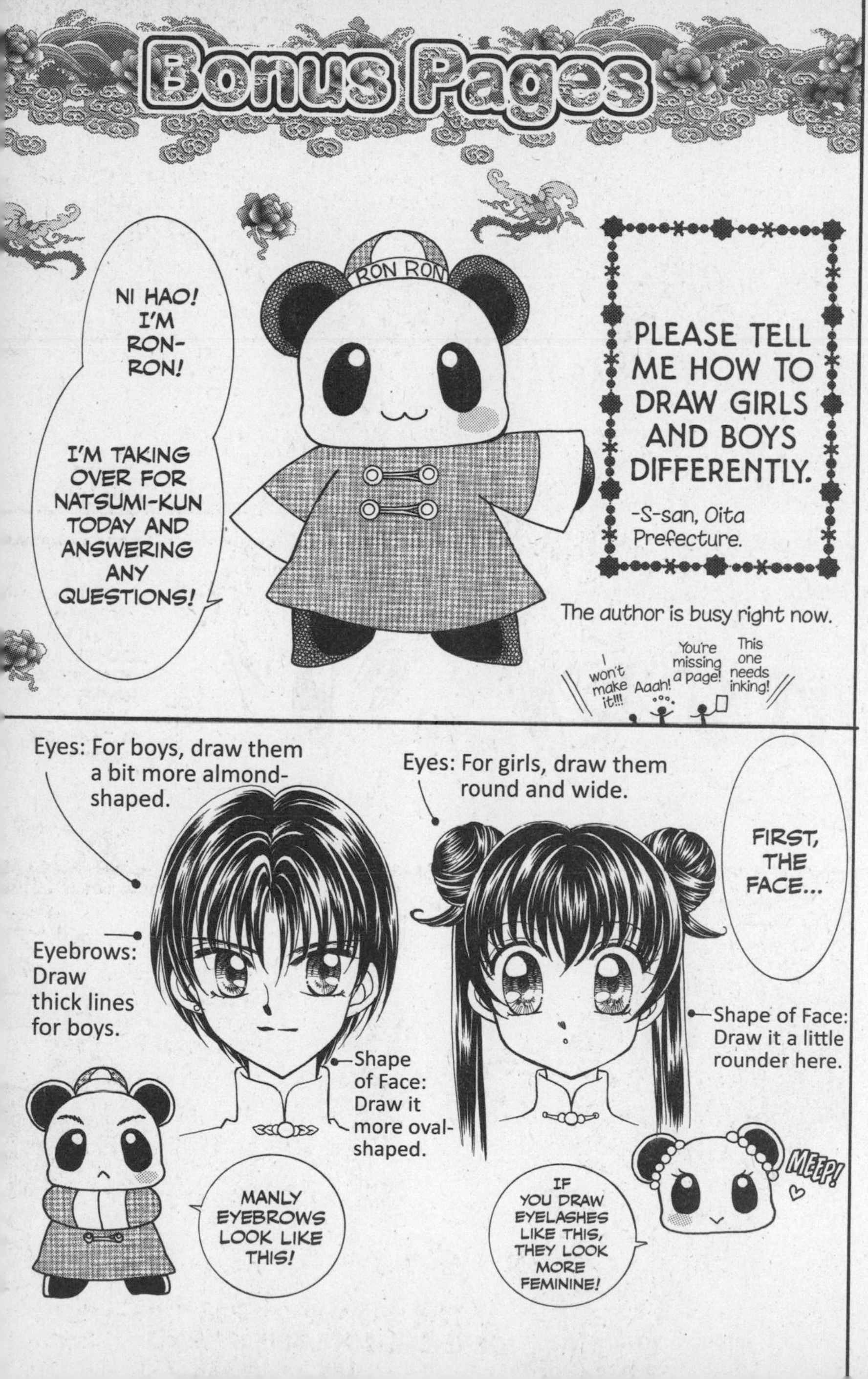
Bonus Pages
PLEASE TELL ME HOW TO DRAW GIRLS AND BOYS DIFFERENTLY.
-S-san, Oita Prefecture.
The author is busy right now.
This one needs inking!
You're missing a page!
Aaah!
I won't make it!!!
RON RON
NI HAO! I'M RON-RON!
I'M TAKING OVER FOR NATSUMI-KUN TODAY AND ANSWERING ANY QUESTIONS!
FIRST, THE FACE...
Eyes: For girls, draw them round and wide.
Shape of Face: Draw it a little rounder here.
MEEP!
IF YOU DRAW EYELASHES LIKE THIS, THEY LOOK MORE FEMININE!
Eyes: For boys, draw them a bit more almond-shaped.
Eyebrows: Draw thick lines for boys.
Shape of Face: Draw it more oval-shaped.
MANLY EYEBROWS LOOK LIKE THIS!

ENTIRE BODIES

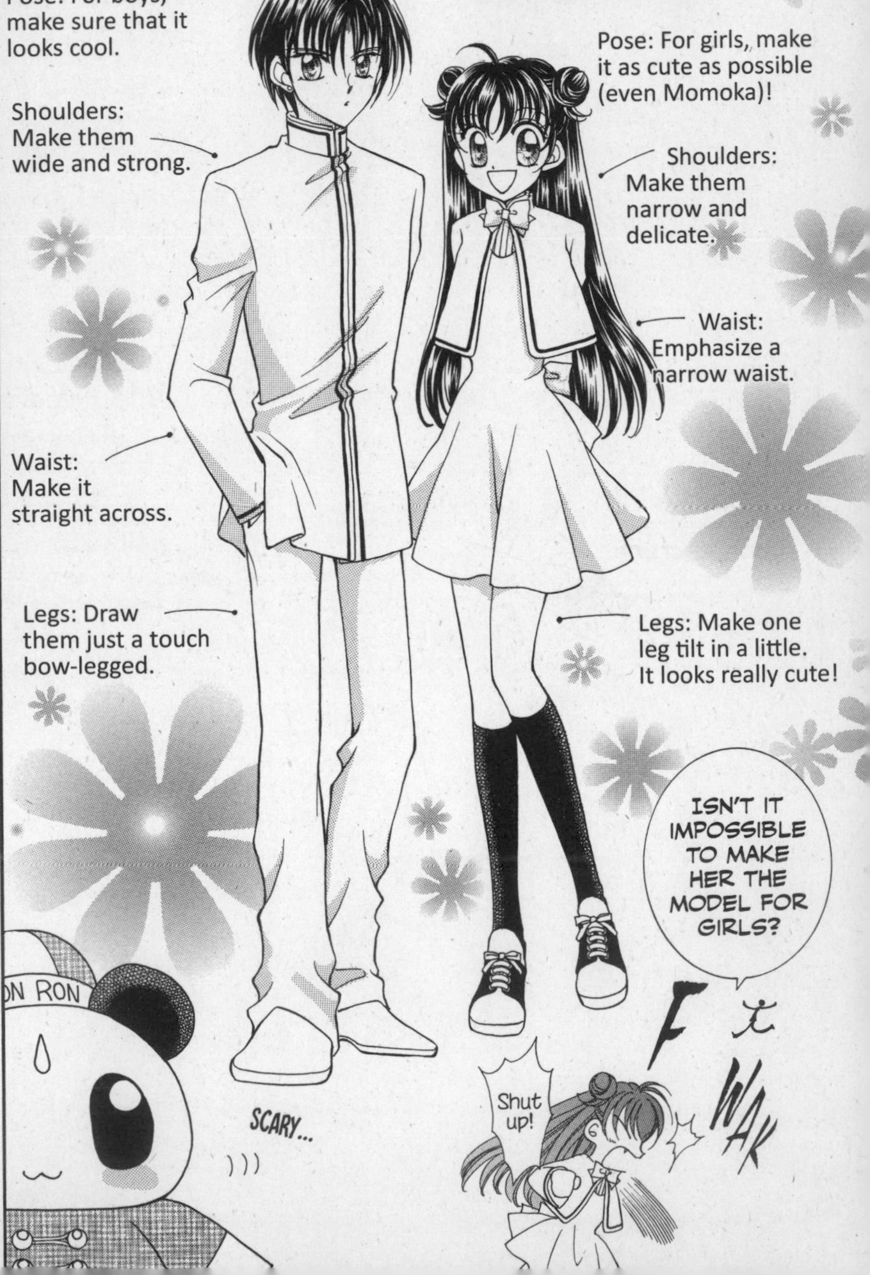
Pose: For boys, make sure that it looks cool.
Shoulders: Make them wide and strong.
Waist: Make it straight across.
Legs: Draw them just a touch bow-legged.
Pose: For girls, make it as cute as possible (even Momoka)!
Shoulders: Make them narrow and delicate.
Waist: Emphasize a narrow waist.
Legs: Make one leg tilt in a little. It looks really cute!
ISN'T IT IMPOSSIBLE TO MAKE HER THE MODEL FOR GIRLS?
WAK
Shut up!
SCARY...
ON RON

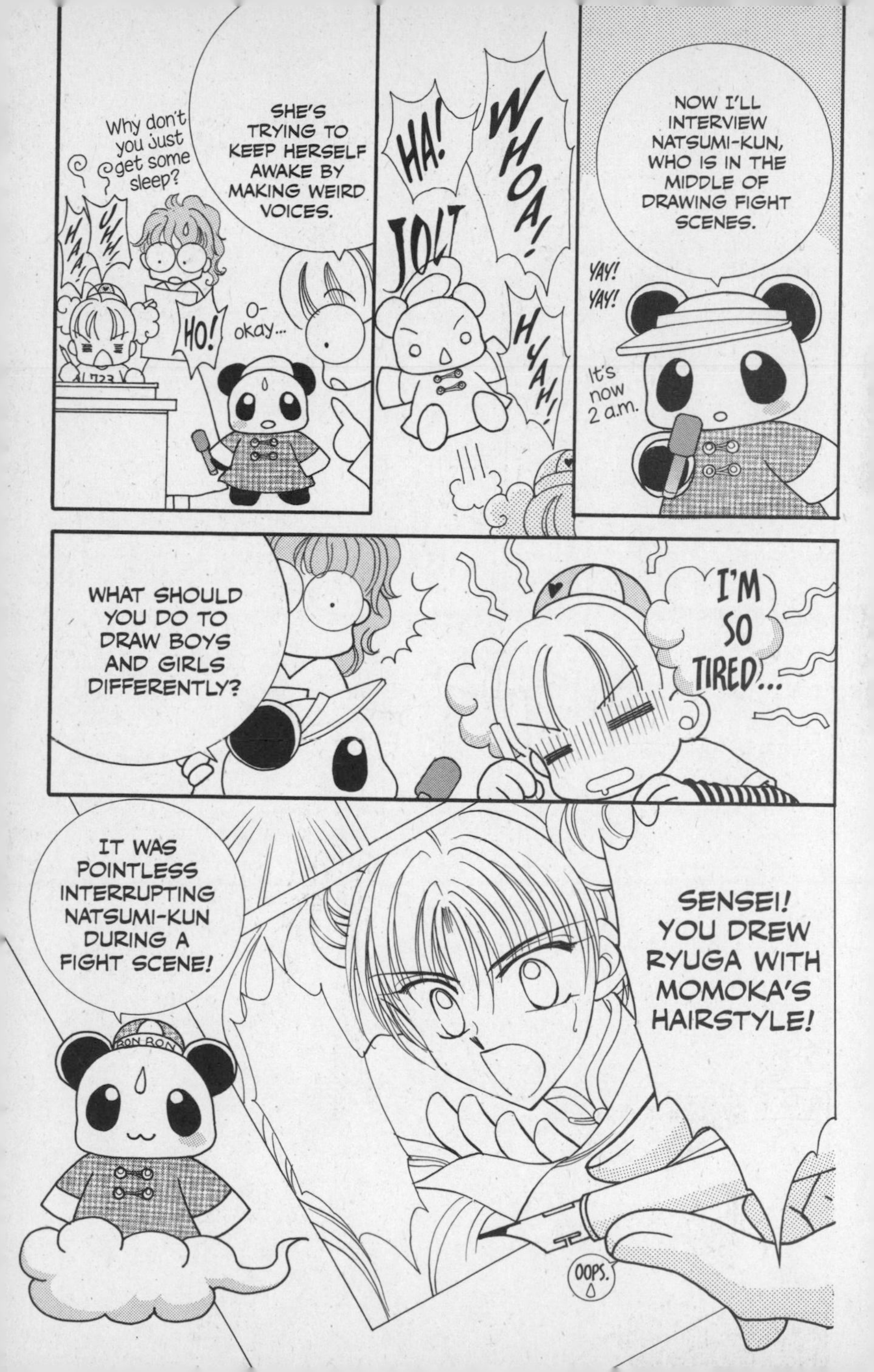
NOW I'LL INTERVIEW NATSUMI-KUN, WHO IS IN THE MIDDLE OF DRAWING FIGHT SCENES.
YAY! YAY!
It's now 2 a.m.
WHOA!
HA!
JOLT
HYAAH!
SHE'S TRYING TO KEEP HERSELF AWAKE BY MAKING WEIRD VOICES.
Why don't you just get some sleep?
UHH
HAA
HO!
O-okay...
I'M SO TIRED...
WHAT SHOULD YOU DO TO DRAW BOYS AND GIRLS DIFFERENTLY?
SENSEI! YOU DREW RYUGA WITH MOMOKA'S HAIRSTYLE!
IT WAS POINTLESS INTERRUPTING NATSUMI-KUN DURING A FIGHT SCENE!
BON BON
OOPS.

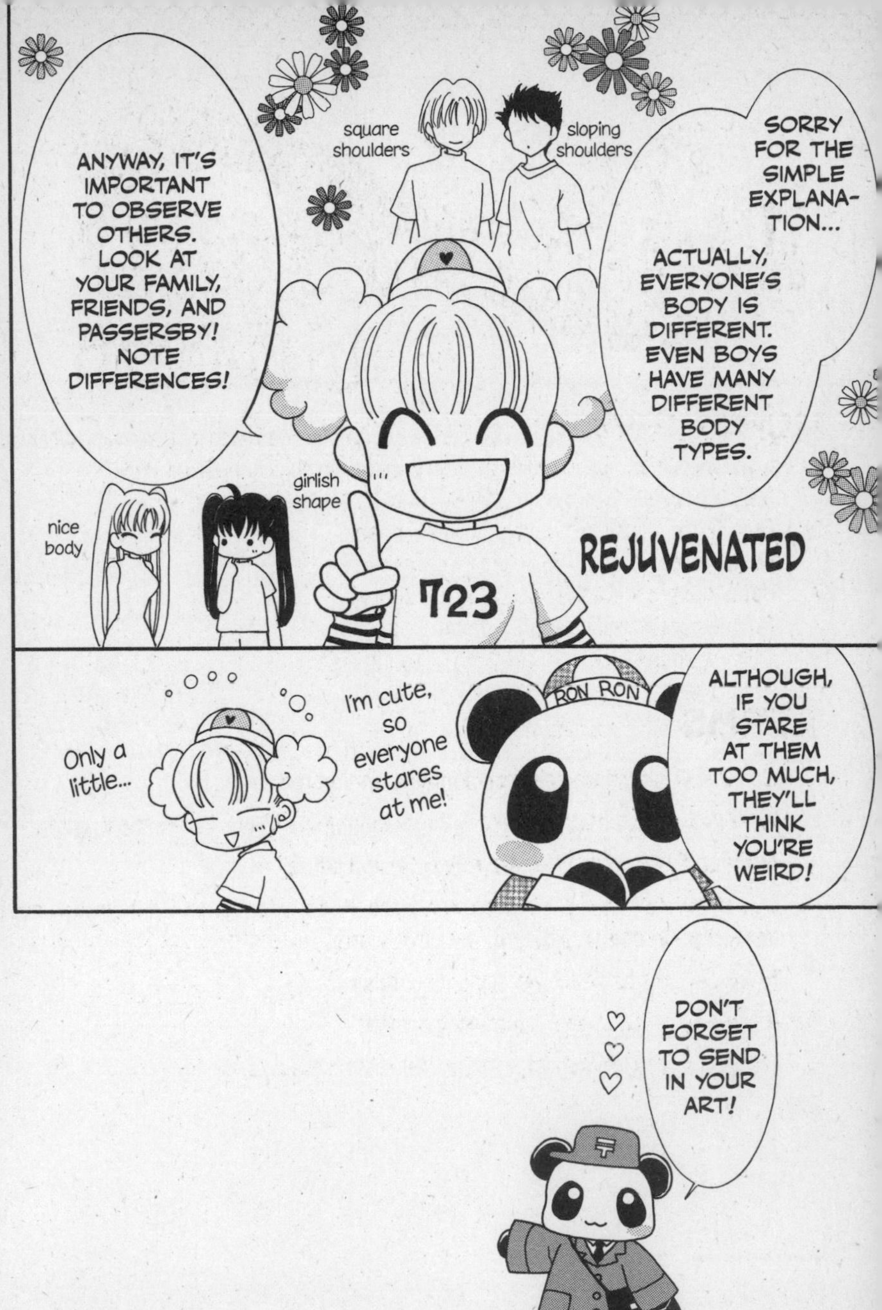
SORRY FOR THE SIMPLE EXPLANATION...
ACTUALLY, EVERYONE'S BODY IS DIFFERENT. EVEN BOYS HAVE MANY DIFFERENT BODY TYPES.
sloping shoulders
square shoulders
ANYWAY, IT'S IMPORTANT TO OBSERVE OTHERS. LOOK AT YOUR FAMILY, FRIENDS, AND PASSERSBY! NOTE DIFFERENCES!
REJUVENATED
T23
girlish shape
nice body
ALTHOUGH, IF YOU STARE AT THEM TOO MUCH, THEY'LL THINK YOU'RE WEIRD!
RON RON
I'm cute, so everyone stares at me!
Only a little...
DON'T FORGET TO SEND IN YOUR ART!

HONORIFICS
In Japan, people are usually addressed by their name followed by a suffix. The suffix shows familiarity or respect, depending on the relationship.

Male (familiar): first or last name + kun
Female (familiar): first or last name + chan
Adult (polite): last name + san
Upperclassman (polite): last name + senpai
Teacher or professional: last name + sensei
Close friends or lovers: first name only, no suffix

TERMS

Doraemon is a character from a manga and anime series.

Kinki Kids is a Japanese pop group. Yousuke Kubozuka is a Japanese actor.

Kamaitachi are wind demons in Japanese folklore.

A *kotatsu* is a table with a heater underneath and a cover on top to trap in heat and keep the people sitting at the table warm.

Enka is a type of traditional Japanese music.

A *yukata* is a traditional Japanese garment.

A *kappa* is a mythical water sprite that resembles a turtle.

FAN ART SUBMISSIONS!

I'm looking for fan art to include in future volumes of the *St. ♥ Dragon Girl* manga.

Please fill out the form on the next page and send it in with your fan art to:

> Nancy Thistlethwaite, Editor
> VIZ Media, LLC
> P.O. Box 77010
> San Francisco, CA 94107

Guidelines:
- All fan art will be presented in black and white, but you can send color art if you want.
- Submissions should be no bigger than 8 1/2" by 11".
- All submissions must have a completed release form (see next page) for consideration.

Please be sure to include the following with your fan art.

FAN ART RELEASE

In exchange for allowing the artwork I submitted with this Fan Art Release ("Fan Art") to be considered for inclusion in the *St. ♥ Dragon Girl* manga series and/or other publications, I hereby irrevocably authorize and grant a non-exclusive, transferable, worldwide, perpetual license to VIZ Media, LLC and others authorized by it, to use, copy, print, publicly display, broadcast and edit the Fan Art and my name, in whole or in part, with or without my name identification, in any and all media now known or hereinafter developed without time, territory or other restrictions and to refrain from doing any or all of the foregoing. I release them all from any claims, liability, costs, losses or damages of any kind in connection therewith, including but not limited to copyright infringement, right of publicity/privacy, blurring or optical distortion. I agree that I have no right to approve any use of the Fan Art or my name as licensed above or the content thereof.

I represent and warrant that I am of the age of majority in my state or province of residence (or, if not, that a parent or legal guardian will sign on my behalf) and that this release does not in any way conflict with any existing commitments on my part. I represent that no other person, firm or entity claiming or deriving rights through me is entitled to grant the rights in the Fan Art I've granted to you (or granted by my parent or legal guardian on my behalf) and that I have the right to license it as outlined herein. I further represent and warrant that I have the full right to enter into this agreement without violating the legal or equitable rights of any third party and that no payments shall be due to me or any third party in conjunction with the use of the Fan Art or my name as outlined herein.

ACCEPTED AND AGREED TO:

Print Name: _____

Signature: _____

(Sign or have your Parent or Legal Guardian do so, if you are a minor)

Address: _____

Date: _____

Finally a *St. ♥ Dragon Girl* full of one-shots! I do like continuing arcs, but it's fun drawing all the different types of stories that appear in one-shots. ♥ Love, friendship, comedy, tears—every month I'd like to write a different, moving story for you!!

—Natsumi Matsumoto

Natsumi Matsumoto debuted with the manga *Guuzen Janai Yo!* (No Coincidence!) in *Ribon Original* magazine. *St. ♥ Dragon Girl* was such a hit that it spawned a sequel, *St. ♥ Dragon Girl Miracle*. Her other series from *Ribon* include *Alice kara Magic* and *Yumeiro Patisserie*. The popular *Yumeiro Patisserie* was made into an animated TV series in Japan. In her free time, Natsumi studies Chinese and practices tai chi. She also likes visiting aquariums and collecting the toy prizes that come with snack food in Japan.

St. ♥ Dragon Girl
Vol. 5
Shojo Beat Manga Edition

STORY AND ART BY | Natsumi Matsumoto

English Adaptation | **Heidi Vivolo**
Translation | **Andria Cheng**
Touch-up Art & Lettering | **Gia Cam Luc**
Design | **Fawn Lau**
Editor | **Nancy Thistlethwaite**

VP, Production | **Alvin Lu**
VP, Sales & Product Marketing | **Gonzalo Ferreyra**
VP, Creative | **Linda Espinosa**
Publisher | **Hyoe Narita**

SAINT DRAGON GIRL © 1999 by Natsumi Matsumoto. All rights reserved. First published in Japan in 1999 by SHUEISHA Inc., Tokyo. English translation rights arranged by SHUEISHA Inc.

The stories, characters and incidents mentioned in this publication are entirely fictional.

Printed in Canada

Published by VIZ Media, LLC
P.O. Box 77010
San Francisco, CA 94107

10 9 8 7 6 5 4 3 2 1
First printing, December 2009

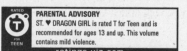

PARENTAL ADVISORY
ST. ♥ DRAGON GIRL is rated T for Teen and is recommended for ages 13 and up. This volume contains mild violence.
ratings.viz.com

www.viz.com

www.shojobeat.com

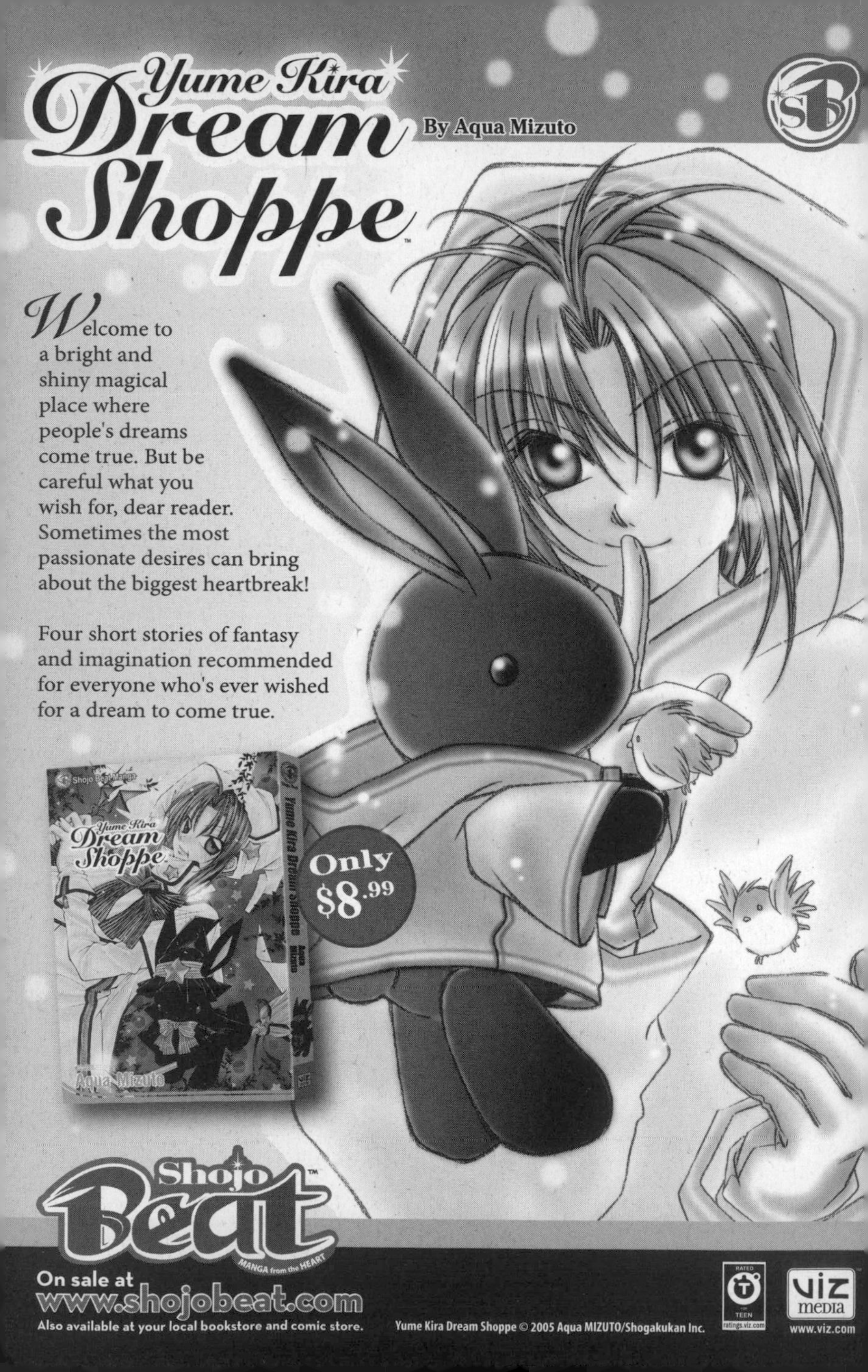

Yume Kira Dream Shoppe™
By Aqua Mizuto
Welcome to a bright and shiny magical place where people's dreams come true. But be careful what you wish for, dear reader. Sometimes the most passionate desires can bring about the biggest heartbreak!
Four short stories of fantasy and imagination recommended for everyone who's ever wished for a dream to come true.
Shojo Beat Manga
Yume Kira Dream Shoppe
Aqua Mizuto
Only $8.99
Shojo Beat™
MANGA from the HEART
On sale at
www.shojobeat.com
Also available at your local bookstore and comic store.
Yume Kira Dream Shoppe © 2005 Aqua MIZUTO/Shogakukan Inc.
RATED T TEEN
ratings.viz.com
VIZ media
www.viz.com